Essays on Opera

WINTON DEAN

Essays on Opera

CLARENDON PRESS · OXFORD

Oxford University Press, Walton Street, Oxford OX2 6DP

Oxford New York Toronto
Delhi Bombay Calcutta Madras Karachi
Kuala Lumpur Singapore Hong Kong Tokyo
Nairobi Dar es Salaam Cape Town
Melbourne Auckland Madrid
and associated companies in
Berlin Ibadan

Oxford is a trade mark of Oxford University Press

Published in the United States
by Oxford University Press Inc., New York

British Library Cataloguing in Publication Data
Dean, Winton, 1916–
Essays on opera.
1. Opera
I. Title
782.1
ISBN 0–19–315265–7
ISBN 0–19–816384–3 (pbk.)

Library of Congress Cataloguing in Publication Data
Dean, Winton.
Essays on opera/Winton Dean.
A collection of essays written between 1952 and 1985.
1. Opera. I. Title.
ML1700.D4   1990   782.1—dc26   89–48621
ISBN 0–19–315265–7
ISBN 0–19–816384–3 (pbk.)

1 3 5 7 9 10 8 6 4 2

Printed in Great Britain
on acid-free paper by
Bookcraft Ltd, Midsomer Norton, Avon

To Stephen

Preface

It will be apparent that these essays were not all addressed to the same audience. Some were designed chiefly for the specialist, others for the more general reader. It seems to me presumptuous to assume that scholarly articles will be beyond the comprehension of the latter, or that the former will not appreciate a little leaven in the musicological lump.

It may not be so necessary today as it was thirty years ago to defend Berlioz and Janáček against the hosts of Midian, but I have not modified the tone of the earlier essays. Nor, for reasons of clarity, have I removed a slight overlap between some of them. I have, however, taken the opportunity to correct errors, add notes, and incorporate fresh information, especially in the more scholarly pieces. Nos. 3 and 6 very considerably, and nos. 2, 13, 14, 26, and 27 to a rather lesser degree, have been revised in this sense. Two paragraphs, previously omitted for lack of space, have been restored to no. 13. I have partially rewritten no. 28 to clarify the argument and incorporate a few details from a later essay, *The Corruption of Carmen: or The Perils of Pseudo-Musicology (Musical Newsletter*, October 1973).

These essays originally appeared in the following books and publications. I am grateful to their publishers and editors for either confirming my copyright or giving me permission to reprint.

Bach, Handel, Scarlatti: Tercentenary Essays, ed. Peter Williams, Cambridge University Press (no. 2).

Studies in Eighteenth-Century Music: A Tribute to Karl Geiringer on his Seventieth Birthday, ed. H. C. Robbins Landon, George Allen & Unwin (no. 3).

New Mattheson Studies, ed. George J. Buelow and Hans Joachim Marx, Cambridge University Press (no. 4).

Essays on Opera and English Music in Honour of Sir Jack Westrup, ed. F. W. Sternfeld, Nigel Fortune, and Edward Olleson, Basil Blackwell (no. 6).

The Beethoven Companion, ed. Denis Arnold and Nigel Fortune, Faber & Faber (no. 14).

Music and Bibliography: Essays in Honour of Alec Hyatt King, ed. Oliver Neighbour, K. G. Saur/Clive Bingley (The Library Association Publications) (no. 17).

Fanfare for Ernest Newman, ed. Herbert van Thal, Arthur Barker (no. 27).

Opera (nos. 1, 10, 18, 21).

The Musical Times (nos. 15, 25, 28).

Music & Letters (nos. 5, 7, 8, 30).
The Listener (nos. 9, 12, 16, 20, 22, 23, 29).
The Haydn Yearbook (no. 11).
Shakespeare Survey (nos. 24, 26).
Proceedings of the Royal Musical Association (nos. 13, 19).

Nos. 1, 18, and 21 were reprinted in *The Opera Bedside Book*, ed. Harold Rosenthal (London, 1965); nos. 6, 8, 19, and 28 in *The Garland Library of the History of Western Music*, ed. Ellen Rosand (New York & London, 1985), volumes 11 and 12; and no. 29 in *Leoš Janáček: Kát'a Kabanová*, ed. John Tyrrell (Cambridge, 1982).

My grateful thanks are due to Elizabeth Gibson and in particular to my son Stephen, who helped in the selection, compiled the index, and has scrutinized every stage in the production of this book with more than filial care and enthusiasm. For this paperback edition I have supplemented Table 4 on page 18 and corrected some errors in no. 3.

W.D.
May 1993

Contents

===

x   Contents

List of Plates

═══

I
Critic and Composer

Between creative art and criticism there is notoriously a great gulf fixed. No one questions its existence or the fact that it has on occasion been crossed; but those who set out to plumb or dredge it are apt to find themselves stranded on sandbanks. A cursory glance at history shows that while a great many artists have operated at some time or another on both sides of the gulf, very few have annexed anything like an equal amount of territory on each bank. The critics are too often numb or inept creators, the creators erratic and unprincipled critics. There is nothing odd in this, since the two functions call into play different areas of the personality, creation depending more on the organization of subconsciously generated material, criticism on the discovery and conscious application of standards, both personal and generic. It is when the two processes are found operating more or less powerfully in the same individual that the question assumes an intense and mysterious fascination. Is the creator helped or hindered by the possession of a trained critical faculty, and vice versa? (The self-criticism of the artist is of course a different matter.) Can any general conclusions be drawn?

The art in which we should expect to find most traffic across the gulf is literature, where creator and critic both express themselves in words. Satire is possible in terms of paint or stone or musical notes, but not criticism, which cannot express its concepts in a sufficiently unequivocal form except through words. Yet even in literature, except perhaps in France, we do not often find an important creative writer also distinguishing himself in criticism. Many great writers have produced critical essays, but they tend naturally to enunciate their own creative principles, sometimes in the form of veiled propaganda (Shelley is an obvious example); and coming from such a source, these essays will be eagerly read and may acquire considerable historical and literary significance. People like to hear the great artist talking about his work and slinging missiles at his fellow-artists, and it would be remarkable if his words contained nothing of interest. But this interest would not be primarily critical.

If we turn to the other side of the medal and glance at the great names in English literary criticism (there is no time to spread the enquiry wider) we find a peculiar state of affairs. They tend to fall into two groups: those who were failures as creative artists, like Addison and Hazlitt, and those who took to criticism after their brief creative flame had burned itself out, like Johnson, Coleridge, and Arnold. This last group includes the only names that have attained high repute in both departments, and without exception their creative output has been small. In fact very few creative writers of the first rank have done any systematic criticism (Shaw is a rare exception); they generally prefer, like Pope and Swift, to express their animadversions on life, art, and other artists by the less intellectually responsible but more potent method of satire. The explanation would appear to be twofold. First, there is seldom time for one man to master and cultivate two disparate growths, even though he may have the seeds of both sprouting vigorously within him. Each requires close and constant attention; time given to the one is inevitably taken from the other. And (secondly) not only time, but energy. There is only one source whence the two headstrong beasts can draw strength and sustenance. And the stronger the creative race-horse grows, the more impatiently will it regard its more laborious stable-companion. Unable any longer to tolerate it under the same roof, it may provoke a struggle that threatens one or other champion with exhaustion.

What has all this to do with music? It was necessary to begin with literature in order to distinguish those parts of the problem that are peculiar to music from those that are generic to art itself. In the former class the main obstacle to the composer-critic is not his need to use two sets of symbols for communication (words and notes), but that *pons asinorum* of all music critics, whether they compose or not —the extreme difficulty of discussing music in words without indulging in a dangerous excess of metaphor. Music, as Mendelssohn said, is on its own territory so much more precise: we might add that if it were not so, it would not be the major art it is. The only extra disadvantage under which the composer-turned-critic labours is that, although he has used words all his life to ask for the mustard and order a new pair of trousers, he has not as a rule cultivated them as a medium of artistic communication (and criticism in its highest form is unquestionably art). We should therefore expect to find a composer's criticism less well expressed than a writer's. But even this is by no means always the case; and it does not affect the central question of the creator-critic.

Thus the basic position in musical history is very much the same as in literature (the lower achievement of musical criticism is due to the *pons asinorum*, whose existence was not recognized before the early nineteenth century and has often been ignored since). Only two composers of the first rank have attained anything like equal status as critics—Berlioz and Schumann. Many others have been part-time writers, whether for money or to relieve their brains of teeming aesthetic matter. Wagner for years bombarded Europe with obscure and inflated propaganda in execrable prose (very interesting as a key to his mind, but disastrously confusing to contemporaries, since he had not yet written the music that justified and explained it). Liszt was a propagandist of a more extroverted and generous type, and so were Weber, who had a feeling for the written word, and Smetana. Tchaikovsky, Wolf, and Debussy all held critical posts for short periods, but these were incidental to their creative careers and did not add anything to their stature. Tchaikovsky enjoyed himself at Wagner's expense, and Wolf at Brahms's, while Debussy carried some part of his impressionist technique from music into letters. All three are amusing and readable, but none was sufficiently systematic to be called a critic in his own right. What they say interests us, either on account of its curious or witty expression, or because it proceeded from the mouths of important composers and not from the babes and sucklings of everyday journalism.

Lest this last remark appear an insult to a fine body of men (and women), it may be mentioned that the ranks of criticism have at various times been swelled by many lesser composers whose creative experience by no means always honoured the status of their second profession. Reyer was a good critic, but Cui and Serov were not; and the incursion of Parry and other composer-moralists into the critical realm often had very unhappy results. On a lighter level, it is related of J.W. Davison, for many years music critic of the *The Times*:

> There once was a J. W. D.
> Who hoped a composer to be;
>   But his muse wouldn't budge,
>   So he set up as judge
> Over greater composers than he.

That is not in itself a bad qualification. None of Davison's compositions appear to be available, but quite a comprehensive collection could be made of the creative works of modern English critics. Tovey of course composed a great deal, including an opera and an endless cello concerto; Professor Dent has given us songs and psalms (we only need sonnets for the completion of Byrd's trilogy); Cecil Gray wrote operas, and a Divertimento for bassoon, cello, and piano has proceeded from Professor Westrup. It is even possible that painstaking research might uncover suppressed masterpieces of the greatest interest by other hands, such as a saxophone concerto by Mr Newman, an Agnus Dei by Mr Blom, or a comic opera by Mr Howes. After all, there is two-way traffic across the gulf.

But that is by the way. The fact that Schumann and Berlioz were contemporaries is significant; the Romantic age saw an attempt by all the arts to emerge from their estuaries and swim out into a common sea. Wagner's art-work of the future, Berlioz's dramatic symphony, and Liszt's symphonic poem were all products of this movement, which sent musicians into literature and men of letters into music on a prodigal scale. All the important composers born between 1800 and 1820, with the exception of Chopin and Verdi, were to be found at some time or another wielding a vigorous pen, and many of the first regular music critics, such as Hoffmann, Rochlitz, the two Rellstabs, and Dickens's father-in-law Hogarth, were originally men of letters. Even Goethe employed a composer—unfortunately an inferior one—to report on musical settings of his poetry. What this Romantic mingling of the arts unhappily did not do was to establish a tolerable liaison between dramatists and composers to the advantage of opera. Third-rate writers like Helmine von Chézy and Planché rushed in to ruin the stage works of Schubert and Weber, but opera had to wait another sixty years for Boito, himself an opera-composer whose muse was disinclined to budge. The trouble was that musical criticism got away to a late start. Having long languished on the windy heaths of eighteenth-century rationalist aesthetics, which can scarcely be said to have been watered by the cool stream of music at all, it toppled straight over the cliff into the Romantic morass, where new aesthetic bases were laid down indiscriminately on the most unsuitable soil. One of the first men to see the necessity for a fresh estimate was Hanslick, but he allowed himself to react too far in the direction of a narrow dogmatism and so egregiously damaged his reputation with posterity. In a complex art like opera, where divergent principles have not only to be thought out but reconciled, the position was of course much worse.

It was natural for Berlioz and Schumann to try their hands at sorting out the mess, and all things considered they made a very good job of it. Schumann was perhaps the more balanced critic, but Berlioz was the more penetrating and by far the better writer. He is the only great composer whose literary gifts might have won him an equal status in another art. It would be worth considering whether this distinction, in conjunction with the Romantic mixture of the arts, did not influence the unique character of his musical genius, with its tendency to jump from peak to peak and leave the connecting matter to perfunctory patching up or even to programme notes. The fact that his criticism scarcely dates is due in no small measure to his style, which combines clarity and a scrupulous care in selecting the right word with a vivid and apposite use of analogy and a subtly allusive wit. His matter is often little inferior to his manner. Berlioz had nearly all the peculiar gifts of the great critic, while lacking some of those frequently to be found in little critics —a situation exactly paralleled in his music. He was intellectually honest, and less disposed than most critics to camouflage his blind spots by special pleading. He lambasted Palestrina and Haydn and likened Handel to a barrel of pork and beer, but he did not assume, as Parry did with opera, that what he disliked must be morally and aesthetically worthless. Berlioz was always fair to contemporaries, despite a temperamental aversion to Rossini and Italian opera. In writing of composers whom he specially admired, such as Gluck or Beethoven, he is often profoundly revealing. Above all, he was brilliantly successful at negotiating the *pons asinorum* mentioned above, the bridge between notes and words. The passage in *À travers Chants* where he analyses the transition from the Scherzo to the Finale of Beethoven's fifth symphony, conveying at the same time the emotional suspense and the technical means whereby it is achieved, without falling into dryness on the one hand or fulsomeness on the other, is nothing less than masterly. (It is interesting to compare E. M. Forster's totally different but equally sensitive treatment of the same passage in *Howards End*.) Berlioz's chief defects as a critic sprang from a lack of historical vision; he was apt to judge the music of the past by inapplicable standards, and so misapprehended nearly all the leading composers of the seventeenth and eighteenth centuries except Mozart and Gluck. Here perhaps he was inevitably hindered by the powerful individuality of his own creative powers.

Schumann was a critic of a very different type. He had a finer historical sense than Berlioz, and a catholic taste in contemporary music (Italian opera again excepted); he was, if anything, too generous in his enthusiasms, for while he detected abundant genius in the early works of Berlioz, Chopin, and Brahms, he claimed almost as much for numerous nonentities long forgotten. What his criticism gained in breadth it lost in depth. Eschewing technical analysis, he attempted to evoke and transmit the content of music through the poetry of words. He regarded 'that criticism as the highest which leaves behind it an impression resembling that awakened by its subject'. But this leads to rhapsody rather than criticism, and Schumann often gives the impression of not getting to grips with the music itself. The famous article on Schubert's C major symphony, so admired by German writers, tells us virtually nothing about that work except that it is long and contains a fine passage for solo horn in the slow movement, and that Schumann liked it. His writings exercised a valuable influence in their time, but their permanent contribution is relatively slight. The critic who blurs the aesthetic outlines, as Schumann does when he discusses music in terms of poetry, is bound to date, for later periods will evolve a new 'interpretation' of their own. Nor does his style always endear him today, with its echoes of the whimsical gush of Jean Paul (a kind of German Leigh Hunt); he describes Schubert's early waltzes as 'little lovely genii floating over the earth at about the height of a flower' and Mendelssohn's 'I waited for the Lord' as 'a glance into a heaven filled with the Madonna eyes of Raphael'. The many literary pseudonyms into which he subdivided his personality are more acceptable in their musical form (in *Carnaval*) than in criticism. Yet the man who wrote that if Liszt 'played behind the scenes, a great deal of the poetry of his playing would be lost' lacked neither sharpness nor humour; Schumann in fact had a positive genius for the sugaring of pills. As a critic he cuts a pleasant and friendly figure; he was completely above professional jealousy, and loved music so much that he always suspected the virtuoso. He is less mordant than Berlioz, more diffused, and though less accomplished a writer, more literary in approach. In reading him it is his character rather than his intellectual equipment that we admire. As in Berlioz, the critic runs parallel with the composer.

The question arises whether the creative work of either composer suffered from his addiction to criticism. Both certainly felt the strain. Schumann edited his *Neue Zeitschrift für Musik* from 1834 till 1844; at least twice during those ten years the inner conflict nearly drove him to abandon criticism, and after giving up the paper he wrote very little for the press. Whether the prolonged strain of serving two masters had any effect on either his mental collapse or the qualitative decline of his creative powers during later life it is impossible to say without fuller evidence. At all events there was never any doubt which of the masters would win. With Berlioz the position is different. For all his genius he was by no means a prolific composer; his last twenty-nine years yielded little more than five big works, one of them an expansion of earlier material. He claimed that his sole motive in writing criticism was money, and never tired of resenting it as a form of slavery. The question has often been asked whether any man could have loathed so much a task he did so well and with such exuberance of style and thought. The answer perhaps is that one half of him did hate it, especially when he had to discuss music he despised. He was divided against himself, like the stable postulated earlier. The creative animal resented criticism as a waste of valuable time; but the critical animal, which might otherwise have gone under (as in Schumann), found reinforcement in that spiritual negative that always lurked in Berlioz's heart. When the question of a new creative work arose, it suggested the reply 'What's the use? No one understands me. My critical articles amuse the public and line my exchequer. *Vive le feuilleton!*' The presence of the creative animal in the next stall would be quite enough to account for the distaste that accompanied every assumption of the critic's pen. If Berlioz the critic had been silenced, we should surely have had more from Berlioz the composer.

On the one hand then we may conclude that while criticism is doubtless an excellent platform for the composer who has a low-powered creative gift or has lost his creative faith, rarely will a major composer prove also a major critic, and then only at some cost. On the other hand, it is dangerous for anyone to undertake art criticism who has not some first-hand acquaintance with the creative mentality. He need not have gained this through practising the same art; indeed there are obvious advantages in his not operating creatively and critically in the same element, at any rate at the same time. He will be more detached from the strong predilections generated by his creative bent, and freer for not being a potential rival—a great deal freer than he probably can know. It goes without saying that he must have a thorough knowledge of the history, technique, and limitations of the art he is to criticize; an awful pit yawns before the writer who treats music as a kind of substitute literary language or a canvas of bright colours. History supplies many instances of this artistic ambivalence. Baudelaire was a distinguished critic of painting; Gautier began as a painter and regularly criticized drama, almost the only form of literature he did not himself practise. Hazlitt too began as a painter, and Ruskin as a poet. Hoffmann, historically very important as a music critic, was primarily a writer of fiction, though he also composed operas. Heine was a lively and successful critic of music. Almost the only perceptive criticism of *Carmen* in 1875 was by a poet, Théodore de Banville. Even Chorley, though too poor a critic to help the argument, was a dramatist, novelist, and poet. But the outstanding instances in music are Romain Rolland and Bernard Shaw, whose fame as creative artists is secure and whose musical criticism has few rivals in either language.

The casual enquirer is apt to forget that criticism is an essentially rigorous occupation, requiring a mind not only broadly based but ever ready to expand; indeed if it is not continually stretched, it automatically contracts. The mentally chair-bound critic (no reflection on academic chairs!) is presently unable to walk without crutches. Nor is it always remembered that it is not the critic's main business to be right before the event, like the football-pool forecaster; the best critic is not necessarily the man whose judgments are least often upset on appeal. His task is (1) to grasp *all* the issues—aesthetic, technical, social—involved in the creation and presentation of a work of art, (2) to set them before the reader with such clarity and vigour that a congenitally slothful person not only cannot take avoiding action but is jostled into thinking for himself, and (3) to make it perfectly clear, in giving his own judgment, on what standards and principles he is relying. He must operate from a base that can be plotted almost as on a map. It is difficult to see a contemporary or near-contemporary work with the eye of history; but no criticism is worth much that does not make the attempt. In past criticism it may well be the 'wrong' judgement that tells us most about the composer, the work, and the period, not to mention the critic. The propagandist exhausts his value at one throw; the critic who plays for safety achieves nothing, since he never lets the ball out of his hand. Composers tend to dislike critics, and are generally right when they insist on telling the composer what he ought to do instead of telling the public what he has done. The composer does what he must, and if it is well done the fact will eventually be recognized, even if traditional furniture has to be overturned in the process. The critic in the long run is less lucky, for though he may enjoy his little fling it is the composer who controls history. How else has it been forgotten that by far the best and most valuable contemporary criticism of Wagner was by Eduard Hanslick?

2
Handel's Early London Copyists

Since Chrysander published his biography and embarked on his monumental edition more than a century ago Handel scholarship has been a grossly neglected area, not least in Britain, which should have taken the lead. Although the vast majority of the manuscript sources are in this country, until very recently no attempt has been made to subject them to a systematic examination or even to draw up an adequate calendar of their contents. The fact that Handel scrupulously dated his principal autographs—which with minor exceptions are all assembled in two places, the Royal Music Collection in the British Library and the Fitzwilliam Museum in Cambridge—has led to the easy but quite erroneous assumption that no problems of chronology arise. Handel constantly revised and altered his works, especially for revivals in the theatre, with the result that a great deal of music, much of it unpublished, is scattered among early copies. An investigation of the copyists, their identity, habits, and dates of operation, is obviously an essential preliminary to the assessment of this material. Yet the only published work of any consequence in the field has come from a Danish and a German scholar.

Until the appearance of Jens Peter Larsen's book *Handel's* Messiah: *Origins, Composition, Sources* (London, 1957), nearly all eighteenth-century Handel copies were ascribed almost automatically to his amanuensis John Christopher Smith, or sometimes to the two Smiths, father and son. Larsen demolished this never very convincing assumption and demonstrated the existence, during the 1730s and later, of a circle of copyists working more or less under Smith's guidance, whom Larsen designated S1 to S13. At the same time he allotted symbols to a number of other copyists according to the libraries where their work is preserved: RM1 to RM10 (Royal Music Library), BM1 to BM6 (British Library, Additional Manuscripts), Hb1 and 2 (Hamburg Staats- und Universitätsbibliothek), Lenn 1 and 2 (Barrett Lennard Collection in the Fitzwilliam Museum), and Fitz 1 (other Fitzwilliam manuscripts). He recognized the existence of many more. Hans Dieter Clausen, in his comprehensive study of Handel's performing scores, *Händels Direktions-partituren ('Handexemplare')* (Hamburg, 1972), added twelve more Hamburg copyists, whom he numbered H1 to H12.

Every Handel scholar is indebted to the pioneering work of Larsen and Clausen, which established an essential foundation on which we can build. It could not be final, for the very good reason that they did not have access to all the manuscripts, especially of the early works. Clausen, though aware of the British Library and Fitzwilliam holdings, restricted himself to the Hamburg scores, where the identification of copyists was only one among many considerations. Larsen used the principal public collections (British Library, Royal College of Music, Fitzwilliam, Tenbury, Hamburg), but was denied access to the bulk of the Aylesford Collection copied for Handel's friend Charles Jennens (then owned by Sir Newman Flower, since 1965 in the Henry Watson Music Library, Manchester), and was unaware of the private collections of Gerald Coke and the Earl of Malmesbury. As it happens these two contain many key manuscripts, in several instances the earliest surviving copies of works whose autographs are missing or defective.[1] Some were dated by the original owners; others can be given a surprisingly precise date from internal evidence. Further unexamined early copies can be found in places as far apart as Oxford, Hereford, Berlin, Munich, Vienna, Washington, and Tokyo—a list by no means exhaustive. Detailed inspection of this material, quite apart from yielding a substantial amount of unknown music, exposes a totally unfamiliar picture of Handel's copyists and the way they worked.

Although the present study is necessarily limited in scope, the whole field is so little mapped and so enveloped in a fog of obscurity and ignorance that some preliminary clearing of the ground may be helpful. In the first place, there have inevitably been a few false identifications. Larsen's and Clausen's lists each contain two duplicates. RM5 and RM6 are the same person; so are RM7 and RM9, H6 and H9, and H11 and H12. Secondly, the widening of the search has helped to distinguish those copyists who were closely linked with Handel's immediate circle from those who were not, and to define the periods during which each one was active. For the present commemorative volume,[2] I had first intended to cover the years up to 1725, but soon found that this would take up more space than was likely to be available. Nevertheless it may be useful if I indicate which of the copyists enumerated by Larsen and Clausen were active before 1725, and their relative importance. All the S series except S2, RM5–10, BM2–6, Hb1 and 2, Lenn 1 and 2, Fitz 1, and H6–12 are later—some of them much later. So far as is known, RM3 and BM1 copied only a single Handel score each, and RM2 two; there is little to connect them closely with the composer. H4 was rather more prominent, but was not in action for long. On the other hand RM1, RM4, H1, H2, H3, and H5—and of course Smith—were important copyists, at least for a time, not only in the number of manuscripts that contain their work but in their relationship to the source, Handel himself. So were several others either wrongly identified or not mentioned by Larsen and Clausen. I hope elsewhere to describe and classify their work, designating them by the letters of the Greek alphabet in the order in which they appear among the sources. Only those having a demonstrable or likely link with the composer will be included in the series. I am conscious that any conclusions reached will always be subject to revision in the light of further evidence or reinterpretaion.

[1] I owe a huge debt to Mr and Mrs Gerald Coke and to Lord and Lady Malmesbury for allowing me on numerous occasions to disturb their households and for making me so welcome in their libraries. Without their co-operation much of my work, in this study and elsewhere, would have been stillborn.
[2] The reference is to the original publication of this essay in 1985.

Handel scholars have for some time been aware of two puzzles posed by the early Smith copies. One is the year of Smith's arrival in England, and therefore the earliest possible date for any manuscript copied by him. According to Coxe's *Anecdotes of George Frederick Handel and John Christopher Smith* (London, 1799), p. 37, Handel, who had known Smith in his youth at Halle, visited him in 1716 at Ansbach, where he was engaged in the wool trade, and invited him to act as his treasurer and secretary; Smith at once threw up his job and accompanied Handel to London, leaving his family in Germany till 'the fourth year of his residence in England'. This has been questioned, especially as Smith in a letter to the fourth Earl of Shaftesbury on 28 July 1743 spoke of Handel's having 'many proofs of my fidelity this 24 years'.[3] The second puzzle is the startling change that Smith's handwriting appears to have undergone towards 1720. Larsen does not give a facsimile of this 'Smith Mark 1' (his first facsimile in fact shows H1's hand), but he reproduces four versions of the C clef on p. 263, and Clausen gives a rather fuller illustration on his p. 269. Some of the discrepancies must raise a suspicion that more than one copyist is involved.[4]

That suspicion can now be enlarged into a fact. The principal Mark I manuscripts relied on by Larsen and Clausen (dated around 1720 by the former, 1716 or 1717 by the latter) are RM19.e.4 (*Il pastor fido*) and RM19.d.5 (*Rinaldo*) in the British Library, and MA/1003 (*Amadigi*) and MB/1570 (Italian duets and trios) in Hamburg. The last is a composite manuscript containing several hands of different dates. The Mark I hand can be found in a number of other manuscripts, listed in full below; there are at least thirty, some written in association with other copyists. Internal evidence proves conclusively that two of them antedate by several years the earliest possible time of Smith's arrival in London. RM19.e.4 must have been copied in October 1712, for its first state reproduces the score of *Il pastor fido* before Handel finished the autograph on the 24th of the month. It contains, as insertions, several pieces sung at the first performance on 22 November 1712, as we know from the printed libretto; they are likewise insertions in the autograph. The earliest of the three scores of *Teseo* in Gerald Coke's collection, in the same hand, provides striking confirmation. Handel finished and dated the autograph of this opera on 19 December 1712, and first performed it on 10 January 1713. The Coke copy contains words and music (subsequently cancelled or folded over) for a character, Medea's confidante Fedra, who was reduced to a mute not only before the first night but before the libretto was sent to the printer. The manuscript can thus be dated within very narrow limits to the last days of December 1712. Fedra's words and music are found nowhere else, since the scenes in which she appears are missing from the very fragmentary autograph.

The Handel manuscripts in the Earl of Malmesbury's collection belonged originally to Elizabeth Legh of Adlington Hall, Cheshire, a friend of the composer and

---

[3] B. Matthews, 'Unpublished Letters Concerning Handel', *Music & Letters* 40 (1959), 263.

[4] In his article 'Probleme der Händel-Überlieferung', *Die Musikforschung* 34 (1981), 137–61, which is partly a review of Clausen's book, Larsen acknowledged the possibility of error here. Of the four facsimiles on his p. 263 only *b* and *c* show Smith's C clef; of Clausen's examples on p. 269 only the three bottom lines represent Smith.

a passionate admirer of his music, who from about 1715 until her death in 1734 ordered copies of all his works and had them specially bound in leather with her coat of arms stamped on the cover. They are still in their original condition. Not only that: Elizabeth Legh added numerous annotations and comments, including indexes for each volume and not infrequently the dates when she acquired them. In two instances she supplied the name of the copyist as well. Her score of *Teseo*, in the Mark I hand, bears the note in her writing: 'transcribed by Mr Linike June 1717'.

Who was this Linike? With Elizabeth Legh's invaluable clue we can discover a fair amount about him. He was probably of German origin, and perhaps related to the Weissenfels family of that name, of which three members—Ephraim, Christian Bernhard, and Johann Georg—appear in *The New Grove*. None of these can be our man: the dates do not fit, although the best-known of them, Johann Georg, who in November 1725 adapted and conducted the first Hamburg production of Handel's *Giulio Cesare*, was in England for a time from 1721. The man we are seeking was a London musician who signed himself 'D. Linike', establishing the authentic form of a name on which other people, true to contemporary practice, bestowed an astonishing variety of spellings: Lynike, Linikey, Leneker, Lenniker, Liniken, Linikin, Lunecan, Lunican, Lunicon, and even Unican. The contexts leave no doubt that this was all one man.

He was primarily a viola-player, though he may well have earned more money as a copyist. We first encounter him in a list of twenty-three musicians who applied for jobs when John Vanbrugh was planning to establish an opera orchestra at his newly built Queen's Theatre in the Haymarket about November 1707.[5] Linike asked for £1 a night. He was not among the first two choices (the orchestra, numbering twenty-five to thirty, never included more than two viola-players), but he is rated at 8s a night in an estimate dating from January 1708, shortly before Vanbrugh's season opened. This fee was confirmed later, and was apparently raised to 10s. about 1709/10. There is documentary evidence that Linike was a member of the orchestra for at least six seasons, and he almost certainly continued until the Haymarket opera closed in the summer of 1717. When the Royal Academy of Music was planning to reopen it in the spring of 1720 we find his name on a roster drawn up by the Duke of Portland on 15 February. Five salary levels appear among the thirty-four (later thirty-two) musicians listed; Linike, the senior of two violas, is placed in the fourth. His proposed salary of £40, apparently covering a total of ninety performances in two seasons, is less than he had received ten years earlier.[6] His activities of course were not confined to the theatre. During the 1711/12 season he was paid 4 guineas for playing at private concerts for the Duchess of Shrewsbury,

[5] J. Milhous and R. D. Hume, *Vice Chamberlain Coke's Theatrical Papers 1706–1715* (Carbondale, Ill., 1982), 31. All information about Linike's activities during these years is taken from this authoritative source. I am indebted to the editors for allowing me to see their proofs in advance of publication, and for a facsimile of Linike's signature. For the 1720 reference, see the same authors' 'New Light on Handel and the Royal Academy of Music in 1720', *Theatre Journal* 35 (1983), 158–61.

[6] Milhous and Hume, in *Theatre Journal* 35 (1983), based on Portland Papers on deposit in Nottingham University Library.

the Italian wife of the Lord Chamberlain.[7] It is his receipt for this sum, dated 24 June 1712, that bears his only known signature.

The earliest reference to Linike's activities as a copyist occurs in a document written by Heidegger on 5 May 1711:[8]

Mr Collier agrees to pay to Mr Lunecan for the Copy of Rinaldo this day the sum of eight pound and three pound every day Rinaldo is playd till six and twenty pound are payd and he gives him leave to take the sayd Opera in his custody after every day of acting it till the whole six and twenty pound are payd.

Collier, the business manager at the Haymarket, was in debt to tradesmen and evidently still owed money to Linike for the score (and parts?) used at the first performance of *Rinaldo* on 24 February that year. This suggests that Linike was the regular theatre copyist at the Haymarket; he was well paid for the job. It is significant that it should have been undertaken by viola-players, who were among the lowest-paid members of the orchestra; another of them, W. Armstrong, received £9 9s. 5d. on 13 July 1708 for copying a score of Bononcini's *Camilla* for the Duke of Bedford.[9] The temptation to identify the score mentioned by Heidegger with RM19.d.5 must be resisted. Both the contents of that copy and Linike's handwriting point to a later date, probably about 1716.

Confirmation that Linike was the principal Haymarket copyist comes from the theatre accounts for the 1716/17 season,[10] which record six payments totalling £17 13s. 0d. 'to Mr Linike for copying Musick'. For similar services 'Mr Davies' received £8 15s. 6d., and 'Mr Smith' (probably yet another viola-player—not Handel's amanuensis) £1 1s. 6d. Further copying bills with no recipient named amounted to £29 0s. 6d; they included the score of a new opera, probably *Tito Manlio*.

Another document connects Linike closely with both Handel and Smith. The autograph of the Chandos Anthem *O be joyful in the Lord* has an inscription on the outside of the fifth gathering (RM20.d.8, f.120), upside down on the page: 'For Mr Smith to be left att Mr Linikey's att ye White Hart in ye Hay Market with Speed'. This anthem was probably composed in September 1717. Although the sentence is not in Handel's writing, it seems likely that the message concerns the copying of the score soon after composition; and the form of words suggests that Smith in his secretarial capacity was to give it to Linike to copy. This agrees with other evidence that Smith was not yet acting as Handel's copyist. As we shall see, there are grounds for supposing that he embarked on this service under Linike's supervision.

Linike's name occurs in several press announcements quoted in *The London Stage*.[11] It was customary for leading singers and instrumental players to enjoy

[7] This document is wrongly dated in Milhous and Hume, *Coke's Theatrical Papers*, 191–3; it cannot refer to the 1712/13 season, because one of the singers listed was then no longer in London.

[8] Milhous and Hume, *Coke's Theatrical Papers*, 176: also (less accurately) in O. E. Deutsch, *Handel: A Documentary Biography* (London, 1955), 40.

[9] G. S. Thomson, *The Russells in Bloomsbury* (London, 1940), 129.

[10] In the Essex (formerly Hampshire) Record Office; I owe this reference to Lowell Lindgren. See also S. Rosenfeld, 'An Opera House Account Book', *Theatre Notebook* 16 (1962), 83–8.

[11] E. L. Avery (ed.), *The London Stage 1660–1800*, Part 2: 1700–1729 (Carbondale, Ill., 1960).

TABLE 1. *Linike Copies*

Date	Source	Work	Remarks
1. Oct. 1712	RM19.e.4	*Il pastor fido*	copied before completion of autograph
2. late Dec. 1712	Coke	*Teseo*	copied before printing of first libretto
3. (1713)	BL Add. MS 5333	Utrecht Jubilate and Te Deum	probably earliest copy
4. (1715)	Coke	*Amadigi*	earliest surviving copy
5. ?1715	Munich, private collection	*Teseo*	unfoliated; p. [1] only; rest RM1, except last two pages added later (S2 and Jennens); ex-Aylesford
6. c.1715–16	BL Add. MS 16024	*Il pastor fido*	appendix RM1
7. c.1716	RM19.d.5	*Rinaldo*	much amended by Handel
8. c.1716	Washington, L. of C. (Landon)	*Amadigi* arias etc.	ff.15–38; additions by Smith (ff.1–14, c.1719) and another (a source recently acquired by the Library, not yet with call number)
9. c.1716	Hamburg MA/1003	*Amadigi*	amended by Handel
10. June 1717	Malmesbury	*Teseo*	dated by Elizabeth Legh; one insertion RM1
11. c.1717	Malmesbury	Ode for Queen Anne's Birthday	
12. 1717	Hamburg MB/1570	Italian duets	dated; pp. 1–100; later additions Newman, Smith, and Hb1
13. 1717/18	Malmesbury	Pieces for harpsichord	dated 1717 and 1718 (i.e. before 25 March 1718); pp. 9–12, 14–20, 76, 91–109; with *Alpha, Beta*, RM1, and RM4
14. (1717/18)	Malmesbury	Overtures etc. for harpsichord	pp. 18–19, 61–80, 129; with RM1; incorporated later in composite volume dated 30 August 1722
15. 1718	Bodleian MS Mus d 61	Italian cantatas	dated; ff. 1–8, 61–121; with RM1 and *Beta*; later additions
16. c.1718–19	BL Add. MS 31574	Italian cantatas	ff.1–40, followed by one cantata in later hand
17. c.1719	Bodleian Tenbury 881	Chandos anthems: *As pants the hart* and *Sing unto the Lord*	ff.1–76; with RM1
18. c.1719	Hereford Cathedral Lib. R.X.XVI	Chandos Anthems: *Have mercy on me* and *O be joyful*	
19. 6 June 1721	Berlin Amalienbibliothek 439b	*Muzio Scevola* (without recits.)	dated by copyist at end
20. c.1725	BL Add. MS 29416	Chandos Te Deum	
21–30. c.1725	BL Add. MSS 29417–26	Ten Chandos Anthems	

benefit concerts, usually in the spring of the year; the receipts, after payment of expenses, went to the beneficiary. Benefits were announced for 'Lenniker' at Hickford's Room on 3 May 1717, for 'Leneker and Mrs Smith' (wife of John Christopher?) at the same place on 18 February 1719, for 'Linike' at the New Haymarket Theatre on 27 March 1724, and for 'the Widow Linike' at Hickford's on 16 March 1726. Linike presumably died during the winter of 1725–6. The programmes consisted of vocal and instrumental music, 'by the best Hands in the Opera' in 1717. Some of Linike's orchestral colleagues are named in the bills: Matthew Dubourg (violin), Pietro Chaboud (German flute and bass viol), and Jean Christian Kytch (oboe). Dubourg played 'several new Solos and Concertos' for Linike in 1717 and 'a new Concerto, Compos'd by Mr Hendel' in 1719.

The Handel manuscripts copied by Linike cover the years 1712–c.25. Since a number of them from 1712 to 1721 are firmly dated, and the date for the c. 1725 group is supported by paper evidence,[12] it is possible by tracing the development of his handwriting to supply approximate dates for the rest. Table 1 lists all those so far discovered; further research may well reveal others. The surest pointers to dating Linike copies are the C clef and the crotchet rest; the detached semiquaver is sometimes a help, though Linike occasionally reverted to his early practice in later copies. As Plates 1, 2, and 3 show, his treble and bass clefs are remarkably constant throughout. The former has a fair rounded figure with a straight stem and no curl at the bottom; the latter is distinctive, with its tail curled neatly round like a seated cat. The C clef, on the other hand, passes through three distinct phases. In the earliest copies up to and including no. 9 it is of a 'comfortable armchair' type, with two short horizontal lines above and two longer ones below, all more or less parallel and at right angles to the downward stems. By 1717 (nos. 10–18) it has grown more flexible, with the short lines in the upper quadrant no longer parallel and modified by an upward curl.[13] In the 1721 copy (Plate 3) and those of c. 1725 it is still more schematic. The crotchet rest in the earliest copies is almost a right angle made up of a horizontal and vertical line, but this soon changes to a more sloping form with a hook emerging by degrees at bottom left and progressively lengthening. There are signs of this in nos. 4 and 5; it becomes more pronounced from no. 6 onwards, but reverts towards its original slope and a smaller size in no. 19. The semiquaver in nos. 1 to 4 is as *a* below; from 1716 it becomes *b* or *c*, but occasional examples

of *a* occur as late as no. 16 and even no. 19. Linike's notes are always clear; so as a rule are his words, which have a forward slant and a certain resemblance to Smith's. However, identification of copyists by their verbal texts needs to be approached with caution, for two reasons; many of them wrote a very similar

---

[12] According to information from Donald Burrows.
[13] Larsen's C clef type *a* (p. 263) and Clausen's top four lines (p. 269) all show Linike's hand. Larsen's *d* is RM1.

cursive hand, and in a fair number of manuscripts music and words were the work of different scribes. The calligraphic Act and Scene headings usual in opera full scores are so similar as to suggest that they either were written by the same man (regardless of who did the bulk of the music copying) or were expected to conform to a prescribed pattern.

As already mentioned, Larsen established the existence of a Smith circle of copyists during the 1730s, with S1 and S2 taking a leading part, aided on occasion by S3 and S4. This is fully confirmed by evidence unknown to Larsen, with the proviso that S2 was working from about 1722/3 and S1 probably by 1728. The manuscripts newly studied reveal that there were at least two earlier circles, one (c.1715–19) based on Linike and another (c.1720–5) based on Smith. During this second period, the early Royal Academy years, there was evidently a great demand for copies and heavy pressure on the scriptorium, with the result that a surprisingly large number of manuscripts show the work of three, four, or even five different hands. They collaborated in various ways. Sometimes they took an act each; sometimes one would break off in the middle of a page and another would carry on. Occasionally the change-over was so frequent, no doubt when pressure was greatest, as to suggest that a second copyist had to take up his pen; however briefly when the first for whatever purpose left the room.

The activities of the Linike circle are most clearly observed in the volumes copied for Elizabeth Legh, which included two now in the Bodleian (MSS Mus d 61 and 62). A volume of harpsichord pieces in the Malmesbury Collection, dated 1718 on the title-page but inscribed by the owner 'Elizabeth Legh her book 1717' (presumably Old Style, i.e., up to 25 March 1718), shows five copyists in action: *Alpha*, Linike, *Beta*, RM1, and RM4. *Alpha* wrote only the first seven pages (p. 8 is blank) and may not have been a member of the circle; I have not found his writing elsewhere. The other four worked closely together, taking turns; each on occasion filled the verso of a leaf whose recto shows the hand of one of the others. Another harpsichord volume in the same collection, mostly arrangements of overtures and instrumental pieces from the operas, is inscribed 'Eliza: Legh August ye 30, 1722'. That date however is misleading. The core of the volume—pp. 1–10, 17–80, and 121–30, of which 10, 17 and 130 are blank—belongs to 1717–18; this is confirmed by the paper, the rastra, and the copyists.[14] In the summer of 1722 Elizabeth Legh evidently had these pages bound up with more than 150 others, of which the majority carried freshly copied music but about 45 were left blank; these in due course were filled with music written on three subsequent occasions, in 1724, 1726, and 1727, the volume being returned each time to the scriptorium. The original 1717–18 section was copied by RM1 and Linike in conjunction. They shared a series of instrumental excerpts from *Rinaldo* (others were added in 1722 by H1 and Smith on the inserted pp. 11–16) and the overture to *Agrippina,* mangled as *Argripini ed Nerone.* RM1 contributed the overtures to *Teseo, Il pastor fido,* and *Amadigi,* and two sinfonias from the last opera; Linike the concerti grossi Op. 3 No.

[14] I am grateful to Terence Best for help with the paper and rastra, and for much stimulating discussion of all the problems involved.

4 (also known as the second overture in *Amadigi*) and Op. 3 No. 2. Bodleian MS Mus d 61, a volume of Italian cantatas (some unpublished) dated 1718, likewise shows Linike, RM1, and *Beta* working together, and has later additions at the end.

The three copyists (apart from *Alpha*) associated with Linike in these manuscripts of about 1718 all occur elsewhere; see Tables 2, 3, and 4. RM4 (*c*.1717–21) has a neat and regular hand with little variation in clefs, notes, or words (he was evidently hurried when he copied the few pages from *Muzio Scevola*); his bass clef is individual, his C clef not unlike Handel's (Plate 4). Although his copies are not numerous, three of them are of substantial works in complete volumes. The other two copyists are decidedly eccentric. *Beta*'s peculiar hand, with a dejected C clef of geriatric aspect (Plate 5), is found in four manuscripts, none of them devoted to a single work and all of about the same date. The two RM volumes are composites assembled years later from copies of various periods; the paper and rastra of *Beta*'s contributions suggest a date about 1717 or a little earlier.

RM1 was much more actively associated with Linike and Handel (and later with Smith and others); he appears in two dozen manuscripts covering the years 1713(?) to 1725, and worked alone and in collaboration. His hand is so erratic as to suggest at first glance the work of several different men, but a comparative study of the large amount of material available leaves no doubt that we are dealing with a single individual, albeit a graphological freak (Plates 6, 7, and 8). All three clefs are subject to extremes of irregularity, depending perhaps on the speed with which he wrote; he often gives the impression of being in a tearing hurry. If the general appearance of his copies is untidy, with casually written key signatures and ill-formed words, the notes at least are legible. The crotchet and quaver rests are small and uneven. When he tries hard he can be reasonably neat, for example at the start of long jobs like the Manchester *Amadigi* and the RM *Teseo;* but the cloven hoof begins to show before long. After he has been copying for a time his clefs begin to run amok, the downward stroke of the treble sometimes completely missing the lower loop and the C clef describing all manner of contortions. He even supplies different clefs for more than one system with a single stroke of the pen. His bass clef nearly always has a somewhat hunchbacked appearance, and is peculiar in other respects. Nothing is predictable about the placing or even the presence of the two dots of the F clef; in a key with one flat they can appear before the flat or after it or be missing altogether, and all three forms are found on the same page (Plate 8). A few extra examples will serve to illustrate some of the wilder fantasies of this protean clefomaniac (see p. 19).

A feature of some RM1 copies is his placing of the clef at the very beginning of the staff, or even partly in the margin, where it is apt to be cut off by the brace (Plate 7). That he was closely associated with Handel there can be no doubt. RM19.e.6 has a number of annotations and corrections by the composer, and may have been used in the 1713 performances of *Teseo*. RM1's career continued throughout the Linike and first Smith periods. The gyrations of his hand make it of little use for dating, but the music he copied generally supplies a limit.

One more early copyist, Thomas Newman, demands a mention. Again Elizabeth

TABLE 2. *RM4 Copies*

Date	Source	Work	Remarks
1. ?1717	Coke	*Rinaldo*, 4 arias	for 1717 revival
2. c.1717	RM19.d.3	*Brockes Passion*	
3. 1717/18	Malmesbury	Pieces for harpsichord	pp. 110–57 and 4 unnumbered; see Linke copy 13
4. c.1717–18	BL Add. MS 47848	*Amadigi*	
5. 1718	Malmesbury	Utrecht Jubilate and Te Deum	dated by Elizabeth Legh
6. (1721)	RM19.c.8	*Muzio Scevola*	ff.1–9 (Amadei); with RM1, H2, and another
7.	Coke	Cantata 'Mi palpita il cor' (HWV 132c)	

TABLE 3. *Beta Copies*

Date	Source	Work	Remarks
1. c.1717	RM18.b.8	Pieces for harpsichord	ff.1–4, 33–57 of composite volume
2. c.1717	RM18.b.4	Sonata for 2 keyboards	ff. 12–20 of composite volume
3. 1717/18	Malmesbury	Pieces for harpsichord	pp. 13, 158–96; see Linke copy 13
4. 1718	Bodleian MS Mus d 61	Italian cantatas	pp. 156–258; see Linke copy 15

TABLE 4. *RM1 Copies*

Date	Source	Work	Remarks
1. ?1713	RM19.e.6	*Teseo*	amended by Handel; ? used in performance
2. ?1715	Munich, private collection	*Teseo*	unfoliated; for p. [1] and later addendum see Linke copy 5
3. c.1716	Manchester MS 130 Hd4 v.46	*Amadigi*	
4. ?1716	BL Add. MS 16024	*Il pastor fido*	appendix (ff. 94–104) to Linke copy 6
5. c.1716–17	Washington L. of C. (Littleton)	*Amadigi*	
6. 1717	Malmesbury	*Teseo*	insertion (pp. 221–3) in Linke copy 10
7. c.1717	Boston Museum of Fine Arts (Edwin M. Ripin MS)	Pieces for harpsichord	pp. 1–103; later additions by S1, Smith, and others

TABLE 4. (Cont.)

Date	Source	Work	Remarks
8. 1717/18	Malmesbury	Pieces for harpsichord	pp. 21–75, 77–90; see Linike copy 13
9. (1717/18)	Malmesbury	Overtures etc. for harpsichord	pp. 1–9, 21–59, 121–8; see Linike copy 14
10. 1718	Bodleian MS Mus d 61	Italian cantatas	pp. 9–60, 122–55; see Linike copy 15
11. 1718/19	Malmesbury	*Acis and Galatea*	dated 1718 (? Old Style); pp. 1–part of 60 (rest Smith)
12. March 1719	Malmesbury	Te Deum in B flat	dated 25 March 1719; p. 1 only (rest Smith)
13. c.1719	Bodleian Tenbury 881	Chandos Anthem: *I will magnify thee*	ff.77–119; see Linike copy 17
14. c.1719	Bodleian Tenbury 882	Chandos Anthems: *Let God arise, My song shall be alway, O come let us sing*	ff.1–56^v, 93–146; last two anthems partly Smith
15. c.1719	Bodleian Tenbury 883	Chandos Anthem: *The Lord is my light*	no foliation; two other anthems Smith
16.	RM19.e.7	Chandos Anthem: *O praise the Lord with one consent*	ff.1–47 of composite volume
17.	Coke	*Amadigi*, second copy	overture only; rest later
18. (1720)	BL Add. MS 31562	*Radamisto* (without recits.)	ff.44^v–81, 107^v–113 (clefs only); rest Smith and another
19. (1720)	Fitzwilliam MS Mus 72	*Radamisto*	no foliation, part of Acts II and III, rest Smith and another; later additions S2 and one more
20. ?1720/1	RM19.d.12	Aria from Bononcini's *Astarto*	ff.66–8 of composite volume
21. (Apr.1721)	Tokyo, Nanki Library	*Muzio Scevola* (incomplete)	last two movements of Act I overture (Amadei), 3 pages; with H2, H1, and another
22. (1721)	RM19.c.8	*Muzio Scevola*	ff.43–7^r (Amadei); see RM4 copy 6
23. c.1722	DSB Mus MS 9042	*Acis and Galatea*	ff.1–26;[2] rest Smith
24. (1722)	RAM MS 140	*Floridante* 1722 additions	ff.83–98 of composite volume
25. mid-1720s	Malmesbury	*Rinaldo*	second appendix (pp. 357–89); rest Smith and S2
26. (1725)	RM19.c.7	*Giulio Cesare*	with 1725 additions at end

[2] Illustrated as KP4 by Wolfram Windszus, *Aci, Galatea e Polifemo*, diss., University of Erlangen (Hamburg, 1979), 143.

Legh identifies him, writing on the title-page of the Malmesbury score of *Il pastor fido* : 'Transcribed by Mr Newman Feb[r] 1715' (this may be 1716 New Style). Newman also copied the Malmesbury *Amadigi* (dated 1716 by Elizabeth Legh), a keyboard fugue in E minor in Berlin Deutsche Staatsbibliothek Mus Ms 9171 ('Fuga di Sr Hendel 1717'), the cantata 'Lungi dal mio bel nume' (HWV 127b) in the Coke Collection, and two Italian duets in Hamburg MB/1570. His writing is neat and clear, with a small 'armchair' C clef and a very distinctive crotchet rest (Plate 9). Although no document connects Newman with Linike, the fact that he copied two complete operas for Elizabeth Legh places him close to the source of supply. We know a little about his career. He was a theatrical prompter, listed in *The London Stage* as attached to Drury Lane in the seasons 1702/3, 1704/5, 1707–9, and 1710–14, and to the Haymarket in 1706/7 and 1709/10. He may have worked at the Haymarket in 1705/6 as well, for the Lord Chamberlain's papers at the Public Record Office contain a complaint from Christopher Rich, dated 9 December 1705, accusing Vanbrugh of trying to entice Newman away from Drury Lane, where Rich was the notoriously unpopular and stingy manager.[15] Several of Newman's copying bills survive in the Folger Shakespeare Library (Washington), the Pierpont Morgan Library (New York),[16] and the British Library (Egerton MS 2159, f.36), the last with a letter complaining about tardy payment. They all date from about 1713–15; they are not concerned with music, but the hand appears to be the same as in the scores.

It remains to discover when and how Smith entered the picture. The earliest identifiable copy with his hand is the Malmesbury *Acis and Galatea*,[17] described on

---

[15] A. Nicoll, *A History of English Drama* 1660–1900, 6 vols. (Cambridge, 1952–9), ii. 289.

[16] I am indebted to Judith Milhous for photocopies of the bills in American libraries.

[17] This score confirms an earlier conjecture that Handel composed the work for only five singers. Each choral part bears the name of a character: 'Canto' = Galatea; 'Basso' = Polypheme; Tenors 1, 2, and 3 = Acis, Damon, and Coridon respectively. 'Would you gain the tender creature?' is for 'Coridon. 3 Tenor'.

the title-page as 'An English Opera Composed by George Frederick Handel Esquire, London, Anno 1718' and by the owner 'Elizabeth Legh her Book 1718' (again this could mean early 1719 New Style). Smith took over from RM1 after the top system on p. 60 and copied till the end of the work (p. 259). A score of the B flat Te Deum in the same collection, dated 25 March 1719, shows Smith again collaborating with RM1. Here RM1 wrote the first page only and Smith the rest. This suggests that he was learning his business, RM1 giving him a start. Smith himself followed the same procedure later, for example in the Bodleian *Giulio Cesare* (MS Mus d 220, c.1725), where Smith began and three other copyists continued, and the Malmesbury *Brockes Passion* (probably late 1720s), where Smith wrote the first page and S1 the remainder.

If Tenbury MSS 881–3 (nine Chandos Anthems; now in the Bodleian) were all copied at the same time, which seems overwhelmingly probable, we find Smith working with Linike and RM1. Two of the anthems in MS 882 are divided between RM1 and Smith. The date is probably 1719. It is worth noting that these three Tenbury manuscripts and Hereford Cathedral MS R.X.XVI of about the same date give the complete series of Chandos anthems without duplication. Tenbury MS 884 ('Opera of Amadis & Other Songs'), an *Acis and Galatea* in the Coke Collection, a fragment of Act 1 of *Agrippina* in RM19.d.12 (ff. 1–17), a duet from *Amadigi* in BL Add. MS 31571 (ff. 1–10), and the first fourteen leaves in the Washington Landon songs from *Amadigi* (see Table 1)—all the unaided work of Smith—belong to the same period and probably the same year. At least four copies show Smith's work in 1720: in Bodleian MS Mus d 62 (Italian cantatas, dated) he collaborates with H1 and S2, the earliest known appearance of either (S2's contribution may be a rather later addition); in the Malmesbury *Radamisto,* likewise dated, he takes turns with another newcomer, *Gamma;* in Fitzwilliam Mus MS 72 (*Radamisto,* datable from internal evidence) he works with RM1 and yet another, *Delta;* towards the end of that year he writes the performing score for Handel's first revival of the same opera[18] on 28 December (Hamburg MA/1043). He probably copied the whole of it, though this cannot be proved owing to the removal of many pages at subsequent revivals.

In all these pre-1721 copies Smith's hand shows certain individual features. His treble clef, taller, narrower, and usually more sloping than Linike's, lacks the characteristic little tail at the bottom of the stem familiar throughout his later work. We can actually watch him starting to develop this appendage in BL Add. MS 16108, a *Muzio Scevola* copy (containing several hands, like most copies of this opera) dating mostly from about April 1721, and in the keyboard volume Drexel MS 5856 in New York Public Library. Occasionally, for example on some pages of Tenbury 884 and Washington Landon, Smith's C clef is close to the second state of Linike's, that in use from about 1717 (Plate 2), though more often it approximates to its later shape. Most remarkable however is the bass clef, which is found in

<hr/>

[18] The original performing score used in Apr. 1720 is lost, and the first version of the opera has never been published. Chrysander's first version reflects Hamburg MA/1044, copied by H1 after Dec. 1720. See also p. 32 ff.

PLATE 1. Linike's handwriting, October 1712:
Il pastor fido (BL MS RM19e.4, f. 71ʳ).

PLATE 2. Linike's handwriting, June 1717: *Teseo* (Malmesbury MS).

PLATE 3. Linike's handwriting, June 1721: *Muzio Scevola* (Berlin SPK MS Am. B. 439b).

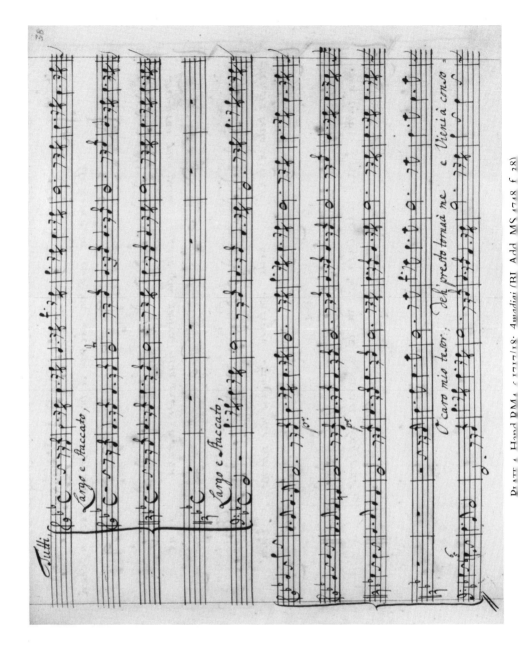

PLATE 4. Hand RM4, c.1717/18: *Amadigi* (BL Add. MS 1748. f. 28)

PLATE 5. Hand *Beta*, 1718: Italian cantata (Bodleian MS Mus d 61, p. 169).

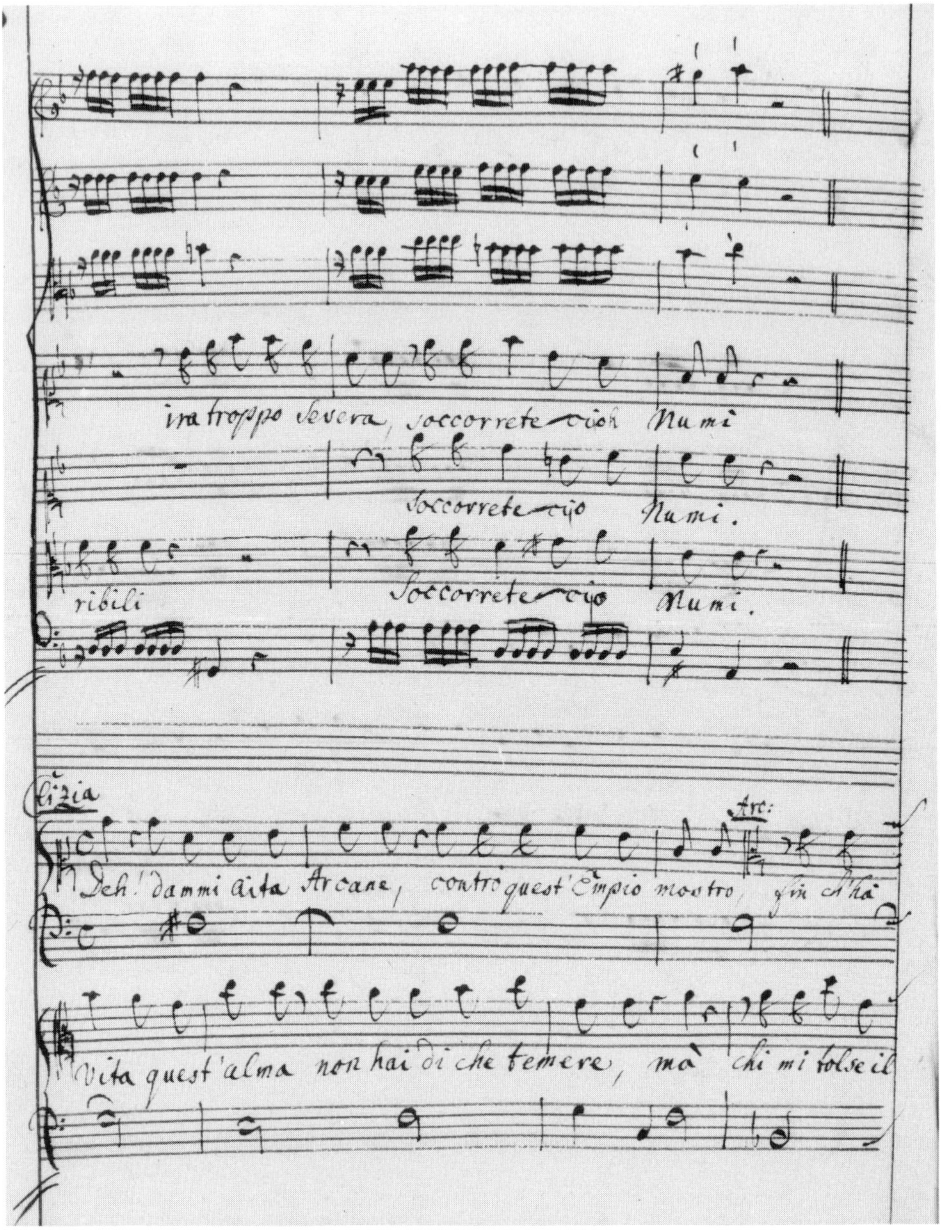

PLATE 6. Hand RM1, ?1713: *Teseo* (BL MS RM19.e.6, f. 74r).

PLATE 7. Hand RM1, *c*.1719: Chandos Anthem 5A
(Bodleian MS Tenbury 881, p. 101).

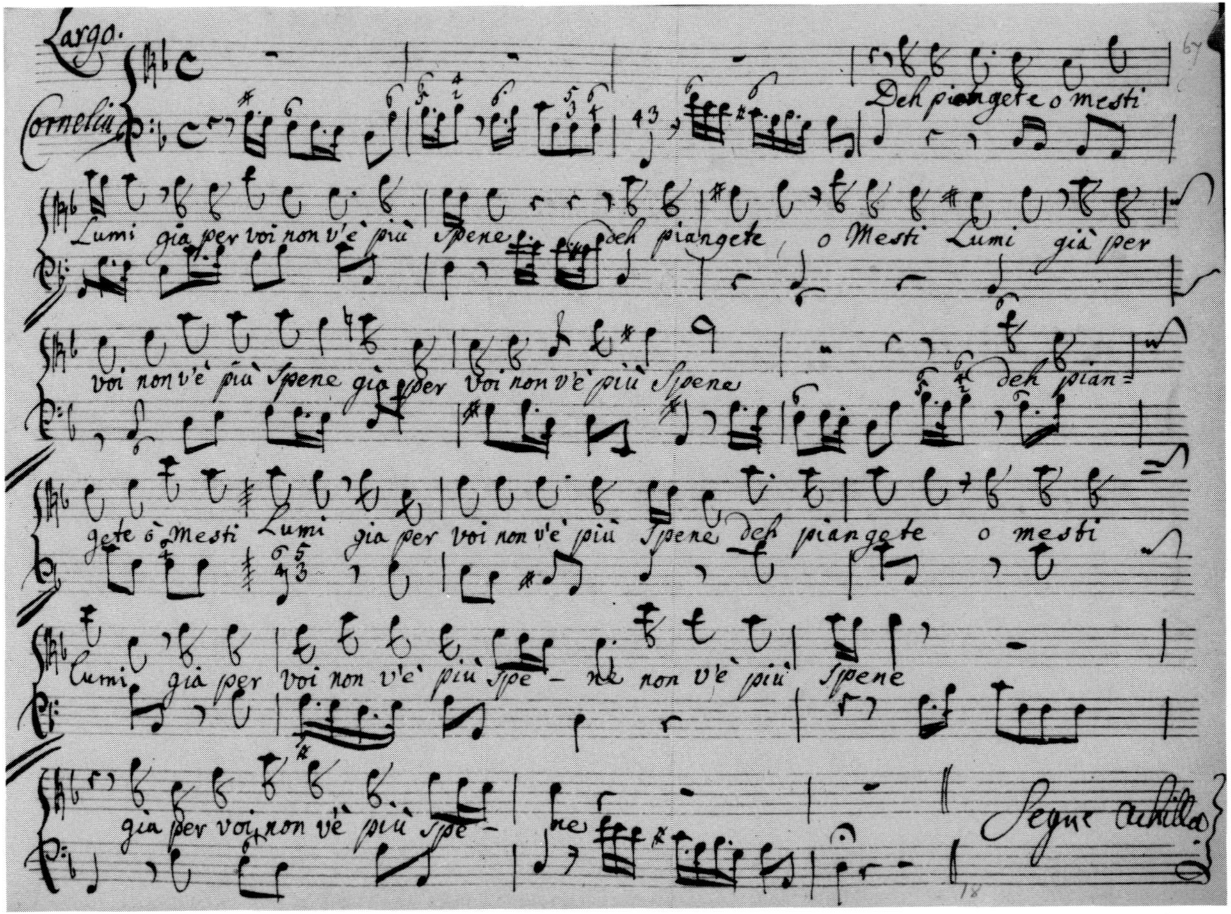

PLATE 8. Hand RM1, 1725: *Giulio Cesare* (BL MS RM19.c.7, f. 67).

126.

PLATE 9. Newman's handwriting, February 1715 (O.S.?): *Il pastor fido* (Malmesbury MS).

PLATE 10. Smith's handwriting, *c.*1719, showing both types of bass clef: *Amadigi* (Bodleian MS Tenbury 884, p. 100).

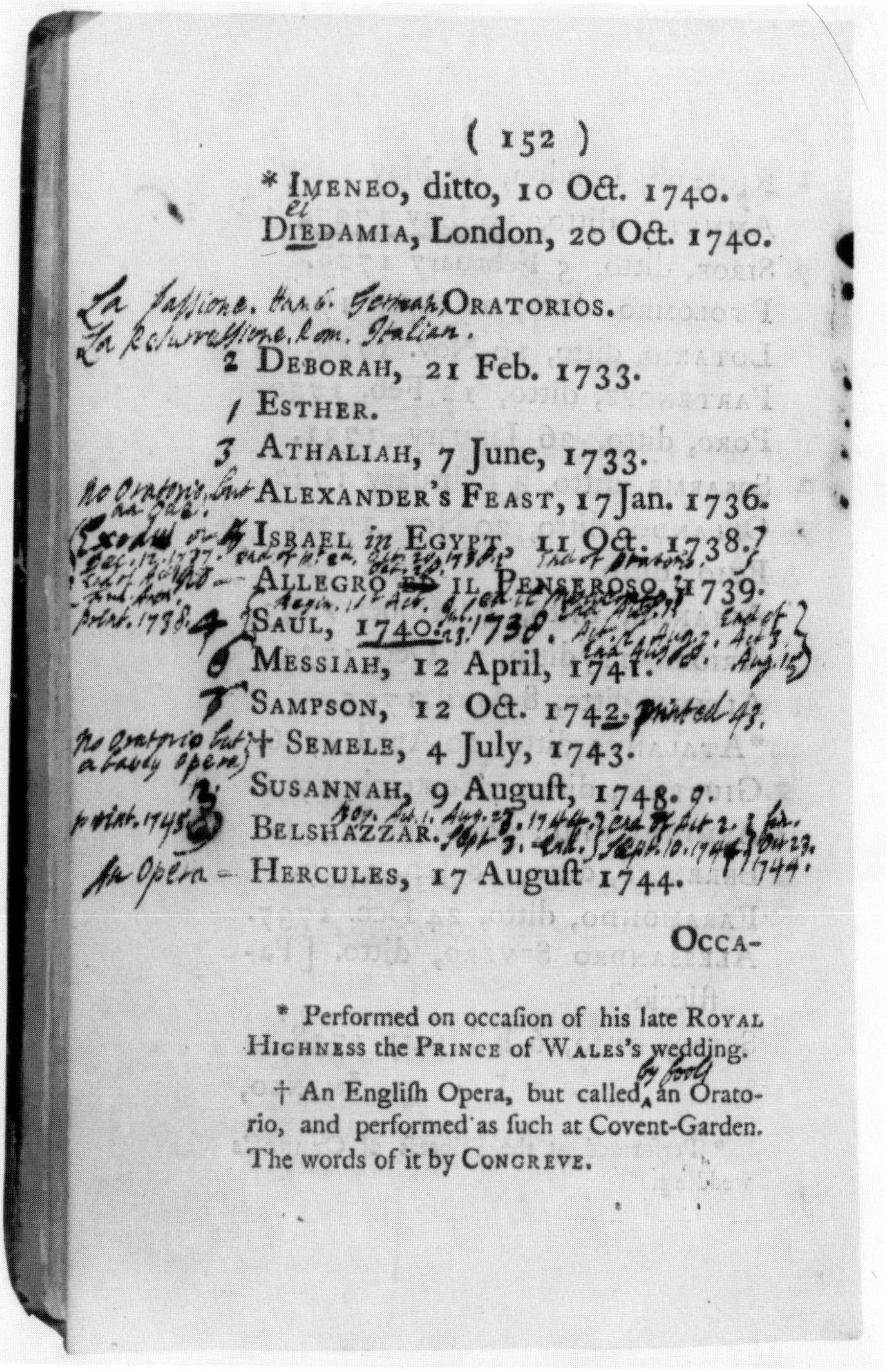

* IMENEO, ditto, 10 Oct. 1740.
ei
DIEDAMIA, London, 20 Oct. 1740.

La Passione. num. 6. German ORATORIOS.
La Resurressione, Rom. Italian.

2 DEBORAH, 21 Feb. 1733.

/ ESTHER.

3 ATHALIAH, 7 June, 1733.

no Oratorio but ALEXANDER'S FEAST, 17 Jan. 1736.

Exodus or ISRAEL *in* EGYPT, 11 Oct. 1738.

ALLEGRO & IL PENSEROSO, 1739.

4 SAUL, 1740.

6 MESSIAH, 12 April, 1741.

7 SAMPSON, 12 Oct. 1742.

no Oratorio but a bawdy opera † SEMELE, 4 July, 1743.

8 SUSANNAH, 9 August, 1748.

BELSHAZZAR.

An Opera — HERCULES, 17 August 1744.

OCCA-

---

* Performed on occasion of his late ROYAL
HIGHNESS the PRINCE of WALES's wedding.

† An English Opera, but called *by fools* an Oratorio, and performed as such at Covent-Garden.
The words of it by CONGREVE.

PLATE 11. Jennens's additions and amendments to Mainwaring's
list of Handel's oratorios.

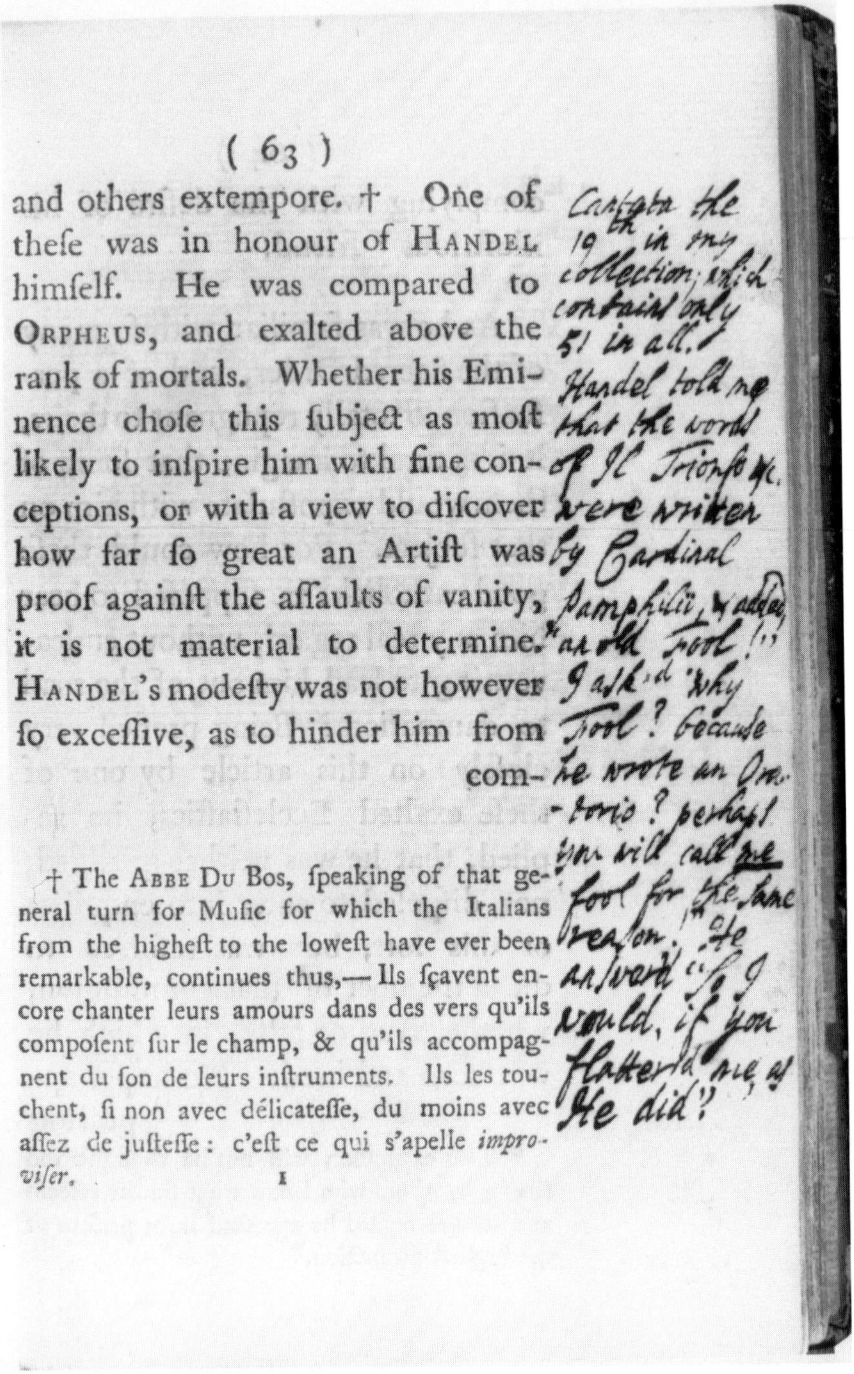

and others extempore. † One of thefe was in honour of HANDEL himfelf. He was compared to ORPHEUS, and exalted above the rank of mortals. Whether his Eminence chofe this fubject as moft likely to infpire him with fine conceptions, or with a view to difcover how far fo great an Artift was proof againft the affaults of vanity, it is not material to determine.* HANDEL's modefty was not however fo exceffive, as to hinder him from com-

Cantata the 19th in my collection; which contains only 51 in all. Handel told me that the world of Il Trionfo &c. were written by Cardinal Pamphilii, which he called "an old fool!" I afk'd "why fool? becaufe he wrote an Oratorio? perhaps you will call me fool for the fame reason." He anfwer'd "fo I would, if you flatter'd me as he did!"

† The ABBE DU BOS, fpeaking of that general turn for Mufic for which the Italians from the higheft to the loweft have ever been remarkable, continues thus,— Ils fçavent encore chanter leurs amours dans des vers qu'ils compofent fur le champ, & qu'ils accompagnent du fon de leurs inftruments. Ils les touchent, fi non avec délicateffe, du moins avec affez de jufteffe : c'eft ce qui s'apelle *improvifer*.

I

PLATE 12. A Handel anecdote recorded by Jennens.

two totally different and unrelated forms in the same manuscripts and often on the same page (Plate 10). One is virtually identical with Linike's; the other is the common type used by Smith himself later and by most other copyists of the time. The choice of one or the other is purely arbitrary. The Linike type, though always outnumbered, occurs sporadically throughout the 1719 copies, notably the Malmesbury and Coke scores of *Acis and Galatea* and the Tenbury *Amadigi*. There are, for example, twenty-eight instances in the 200 pages of the Malmesbury *Acis and Galatea* written by Smith, and seven in the seventeen folios of the *Agrippina* fragment in RM19.d.12. In 1720 it begins to die out. Two specimens appear suddenly on p. 41 of the Malmesbury *Radamisto*, just before Smith gives way to *Gamma*; six in the Fitzwilliam *Radamisto*; nine (five in one aria) in the December performing score of that opera; five (four in one aria) in the Hamburg *Floridante* (1721); three in Drexel MS 5856; none in the Smith sections of Bodleian MS Mus d 62. Single isolated specimens occur in the Hamburg scores of *Ottone* (Act III only) and *Flavio*, and in the Malmesbury copies of the same operas (1724 and 1723 respectively). The last three were partly copied by others.

What conclusions can be drawn from this? First, that Smith, who was not originally a copyist or even a musician (or of course an Englishman; several of these early copies contain jottings by him in German), was enlisted in the Linike circle about the end of 1718. He was already Handel's friend and trusted secretary, and by 1720 was concerned in a music shop in Coventry Street off the Haymarket.[19] It was becoming apparent that Handel's large output and the growing demand for copies, both for performance and for sale to patrons (accentuated by the failure of Walsh or any other publisher to print anything more than a few truncated arias in the nine years between *Rinaldo* and *Radamisto*), required the services of more and more scribes. Although there was no opera between 1717 and 1720, Linike was doubtless busy playing in concerts; in any case, like Smith later, he could not carry the full load of work. My second conclusion is that Smith, perhaps at Handel's suggestion, learned the copyist's trade under the guidance or tuition of Linike, whose idiosyncrasies in such matters as clef-formation he would naturally begin by imitating. His musical hand soon developed greater assurance and characteristics of its own. By 1720 he was ready to succeed Linike in command of Handel's scriptorium, a position he occupied until his death in 1763. We may be thankful that he modelled his style on Linike and not on RM1.

[19] He and Richard Meares issued the first volume of Handel's *Suites* for harpsichord and the score of *Radamisto* in Nov. and Dec. that year.

3
Vocal Embellishment in a Handel Aria

Amadigi di Gaula, Handel's fifth London opera, was produced at the King's Theatre in the Haymarket on 25 May 1715. It is one of three surviving Handel operas of which the autograph has vanished without trace,[1] though early manuscript copies are more numerous than for any other Handel opera. The only autograph material for Amadigi, apart from a keyboard arrangement of the overture[2] dating from about 1725 and some modifications in the Hamburg copy, is a single aria among the miscellaneous fragments in the Fitzwilliam Museum, Cambridge (Mus MS 256, pp. 41–3).[3] This is neither a sketch nor a portion of the original score, as Handel's heading 'Aria dell' Opera d'Amadigi' sufficiently indicates. A. H. Mann in his Catalogue[4] conjectured that Handel wrote it out 'for the soloist to study the song from', and remarked that 'the vocal part is more florid than the printed'. This statement is reasonable as far as it goes, but the manuscript has puzzling features and others that throw light on Handel's artistic intentions and methods of work.

The aria is 'O caro mio tesor', a love song addressed by the heroine Oriana to Amadigi in Act I. The part was written for the soprano (later contralto) Anastasia Robinson, a young singer about 20 years old who had made her début the previous year. A comparison between the Fitzwilliam manuscript and the aria as it appears in the Chrysander score[5] and the early copies reveals many differences.

(1) The Fitzwilliam manuscript has an accompaniment for figured bass only (except for a violin part in the ritornello after the A section), whereas in Chrysander there are parts for two violins (doubled by oboes)[6] and viola.

(2) The opening ritornello (bars 1–8) is omitted, and the ritornello after the A section reduced from eight bars to four by the suppression of bars 52–5. The bar numbers cited here apply to the full (Chrysander) version.

(3) The tempo mark is Larghetto, not Largo e staccato.

[1] The others are Almira and Admeto.
[2] Printed by Terence Best in Twenty Overtures in Authentic Keyboard Arrangements (Novello, 1987), vol. i.
[3] It is reproduced in facsimile in the Hallische Händel-Ausgabe score of the opera.
[4] J. A. Fuller-Maitland and A. H. Mann, Catalogue of Music in the Fitzwilliam Museum, Cambridge (London 1893), 171.
[5] Chrysander's text is based on the Hamburg copy MA/1003, which is not the 1715 performing score but dates from about 1716–17. Some of the other copies are earlier; there are however no material differences in this aria.
[6] Chrysander misinterpreted the oboe parts. Both should double the first violins.

(4) The principal rhythm of the accompaniment is phrased ♩. ♪♩. ♪

not ♩. ⅞♪♩. ⅞♪

(5) There are many minor differences in note-values; for example where the bass note is repeated Handel sometimes writes ♩ instead of ♩. ♪

(6) The vocal line, as Mann noted, is more elaborate. This is discussed in detail below.

(7) There are a number of changes in the bass (bars 13, 22, 24, 28–9, 42–3, 48–9, 62, 64–5, 67, 71–3, 75–6). In the first part of the aria these are mostly different inversions of the same chords; in the B section they range further afield.

If we assume that the Chrysander score is essentially correct, it is obvious that Handel was not copying. He was writing out the aria from memory. Even if the change of tempo was deliberate, the numerous altered note-values (5) are a clear indication of this (see Exx. 1 and 3). A point of some interest for performance practice is that in Chrysander all four instrumental parts have the principal rhythm (4) in its double-dotted form (more strictly a dot followed by a pause of articulation), whereas the voice has dotted crotchets followed by quavers, like both parts in the Fitzwilliam manuscript. At first glance this looks like an ingenious type of syncopation, especially as the notation is consistent throughout. But a performance of the music as written, with every alternate chord entering a quarter of a beat after the voice, would not be satisfactory. The discrepancy can be reconciled if the voice conforms to the instrumental rhythm (Ex. 1c), omitting the pauses, which would produce a singularly jerky delivery for a love song.

There is much to be said for Mann's suggestion that Handel intended the Fitzwilliam copy for a singer. Points (1) and (2) are consistent with this, though, as we shall see, (7) presents certain difficulties. Moreover most of the variants under (4) are undoubtedly vocal embellishments. As such they are very valuable. Handel's autograph scores contain plenty of decorative writing for the voice, chiefly in the form of coloratura; occasionally he indicates appoggiaturas and cadential trills; but he never writes out the optional ornamentation regularly added at this period, especially in da capos, because this was the province of the individual singer. A part so embellished by Handel suggests exceptional circumstances, such as a projected performance by an artist with little experience of the Italian operatic style.

The closest parallels to the Fitzwilliam 'O caro mio tesor' are another of Oriana's arias, 'S'estinto è l'idol mio', in the Malmesbury score of *Amadigi*, copied by Thomas Newman in 1716, and a copy (by Smith and ?H3) of five arias from *Ottone* in the Bodleian Library (MS. Don.c.69).[7] The embellishments to 'S'estinto è l'idol mio' were probably written by Handel's friend Elizabeth Legh for whom the score was copied. Handel himself embellished four of the *Ottone* arias. All five belong to the soprano part of Teofane, composed for Francesca Cuzzoni and sung by her in the seasons of 1723 and 1726. In the Bodleian copy they are transposed down a fourth or a fifth for contralto. This could have been for the hurried revival in April 1727, when Faustina and Cuzzoni in turn were

[7] First described by J. S. and M. V. Hall in 'Handel's Graces' (*Händel-Jahrbuch* 1957), 25–42; printed in G. F. Handel, *Three Ornamented Arias*, ed. W. Dean (Oxford, 1976).

Ex.1

(a) Chrysander

Largo e staccato

O ca - ro mio te - sor, deh! pre - sto tor - nia me

(b) Fitzwilliam

Larghetto

O ca - ro mio te - sor, deh! pre - sto tor - nia me

(c) (upper parts omitted)

O ca - ro mio te - sor, deh! pre - sto tor - nia me

incapacitated by illness, or perhaps for an abortive revival in May or June 1733 whose cancellation may have been due to the illness of Anna Strada.[8] Whatever the occasion, Handel left the job unfinished. Of the five arias, two are ornamented throughout, one in the A section only, one has a single ornament on the voice's first phrase, and one is untouched. It seems probable that Handel added the ornaments in the Bodleian copy for the benefit of an inexperienced (perhaps English) singer who had to learn the part in a hurry (but in the event was not required to sing it). Can some such explanation account for the Fitzwilliam copy of 'O caro mio tesor'?

Before considering the possibilities it may be as well to look more closely at the manuscript. It has several interesting features. In the first place, both parts of the aria are affected, though the embellishments in the A section must be presumed to apply to the da capo, which of course is not written out. This agrees with Tosi's opinion about the decoration of da capo arias: 'In the second [part] they expect, that to this purity some artful Graces be added, by which the Judicious may hear, that the Ability of the Singer is greater; and, in repeating the Air, he that does not vary it

---

[8] See W. Dean and J. M. Knapp, *Handel's Operas 1704–1726* (Oxford, 1987), 402, 439–40.

for the better, is no great Master.'[9] Secondly, in none of these manuscripts are
there any cadenzas, though the B section of 'Benchè mi sia crudele' has a brief
flourish at a fermata (bar 112). This should not be taken as evidence that Handel
never tolerated cadenzas, though it may suggest that he preferred them to be
very short. In some arias they are clearly implied; but Burney's remark about
'Rival ti sono' in *Faramondo*, that 'in the course of the song [Caffarelli] is left *ad
libitum* several times, a compliment which Handel never paid to any ordinary
singer',[10] probably indicates the general trend. Cadenzas were certainly not
obligatory; the Fitzwilliam version of 'O caro mio tesor' even simplifies the
closing vocal cadence of the B section. Thirdly, and most important, Handel's
embellishments never confuse or deface the vocal line, though they occasionally
modify it in detail for expressive purposes. (This is true even of the most
elaborate, in Teofane's 'Affanni del pensier', where he shows himself not averse
to harmonic clashes.) They occur most frequently in the approach to cadences
and in melismatic passages, and they are carefully graded: little or no ornament
when the material is first sung (in the da capo), considerably more when it is
repeated or varied.

The first twelve bars of the voice part (10–21) are untouched. The cadential
figures in bars 22, 24, and 30 are lightly decorated, those in bars 28 and 37–8 receive
more elaborate treatment. Towards the end of the first part, with the ideas now
familiar, the ornament becomes more ambitious. When the triplet figure first heard
in bars 26–8 is repeated in bars 40–2[11] Handel recasts it in a flowing quaver
movement and intensifies the approach to the cadence by changing the rising
seventh in bar 43 to a ninth, as in bar 29. This however anticipates and devalues
the quaver figure in bars 46–8, which is replaced by a charming rhythmic variation
adorned with trills. And having twice employed the rising ninth before cadences
Handel reverts to the seventh in bar 49. Ex. 2 shows all the ornamentation in the
first part of the aria, with the Chrysander vocal line for comparison; the bass is the
same except where indicated.

The opening of the B section (59–64) also remains unadorned. In bars 65 and 68
(and later 77) we find the same type of simple ornament as at corresponding points
in the first part, though bar 65 has a new bass. A change in the vocal line of bar
70 (g″ for d″ on the third beat) might be considered an improvement rather than
a decoration. But the most interesting modification occurs towards the end (bar 71
ff.), where not only the vocal line but the harmonic movement is radically altered,
and with it the whole approach to the D minor cadence (Ex. 3).

This goes beyond mere embellishment and brings us back to point (7). What
exactly was Handel doing? It is obvious here that the voice and bass of the
Fitzwilliam version would require considerable alteration of the upper parts in the
Chrysander score if they were to be used together. This is by no means the only

[9] P. F. Tosi, *Observations on the Florid Song,* trans. J. E. Galliard (London, 1743).

[10] *A General History of Music* (London, 1935), ii. 819.

[11] It is interesting to find that Handel originally copied the triplet on the first beat of bar 40, followed
by a crotchet rest, exactly as in bar 26. The variation evidently occurred to him as he wrote.

Ex.2

Chrysander

Ex.3

(a) Chrysander

rar   il tuo   sem - bian   -   te.

(b) Fitzwilliam

discrepancy: the changed bass in bars 28–9, 42–3, 48–9, and 63–5 would produce consecutive octaves or other anomalies when associated with the upper parts. Although Handel was no pedant in such matters he would scarcely have tolerated such a crop of them, even without the evidence of bars 71–3. Any singer who tried out the ornamented version with Chrysander's instrumental parts would be in for a rude surprise.

It is difficult to resist the conclusion that in writing out the aria Handel was not only using his memory but to some extent recomposing the music. This is consistent with what we know of his method of composition, in which there was always a strong element of improvisation. Much reworking of old material seems to have arisen from just this type of situation; he begins by quoting more or less exactly, and as his pen runs over the paper his inventive power leaps into activity, like the engine of a car running down hill, until reproduction turns into new creation. The

Amadigi aria does not take this process very far; indeed, it may have been un-conscious. But, as we know from other contexts, the Habermann borrowings in *Jephtha* for example,[12] Handel found it difficult even to copy another man's music without making adjustments and improvements.

For what singer, and on what occasion, did he prepare the Fitzwilliam copy? In some respects the original Oriana, Anastasia Robinson, who was young and inexperienced and whose Italian training was confined to what she picked up from Pier Giuseppe Sandoni in London, would seem to fill the bill. Another possibility is the unkown substitute who replaced her after the first performance in 1715. But it seems unlikely that Handel, so soon after composing the opera, would give either artist a version materially different from that of the full score, unless he intended to modify this; and there is no evidence from the copies that he did so. A more tenable solution is that Handel wrote out the aria for some singer who was to be accompanied only by continuo, perhaps at a concert. This might have happened at any period, before or after his last revival of *Amadigi* in 1717, or even when his memory of the original detail had begun to fade.[13] The heading 'Aria dell' Opera d'Amadigi' might be taken to support a date after the production of the opera. We shall probably never know the answer. But the manuscript deserves to be published in a critical edition; the vocal line could then serve as a model for singers and conductors who wish to recreate the correct style of embellishment in Handel's operas. Together with the other arias mentioned above it supplies the only positive evidence we have for what he considered suitable. It gives no support whatever to the wild ornamentation—or all too often recompositon—distressingly common in modern revivals.

[12] See W. Dean, *Handel's Dramatic Oratorios and Masques* (London, 1959), 624.

[13] The paper, type Cb, would fit any date up to 1731.

4

Mattheson's Arrangement of Handel's *Radamisto* for the Hamburg Opera

It is well known that soon after Handel established himself as a dramatic composer in London his operas became increasingly popular in Hamburg. Between 1715 and 1734 fifteen of them, including the Venetian *Agrippina,* were staged there, and several remained in the repertory until the closure of the Hamburg Opera in 1738. Apart from Brunswick, which had connections with the English court after the accession of the Elector of Hanover as King George I, Hamburg saw far more contemporary Handel productions than any other city on the Continent. There were obvious reasons for this. As a free city it had close commercial and cultural links with England. The young Handel had spent three impressionable years there, playing in the theatre orchestra, learning his trade, and composing his first operas. And several influential friends and colleagues were active in Hamburg, among them Keiser, Mattheson, and Telemann, each of whom was concerned in the introduction of one or more of Handel's London operas.

Although librettos for all these productions survive, most of the scores have been lost. It is clear, however, that they had to be adapted for the Hamburg public. Apart from *Agrippina* and *Muzio Scevola,* which were given in Italian throughout, they were sung in a mixture of two languages, the regular Hamburg practice: the recitatives and on occasion some of the arias in German, the majority of the arias and set pieces in the original Italian. The librettos printed a German translation, generally in prose, alongside the Italian arias. The degree of rearrangement to which the operas were subjected varied widely. While the recitatives had to be recomposed, some productions retained the original plots and most if not all of Handel's arias and set pieces. Others were changed, sometimes very considerably. The Hamburg public liked not only spectacle, of which there was plenty in the London theatre, but choruses, extra ballets, and if possible comic relief; and they were developing a taste for that Italian curiosity, the pasticcio. There was a tendency to divide the music as evenly as possible between the available singers, regardless of their importance in the plot. This was common in Italy too, but it was very different from Handel's own practice when he adapted old Italian librettos for his operas in London.

As early as 1717 the magic opera *Amadigi,* produced in Hamburg under the title *Oriana,* received three extra characters, including a buffo servant who consoled himself with drink; most of the new music was by Keiser. J. G. Linike added choruses of concubines and comic peasants and extra music for minor characters to

Giulio Cesare. Telemann in particular was inclined to dilute Handel's most serious and tragic operas with extravagances of this kind. He introduced a scene at the foot of Mount Olympus, with a ballet of Highlanders and their women, into Act I of *Tamerlano,* and a Tartar dance at a most unsuitable moment in Act II. His version of *Ottone* is virtually a pasticcio, with an extra character and additional arias not only by Telemann himself but by various Italian composers. The most extreme case is *Riccardo Primo,* where the degree of buffoonery almost approaches that of Telemann's own *Der geduldige Socrates.*[1]

None of this is surprising. Probably no one at that period regarded an old opera as a work of art whose integrity had to be respected in revivals. That is a modern conception. In any case, it would not have been practical in the present instance. All Handel's operas after he left Hamburg were composed according to the Italian *opera seria* convention (admittedly with variations of his own), many of them for the greatest singers in Europe. A central feature of this tradition was that the heroic parts were designed for high voices, sopranos or altos, and sung by castratos or women—often by both in different performances. The Hamburg company was very differently constituted. Castratos did appear there occasionally: Valentino Urbani in 1722, Campioli from 1722 to 1726. (Both sang under Handel in London.) Male parts were sometimes sung by women, for example Julius Caesar by Domini-china Pollone in 1729.[2] But the usual practice was to transpose these heroic parts down an octave for tenors and basses, simply because more of them were available. The implications of this are considered below.

Mattheson's version of *Radamisto,* one of five Handel operas of which the Hamburg score survives,[3] was produced in January 1722 under the title *Zenobia, oder das Muster rechtschaffener ehelichen Liebe.* It enjoyed considerable success, with at least thirty performances, most of them in the first two seasons; there was a ten-year gap before its last revival in 1736. Before examining Mattheson's treatment of the score, and how it conformed with the work of his Hamburg contemporaries, it is necessary to say something about the opera itself and its early history. *Radamisto,* composed for the first season of the Royal Academy, the most ambitious of all attempts to establish Italian opera in London, is one of Handel's grandest and most heroic operas. There is no light relief at all. The characters, all of royal or princely blood, are torn by the most passionate emotions (Fig. 1 shows their relationships), and the plot is full of threatened and actual violence. The villain Tiridate, king of Armenia, is married to Radamisto's sister Polissena but lusts after his sister-in-law Zenobia, Radamisto's wife. In order to gain his desires he makes war on his father-in-law Farasmane, king of Thrace, conquers all his dominions except the capital city in which Radamisto and Zenobia are besieged, captures the old king himself, and tries to blackmail Radamisto into surrender by threatening to kill his

[1] See E. Dahnk-Baroffio, 'Händels *Riccardo primo* in Deutschland', in W. Meyerhoff (ed.,) *50 Jahre Göttinger Händel-Festspiele* (Kassel, 1970), 150–66.

[2] K. Zelm, 'Die Sänger der Hamburger Gänsemarkt-Oper', in *Hamburger Jahrbuch für Musikwissenschaft* 3 (1978), 35–73, on p. 65.

[3] The others are *Almira, Ottone, Riccardo Primo,* and *Poro.*

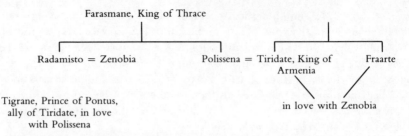

FIG. 1. Relationships between the characters in *Radamisto*.

father before his eyes and put the city's whole population to the sword. Among
Tiridate's allies are two other princes: Tigrane, who loves Polissena but tries to win
her by persuasion rather than force, and Tiridate's brother Fraarte, who in Handel's
first version also loves Zenobia. The events of the opera include Tiridate's capture
of the city, the escape of Radamisto and Zenobia, her attempted suicide by jumping
into the river Araxes, the faithful Polissena's denunciation of her husband when he
refuses to pardon her brother, and a revolution led by Tigrane and Fraarte who,
sickened by Tiridate's cruelty, bring the tyrant to his knees. He confesses and, to
his surprise, is forgiven. This ensures the statutory happy end.

   By the time of the Hamburg production Handel had performed the opera in
three London seasons, in April 1720, December 1720, and November 1721, and he
was to revive it again in January 1728. Each production saw changes in the music
and the cast, and the first two—in April and December 1720—were radically
different. Even the plot was altered: in December Fraarte was no longer Tiridate's
brother but his minister, his love for Zenobia was cut out, and the action of the third
act was greatly tightened up. The casts are listed in Table 1. It will be seen that of
the seven singers in April only one, the bass Lagarde in the small role of Farasmane,
retained the same part in December. Two others, the sopranos Durastanti and
Galerati, were still in the cast but sang different roles. Three important characters
had a new vocal pitch: Radamisto, composed for a woman soprano, was sung by
an alto castrato; Zenobia, a contralto, by a soprano; and Tiridate, a tenor, by a bass.
It is worth noting, as typical of Handel's practice, that during the year 1720 all three
male soprano roles were sung both by women and by castratos.[4]

   To accommodate the new singers in December 1720 Handel was not content
simply to transpose the old arias; he rewrote many of them, and composed twelve
new pieces, including a magnificent quartet, one of the most elaborate ensembles
in any of his operas. But the matter is more complicated than that. There are five,
not four, versions of *Radamisto*, quite apart from changes made before performance,
and no accurate printed score of any of them. The version staged in April 1720,
representing Handel's original conception, which includes three ballet suites, has not
been published at all.[5] Chrysander's first version is based on Hamburg MS MA/

---

   [4] Deutsch (*Handel: A Documentary Biography*) is wrong in listing Baldassari and Berselli as tenors, and
in doubting whether the 1728 revival took place. Chrysander (in the Preface to the Händel-Gesellschaft
score) is wrong in saying that Fraarte was cut in December 1720.
   [5] It survives complete in a single manuscript in the possession of the Earl of Malmesbury.

TABLE I. *Cast changes for Radamisto–Zenobia productions*

	Radamisto					Zenobia
	April 1720	Chrysander's first version	December 1720	November 1721	January 1728	Hamburg, January 1722
Male						
Radamisto	Durastanti (soprano)		Senesino (alto castrato)	Senesino	Senesino	Bass
Tigrane	Galerati (soprano)		Berselli (soprano castrato)	? Baldassari (soprano castrato)	Baldi (alto castrato)	Tenor
Fraarte	Baldassari (soprano castrato)		Galerati (soprano)	—	—	Tenor
Tiridate	Gordon (tenor)		Boschi (bass)	Boschi	Boschi	Bass
Farasmane	Lagarde (bass)		Lagarde	? Lagarde	Palmerini (bass)	Tenor
Female						
Zenobia	Anastasia Robinson (contralto)		Durastanti (soprano)	? Anastasia Robinson	Faustina Bordoni (soprano)	Soprano
Polissena	Ann Turner Robinson (soprano)		Salvai (soprano)	Salvai	Cuzzoni (soprano)	Soprano
Version of score	1	2	3	4	5	

1044, which he assumed to be the April performing score. It is not a performing score, it is not the April version, and it is not a Smith copy. It was written by another copyist[6] about 1721, apparently because Handel wished to preserve a clean pre-December score for his library. It reflects not what was performed in April but the score as altered either during the original run or a little later, but before December 1720. These alterations included the omission of the ballet suites and a number of modifications both to words and to music. Most unusually Handel entered some of these in the original autograph: but the survival of material cancelled there both in the first printed score and in a number of early copies proves that he must have done this after the April production.

Chrysander's first version is thus no. 2 in Table 1 and corresponds to no known performance. His *Seconda e Terza Versione* is a confusing jumble of nos. 3, 4, and 5—the versions performed in Handel's three revivals—none of them printed or indicated in full. Moreover Chrysander also backdated into his first version—no. 2—some minor changes that belong to Handel's later productions.

Mattheson's Hamburg score, now in the Berlin Staatsbibliothek (Mus. MS 9051), differs from all of Handel's. That almost certainly was not Mattheson's intention, apart of course from the recitatives and vocal transpositions. It can be shown that he obtained three separate sources from London; a manuscript full score of the April version, the printed libretto of the December 1720 revival, and a manuscript full score of Handel's twelve new pieces composed for that occasion. He must have obtained the music from Handel himself, or at least with his consent. He cannot have relied on the Meares printed scores of either April or December,[7] since as usual they were incomplete, omitting many of the orchestral parts, and Meares did not print the quartet at all. There is no evidence that Mattheson knew the November 1721 score (no. 4), which omitted Fraarte altogether.

What he tried to do was to reproduce Handel's December version by grafting the twelve new pieces on to the April score. He needed the December libretto to know where to place them—not at all a simple matter—and he did this correctly; Chrysander prints three of them in the wrong place. But Mattheson obviously knew nothing of the other alterations and revisions made by Handel in December; nor did he know Handel's transpositions of the arias he retained. None of these appears in his *Zenobia* score, which (apart from the twelve new pieces and the recitatives) follows the April version without the ballet suites. One of Polissena's arias in Act II, 'Non sarà quest'alma mia', received a new and stronger text in Handel's December revival, beginning 'Che farà quest'alma mia'. Mattheson realized that it was essentially the same piece, so he fitted the December words to the April music, unaware that in the meantime Handel had rewritten and improved the aria, especially the orchestration.

Table 1 shows that Mattheson gave six of the seven characters a different voice from Handel's April score, only Polissena retaining her original pitch. She remained a soprano in all Handel's versions too, though he lowered the tessitura a little for

---

[6] H1 in Clausen's enumeration (see p. 8). Chrysander used this manuscript as copy for his edition.
[7] Published in December 1720 and March 1721 respectively.

Salvai and raised it again later for Cuzzoni. Mattheson set about his task in a rather strange manner. The three high male parts—Radamisto, Tigrane, and Fraarte— were all put down an octave, though Radamisto now had five arias and one duet from the soprano version of April, and two arias, one duet, and the quartet from the alto version of December. Farasmane's single aria, for bass, had its voice part adjusted for tenor in the original key. Zenobia's six alto arias were simply written out at the same pitch in the soprano clef; she also had one soprano aria, 'Fatemi, O cieli', the only new one composed for her in December, and incidentally the only aria of hers in that revival whose exact pitch we know. All Zenobia's other arias in Chrysander's *Seconda e Terza Versione* are adaptations for Faustina Bordoni in 1728 (version 5). For Tiridate, Mattheson had one bass aria from December and two tenor arias from April, both of which Handel had since rewritten with more elaborate scoring and striking improvements. Mattheson could not know this; he simply retained the tenor versions, and his copyist put the voice part of one into the bass clef, but for some obscure reason not the other.

This resulted in some odd inconsistencies of tessitura. Occasionally another hand made adjustments in the manuscript, generally shifting phrases at either end of the vocal compass up or down an octave, which does not improve the vocal line. One of Zenobia's April arias, the fiery 'Già che morir non posso', is very awkward for a soprano at the original pitch, so many phrases in both sections were put in the higher octave. One of Tiridate's, 'Si che ti renderai', and one of Radamisto's, 'Vanne sorella ingrata', underwent the opposite procedure, their highest phrases going down an octave. Others, on the face of it equally uncomfortable for the singers, remained untouched. If the opera was sung as it stands in the score, some of the voices must have been subjected to considerable strain. This is particularly true of Radamisto's part, which veers between a high baritone and a bass. It is not at all clear why Mattheson did not have some arias transposed into more convenient keys before the score was copied. He may not have known who was to sing in the opera. He may even have delegated the whole job of reconciling the scores to the copyist and confined himself to translating and setting the recitatives. Unfortunately we know nothing of the Hamburg casts, except that Signora Stradiotti, a soprano who had sung in London (though not under Handel), appeared in *Zenobia* in 1724.

Apart from annotations for revivals and the tessitura changes just mentioned, Mus. MS 9051 is in the hand of a single theatre copyist. The bass is fully figured. On one page of Fraarte's first aria, 'Deh! fuggi un traditore', the copyist forgot to alter the voice clef from soprano to tenor, and no one bothered to correct the mistake. Another aria for Fraarte, in the first scene of Act III, is in the soprano clef throughout. Apart from the recitatives, it is the only music in the manuscript not by Handel. Fraarte had an aria here in the April version, 'S'adopri il braccio armato', but not in December. Mattheson decided to give him one, but instead of restoring Handel's he chose a piece very similar in style and mood both to 'S'adopri' and to 'Deh! fuggi un traditore', which Reinhard Strohm has identified as from Bononcini's *Etearco*. However, Mattheson then thought better of this, for the copyist never supplied the words, and the aria was apparently concealed or pasted down before the performance and not sung.

The modifications made for later Hamburg revivals include the omission of Farasmane's single aria, two of Tigrane's, and the remaining two of Fraarte's, though all seem to have been subsequently restored. The 1726 edition of the libretto omits Fraarte's first two arias but includes 'S'adopri'; this may be a mistake, or the aria may have been inserted on loose pages and subsequently lost. Three of Tigrane's arias were marked for transposition, 'L'ingrato non amar' from G minor to C minor, 'Vuol ch'io serva' (which has a high tessitura) from G to A, and 'La sorte, il ciel' from B flat to F, either for an alto or a bass. The magnificent aria 'Barbaro, partirò', in which Polissena finally denounces her brutal husband, copied in its December 1720 key of A major (not Chrysander's B flat, which belongs to Cuzzoni in 1728), may on some occasion have been replaced by the original April aria, 'Sposo ingrato,' a much weaker piece; someone wrote those words in the margin, but the music is not in the manuscript. Another revival change was the raising of two of Zenobia's arias, 'Fatemi, O cieli' and 'Empio perverso cor,' by a third. Handel himself made these transpositions, but not until 1728, when he transferred 'Fatemi, O cieli' to Polissena.

The manuscript also contains the first words—not the music—of several arias that do not belong to any version of Handel's opera. They come from Zeno's *Caio Fabrizio,* first set by Caldara for Venice in 1729, and can only apply to the last revival of *Zenobia* in 1736, turning it into a pasticcio. Whether Mattheson was concerned with this performance we cannot tell; but his 1722 copy was still in use, though the inserted music has been lost.

Mattheson's recitatives are considerably longer than Handel's both in the words and in the music. The first of all, after Polissena's cavatina 'Sommi Dei', has twenty-six bars in Handel's April score, twenty-eight in December, and thirty-eight in Mattheson's. Over the whole opera, on a rough estimate, Mattheson's recitatives exceed Handel's by at least 20 per cent. Their actual performance time must have been longer still. Apart from the fact that the German language does not trip so lightly off the tongue as the Italian, much of the tessitura of Mattheson's recitatives is pitched very high, especially for the basses Tiridate and Radamisto, who often go up to top F sharp and G. This would require a more declamatory delivery than the quick parlando of the Italian style that Handel always adopted in his operas. Mattheson's recitatives are also slower in harmonic movement and less bold in their progressions, with little of the rapid cut and thrust characteristic of Handel's. This is perhaps what we should expect; no one has claimed that Mattheson possessed Handel's dramatic genius. But it means that the pacing of the opera, the fine balance between the lyrical and the dramatic sections, is seriously disturbed.

Mattheson clearly tried to reproduce Handel's December 1720 score as accurately as possible from the resources at his disposal; he preserved its serious heroic tone and did not dilute it with comic subplots or extraneous spectacle, as Telemann did with *Tamerlano* and *Riccardo Primo.* He may have grasped the grandeur of Handel's conception in one of the noblest of all Baroque operas. But here we must consider the effect of the vocal transpositions. One thing that modern revivals have proved beyond all dispute is that Handel's extraordinarily subtle insight into character and his acute feeling for the balance of vocal and instrumental texture—qualities in which he has had few rivals in any age—can be appreciated at their full value only if the original voice pitches are retained. In the nature of things that was impossible at Hamburg. By making Radamisto's old father a tenor and Radamisto himself, the young and vulnerable hero, a bass, Mattheson subverted their entire relationship as depicted in the music. The two Senesino arias in particular, with their very long low-lying coloratura divisions, lose all their brilliance when sung by a bass in the lower octave; they sound more like a man with a sore throat gargling in a bathroom. In the beautiful duet at the end of Act II Radamisto is the soprano, Zenobia the alto, in Handel's April score that Mattheson was using. In his *Zenobia* manuscript Radamisto's part is in the bass clef, Zenobia's in the soprano, so that all the intervals between them are inverted. Someone later changed the names round, giving Zenobia's original part to the bass. This makes little dramatic difference, since both are uttering the same sentiments, but it sometimes places the voices more than two octaves apart and carries the lower one below the written bass line.

The purpose of this inquiry is not to decry Mattheson or his Hamburg colleagues but to discover how they set about adapting an Italian *opera seria* composed for London to the conditions of performance in Hamburg. He turned it into a different kind of opera, a hybrid neither Italian nor quite German, like the other Hamburg arrangements. The use of two languages made this inevitable, and the more deliberate pacing of the recitatives and the vocal transpositions accentuated it, though Mattheson was more faithful to Handel than Telemann was. His arrangement served its purpose by making some magnificent music familiar to German audiences. But *Radamisto,* whether in its April or its December version, is much more than a collection of fine arias. It is a closely organized masterpiece in its own right. We should be doing little service to Mattheson, and none at all to Handel, if we were to revive this version of *Zenobia* today.

5

A French Traveller's View of
Handel's Operas

The Handel Collection of Mr Gerald Coke, to whom I am indebted for permission to publish the quotations that follow, contains a neatly written manuscript volume of 250 pages, in contemporary calf binding, entitled 'Voiage d'Angleterre d'Hollande et de Flandre fait en l'année 1728 Par Mr Fougeroux Pierre Jacques'. It is in the form of six extensive letters addressed to an unknown friend or patron in France, and gives an elaborate account of the topography, buildings, and art collections of London and parts of the surrounding country, and of the life, habits, and pastimes of the people. While I must confine myself here to the few pages dealing with music and the theatre, the whole volume is of such wide interest, especially to the social and art historian, that it seems worth while to give a short description of its contents.

Little is known of the author; but both his son Auguste-Denis Fougeroux de Bondaroy (1732–89) and his brother-in-law Henri-Louis Duhamel du Monceau (1700–82) were well-known botanists and agronomists. The elder Fougeroux married Angélique Duhamel. The younger was much influenced by his uncle, who established a botanical garden, to acclimatize exotic trees and improve the quality of fruit, vegetable, and cereal crops, on his estate at Denainvilliers in the Gâtinais, and wrote a six-volume treatise (1750–61) that exercised considerable influence on the subsequent history of French agriculture. Uncle and nephew shared that universal interest in the sciences characteristic of the age of the encyclopaedists. Auguste-Denis Fougeroux published researches on the formation of bones in animals and on geological and archaeological subjects (including the ruins of Herculaneum), and was encouraged in chemical experiments by his friend Lavoisier. He inherited his uncle's property at Denainvilliers and continued to develop it on the same lines. At the end of his life, when living in Paris a stone's throw from the Bastille, he kept a diary describing the events of the first weeks of the Revolution (12 July–29 August 1789). This valuable historical document was published by Lucien Scheler in 1960. It seems likely that Duhamel was the recipient of Pierre-Jacques Fougeroux's 'Voiage d'Angleterre', which may, like his son's 1789 diary, have come on the market when the Denainvilliers archives were dispersed in the 1950s.

The author left Paris with two friends at the beginning of April 1728 'dans l'idée tous trois de ne rien obmettre de tous ce qui peut regarder les beaux arts'. The first letter describes their journey by way of Beauvais, Abbeville, Montreuil, Calais,

Dover, Canterbury, and Rochester; the last their return by the same route as far as Calais and then through what is now Belgium and Northern France. On arrival in London they were greeted by 'la fumée du charbon', which almost concealed St Paul's and which, as soon as they reached their lodgings, 'nous commençâmes à sentir violemment . . . Donnez nous le temps de respirer s'il vous plaît.' The second letter is a topographical survey of London, its principal public and private buildings, palaces, churches, hospitals, squares, and gardens, and all manner of functional services from prisons to synagogues. The third deals with the art collections: Fougeroux had obtained introductions to many private patrons and collectors, including the Dukes of Devonshire, Rutland, and Somerset, the Earls of Pembroke and Burlington, Sir Robert Walpole, and the painter Jonathan Richardson. The fourth letter describes the towns and great country houses outside London to which Fougeroux made sight-seeing excursions. The former included Oxford (where he visited the 'Collège d'Alsold'), Cambridge (where he climbed to the roof of King's College Chapel and saw George II confer degrees), Northampton, Salisbury, and Windsor. Among the country houses were Wanstead, Audley End, Wimpole, Kimbolton, Broughton, Blenheim, Wilton, Cannons, and Burlington's villa at Chiswick. He also visited Newmarket for the races, Stonehenge, Hampton Court, and Chelsea and Greenwich Hospitals. Wherever he went he recorded his impressions, often in minute detail. The fifth letter, perhaps the most entertaining of all, contains his view of the English character and the manner in which it revealed itself in all manner of pursuits, from costume and cooking to the law, trade, armed services, arts, sciences, and many forms of sport. Fougeroux was nothing if not comprehensive: a detailed section on prostitutes, including their method of provoking persons put in the stocks for sodomy, is immediately followed by one on religion. The English addiction to fighting (with each other and with animals), hunting, and ball games is duly noted; in particular the winter sport of football in the streets, which often smashed the windows of houses and carriages.

It is this fifth letter that contains the passages on music and the theatre. I give the musical section in full, beginning with the description of the opera house (the King's Theatre in the Haymarket), but have summarized the paragraphs on the other theatres, apart from the account of *The Beggar's Opera* with which this part of the book closes. Fougeroux is sparing of dates, but seems to have reached London about the end of the first week in April and stayed at least two months. He is an acute if sometimes prejudiced observer with a good eye for detail that supplies valuable fresh information about the performance of Handel's operas. He can turn a pretty phrase, as when he compares the chandeliers in the King's Theatre to puppet dancers on strings, and he is often (perhaps unintentionally) amusing: witness his statement that the English translations in the printed librettos on sale at the opera house were intended for the ladies and his remarks on the efficacy of music in France for keeping the young out of debauchery. He was a cultivated man, but not a professional musician. He had never heard of Handel, whose name he spells phonetically. His punctuation, capitalization, and accentuation are often erratic and inconsistent; I have regularized them, but not attempted to standardize the spelling except where he makes obvious slips of the pen (Senesino for example sometimes appears as 'Sanesino').

Fougeroux was, of course, wrong in supposing that the opera had been a considerable spectacle for only three years. The Royal Academy had opened in 1720; but he may be dating its great days from Faustina's arrival in the spring of 1726. Of the three operas he attended, *Siroe* (which he must have seen first) had eighteen performances between 17 February and 27 April, *Tolomeo* seven between 30 April and 21 May, *Admeto* three between 25 May and 1 June. The first two were new works, the third a revival. The three leading singers, Senesino, Faustina, and Cuzzoni, require no introduction. Fougeroux's opinion of their relative merits is interesting, but he is unlikely to have heard all three in Venice twelve years earlier. Faustina had sung there in 1716–25, Cuzzoni in 1718–22; Senesino's last known appearances in a Venetian theatre had been in 1713–14. Fougeroux could have heard the rival prima donnas together in 1718–19, when they sang in three operas, including C. F. Pollarolo's *Ariodante* on a libretto subsequently adapted for Handel. The second castrato was Antonio Baldi, whose career spanned the years 1722–35; he sang in London throughout the last three seasons of the Royal Academy (1725–8), appearing in fourteen operas, ten of them by Handel. Giovanni Battista Palmerini was not a castrato but a second bass; both he and Boschi would have been called baritones today. Palmerini sang in six London operas in 1727–8; he had small parts in *Siroe* and *Admeto*, but was not in *Tolomeo*. The only singer not mentioned by Fougeroux was the English soprano Mrs. Wright, who played the small part of Orinda in the revival of *Admeto*. 'Santine' was probably Santa Stella, a successful soprano who married the composer Antonio Lotti. The salary of £1,600 ascribed to the three principal singers is £400 lower than Deutsch's figure (*Handel, a Documentary Biography*, p. 195); the most reliable contemporary estimate is 1,500 guineas. Fougeroux was voicing a common opinion in finding it exorbitant, and the reports he heard about the instability of the opera were true. This was the Academy's final season; Fougeroux heard one of the last three performances.

The most important new evidence concerns Handel's orchestra, though Fougeroux must be wrong in two respects. His list of instruments—24 violins, 2 harpsichords, 1 archlute, 3 cellos, 2 double basses, 3 bassoons, with occasional flutes and trumpets (and horns, mentioned two paragraphs later)—makes no reference to violas or oboes, which were certainly present. The former no doubt were included among the violins. It is possible that Fougeroux wrote 'clairons' by mistake for 'hautbois'—trumpets appear in none of these three operas—or even that he mistook Handel's vigorous oboes for trumpets. The opera with horns in the overture and final chorus was *Tolomeo*, and the 'morceau de someil' presumably the hero's 'Tiranni miei pensieri' in the same opera. *Admeto* also contains horns; a single flute part appears in *Admeto* and *Tolomeo*, and two recorders in the latter; *Siroe* uses none of these instruments. The Castrucci brothers, Pietro and Prospero, led Handel's orchestra for many years; they were primarily violinists, but also played the *violetta marina*, a variant of the *viola d'amore* of their own invention, for which Handel wrote special parts in *Orlando* (1733). For Sir John Clerk's similarly detailed account of the orchestra in *Orlando* on 1 May 1733, see J. Simon (ed.), *Handel: A Celebration of his Life and Times*, Catalogue of Exhibition at the National Portrait Gallery, London, 1985.

Fougeroux's account is the only confirmation we have that Handel used two harpsichords and an archlute in *secco* recitatives. Presumably one harpsichord accompanied each singer in dialogue. The cutting off of the sound of each chord should be noted by continuo players who like to spray a modern audience with arpeggios. Fougeroux disapproved because his ear was attuned to the slower, sustained, and declamatory recitative of French opera. Likewise his statement that there were no middle parts except those supplied by the continuo instruments was conditioned by his familiarity with the five-part string writing of the school of Lully. It is perhaps not surprising that he failed to notice Handel's discreet use of the violas, so often confined to the main ritornellos. His tribute to the extreme brilliance of the violin-playing and the 'grand fracas' made by the orchestra as a whole is striking. Comparison with the Paris Opéra must also have been responsible for his criticism of the decorations in the King's Theatre, both on the stage and in the auditorium. No doubt the Royal Academy, committed to a huge outlay on singers, was by this time retrenching on scenery and spectacle; neither of the two new operas requires anything elaborate—they were probably given with old sets and costumes—and the Hades scene in *Admeto*, if it retained its flying Furies of the previous season, cannot have impressed Fougeroux. A Frenchman used to the spectacle of the Académie Royale would naturally regard an opera without ballet, machines, choruses, and supers, and wholly dependent on singers, as little better than a concert in costume. An interesting detail is the use of a small bell instead of the usual whistle as a signal to the stage-hands to change the scenery; this was done of course with the curtain up.

The first concert mentioned by Fougeroux was perhaps that given at York Buildings on 12 April, with 'Vocal and Instrumental [music], particularly several favourite Ballads by Mr Mountfort'. It was given for the benefit of one Carter, and the tickets cost five shillings. There were others at York Buildings and Hickford's Room during this period, but most of them seem to have been purely instrumental, and none fits so well Fougeroux's mention of 'des vaudevilles anglois et allemands'. The Great Room in York Buildings, Villiers Street, sometimes known as Sir Richard Steele's Great Room, had been in use for concerts and meetings since the beginning of the century. The Thursday concert at which the violins of the opera orchestra appeared and a clergyman played the cello was probably a meeting of one of the private music clubs, with mixed professional and amateur membership, that assembled regularly in taverns—perhaps the Castle Society, which from 1724 met at the Castle in Paternoster Row and whose orchestra was for some years led by Prospero Castrucci.

After describing operas and concerts Fougeroux goes on to deal with the other theatres, Drury Lane and Lincoln's Inn Fields, of which he is decidedly contemptuous. He begins with the startling statement:

Leur meilleurs comiques comme Benjonnson Scakespeer insultent Molière et nos grands auteurs et les pillent toujours. Leur Comique est sans aucune galanterie, toujours remply d'ordure et de mauvaises pointes d'esprit . . . Dangereuse école pour les femmes et pour la jeunesse.

He may have been thinking of the comedies of Vanbrugh, Farquhar, and Congreve, several of which were performed at this time. He saw a number of farces, including John Thurmond's popular 'Grotesque Entertainment' *Harlequin Doctor Faustus* (given at Drury Lane on 17 and 29 May), and thought the English dancers pitiable. He could have seen *Volpone* and at least five plays by Shakespeare; the only one he mentions is *Henry VIII* (Drury Lane, 14 May), of which he gives a long description. He was impressed by the costumes and the ceremonial processions, 'suivis des trompettes et des tymbales', but found the play full of death sentences which he expected to see carried out on stage; 'mais il n'a pas plus au poète de nous donner ce plaisir'. He described the theatres as like the opera house but smaller and less ornamented, with Lincoln's Inn Fields the prettier of the two. At Drury Lane 'l'orchestre est très garni mais fort médiocre'. That at Lincoln's Inn Fields was no better, and he despised the music it played in *The Beggar's Opera*. He saw one of the performances in the original run of this famous work (first produced on 29 January 1728), with Lavinia Fenton (later Duchess of Bolton) as Polly.

L'opéra, qui autrefois n'étoit rien, est devenu depuis trois ans un spectacle considérable. Ils ont fait venir d'Italie les plus belles voix [et] les plus habiles symphonistes et y ont ajouté ce que l'Allemagne a de meilleur. Cela leur coûte tant qu'on parloit à mon départ de Londres de la rupture de cet opéra. Il n'y avoit que six voix, dont trois étoient excellentes, la fameuse Faustine de Venise, la Cuzzoni et Senesino fameux Castratte,—deux autres Castrattes, Balbi [*sic*] et Palmerini, et Boschi pour la basse, autant bon que peut estre un italien pour cette partie, qui est très rare chez eux. J'avois déjà entendu à Venise les trois belles voix, et comme il y a douze ans elles étoient encore meilleures qu'à présent. La Faustine a un gosier charmant et la voix assez grande mais un peu rude, sa figure et sa beauté sont des plus médiocres. La Cuzzoni quoique d'une voix plus foible a une douceur qui enchante avec des passages divins, après la fameuse Santine de Venise qui ne joue plus. Présentement, l'Italie n'a point eu des plus belles voix que les deux femmes: le Senesino est tout ce qu'ils ont eu de meilleur, bon musicien, beau gosier et assez bon acteur. On donnoit à Senesino 1600 pièces ou livres sterlings valent 35000 ff monoye de France et 1600 pièces à chaques des deux actrices, quoique l'opéra ne se joue que deux fois la semaine, les mardys et les samedys, et qu'il cesse pendant Lente. C'est un prix exorbitant et le moyen dont ils se font service pour enlever tout ce que l'Italie avoit de meilleur.

L'orchestre étoit composé de vingt-quatre violons conduits par les deux Castrucci frères, deux clavessins, dont Indel allemand grand joueur et grand compositeur en touchoit un, un archilut, trois violoncelles, deux contrebasses, trois bassons et quelquefois des flûtes et des clairons. Cet orchestre fait un grand fracas. Comme il n'y a point de partie du milieu les vingt-quatre violons ne jouent ordinairement que le premier et le second dessus, ce qui est extrêmement brillant et d'une belle exécution. Les deux clavessins [et] l'archilut font les accords et les parties du milieu. Il n'y a qu'un violoncelle, les deux clavessins et l'archilut pour le récitatif. La musique en est bonne et tout au fait dans le goût italien, à l'exception de quelques morceaux tendres dans le goût françois. C'est Indel qui a composé les troix opéras que j'ay vu. Le premier étoit Ptolemé Roy d'Égypte, le second Siroé Roy de Perse, et le troisième Admette Roy de Tessalie. C'étoient d'anciens opéras italiens pour les paroles que l'on avoit traduit en vers anglois à coté de l'italien en faveur des dames. Comme il n'y a aucun spectacle en danses en décorations en machines et que le théâtre est dénoué de choeurs[1] et de cette multitude d'acteurs qui décorent la scène, on peut dire que le nom d'opéra est mal appliqué à ce spectacle, c'est plutôt un beau concert sur un théâtre.

La salle en est petite et d'un goût fort médiocre, le théâtre assez grand avec de mauvaises décorations.[2] Il n'y a point d'amphitéâtre, ce n'est qu'un parterre, où sont de grands bans ceintrez jusqu'à l'orchestre où les hommes et les femmes sont assis pesle-mesle. Les loges sont louées à l'année. Au fond de la salle il s'élève une galerie ceintrée soutenue par des piliers qui donnent dans le parterre et élevée comme nos secondes loges. C'est pour la petite bourgeoisie, on y donne cependant cinq schelings qui font 5^{ff} m^e de France. Les places du parterre sont d'une demie guinée valent 11^{ff} 10. Le Roy a deux loges contre le théâtre, il y vient deux fois avec la Reine. Les princesses étoient vis à vis dans une autre loge. On bat des mains quand le roy arrive, et on les salue en sortant; il n'avoit que deux hallebardiers pour toute garde. Les bords du théâtre sont ornez de colones, le longs desquels sont attachez des miroirs avec des bras et plusieur de bougies, ainsi qu'aux pilastres qui soutiennent la galerie du fond de la salle. Au lieu de lustres ce sont de vilains chandeliers de bois, soutenus de cordes comme on en voit aux danseurs de cordes. Rien n'est plus vilain, ce sont pourtant des bougies par tout.

Comme vous n'estes pas sectateur de la musique italienne, je n'ose pas vous dire, Monsieur, qu'excepté le récitatif et la mauvaise manière d'accompagner en coupant le son de chaque accord, il y a des ariettes magnifiques pour l'harmonie avec des accompagnements de violons qui ne laissent rien à souhaiter. Les ouvertures de ces opéras sont des espèces de sonates en fugues fort belles. J'y entendis un morceau de someil imité de ceux que vous connoissez dans nos opéras. On avoit meslé dans une de ces ouvertures des corps [sic] de chasse ainsi que dans le Chorus[3] de la fin, ce qui faisoit des merveilles.

Les Concerts. Pendant que nous sommes sur la musique, il faut vous parler des concerts publics de Londres, qui sont peu de chose en comparaison des nôtres. Nous en entendimes[4] un qui se tint dans une salle basse, toute peinte mais fort noircie, qui sert ordinairement de salle à danser; il y a une tribune au bout où l'on monte quelques marches, c'est où se met la musique. On y joua quelques sonates et l'on y chanta des vaudevilles anglois et allemands: on paye pour ces mauvais concerts cinq schelings qui valent 5^{ff} 10^s. Nous entendimes encore un autre concert au premier étage dans un caffé, où les violons de l'opéra s'exercent tous les jeudys. Il n'avoit que des allemands qui exécutent fort bien, mais qui jouent durement, un entre autres joua très bien de la flutte allemande. Nous y vismes aussi un ministre jouer du violoncelle.

Vous serez surpris, Monsieur, de ce que je vais vous dire, que parmy les gens de qualitez hommes et femmes il y en a peu qui s'attachent à la musique. On ne scait ce que c'est que de concerter ensemble, tout le plaiser consiste à bien boire et à fumer; vous scavez, Monsieur, combien l'occupation de la musique en France détourne la jeunesse de la débauche et de quel commerce elle devient par tous . . .

On y jouoit une espèce d'opéra comique, appellé l'Opéra des gueux, à cause qu'on y représentoit une bande de voleurs des grands chemins avec leur Capitaine, dont il n'y avoit que deux acteurs de bons et une fille appellée Fenton assez jolie. L'orchestre est aussi mauvais

[1] Il n'y a qu'un trio ou quatuor à la fin et deux duo dans tout l'opéra.
[2] Dans les changemens de décorations on se sert d'une sonette au lieu d'un siflet.
[3] Le Chorus est composé seulement de quatre voix.   [4] Contre la pompe à feu.

que l'autre [at Drury Lane]. Tout est en vaudevilles avec de méchante musique. On prétendoit que le poète avoit fait quelque application au gouvernement présent. On y boit à chaque moment, on y fume, et le Capitaine avec huit femmes qui luy tiennent compagnie dans la prison les baise à plusieurs reprises. On alloit le faire pendre au cinquième acte, mais avec de l'argent il a l'adresse de se sauver du gibet. C'est par où l'opéra finit. Je vous ennuyerois de vous parler des contredanses de la fin.

6

Handel's *Sosarme*, a Puzzle Opera

In a sense nearly all Handel's operas are puzzle operas. In a surprising number of instances the source of the libretto has been identified wrongly or not at all,[1] and we do not know who adapted it for Handel. No correspondence survives to throw light on the reasons for the choice, or the part played by Handel in the adaptation, though in some operas this must have been appreciable.[2] The music too raises many questions that have never been answered or fully investigated. Yet there is enough material to keep a posse of musicological detectives at work for years. By the study of autographs, sketches, performing scores, other manuscript copies, parts, printed librettos and early musical editions, evidence of the capacity of singers, and various other sources, it is possible to plot in detail the history of almost every major work from the moment Handel put the first note on paper to the last revival during his life. Few great composers other than Beethoven have left so many clues to the inner working of their creative processes. The amount of unpublished music, whether rejected by Handel or omitted or not discovered by Chrysander, is enormous, and the conclusions to be drawn are nearly always illuminating and occasionally startling.

Sosarme is something of a problem child. No one would rank it among the greatest of Handel's operas, which are landmarks in the history of the art. It has had an indifferent press from historians and scholars. Burney, it is true, ranked it among Handel's 'most pleasing theatrical compositions', but he judged by standards that satisfy few critics today, assessing each opera as a string of arias written for particular singers rather than a musical drama based on the conflict of character and emotion. To Streatfeild *Sosarme* was 'another of Handel's less important operas', to Dent 'another unsatisfactory opera'. Between Handel's only revival in 1734 and Alan Kitching's Abingdon production in September 1970 it was never performed in the theatre[3] despite the widespread enthusiasm that has resurrected all but one of Handel's thirty-nine surviving operas, many of them repeatedly, on modern stages. Yet it was one of the first to be broadcast by the BBC and made available on the

---

[1] Since this was written the researches of Reinhard Strohm have filled most of the gaps: see 'Handel and his Italian Opera Texts' in *Essays on Handel and Italian Opera* (Cambridge, 1985), earlier version in *Händel-Jahrbuch* 1975–6; also Dean and Knapp, *Handel's Operas 1704–1726*.

[2] No one else could have introduced words as well as music from works of the Italian period into operas written for London, a not infrequent occurrence from *Rinaldo* to *Alcina*. For further discussion of this point, see my *Handel and the Opera Seria* (London, 1970), 41–2.

[3] It has since been staged at Göttingen in 1973 and Birmingham in 1979.

gramophone (Oiseau Lyre, 1955, conducted by Anthony Lewis), and the first in which the voices (with one minor exception) were recorded at their original pitch. Most people who know the score or the recording would probably agree that it is full of magnificent music, whatever their reservations about the libretto.

It is this libretto that presents some, though not all, of the problems. Before reviewing them it is necessary to summarize the plot and the early history of the opera. There are discrepancies between Chrysander's edition (*HG*), the 1732 printed libretto, and the autograph as Handel left it, especially in the matter of stage directions. Those printed here in italics are from the libretto, except where stated; most of them are in the autograph too. Chrysander omits a fair number, among them the description of the duel in which two of the principal characters are wounded.

The background of the story is difficult to grasp without the aid of the Argument, given in Italian and English in the libretto on sale in the theatre but never reprinted:

Sosarmes King of Media falling in Love with Elmira, Daughter of Haliates King of Lydia, at the Report he heard of her Beauty, demanded her in Marriage of her Father, who readily assented: But about the Time that Elmira was preparing for her Departure to her Husband, a cruel Rebellion broke out in Lydia, which obliged the Princess to defer her Journey. The Author of this Rebellion was Argones, the eldest Son and Successor of Haliates, prompted to it by Jealousy he entertained, that his Father intended to advance his natural Son Melus, whom he tenderly lov'd, to the Throne. When Argones had openly declared himself a Rebel against his Father, the latter was obliged to take up Arms, and besiege the City of Sardis, where his Son and the Rebels had shut themselves up, and by Treachery made themselves Masters of the Palace itself. Both the Besiegers, and those they besieged were equally obstinate . . .

We learn in the course of the opera that Melo's mother was Anagilda, daughter of Haliate's trusted but treacherous old counsellor Altomaro. Elmira and her mother Erenice, Haliate's queen, are prisoners in the palace seized by Argone, whereas Sosarme and his forces are with Haliate's besieging army.

ACT I opens in *the great Square of Sardis, with Soldiers drawn up in Battalia.* The city has withstood every assult, but is in danger of succumbing to famine. Argone proposes a sortie to seize supplies from the enemy. He *draws his Sword, the Soldiers doing the same,* and after a brief military chorus all depart. Within the palace Erenice tells Elmira of a dream in which Hecate told her to cease weeping, since the war shall be ended this day by 'the Royal Blood thy Son shall shed'. Erenice fears the death of husband or son. Elmira tries to reassure her and leaves, but returns at once *with an afflicted Air*: Argone is preparing a sortie. Erenice's fears are reinforced, and Elmira goes off to try to dissuade her brother. Erenice follows: if Argone will not yield to her tears, he must kill her first. The scene changes to *an Incampment* outside the city. Altomaro compares his grandson's mental confusion to that of a moth when the light has gone out. Melo discusses the political situation with Sosarme, who finds him more worthy of the throne the more he scorns it. Melo supports Sosarme's mission to reconcile the warring parties, but this receives an immediate setback from Haliate, who swears to exact condign vengeance on Argone and his supporters without respect for sex, consanguinity, age, or innocence. In that case, Sosarme replies, he will no longer be Haliate's son-in-law but his mortal enemy. Haliate's rage against Argone's insults and pride continues unabated. The next scene reverts to Sardis: *a Royal Court-yard. Argones armed with Soldiers and Officers.* He is still planning his sortie. *As he retires he meets with Erenice and Elmira,* who both beg him to abandon the enterprise. When Erenice bids him trample on the bosom that gave him life, *he continues in Suspense* until a repetition of the military chorus in the first scene recalls him to his resolution and he departs *in haste.* Erenice is desolate: whoever slays the other will rob her of half her happiness. Elmira asks Hecate how the shedding of royal blood can bring reconciliation: if that is the way the fates announce peace, how would they predict war?

ACT II. Elmira in the palace dreads the loss of father, brother or husband. She describes to Erenice the sortie from Sardis and the fight with Sosarme's soldiers, but dust and smoke prevent her seeing the result. *A warlike Symphony is heard*; Argone enters, his sword covered with blood. He says it is royal, and Sosarme's; *Elmira swoons*[4] *in the arms of Erenice.* Erenice charges Argone with three murders, 'one with thy cruel Sword, and two with Grief', and blushes 'to have a Monster for my Son'. *Elmira is carry'd away in a Swoon by her Ladies.*[5] Argone tries to explain, but Erenice dismisses him as a traitor to love and duty. In a *garden*[6] Haliate is unmanned by his defeat. Melo reports that Sosarme's Medes have mutinied and are demanding the rescue of their captured king. Altomaro accuses Melo of engineering the mutiny, and Haliate denounces both his sons: one is a rebel, the other wants to see him scorned and unavenged. Melo denies this; Altomaro emphasizes the duty of monarchs to quell the haughty. Haliate suddenly changes his mind and orders Altomaro to offer peace and pardon to Argone. Altomaro again chides Melo for abjuring his own greatness. Melo is convinced that providence punishes the guilty. Altomaro, all the more determined to place Melo on the throne, rejoices that his genius has discovered the means. The scene changes to *a Closet*[7] [in Sardis]. *Sosarme reposing on a Bed, and Elmira applying Remedies to his Wound.* He rejoices that so slight an injury should have brought him so great a reward. Both agree that the path to happiness passes through pain. Erenice reports the arrival of Haliate's peace offer and asks Sosarme to urge its acceptance on Argone. He says he came to Sardis and allowed himself to be captured for that very purpose; honour is the sole motive for military glory. In *a Room of Audience with a Throne* Sosarme persuades Argone to receive Haliate's envoy. *An Officer goes out to introduce Altomarus.* Argone promises to beg Haliate's pardon in return for the restoration of his right to the succession. Altomaro enters and says that Haliate will conclude peace if Argone first fights him in single combat. *Argones appears astonish'd*; Elmira, Erenice, and Sosarme are outraged. Argone bitterly accepts the challenge. He and Altomaro depart in

---

[4] '*Viene*' (HG) should be '*sviene*'.
[5] 'Knights accompanying Argone' in Handel's autograph.
[6] 'A royal pavilion' in the autograph.
[7] The autograph has '*Fonderia Reale*'.

opposite directions.[8] Erenice, recommending Argone to Sosarme's care, sets off for Haliate's camp to soften his rage. Sosarme promises to appease Argone and then return to Elmira's arms for ever. Elmira hopes that Erenice and Sosarme will prevail and bring back Argone like a bird to its nest or a tigress to her young.

ACT III. *The Suburbs of Sardis, with Military Tents at a Distance.* Altomaro tells Haliate that Argone not only spurns his peace offer but challenges him to single combat, set on by Erenice 'with all the Art of Language'. Haliate once more hardens his heart. When Erenice enters he has her arrested and put in Melo's charge: whether he himself or Argone is killed, the survivor will always be a source of remorse to her. Melo soon discovers Altomaro's perfidy from Erenice and sends her to his tent *attended by the Guards.* He means to expose Altomaro by taking his father's place in the duel, dropping his sword, and embracing his brother. The scene changes to *a Royal Garden. Argones attended by an Officer, with two Swords . . . . As he is going out, he's stop'd by Elmira and Sosarmes*, who try vainly to detain him. He departs *in a Rage.* Sosarme follows, promising to quench Argone's fury with his own blood. Elmira, banishing tears, screws up her courage to confront Argone: pleasures are seasoned by the pain that precedes them. In *a Field appointed for the Duel* Haliate orders Altomaro to keep the lists clear and allow no one to obstruct his chastening wrath. Altomaro compares Haliate to Jove and bids him destroy his 'impious Offspring'. Haliate rejects Melo's pleas to take his place. *Altomarus with two Swords, Haliates, Argones, with an Officer bearing two Swords.* After an exchange of insults Altomaro *presents a Sword to Argones whilst the Officer presents another to Haliates: They afterwards put themselves upon their Guard, and begin the Combat. The aforesaid, and Erenice, who advances to Argones and Melus, who goes to Haliates, and both of them are wounded* [*disgraziatamente feriti*], *the Mother by the Son, and Melus by the Father.* Altomaro declares that all is lost and *betakes himself to Flight, and Erenice goes to Haliates, whilst Melus advances to Argones. . . . They throw away their Swords and stand in Suspense.* Melo explains Altomaro's deception, presently confirmed by Sosarme and Elmira. Sosarme reports Altomaro's suicide, and all are reconciled.

Handel completed the score on 4 February 1732; there is no date at the beginning. The first performance took place at the King's Theatre on 15 February with the following cast:

Sosarme	Francesco Bernardi, known as Senesino	Alto castrato
Argone	Antonio Gualandi, known as Campioli	Alto castrato
Elmira	Anna Strada	Soprano
Erenice	Anna Bagnolesi	Contralto
Melo	Francesca Bertolli	Contralto
Haliate	Giovanni Battista Pinacci	Tenor
Altomaro	Antonio Montagnana	Bass

There were eleven performances during the season, and the reception was enthusiastic; Viscount Percival, Francis Colman, Burney, and the anonymous author of a

---

[8] This detail is in the autograph but not the libretto.

pamphlet, *See and Seem Blind*, are all in agreement on this. The two duets for Elmira and Sosarme were especially popular; 'Per le porte del tormento' was sung at least six times during the 1733–4 season, in the intervals of various plays at the King's Theatre and Drury Lane, by 'Miss Arne and Young Master Arne', the future Mrs Cibber and the younger brother of the composer. Handel was to introduce it into *Imeneo* in Dublin in 1742. He revived *Sosarme* for three performances in 1734, the first on 27 April, at a time when his rivalry with the Opera of the Nobility was at its height and both companies were in low financial water. No printed libretto has been found. The future Mrs Delany, who heard it twice, considered it 'a most delightful opera' and 'a charming one, and yet I dare say it will be almost empty! Tis vexatious to have *such music* neglected.' Her misgivings were well founded; *Sosarme* was not heard again for more than 200 years.

The autograph shows that two strange things befell the opera before the score was even finished. For the greater part of two acts the original scene of action was not Sardis but Coimbra in Portugal; the title was *Fernando rè di Castiglia*, and with the exception of Altomaro the characters all had different names. Sosarme was Fernando, Argone Alfonso, Melo Sancio, Haliate Dionisio, Elmira Elvida, and Erenice Isabella. Barclay Squire is not quite correct in saying that 'the first two acts were set to this book'.[9] When Handel transferred the scene from Iberia to Asia Minor, which he did by changing every name in the autograph up to the point he had reached,[10] Act I ended with Isabella's aria 'Due parti del core', the soprano aria 'Vola l'augello' (later the finale of Act II) occurred at Elvida's exit in I. iii, and 'Il mio valore' was probably not present, at least in the form we know.[11] Act II went as far as 'Vado al campo'; scenes xiii and xiv did not exist. The music had already undergone important revision, and the recitatives were much longer. This drastic abridgment of the recitatives, after they had been fully set, is the second strange fact. It did not tighten up the action; on the contrary, it obscured the motivation and rendered a none too convincing plot almost comically inconsequent. Chunks were removed from six scenes in Act I, and five in Act II, and every character in the opera was affected. The cuts amounted in all to 134 bars, more than a hundred of them in Act I. Argone and especially Melo were more fully treated in the original version; Melo's resistance to Altomaro and sympathy with Sosarme were established with greater firmness. But the character who suffered most was Haliate. His sudden change of mind towards Argone in II. v had been prepared by a much more extended treatment of his recitative in I. viii. Instead of the perfunctory eight bars that now stand in the score he had a prolonged soliloquy of 50 bars, in which he vacillated between thirst for revenge and the natural urge to spare and come to terms with his rebellious son; in the middle, when he has apparently decided on pardon, we find the direction *Stà un poco sospeso, poi infuriato*. This is a turning-point in the action, and we might have expected Handel to give it a string accompani-

[9] *Catalogue of the King's Music Library*, i (London, 1927), 83.

[10] He made one or two other small changes; Isabella in her dream (I. ii) did not see 'Hecate . . . spuntar dal Cielo', but 'Irene . . . sorger dall'acqua'. This is the reading of the source libretto.

[11] It bears the name of Sosarme, not Fernando.

ment. He did not do so, but his setting is highly dramatic, and its suppression a serious loss.[12]

Already at least seven questions present themselves. (1) What was the original source of the libretto? (2) Who were the historical persons involved? (3) Who adapted it for Handel? (4) Why did Handel put himself to the trouble of altering nearly all the names half way through the composition? (5) Why did he injure the opera by decimating the recitatives? (6) When did he carry out these two operations? (7) What exactly happened in 1734, when his company included only one of the 1732 cast and several of the other voices were of different pitch?

Of the seven questions, only the first has until recently received a firm answer —and it is wrong. According to Burney, Chrysander, Loewenberg, and William C. Smith the source libretto was Matteo Noris's *Alfonso Primo*, set by Carlo Francesco Pollarolo for Venice in 1694. There is a copy of Noris's work in the Library of Congress, and it has no connection with *Sosarme* either in character or plot. The true source libretto, identified by Reinhard Strohm, was *Dionisio rè di Portogallo* by Antonio Salvi, set by G. A. Perti and performed in Ferdinando de' Medici's private theatre outside Florence on 30 September 1707. Handel, whose first Italian opera *Vincer se stesso è la maggior vittoria (Rodrigo)*, also written for Ferdinando, was produced at the Cocomero theatre in Florence only a few weeks later, probably saw Perti's opera and almost certainly obtained a copy of the libretto at that time.[13] By changing the title in his autograph to *Fernando rè di Castiglia* he introduced a red herring.

Noris's title led Dent to propose Alfonso I, first king of Portugal, as the original of Argone. This is another red herring. Iberian history is so full of Fernandos, Alfonsos, and Isabellas that it would be difficult to date the action from these names alone; but Dionisio gives the clue. He is Diniz, also known as Dionysius, king of Portugal from 1279 to 1325 and founder of the University of Coimbra. The other potentates are his son and successor Alfonso IV (the Fierce), chiefly remembered as the murderer of his son's mistress Ines da Castro, and Ferdinand IV, king of Castile from 1295 to 1312. This places the action closer to Handel's time than that of any of his other operas except *Tamerlano*. The point is academic; even the transmogrification of Portuguese into Lydians and Castilians into Medes makes very little difference in an *opera seria* of this period.[14]

When I first published this study I was inclined to see a possible clue to the identity of Handel's collaborator in II. v, where Altomaro fans the flame of Haliate's revenge with the words 'Debellar i superbi, è virtù regia'. This echo of Virgil's famous line in the *Aeneid*, 'Parcere subjectis et debellare superbos', is paralleled in

[12] This longer recitative was new in Handel's libretto; it is not in the source.

[13] He adapted an aria from it for the 1728 revival of *Admeto*. Much earlier the text of the duet 'Per le porte del tormento' had been used for the final *coro* of the London pasticcio *Almahide*, first produced in January 1710.

[14] Parts of *Siroe* (1728) and *Ezio* (late 1731), like *Sosarme*, were originally composed to different librettos.

two earlier Handel librettos, *Alessandro* and *Riccardo Primo*, both free adaptations of earlier material by Paolo Rolli. But the line is in Salvi's libretto, and although the creaking mechanism of the plot is typical of Rolli, the method of adaptation is not.[15] On the other hand my conjecture that the source might prove to be a much more coherent piece of work than *Sosarme* as we have it was correct: see below, p. 59.

The reason for the change of names was almost certainly political. King John V of Portugal, who reigned from 1706 to 1750, was the richest ruler in Europe, thanks to the mineral wealth of Brazil, and a man of excessive punctilio in matters of status, who in 1729 had arranged a dynastic marriage with the Spanish royal family.[16] The Portuguese were Britain's oldest allies. A libretto that presented them in a most unflattering light, their king engaged in an undignified civil war with his son and requiring to be rescued by his neighbour of Castile, might well cause apprehension at the court of George II. Handel was not a political animal; it seems likely that his attention was drawn at a late stage to the risks of offending a friendly but touchy ruler and that this explains the abrupt translation of the story from the Iberian peninsula to a remote Sardis. The name Sosarme seems to have been invented for the occasion.

This does not account for the abridgment of the recitative. Here the decisive factor was beyond question the resounding failure of *Ezio*, produced exactly a month before *Sosarme* on 15 January 1732; it enjoyed fewer performances (five) than any of its predecessors—or indeed any of its successors before *Berenice* in 1737. London audiences were very critical of Italian *secco* recitative, which they found tedious if not positively absurd. Handel's natural reaction to failure would be a retrenchment in this direction. From about 1731 the proportion of recitative in his operas, whether new works or revivals, declined steadily and sometimes steeply from what it had been during the Royal Academy years. The point could be illustrated from almost any production of the period, especially after *Ezio*. The consequences are often baffling to anyone concerned to follow the development and motivation of the plots; but contemporary listeners were more interested in arias and singers, and they were helped by the explanatory Argument as well as the text (including some omitted passages) in the printed libretto.

The autograph makes it clear that the change of names and locale and the shortening of the recitatives were carried out at the same time. There are no recitative cuts in Act III other than four or five lines in the last scene that Handel wrote out but never set, a frequent occurrence in the autographs. At first glance it might be tempting to conjecture that the proto-*Sosarme* dates back to the Royal Academy period, before John V's Spanish marriage, but the compass and tessitura of the vocal writing make this untenable. The part of Altomaro was certainly composed for Montagnana, who did not arrive till the autumn of 1731; Boschi, a

---

[15] Rolli, unlike Handel's other collaborators, notably Nicola Haym, preferred to supply new aria texts of his own. Handel's assistant in *Sosarme* remains unidentified. Haym had died in 1729.

[16] I am indebted to Professor Hugh Trevor-Roper for enlightenment on the historical background here.

high baritone, could never have sung it. Although the autograph bears no initial date, it is likely that Handel began *Sosarme* in late December or early January and finished it after the production of *Ezio*, slashing the recitative in a desperate attempt to save it.

For the 1734 revival we must rely, in the absence of a libretto, on the two scores used by the continuo players in the theatre. Fortunately both survive, one among the collection of performance copies in the Staats- und Universitätsbibliothek, Hamburg, the other in Chrysander's private library, now deposited at the same place. The first, MA/1054 (henceforth cited as *H*), is a Smith copy begun while Handel was still at work on the autograph. The second, MA/185 (henceforth *C*), was copied a little later, probably from *H*, by more than one hand: Act I by H8, Act II by an unidentified copyist, Act III possibly by S4. After the 1732 run, when both copies were used, Handel jotted down his alterations for 1734 in *H*, more than once having second thoughts. His final decisions were then incorporated in both scores, by Smith and S1 in *H*, by S1 alone in *C*.

From these scores it is possible to deduce not only what Handel performed in 1734, but a number of expedients that he considered and subsequently rejected. He now had a company comprising three sopranos, three altos, and a bass, compared with one soprano, four altos, a tenor, and a bass two years earlier. Strada was available to sing Elmira, but the second castrato was a soprano and there was no tenor. Several solutions were open to Handel; the one he adopted was almost certainly that given by Otto Erich Deutsch,[17] though where Deutsch found it is a mystery he was unable to elucidate in response to an enquiry some years ago.[18] It is possible that he discovered a libretto. This is his cast (the voices are the same as in 1732 except where stated):

Sosarme	Giovanni Carestini	Mezzo-soprano castrato
Argone	Carlo Scalzi	Soprano castrato
Elmira	Strada	
Erenice	Maria Caterina Negri	
Melo	Rosa Negri	
Haliate	Margherita Durastanti	Soprano
Altomaro	Gustavus Waltz	

Before settling on this it is clear from various transpositions scribbled in *H* that Handel considered a different arrangement. He marked Haliate's second aria up a sixth for contralto, probably Maria Negri, and several pieces in Erenice's part, including the duet with Argone, up a tone, which would take it outside the compass of either of the Negris. It seems to have been intended for Durastanti, whose voice had dropped nearly to mezzo-soprano; in the event she probably sang the tenor part of Haliate an octave above its written pitch, though the evidence is not absolutely conclusive. Several of these transpositions were indicated by Smith on the other copy (*C*) but later cancelled.

[17] *Handel, a Documentary Biography*, 364.
[18] Nor is the answer to be found in the materials for his book, now in the Gerald Coke Collection.

Handel's difficulties were not yet solved. Carestini's voice, a coloratura mezzo-soprano similar in range to that of many Rossini heroines, was higher and wider in compass than Senesino's. Scalzi was not only a soprano but a far better singer than Campioli, an artist of such dubious attainments that Handel never composed an aria for him. Maria Negri was scarcely up to the standard of Bagnolesi, her sister Rosa well below that of Bertolli. Durastanti had been a fine singer (she was the original Agrippina in 1709, and Handel had composed many cantatas for her as early as 1707),[19] but her voice had declined in reliability as well as pitch, as all her parts at this period testify. Waltz was no Montagnana and in no position to tackle the tremendous span of 'Fra l'ombre'. Every one of these limitations was catered for by Handel with characteristic professional skill, though sometimes with more care for the voices than for the drama.

All *Sosarme*'s music outside the recitative was modified for Carestini. In the two duets with Elmira Handel simply wrote (in pencil in *H*) higher alternatives for the low-lying passages; they appear in small notes in *HG*. 'Alle sfere' was put up a tone to G major (requiring the use of brilliant horns in G, which Handel employed to such splendid effect in *Giulio Cesare, Alcina*, and elsewhere), the very low-pitched 'In mille dolci modi' up a fourth,[20] also to G major. 'In mio valore' was replaced by 'Agitato da fiere tempeste', 'M'opporrò' by 'Nube che il sole adombra'. Both these arias had been written for Senesino in *Riccardo Primo* (1727), and each was transposed up a major third, to D and G major respectively, with the words modified in places to fit the new context. The effect was to shift the balance and character of *Sosarme*'s part, now confined to the major mode, in the direction of extrovert bravura and sharp keys. 'Agitato da fiere tempeste' can scarcely be considered a suitable introduction for a would-be peacemaker.

Scalzi as Argone received three arias: 'Corro per ubbidirvi' in I. i between his accompanied recitative and the *coro militare*; Sosarme's 'Il mio valore', transposed up a tone to A minor, in place of the duet with Erenice in II. iii; and 'Quell'orror delle procelle' in F major at the end of III. vi (*HG*, p. 93, after Elmira's 'T'arresta'). The first and third of the inserted pieces are again from *Riccardo Primo*, an opera composed for a specific occasion that Handel never intended to revive and cannibalized freely in subsequent works. They had been sung by Faustina and Senesino respectively, the former at the same pitch (A major), the latter a fourth lower in C. The verbal changes disturbed the initial words, which in *Riccardo* are 'Vado per obedirti' and 'All'orror delle procelle'. In 'Corro per ubbidirvi' the music too was altered, the B section (before the return of the first line of text) being reduced from eighteen to seven bars. Handel's pencil annotations in *H* show that he took some time to make up his mind about the substituted arias. He allotted 'Agitato da fiere tempeste' to Argone in I. i and to Sosarme in I. vii, 'Il mio valore' to Argone in III. vi, and something now indecipherable to Sosarme in III. vii before settling on

---

[19] Ursula Kirkendale, 'The Ruspoli Documents on Handel', *Journal of the American Musicological Society*, 20 (1967), 222.

[20] Handel changed his mind more than once about the interval, noting the new key first as G, then as F, then again as G.

the ultimate positions. When 'Il mio valore' was recopied in A minor for *H* the violin part was adjusted in the fourth bar and later to avoid high e'''; Handel usually treated d''' as the violins' top note.

The other parts—except Elmira, which Strada sang unchanged except for a seemingly pointless cut of five bars in 'Padre, germano' (*HG*, pp. 42–3)—were all significantly shortened. Erenice lost the duet with Argone and 'Cuor di madre'. Melo lost 'Sò ch'il ciel' and the two passages in 'Sì, sì minaccia' bracketed in *HG*. Altomaro lost 'Fra l'ombre'. For Durastanti Handel made extensive cuts in the long and brilliant 'La turba adulatrice': not only the three indicated in *HG* but two more, bars 28 and 29 (*HG*, p. 29) and no fewer than seventeen and a half bars in the B section, from the middle of bar 81 to the end of bar 98. This eased the veteran singer's task, incidentally removing the only top A in the aria—a note no longer accessible to Durastanti[21]—and involved alterations and rebarring at the end of the B section (of which more below). 'S'io cadrò' was probably also cut; Durastanti could not have sung it untransposed, and the note 'Segue l'aria' before it is crossed out in *H*. The words 'Haliate D' in the margin of *C* at the end of III. x (*HG*, p. 100, first bar), preceded by a modified cadence, suggest that Handel considered compensating her here; but there is nothing in *H*.

Handel's method of indicating cuts is worth comment. He did not remove or cancel whole arias, presumably because they might be reinstated, though he sometimes ran a pencil across the first or last page for the convenience of the continuo player. As a rule he made things doubly clear in *H* by marking an exit for the character (*Parte*) in the recitative, e.g. for Altomaro before 'Fra l'ombre', Melo before 'Sò ch'il ciel', and Erenice before 'Cuor di madre'. For recitatives and cuts within the set pieces the procedure was different. Handel crossed out what was to be omitted in pencil in one or both copies, and blank paper was then pasted over the music. Slight changes and modified cadences were sometimes necessary. Chrysander did not always record them. When Handel made the bracketed cut on *HG*, p. 12, he altered the notes to which the words 'il ciglio' were set from a'–b'–b' to b'–e–e. Chrysander prints only the 1734 version.

The recitatives were treated even more ruthlessly in 1734 than they had been before the score was finished. Handel removed not only the eleven passages indicated in *HG* but several others (some 168 bars in all): the last five bars in II. vi (after 'colla perfidia', *HG*, p. 52), the eight bars from 'ma di pietà' to 'quest'alma' in II. viii (*HG*, p. 59), the first three words of II. x (*HG*, p. 72), the first six bars of III. iii (*HG*, p. 86) and the last eight in III. iv (after 'perfido Altomaro', *HG*, p. 90). Several of these cuts involved autograph changes in *H*, and the last of them evoked a new cadence in B major, written by Handel over the old recitative and copied on a fresh page in both copies, by Smith in *H*, by S1 in *C*.

By this time the reader may be wondering why Chrysander in *HG* chose to indicate some of the 1734 cuts and one of the transpositions ('In mille dolci modi'),[22]

---

[21] Handel had not written it for her since *Radamisto* in April 1720, though she reached it once in the 1722 revival of *Floridante*.

[22] In the 'A' version of the recitative before this aria the penultimate note in the bass should of course be C♯, not C♮ as printed.

but ignored seven other internal cuts, two transpositions, one aria transferred to another character, and four inserted from another opera, all modified from their original form. To which there is no satisfactory answer, except that it is typical of his editorial method. There is no means of predicting how much he will print of what lies before him, whether in autographs, performing scores or other sources, and he offers no explanations. In some operas (*Ottone, Tamerlano, Scipione*) he prints music from the autographs that Handel rejected before performance; in others (*Flavio, Giulio Cesare*) he omits similar pieces of equal or superior quality as well as material in the performing score. Elsewhere (*Muzio Scevola*) he excludes music that was not only performed but printed in Handel's time, and gives one whole character to the wrong voice. Of two arias unperformed in *Ariodante* one is left and the other taken. Very seldom are we offered all the available material. The procedure seems totally haphazard.

This arbitrary method leads to an anomaly in 'La turba adulatrice', where Chrysander prints a conflation of two versions containing a floating half bar (bar 99, *HG*, p. 33). It is not inconceivable that Handel might have allowed this; in fact he took special care to avoid it. The autograph version (Ex. 1*a*), followed by the early copy (without recitatives) British Library RM19.a.5[23] and the parts in the Newman Flower Collection (S2), was altered in 1734: when he made the long cut mentioned above, Handel removed half a bar at the cadence and shifted the intervening bar-lines (Ex. 1*b*). This change is made by careful erasures and insertions in both performing copies, though there is a mistake in *C*, which has the equivalent of *HG*'s short bar 99 included in the cut.

Another type of error springs from Chrysander's exaggerated faith in the performing scores as against the autographs, based perhaps on a misapprehension of their purpose. Although one at least was always a full score,[24] they served in performance as continuo parts; there was of course no conductor wagging a stick and making sure the orchestra played what he had before him. If Smith made a mistake in copying the upper parts it might well remain unnoticed, or at least uncorrected;[25] the individual parts would naturally be put right. When Handel marked 'Alle sfere' for transposition up to G major, Smith, finding a convenient blank stave at the bottom of each page in *H*, copied the bass part a second time in the new key, leaving the rest of the aria in F. Where the reading of the performing score differs from that of the autograph, unless a later change has been introduced in the former or Handel has made an obvious slip of the pen in the latter, there is an overwhelming presumption that the autograph will be correct: it is unlikely that Handel would have given Smith—who was a copyist, not an editor—verbal instructions to modify the text in detail. In taking the contrary view Chrysander sometimes perpetuated Smith's mistakes, even when they make no musical sense. There is an example in bar 26 of Erenice's aria 'Cuor di madre' (*HG*, p. 88), where

[23] This was a collaborative effort written by S1, S2, S3, and H8.

[24] The other often was not; *C*, originally (like *H*) a full score of the 1732 version, has only the voice part and bass of the inserted and some of the transposed arias, written by S1.

[25] Chrysander himself quotes an instance of this in his preface to *Il pastor fido*, second version (1890).

Ex.1

the autograph, RM19.a.5, and the Flower parts all have obviously the correct reading (Ex. 2*a*), whereas in *HG*, following *H* and *C*,[26] the two lower violin parts are different (Ex. 2*b*). What must have happened is that Smith accidentally jumped a chord, and the other copyist transferred the mistake from *H* to *C*.

The first performing score (*H*) confirms the evidence of *Floridante* and *Giulio Cesare*, among other works, that Smith sometimes began to copy long before Handel had finished the labour of composition, perhaps when his ink was scarcely dry. In view of the exiguous interval of time that often separated the completion of a score from its first performance this was no doubt a necessity, since the parts for singers and instrumentalists had to be taken from Smith's copy. At least four surviving pages in *H* carry sections of the recitatives suppressed when Handel changed the names of the characters. Most of them were blocked out later, but on one page (f. 30) the original names remain uncancelled (the whole page was presumably covered up). Another (f. 77) has the longer recitative without any

---

[26] The Lennard and Coke copies and the Walsh and Arnold scores are also wrong. Presumably they derive from *H*.

Ex.2

(a)

(b)

names; perhaps Handel had become alert to the danger of ruffling John V's feathers but not yet received the new names from the librettist. In 'Dite pace' Smith reproduced three single bars which are cancelled in the autograph; he pasted them out later, but he must have copied the aria before Handel had finalized it. By the time C was prepared these early variants had disappeared and the text had settled into its 1732 form.[27] The turnover in both copies was always arranged at the same point, to facilitate the transference or substitution of material. The scores were not bound or foliated until after they had ceased to be used. A curious point in connection with the names is that in Arnold's score (1788) Sosarme is on one occasion (II. xii, *HG*, p. 74) addressed as 'Fermando' (*sic*) and Haliate appears in the preliminary list of characters (though not in the text) as 'Corrido'. Arnold printed only four of the operas, and his text for *Sosarme* is peculiar. He gives the complete 1732 versions of the arias, except 'La turba adulatrice' and 'Padre, germano', but (except at three points) the shortened recitatives of 1734. There are numerous mistakes, and the *coro militare* is omitted altogether; but Arnold, unless he used a peculiar copy that has since disappeared, must have collated at least two and possibly three sources,[28] one of them reflecting material from before the first performance. That is the only explanation of 'Fermando', which is not in either of the performing scores at this point; 'Corrido' could be a mistake or a name temporarily alloted to Dionisio before he became Haliate.

Something needs to be said about the Flower parts, now in Manchester Public Library, which have only been open to inspection since 1965. They exist, sometimes accompanied by a score, for all the operas except *Almira* and for many other works, but have not yet been subjected to a thorough scrutiny. Conclusions must therefore remain in some respects tentative. The parts were supplied to Charles Jennens, the

[27] Chrysander used C for preparing his edition, but it was not the printer's copy, since many of the 1734 cuts are still pasted out. It bears many annotations in his hand, as do a number of manuscript copies in the Royal Music Library.

[28] The copy used for his edition of *Teseo* has been identified: see *Handel's Operas 1704–1726*, 252–3. It was written by Linike before the performance of the opera.

original owner of the Aylesford Collection, by Handel's copyists, most of them the work of S2. They were not used in performance, and it is difficult to see what practical purpose they were intended to serve. There are no voice parts for the operas (though there are for most of the oratorios). The continuo never includes *secco* recitatives (which could, however, have been played from a score), and all the parts frequently omit other movements, including important arias; this is not due to incomplete survival, for each piece is numbered in sequence, and accompanied recitatives and sinfonias are often incongruously linked with arias in circumstances that make neither dramatic nor musical sense. The parts of different works reflect and sometimes combine various stages of the text; they include pieces rejected before performance, alternatives, versions otherwise unknown, arias added for revivals, and inconsistencies of pitch in the music of the same character.

It is tempting to suppose that they were copied from Handel's theatre parts (now all lost), which would give them considerable weight; but this seems unlikely. If they were, the theatre parts were startlingly inaccurate. In at least one opera (*Giulio Cesare*) it can be shown that the Flower parts were copied from a surviving manuscript score. This could be true of *Sosarme*, where they share many singularities with RM19.a.5, including repeat marks after the G major chord in bar 12 of the Act III sinfonia, found in no other source. On the other hand this copy includes the whole score except *secco* recitatives, whereas the parts omit the overture, Argone's accompanied recitative, the *coro militare*, and a random group of five arias. The text is that of the 1732 performances. One of the most controversial features throughout the corpus is the treatment of the oboe parts, which often differ not only from *HG* but also from the autograph, performing scores, and all other sources. The principal crux concerns their divergence from the violins where the staves carry a tutti mark; but sometimes they are given parts where other sources indicate violins only, and vice versa. The general, though not invariable, practice was for the oboes to hold their peace in tutti arias while the voice was singing, and more often than not the Flower parts conform to this. In *Sosarme* the oboes are silent in bars 14, 15, 25–8 and 36–41 of 'Forte in ciampo'; in 'Se discordia' they play only during the ritornellos, including bars 46–50; in 'Vorrei nè pur saprei' they play in the ritornello after the A section as well as at the beginning. On the other hand they are in continuous action throughout 'Tiene Giove', taking the higher octave in phrases where the tutti part goes below middle C. Here they contradict not only both performing scores but the autograph. (There are no parts for 'Il mio valore', 'Due parti del core', or 'M'opporrò'.) The most probable explanation, which seems to fit all the facts, is that the copyist was told to extract parts from a score and used his own judgment when he found no guidance in his source. It follows that the parts have no overriding authority. Nevertheless they are interesting as an indication of how a contemporary tackled an important matter of orchestration that bedevils many modern editors and performers. A parallel situation arises with the bassoon and cello parts, which regularly share the same stave, often with no indication as to when one or other instrument is to be silent; but the cello part of *Sosarme* makes no specific mention of the bassoon.

It remains to offer a critical estimate of the opera. The libretto as performed in 1732 —and that is the version we must judge—presents little for admiration. The two principal limbs of the plot, Argone's rebellion against his father and Altomaro's attempt to use this to place Melo on the throne, are poorly articulated. We are given no reason for Argone's rebellion except the statement in the Argument that Haliate intended to make Melo his heir; but this is never made clear in the opera, and Melo's whole attitude undermines it as a dramatic motive. Argone is far too sketchily drawn, without a single aria. Altomaro has a motive of a kind, but it is not clear how such a rascal contrives to hold his job as Haliate's counsellor or how he expects to get away with his nefarious scheme, which a word from any of the other characters could expose at once. (The music further diminishes his credibility, but the libretto cannot be blamed for that.) Neither of the instigators of the action thus carries conviction. Moreover the role of the eponymous hero as potential peace-maker and lover of Elmira is largely passive. He comes tardily on the scene with an aria towards the end of Act I, and does not appear again until II. viii. Thenceforward he is more prominent, but much too late to justify his assumption of the title role. The librettist should have allowed him to take the lead early in the opera. Alternatively he could have expanded Melo into the true hero, a status his conduct certainly justifies. This, however, would have meant promoting a bastard above two kings, a consideration calculated to inspire Handel but a flouting of the conventions of dynastic *opera seria*. Elmira is a delightful heroine, and Melo and Haliate potentially interesting figures; but they remain stunted in the absence of an organic dramatic framework.

Such a framework is present in Salvi's *Dionisio* libretto, which makes it clear from the outset that the rebellion of Alfonso (Argone), the rightful heir, has been provoked by his father's unjust action in disinheriting him at the instance of his scheming minister Altomaro, who covets the throne for his grandson Sancio (Melo). It is a drama of family quarrels and political intrigue; the love interest is secondary, although Salvi has an extra character in Alfonso's general Ramiro, a rival suitor for the hand of Elvida (Elmira). Fernando (Sosarme) is by no means the most prominent character; although he shares two duets, he has fewer arias than Elvida, Isabella (Erenice), Sancio, or Ramiro. All eight persons are clearly drawn; the most interesting are the half-brothers Alfonso and Sancio, the latter an even more attractive figure than Handel's Melo. After doing his utmost to prevent the duel, he offers to die in Alfonso's place. Altomaro's cynical opportunism is entirely convincing.

Handel[29] undermined this excellently balanced libretto by (*a*) greatly reducing the explanatory background even in his first version (Ramiro, otherwise no great loss, is useful in clarifying the plot), (*b*) suppressing all Alfonso's arias, (*c*) reducing Sancio's role, (*d*) expanding Altamaro's and giving him totally unsuitable aria texts (he has only two arias in *Dionisio*, but both round out his character). The explanation is not far to seek. Argone was allotted to an incompetent singer, Melo to a secondary one; Sosarme had to be expanded for Senesino and Altamaro to exploit

---

[29] He cannot be allowed to shelter behind the librettist; we know he took the lead in such matters.

the peculiar gifts of Montagnana; neither character had an aria in Salvi's third act, whereas Sancio had two. Handel regularly made such adjustments for his singers, but the extent to which, in *Sosarme*, he sacrificed dramatic potency and artistic unity to expediency is not characteristic of his usual practice.

Of the twenty-five set pieces in Handel's opera, other than the two *cori*, seventeen take their texts from Salvi, some in modified form. 'M'opporrò' was a duet for Elvida and Fernando, 'In mille dolci modi' an aria for Sancio; it refers to his reconciliation with Alfonso and has nothing to do with love. The new pieces, some of them insertions and some substitutions, are all three of Altamaro's arias, two of Elmira's ('Vola l'augello' and 'Vorrei, nè pur saprei'), two of Sosarme's ('Il mio valore' and 'Alle sfere'), Melo's 'Sincero affetto', and the Act III love duet.

Handel's score is tantalizing. Dent calls it 'very unequal', too severe a judgment when almost every number exhibits some striking felicity of invention. Yet it scarcely fulfils the ideal of amounting to more than the sum of its parts. *Sosarme* does more honour to Handel as a musician than as a dramatist. The tension does not build up from scene to scene, because the behaviour of the characters inhibits presentation in depth. They sing exquisite music, but their conflicts seem contrived and artificial, like the manœuvres of chessmen. This is presumably what Streatfeild meant in saying that the libretto contains 'no dramatic situations worthy of the name'. Burney's estimate, as we have seen, was higher; and time has not disturbed his conclusion that 'it seems impossible to name any dramatic composer who so constantly varied his songs in subject, style, and accompaniment'. The manifold resource in rhythm, melody, harmony, and design is as striking as in any of Handel's operas. All three duets and the final *coro* are of exceptional merit. Yet *Sosarme* remains too close to the received idea of *opera seria* as a disjointed string of unmatched pearls.

The hero, already handicapped by the libretto, receives an uncertain start from Handel. His Act I aria, 'Il mio valore', is dramatically vital. It should establish him as a champion of human rights against cruelty and injustice; but despite expressive details, such as the upper violin pedals in the A section, it makes a somewhat negative impression. This is exceptional; Handel very rarely fails to establish a major character firmly in his or her first aria. We gain no clear view of Sosarme until he lies wounded half way through Act II. From this point his music, all in major keys, is consistently first-rate. As in so many Senesino parts, it is that of a youthful and eager lover rather than a soldier; he is an attractive but not a dynamic figure. His three remaining arias are all sublimated dances. 'Alle sfere della gloria' resembles Trasimede's 'Se l'arco avessi' in *Admeto* in the great length of its initial ritornello and A section (36 and 162 bars respectively) and the delightfully rich yet open texture for horns, oboes, and four-part strings variously contrasted and combined. The six-bar main theme with its springy rhythm, besides impelling the music forward in irregular periods, reinforces the impression that Sosarme regards the pursuit of glory as an extension of the hunting season. The B section lacks horns, but the oboes and violins toss the same material to and fro in insouciant fragments, and the da capo is neatly foreshortened.

'In mille dolci mode' has one of Handel's loveliest minuet melodies, exquisitely refined by art. The rare choice of rondo form, in which Handel always excelled, may have been suggested by the words: Sosarme pledges his love 'In a thousand sweet ways', and the music suggests some of them. The long phrases of the D major main theme (6 + 8 bars in the ritornello, 8 + 10 + 4 + 8 for the voice) build up to a rapturous paragraph of devotion, balanced by two shorter episodes in F sharp minor and B minor. The final return is enriched at the start by the earlier octave doubling of the voice and violins, and at the end by two subtle strokes: the entry of the ritornello on a high A before the vocal cadence and the arrival of the climactic D, the top note of the melody, four bars later. Both have been adumbrated at bar 22, but their novel spacing here sets the seal on a sublime inspiration. Handel did not hit the target first shot: the autograph contains a cancelled opening ritornello on the same material, but less expansively treated in ten bars instead of fourteen and with a conventional two-bar formula at the start (Ex. 3). The seeds go back earlier still, to a suppressed aria, 'Questo core incatenato', in the original Act I of *Giulio Cesare* (1723), where the time, key, some of the rhythms and the upward octave leap are already established (Ex. 4). This in turn is based on the first phrase of an aria, 'Sei pur bella', in a continuo cantata (HWV 160c) (Ex. 5). Handel also used the material, in E flat and with further variants, in the first of the nine German arias on texts by B. H. Brockes, 'Künft'ger Zeiten eitler Kummer', dating from the mid-1720s; the autograph is on 'Cantoni Bergamo' paper, which he was using in 1725–6.

Burney oddly allows 'great theatrical merit' to 'M'opporrò da generoso' on account of 'the agitation and fury of the character for whom it was composed'. The

Ex.3

Ex.4

catchy tune suggests rather the jaunty self-confidence of the sportsman as Sosarme sets out to intervene in the duel between father and son. It is in effect a gavotte with extra bar-lines changing the time to 2/4; Handel first wrote a common-time signature against the top part. Again the ritornello is long, and the squareness of the melody is dissolved in long melismas for the voice.

Sosarme's two duets with Elmira are marvels of beauty; it is difficult to know which to rank the higher. 'Per le porte del tormento' is one of those touching scenes for lovers in misfortune in which Handel's operas abound; but unlike the great examples in *Tamerlano, Rodelinda*, and *Tolomeo* it is in a major key (E), and one generally associated with confidence and serenity. The lovely lilting tune with its exquisite part-writing and characteristic melodic extensions (in particular the prolonged cadence before the Adagio at the end of the A section) seems to hold time suspended, as if the lovers sought to preserve the moment for ever.[30] They do sustain it for a very long time, but we cannot wish it shortened, even if the twelve-bar B section seems little but an excuse to hear the first part over again. 'Tu caro sei' expresses the lovers' relief after their trials are over with a light-heartedness that never descends to triviality. Perhaps no dramatic composer except Mozart rivals Handel's power to combine sublimity with good humour. As so often, the motive force is primarily rhythmic and structural. The ideas are clichés, but the impact is wholly fresh. Handel used several of them elsewhere, sometimes in very different contexts; the contour and syncopated rhythm of the first bar in the early psalm 'Laudate pueri' and the Second Harlot's air in *Solomon*, the rocking sequence in thirds that enters so unexpectedly at 'd'un alma amante' in *Rodelinda* ('Spietati')[31] and the chorus 'When his loud voice' in *Jephtha*. Even the time-worn cadential figure when Sosarme gives the expected answer to Elmira's question (last four bars of *HG*, p. 102) chimes in with a delicious aptness. The orchestra, though it occupies but three staves (for a time only two), reflects the touch of a master. Handel divides it into two groups, each with its own harpsichord: Elmira is supported by unison violins 'pianissimo' and 'Cembalo primo con i suoi Bassi, piano', Sosarme by four violas in unison and 'Cembalo secondo colla Teorba, e i suoi Bassi'. When at length the voices sing together the groups combine ('Tutti, mà pp' in the bass). The oboes double the violins in the fore and aft ritornellos, and at one point the bassoons leave the bass to join the violas.

Elmira's part is as rewarding as Sosarme's; like him she has a single aria in the minor (the last instead of the first), but her five solos, one a cavatina, are well varied and all of the highest quality. 'Rendi'l sereno al ciglio', later to win wide popularity yoked to the unsuitable words 'Lord, remember David', is the only aria Handel ever wrote in B major.[32] The tempo mark too, Largo assai, is very rare. It is brief and touchingly direct, as befits a daughter comforting her distraught mother: two bars of ritornello, ten bars in the first part, three in the B section, no ritornello before the da capo. (Chrysander's omission of stage directions obscures the fact that this is an exit aria; Elmira goes out, but returns *with an afflicted Air* ('affannata') after Erenice's next line of recitative.) Such inspired simplicity, the prerogative of the greatest artists, defies analysis; but one notes the suppression of harpsichord and bassoons after the ritornello (at first Handel omitted them here too), the exquisite entry of the violins with a high B 'un poco forte' on an off-beat at the end of the first part, echoing at a higher pitch an earlier phrase of the voice, the allusion to this by both violins in thirds in the B section, and the beautifully judged return *dal segno*. This feature anticipates 'Angels, ever bright and fair' and 'Waft her, angels', of

---

[30] At bar 33 there is a parallel with the duet 'Una guerra' in the cantata *Apollo e Dafne*, where, however, the mood and (implied) tempo are very different.

[31] This also uses the syncopated rhythm in bars 4–6, and later in the voice, but the line is different.

[32] It borrows from, but transcends, an aria in Keiser's *Claudius*, 'Plagnati del destino': see J. H. Roberts (ed.), *Handel Sources* (New York and London, 1986), iii. 27.

which 'Rendi'l sereno al ciglio' is a worthy forerunner. The similarity between the opening bars and a phrase in the duet 'Per le porte del tormento' is no doubt an accident, but a happy one. 'Dite pace' also looks forward to the late oratorios, especially *Theodora*, in its use of contrasted tempos and textures within the A section. This was of course suggested by the words ('Dite pace, e fulminate') and is a convention Handel had employed as early as *Teseo*; but there is greater depth and subtlety here. The first Adagio begins on a first inversion and returns later over a dominant pedal. The singer should be chary of ornaments, even in the da capo; to do otherwise would wreck the antithesis between this smooth legato and the lively violin figures and agile coloratura of the Allegro with its octave leaps and semiquaver runs. The modulations and chromatic restlessness of the B section have an almost Mozartian emotionalism. The return, though quite literal, achieves an effect of touching surprise through the juxtaposition of two Adagios.

The second act, like the first, is framed—so far as the set pieces are concerned —by two solos for Elmira. Handel wrote few lovelier cavatinas than 'Padre, germano, e sposo'. Vocal line and accompaniment are perfectly balanced, internally and against each other. The ritornello presents the three main orchestral elements in concentrated form: a much ornamented violin line, sharply dotted figures, and steady quaver movement. The last two alternate throughout between treble and bass while the voice pursues its independent way, moulding the initial broken phrases of grief into a sustained paragraph that mounts to a wonderful climax with the romantic aid of Neapolitan harmony. Behind Elmira's suffering we sense a sterling courage. 'Vola l'augello' is more relaxed. The transference of the aria from Act I has left a slight incongruity: while the smile is a valid symbol of hope, Elmira should surely be thinking of her wounded lover rather than her brother. Nevertheless, criticism collapses before the seductive charm of the music, which crowns a superlatively rich act. Handel's bird songs are not all as captivating as this. There is no risk of vapid chortles marring the design based on pedals, trills, and the conjunct motion of voice and violins in unison, thirds, sixths, and tenths. Handel varies this with such delicacy, placing the violins sometimes above and sometimes below the voice, as to convey an impression of sumptuous texture in the almost total absence of inner parts. The brief B section is more passionately engaged—just enough to circumvent the danger of facile uniformity.

Elmira's Act III aria, 'Vorrei, nè pur saprei', though Burney considered it of slight importance, once more raises the simple to the sublime with the predictable aid of rhythmic flexibility. The ritornello has two unequal limbs, of three and six bars; the latter, with its leaping fifths and sixths and sudden climb from the leading note to the subdominant a diminished twelfth above, is an unforgettable inspiration that might have sprung from Bach. It never occurs in the aria itself. After the same initial three-bar figure the voice introduces a new phrase, an unadorned rising sequence in the relative major ('che la speme del mio core'), that by some mysterious magic clutches at the heart. Like so many such details it was an afterthought. Although the phrase occurs once in the B section ('questi solo fanno avere'), its place here was at first occupied by a less memorable sequence used in slightly different form after

Ex.6

the repeat (Ex. 6). This internal redistribution of ideas was the making of the aria, which has no further resources. The first part is in binary form with repeats, the B section uses the same material. Elmira is a heroine worthy of a greater opera.

Dent calls Erenice a managing matriarch, not a common type in Handel (despite Gismonda in *Ottone*, Matilde in *Lotario*, and perhaps Storgè, who has cause enough for indignation). This is scarcely fair to a woman whose husband, son, daughter, and prospective son-in-law are in constant danger of violent death. Her report of Hecate's words in her dream exhibits that unfailingly expressive choice of chords that is as characteristic of Handel's accompanied recitatives as of Bach's chorales; but neither of her arias in Act I transcends routine. The duet with Argone in II. iii is a spirited piece of theatrical action, unorthodox in design despite the regular da capo. Argone begins without ritornello, but it is Erenice who takes command. She never allows him more than two or three words, and those at irregular intervals, interrupting on each occasion with angular phrases of scorching contempt and finally driving him out. As in most of Handel's ensembles where the characters are at odds, the orchestral parts are largely independent of the voices, the violins reinforcing Erenice's objurgations with fusillades of semiquavers. The modulations to flat minor keys (F major to C minor and F minor) strengthen the impact.

'Vado al campo' finds Erenice equally resolute. The Presto opening without ritornello, the first violins and bass in free imitation while the middle parts keep up a buzz of repeated quavers, propels the music with a vigour that the striding first violin figuration and rising vocal sequences never allow to slacken. The progression in bars 14–23, moving in a long crescendo from E flat to F, generates intense energy. The ritornello design assists the forward movement: nothing at the start (where Erenice's decision brooks no delay), but ten bars extending and developing the main theme after the first part, and five in G minor, the key in which the B section ends, before the brisk resumption of the da capo in E flat. This aria too was transformed during composition. The tempo was quickened from Allegro to Presto, and the layout of the bass altered from a procession of even quavers unbroken throughout the A section except at the Adagio cadence. The new angular bass at each entry of the main theme was a multiple improvement: it strengthened the contrapuntal interest, let air into the texture at the vital words 'Vado al campo', deposed the regular symmetry (the dotted rhythm lasts for three, two, and seven bars at its three incursions), and gave Erenice's bold purpose an extra urgency and rhythmic momentum. We can observe Handel's genius breaking up the settled routine of the new Neapolitan idiom. The upper notes for the voice in the first two bars, added in *H* in 1734, may be seen as a further improvement. Perhaps finer still is Erenice's last aria, 'Cuor di madre', in which the prospect of the duel between husband and son wrings from her a desolate F sharp minor lament. In each section Handel deploys an obbligato for solo violin (played by Castrucci), whose long curling phrases, contrasted with the ejaculations of the voice (twice extended in irregular periods of five and six bars), would not be out of place in a Bach sacred cantata. Handel originally included the voice at the start, as in bars 9 and 10, but crossed it out almost at once.

Of the other two altos, Argone remains a cipher. Even so Handel made capital out of Campioli's inadequacies, while confining him to the few abortive but cunningly placed phrases in his duet with Erenice and an accompanied recitative with the appropriate rhetorical gestures at the start of the opera. Melo is a much more individual figure, who would have repaid fuller treatment. He has two arias in minor keys that bear witness to Handel's interest in the bastard son who proves so much more sympathetic than his legitimate brother. In neither does the text imperatively demand the emotional treatment it receives. Both, like 'Cuor di madre', have a flavour of Bach, an accidental peculiarity that suffuses a number of Handel's works at different periods; *Tamerlano* and *Theodora* are notable examples. 'Sì, sì, minaccia' is built round another violin obbligato (unison, not solo), in which a short rhythmic pattern of graceful filigree work is repeated many times. The vocal divisions are very expressive, and the aria has an undercurrent of profound sadness, though Melo is merely urging Sosarme to take a strong line in reconciling Argone and Haliate. This assumes a colour of sombre, even tragic anguish in 'Sò ch'il ciel'. Here the autograph brings one of those major surprises that not infrequently make the Handelian scholar hold his breath in amazement. The words express confidence in heaven's power to frustrate the wrongdoer, and Handel originally set them, not to this music (Ex. 7a) but to that of Altomaro's following aria, 'Sento il cor' (Exx. 7b, c), which on a superficial reading they fit much better. This transference explains the similarity of the words, especially the rhymes, in the two arias; Handel must have asked the librettist to supply the second text for music already written. It also accounts for the appearance of downward scale figures, suggested by the line 'far cader l'indegna frode', at the same point in both. Only the first page (16 bars) of the version shown in Ex. 7b survives, apparently due to the accident that Handel used the other side for modifications to a recitative in another part of the opera. It differs from the bass setting in a number of minor but interesting particulars: the ritornello is one bar shorter, and the octave and unison doubling of the voice and the extension of its second phrase from four to five bars are not yet present. The circumstances suggest that other substituted drafts, not to mention sketches, could have vanished when he sorted out the autograph. There are more indications to this effect, such as the chance survival of part of Daniel's 'Chastity, thou cherub bright'

Ex.7

(a)

(b)

- de

- de - gna fro - de——— sù l'au-tor che l'in - ven - tò

(*c*)

Allegro

Vns. 1, 2

Va.

Altomaro

Sen - tò il cor che lie - to go - de

Bass

di   tro-var si bel - la fro - de——— per-chi an-cor— la

dis - prez - zò.

in *Susanna* set to the music of his other aria, "'Tis not age's sullen face'. By no means every stage of Handel's composing process is open to our inspection.

Why did he undertake this extraordinary metamorphosis? He must have changed his mind completely about Melo, converting him from an extrovert into an introvert; for no two settings could be more utterly opposed in mood. He is more than justified in the event. The counterpoint of words against music in the G minor 'Sò ch'il ciel' is profoundly moving; it suggests that Melo for all his faith has little confidence in the outcome. We are reminded of the *coro* at the end of *Tamerlano* and of Bajazet's 'A suoi piedi' in the same opera. In both arias the Bach parallels are striking. 'Sò ch'il ciel' has another violin obbligato of the type mentioned above, but still more eloquent. The broken figuration in the ritornello ranges over two octaves and a fifth, with leaps of a twelfth and a tenth. The angular vocal intervals over a chromatic bass, interrupted cadences, and tense sequences might have served for a mediation on the crucifixion (Ex. 8). The B section all but quotes the chorus at the end of Part I of the St Matthew Passion, which Handel cannot have known.[33] Much of the texture in the first part has the sonorous economy one associates with Bach's solo violin sonatas; that of the B section, with the violins divided and constantly crossing over a slow and irregular rising chromatic scale in the bass, suggests a magical vista of clouds dissolving beneath the warmth of the relative major key, only to re-form as the music droops towards D minor before the da capo. The treatment of the violins in slurred semiquavers, often in thirds, makes a wonderful contrast with the earlier anfractuosities. Melo's Act III aria, 'Sincero affetto', has a simple straightforwardness (violins doubling the voice at the octave) that illustrates the words very prettily. But it is superficial in comparison with his earlier music; Melo is a character whose mettle shines brightest in adversity.

Haliate is one of several tenor potentates from the Second Academy period, when Handel enjoyed the services of Fabri and Pinacci. The plot forces him into wooden postures, but his three arias are all excellent. Two of them, as with Melo, are in minor keys. 'La turba adulatrice' is a C minor vengeance aria on the grand scale, an immensely powerful piece based on a typical series of contrasts. The

[33] The even more remarkable parallel in 'A suoi piedi' precedes the composition of Bach's work by several years. See *Handel's Operas 1704–1726*, 540.

Ex.8

ritornello has at least five ideas: a smooth half-sinister opening over a pedal, arpeggio and scale figures in rugged octaves, string tremolos over a marching bass, an angular gesture signing off with a trill, and a dotted cadential formula. They appear in the aria in a different order and all manner of transformations, the dotted figure supplying the seed of much of the B section. The first phrase is lengthened by imitation at the vocal entry and provided with a suave cadence in the relative major, making three and a half bars instead of one and a half. Later it appears in E flat throughout, lengthened by yet another bar, after a furious outburst of G minor semiquavers; the effect is of formidable reserves of strength. The voice has some lively coloratura of a type associated with tenor and bass tyrants. The B section is extensively developed, with much new material and further contrasts, the orchestra confined to sharp expostulations while Haliate works off his anger in phrases of every length from two beats to extended melismas of four and five bars. There are traces in this aria, and elsewhere in *Sosarme*, of the new homophonic style current in Italy, which Handel had known at least as early as his Vinci-based pasticcio *Elpidia* of 1725, but he uses it with a resilient strength seldom if ever attained by Vinci or Pergolesi.

In Act II this explosive monarch relaxes in an aria of equal rhythmic and thematic resource but very different temper. 'Se discordia' has a gracious melody of the same family as the duet 'Cease thy anguish' in *Athalia* and the minuet in the overture to *Berenice*. The four-bar opening phrase of the ritornello is answered by one of no fewer than fourteen bars containing a remarkable proliferation of rhythmic patterns. This flexibility extends throughout the aria, whose voice part falls into phrases of approximately the following bar-lengths: 4, 3, 2, 6, 5, 5, 10 (with a beautiful hemiola extension), 9, 5, 6, 5, and 4. Yet the result is a seamless paragraph, the orchestra constantly overlapping the voice in a masterpiece of sustained articulation. The afterthought here, which extended the second limb of the ritornello by two bars and was grouted in two places later, was the three-bar sequence of slurred semiquavers in thirds (bars 13–15, 66–8, 95–7). The B section, with a particularly happy spacing of the string parts, is little inferior. 'S'io cadrò' finds Haliate in a mood of bitter reproach, conveyed by short phrases and a jagged violin obbligato extending over three octaves. Again one catches a glimpse of 'A suoi piedi' at the back of Handel's mind. The major key of the B section, on similar material, brings a moment of calm, but it is soon dissipated. The silent bar with fermata at the bottom of *HG*, p. 85 replaced three bars for voice and bass; Handel was never averse from allowing his singers a cadenza at appropriate moments.

It is difficult to know what to make of Altomaro. Here is a double-dyed villain, an unscrupulous bully, liar, and potential murderer, who expresses himself in music of mellow gravity or bluff exuberance, always in major keys with no chromatic inflections. It is just possible that Handel meant to draw a superficially jolly old scoundrel, an honest Iago whom no one could suspect; but this seems unlikely, especially as two of his three arias originated in other mouths. Probably Handel gave him up as a character and allowed himself to exploit the sonorous voice of his new singer, Montagnana, a true *basso cantante*, not a blustering baritone like Boschi. It was to Montagnana's singing in this part, his first aria in particular, that Burney applied the words 'depth, power, mellowness, and peculiar accuracy of intonation in hitting distant intervals'. 'Fra l'ombre' is certainly a challenge in these respects (Ex. 9). Handel adapted this from an aria for Polifemo in the 1708 Naples serenata *Aci, Galatea e Polifemo*, where the words and the musical material are almost the same but the vocal line, characterizing the clumsy vastness of the giant, is still more ungainly and a fifth wider in compass.[34] The cadences at the end of each section must be among the most eccentric ever written (Ex. 10). A comparison between the two versions offers a fascinating insight into Handel's methods in recomposition. The 1708 aria is strangely scored for two muted violins, viola, and 'Violono grosso senza Cembalo'; the violins' semiquaver figures are not present; and the initial imitations, begun by the voice, are successive instead of overlapping. In 1732 Handel made the texture smoother, tauter, more contrapuntal, and more sensuous. The grotesquerie has disappeared. The opening, where the falling arpeggio of the

---

[34] The part was probably written for Antonio Francesco Carli, who later sang Claudio in *Agrippina*.

Ex.9

Ex.10

instrumental bass is freely imitated in turn by voice, first violin, viola, and second violin, has a concentration preserved throughout with the aid of intricately crossing string parts (once the viola finds itself at the top and the first violin nearest the bass) and deep pedals. The B section is equally fine and returns to the da capo by way of fresh development. Most of these features were new in 1732. It is a superb piece of music, but Streatfeild's opinion that it 'seems to be enveloped in a weird atmosphere of guilt and horror' is difficult to sustain. The mood is rather of timeless serenity, as of some aged philosopher contemplating the remote past. So might Handel himself have looked back to his youth in Italy.

'Sento il cor' would have made an admirable drinking song. It is a very odd response to Melo's defiance, but as we have seen it was conceived for Melo. The descending scale figures in the bass and the leaping octaves associated with them are apt enough, though the image of falling that inspired them has gone. Handel used both ideas with characteristic resource, especially in the ritornello after the A section, where the scale tumbles down more than two octaves instead of an eleventh. Rollicking rhythms, which often take an unexpected turn, lively sequences and coloratura, and a B section that neatly combines the old with the new distinguish an aria more suited in its bass form to a bibulous clown, some Polyphemus guiltless of his fellow shepherds' blood, than to a crafty conspirator. The same is true of 'Tiene Giove', a genial gavotte with a ritornello melody of six bars that the voice promptly extends to sixteen. This jolly dance is the last piece before the duel and Altomaro's suicide. If Handel meant it for dramatic irony, he missed the target by a mile.

Sosarme has a fine and carefully composed overture. The preamble is not the usual dotted introduction but a stately sarabande in 3/2. This may be a link with the original Iberian venue; one recalls the sarabandes in Handel's earlier Spanish opera *Almira*. The Allegro, more genuinely fugal than usual, has a springy subject related to the familiar melody used in the D major violin sonata and the symphony for the Angel's appearance in *Jephtha*. The minuet plays off a short-breathed tune with a rhythmic resemblance to 'God save the Queen', divided between woodwind and full orchestra, against a flowing counterpoint in slurred quavers for the first violins. The opening of Act I is theatrically effective, with two accompanied recitatives (the only examples in the opera) and a *coro militare* full of fanfares and flourishes before the first aria. The *coro* was sung by the soloists, presumably offstage, and it is repeated later in the act (I. x), where it dramatically buttresses the hesitant Argone's resolve to lead the sortie. There was an interesting minor change here in 1734. In 1732 the D major *coro* followed a cadence in the dominant[35] (*HG* version 'A'); when Handel shortened the recitative to *HG* 'B' he cadenced in E, after which the entry of the *coro* comes as a sharper surprise. This reflects the stage direction in libretto and autograph *Mentre stà sospeso si senta il coro militare ad invitarlo*, which Chrysander omits. The final *coro*, like many others at this period, is a substantial movement, though in regular da capo form. The deceased Altomaro supplies the bass from the wings. It is a delightful pastoral in rare 9/8 metre, with a strong foretaste of the duet 'O lovely peace' in *Judas Maccabaeus*. The texture is very rich, with copious double thirds for violins and oboes and the mellow reinforcement of horns. The B section, as so often in this opera, is developed at length, moving from the relative (D) minor to E major as the dominant of A minor. A ritornello in the latter key replaces the opening and drops straight back to the reprise in F major, supplying with the same stroke fufilment, continuity, and surprise.

The orchestra has no flutes or recorders, but the presence of trumpets and horns (each in two movements), the divided forces with theorbo in the duet 'Tu caro sei', and the full four-part accompaniment in the great majority of the arias leave an impression of exceptional amplitude. The unusual balance of voices in Handel's company during the years 1729–32, when he had several altos with a single soprano, tenor, and bass, makes for further variety. *Sosarme* is the only opera he wrote for the particular combination SAAAATB. It is also the only one in which nine different major keys occur in set pieces; he never used D flat and F sharp outside recitatives, and A flat only in *L'Allegro*. The minor mode is less prominent than usual in the last two acts (five times in twenty numbers); Act II, the finest of the three, ends with six consecutive movements in major keys. No overall key pattern is discernible; in this, as in other respects, *Sosarme* is something of a sport among Handel's mature works.

[35] In the first draft of the autograph it was in the mediant, F sharp minor.

7

Charles Jennens's Marginalia to Mainwaring's Life of Handel

====

By courtesy of Mr Robin Golding I was recently allowed to examine a copy of John Mainwaring's *Memoirs of the Life of the late George Frederic Handel* (1760) containing marginal comments in an eighteenth-century hand. The writing was familiar, and a cursory inspection of the comments made it clear that their author was not only acquainted with the composer but was one of his oratorio librettists. Comparison with the fly-leaves in the many volumes of manuscript copies of Handel's music from the Aylesford Collection in the British Library quickly put the identification beyond doubt. The writer was Charles Jennens, Handel's collaborator in *Saul*, *L'Allegro*, *Messiah*, and *Belshazzar*.

Jennens's notes are found on twenty-two pages of the book, and all except one (a single word) are in ink. They range from the solitary letter Q (= Query) to a passage of more than sixty words. While most of them are corrections of mistakes or omissions by Mainwaring, they add several facts to our knowledge about Handel, including the name of one of his anonymous poets, and one splendid and characteristic anecdote. They also throw light on Jennens himself, whom far too many writers on Handel have dismissed as a pompous buffoon. Though no poet, he was a man of taste and considerable literary skill, as his librettos repeatedly demonstrate. These terse notes reflect a trenchant and scholarly mind and a gift for the deflation of humbug. Handel's nine surviving letters to him are full of respect and affection, and it is easy to imagine such a man sharing a twenty-five-year friendship with the genial if explosive composer.

Mainwaring's book falls into three parts: the Memoirs proper (pp. 1–143), the Catalogue of Works (pp. 147–55), and Observations on the Works (pp. 159–208). Jennens makes only one note on the last, the correction of a reference in Longinus. The Catalogue is heavily encrusted with comments in small writing—so heavily that in places the ink has eaten holes through the paper. They are a mixture of addenda, corrigenda, and explanation. Jennens inserts a number of works omitted by Mainwaring: 'Silla' (correctly placed but without date) among the operas; 'La passione. Hamb. German.'[1] and 'La Resurressione. Rom. Italian.' at the head of the oratorios (see Plate 11); 'Dryden's Song or lesser Ode for St Cecilia's day' with the serenatas; 'Mottetti' under church music. He amended '*Three* more Te-Deums' to

---

[1] This of course is the Brockes Passion, not the misattributed 'St John', now thought to be by Mattheson.

'*Four*', and expanded Mainwaring's reference to 'a Funeral Service for her late MAJESTY Queen CAROLINE' to 'Funeral Anthem for Q. Caroline afterwards perform'd as the 1st Part of Exodus, or Israel in Egypt', repeating this information against the list of oratorios and adding the date of completion of each part. He gives precise dates of this kind for three other oratorios: *Saul*, *Belshazzar*, and *Judas Maccabaeus*, but surprisingly not for *Messiah*. Indeed it is amusing to find that this of all oratorios is wrongly dated by Mainwaring and the error was not spotted by Jennens. Mainwaring's dates, where they specify month and day, derive from Handel's autographs; they are generally those of completion, whether of the first draft or of the final filling-in. For *Messiah*, however, he gives 12 April 1741 (before the oratorio was begun), a confusion between the date of completion (14 September 1741) and that of the first performance (13 April 1742).[2]

Jennens's dates for *Saul* and *Belshazzar* are important, for they supply information not otherwise available and not to be found in the autographs. Mainwaring lists simply 'SAUL, 1740' and 'BELSHAZZAR' without date (between *Susanna*, wrongly dated 9 August 1743, and *Hercules* with its correct date, 17 August 1744). Jennens notes against *Saul*:

print. 1738. begin. 1st Act. Jul. 23, 1738. End Aug. 1. Act. 2 Aug. 2, End Aug 8. End of Act 3, Aug. 15.

Of these dates only 23 July and 8 August are in the autograph (according to which Handel completed the filling in of Act II on 28 August and of the whole work on 27 September). The dates for the end of Act I and the beginning of Act II Jennens took from his own copy, now in the Flower Collection in Manchester Public Library (vols. 269 and 270), where he had himself recorded them. There is no date at the end of Act III (vol. 271), though it is likely enough that Handel finished the first draft on 15 August. (*Saul* was planned to end, as *Israel in Egypt* was to begin, with the Funeral Anthem for Queen Caroline.) He had by then got the autograph into a rare tangle, and dropped it to start work on *Imeneo*, before returning to *Saul* after a visit from Jennens on 18 September.

For *Belshazzar* Jennens notes:

print. 1745. Beg. Act. I. Aug. 23, 1744. Sept. 3, end. end of Act 2. Sept. 10. 1744. fin. Oct. 23, 1744.

These dates, except the last, are those of the first draft. Hitherto the date of completion could only be guessed, since the final chorus, adapted from the Chandos anthem *I will magnify thee*, is not in the autograph, and Jennens's manuscript copy is missing from the Flower Collection. The word 'print.' in the last two entries refers to the librettos, of which Jennens was the author. The first edition of *Saul* is dated 1738 (Old Style), although the oratorio was not performed until 16 January 1739.

Predictably Jennens amends the title of *L'Allegro ed il Penseroso* by adding his own 'ed il Moderato'. Three works in Mainwaring's list of oratorios he qualifies, quite

[2] It was originally announced for 12 April.

properly. *Alexander's Feast* is 'No Oratorio, but an Ode', *Hercules* 'An Opera', *Semele* 'No Oratorio, but a baudy Opera'; and he amends Mainwaring's footnote on the last by inserting the two words in italics: 'An English Opera, but called *by fools* an Oratorio, and performed as such at Covent-Garden' (see Plate 11). Against the *Occasional Oratorio* he places the concise comment: 'Nothing'. His emendation of Mainwaring's dates is invariably accurate (his 1749 for *Susanna* and *Solomon* refers to first performance, not composition), and in two further instances he adds dates not available in the autographs: 28 November 1721 for *Floridante* (Mainwaring gives the year 1723 only) and 10 November 1726 for *Admeto*. The autograph of *Floridante* lacks the final *coro*, which must have been detached before 1760 (it reappeared much later and came to the British Library with the gift of the Stefan Zweig Collection in 1986); that of *Admeto* is lost. As with *Saul*, Jennens supplied both dates from his own addenda to the manuscript copies in his library (Flower, vols. 2 and 131).

Mainwaring's list of chamber music concludes with 'Serenatas, [most of them made abroad, and some few at his first coming to England, one of which was for Queen Anne, and performed at St James's, but afterwards lost]' (square brackets original). Jennens makes two comments here: after 'Queen Anne' he added ''s Birthday, the words by Ambr. Philips', and after 'lost' 'no such matter: for I have it transcrib'd from a copy which belong'd to L^d. Radnor'. Hitherto the authorship of the Birthday Ode ('Eternal source of light divine!') has been unknown. Ambrose Philips (1674–1749), a friend of Addison and Steele and for some time MP for Armagh, wrote plays and pastorals. The latter were published in 1709, the same year as Pope's, and not surprisingly they drew Pope's fire. 'From that time', says Johnson in his characteristically pithy life of Philips, 'Pope and Philips lived in a perpetual reciprocation of malevolence'. The victim ('slow Philips') appears twice in *The Dunciad*. The nickname 'Namby-Pamby' bestowed on him by Henry Carey added a new word to the English language. Johnson says that, though a good man with the sword, 'in conversation he was solemn and pompous'. The poetical content of the Birthday Ode is all too compatible with these strictures.

About half Jennens's remarks on the Life are criticisms of omission or corrections of fact:

Why are Esther & Deborah skipp'd (p. 119).
Handel's Arianna was perform'd in the Hay-market, & Porpora's in Lincoln's-Inn-fields (p. 119).
Messiah was not perform'd in London till after his return from Ireland. And Samson was perform'd before it, the same season, with prodigious success (p. 130).

Mainwaring's remark that 'these early fruits of his studies [in Italy] would doubtless be vast curiosities could they now be met with' is glossed: 'Some of them we have' (p. 67). Jennens rightly queries the statement that Handel wrote *Faramondo* and the pasticcio *Alessandro Severo* in 1737–8 for Lord Middlesex (p. 124). Another Q adorns the description of oratorio, 'more suited to the native gravity and solidity of the English', as 'borrowed from the *concert spirituel* of their volatile neighbours on the continent' (p. 126). When Mainwaring, writing of the Italian period, contrasts English unfavourably with Italian as a vehicle for singing and animadverts on 'the disadvantages of a language less soft and sonorous, and of Dramas constructed without art or judgment, order or consistency', Jennens enters two protests: 'The language was no hindrance to his genius', and 'Too generally, & therefore falsely, asserted; falsely, in particular, of the English Acis & Galatea' (p. 66). One can only applaud, noting that this supposedly vain man did not choose his example from one of his own librettos or defend his own dramas.

In writing of Handel's rivalry with the Opera of the Nobility Mainwaring falls into a vein of flatulent moralizing that evidently grated on Jennens. Twice he brings the author sharply to heel. Mainwaring writes:

But it is a principal part of prudence, to command our temper on any trial we may chance to receive; a part of it which, to say the truth, he never practised or professed. This omission involved him in misfortunes, which taught him another part of prudence (if it must be called so) which he never ought to have practised, much less professed, that of consulting his interest at the expence of his art (p. 116).

Jennens comments: 'Explain your self, if you can!' Again:

He could have vanquished his opponents at their own weapons; but he had the sense to discover, that the offended and prejudiced side would never have acknowledged his victory however decisive; and that his new friends, for want of understanding the nature and use of such weapons, would not have discerned it however obvious (p. 118).

The comment: 'Explain again!'

Lastly the anecdote, which alone makes the discovery of the volume a memorable event. On pp. 62–3 Mainwaring writes of Handel's dealings with Cardinals Colonna and Pamphilii in Rome:

The latter had some talents for Poetry, and wrote the drama of IL TRIONFO DEL TEMPO, besides several other pieces, which HANDEL set at his desire, some in the compass of a single evening, and others extempore. One of these was in honour of HANDEL himself. He was compared to ORPHEUS, and exalted above the rank of mortals.

Jennens adds:

Cantata the 19th in my collection; which contains only 51 in all.[3] Handel told me that the words of Il Trionfo &c. were written by Cardinal Pamphilii, & added, 'an old Fool!' I ask'd 'why Fool? because he wrote an Oratorio? perhaps you will call *me* fool for the same reason!' He answer'd 'So I would, if you flatter'd me, as He did'. (See Plate 12.)

[3] The collection (Flower, vols. 77 and 78) contains in fact 50 cantatas; although numbered 1–51 it has no number 38. 'Hendel, non può mia musa' is No. 19. Mr Arthur D. Walker kindly checked these details for me.

8

The Performance of Recitative in Late Baroque Opera

The revival of almost any serious opera composed before 1750 presents major difficulties, which arise from the total disappearance of this repertory for the greater part of two centuries and to some extent also explain it. The French style, which has its own peculiarities and problems, is a separate subject not considered here. The rest of European opera, with rare exceptions, was Italian in form and generally in language too. The German opera at Hamburg, which lasted from 1678 to 1738, fell more and more under Italian influence, to the extent of presenting a bilingual text in the works of Keiser, Mattheson, and Telemann and in Handel's early productions, of which only *Almira* survives complete. English opera scarcely got off the ground: Purcell's *Dido and Aeneas* is unique, not only in its genius but in the circumstances of its composition for a girl's school, which by a happy accident brought it comfortably within the scope of modern performance and appreciation. The present enquiry, provoked by attempts to grapple with the revival of Handel's operas, is concerned with the *opera seria* of the first half of the eighteenth century.

The principal obstacles are the castrato voice, the rarity or total absence of ensembles and choruses, the stereotyped form of the da capo aria, and the extensive acreage of simple or *secco* recitative. The fact that plot development was virtually confined to the recitative (the outer action) and emotional expression to the arias (the inner action) imposed further conventions that modern audiences find unsympathetic. If the opera was to assume any kind of continuity and consistency (the possibility has often been denied), the characters could only be built up facet by facet, since each aria presented a single aspect or *Affekt*; when occasionally the second part or B section introduced another, the aria had still to revert to square A in the da capo. There could be few set-piece conflicts, as in the operas of Mozart and his successors. The plot had to be carefully manipulated to yield aria texts in as many different moods as possible, and to allow each singer the proportion due to his status.

In modern revivals these problems have been widely recognized, frequently shirked, and seldom solved. With a great composer like Handel, who evolved his own method of turning conventional limitations to positive advantage, a solution is certainly possible if the conventions are understood and respected. There is a growing consensus that heroic male parts, not all written for castratos, must be sung at the original pitch, that the formal monotony of the aria becomes less obtrusive if the singer embellishes the da capo in the correct style (of which we now have examples by Handel himself),[1] and that if the score is not barbarously cut the cumulative characterization can carry conviction—so much so that neither the scarcity of ensembles nor the absence of conflict outside the recitative emerges as a disadvantage. Yet many listeners and performers still find the *secco* recitative rebarbative: tedious in itself, absurd when two antagonists quarrel or fight and then desist to make way for an actionless aria, and hopelessly destructive of the continuity and structural unity of the opera.

This problem too has a solution. The reason why it has not been found is that the traditional method of performing recitative is based on misconceptions deriving not from Baroque practice but from that of the second half of the eighteenth century or even later. Nearly all revivals, on the Continent, in Britain, and in the United States, go seriously astray in several important respects. With few exceptions, neither singers nor continuo-players nor conductors (in their capacity as musical directors, for *secco* recitative should never be conducted) interpret their functions correctly.[2]

The first rule for *secco* recitative (accompanied recitative, involving the participation of the orchestra, is a different though related matter) is so obvious that it would be supererogatory to mention it but for the frequency with which it is neglected or only partially observed. All eighteenth-century theorists and practical musicians (generally the same people), followed by the best modern authorities, agree that *secco* recitative in the theatre, despite its regular 4/4 notation, must never be sung in strict time. The tempo should be fluid and flexible, faster or slower according to the sense of the words. Many singers, trained or accustomed to sing notes as written, seem to be mesmerized by the sight of a bar-line after every fourth beat and, half-unconsciously perhaps, distribute their note-values and their emphasis accordingly. This is particularly true of Germany, where some conductors have the deplorable habit of beating time instead of leaving singers and continuo-players to work out their own pace.

Not only should there be no regular pulse; there should be no singing in the sense that arias are sung. Recitative was defined as a form of musical speech and should be delivered *parlando*, not with the full voice. This has the added advantage of making the words more audible. Pier Francesco Tosi, a singing-teacher whose book is of the first importance for our understanding of the Baroque singer's art and practice, and who distinguishes between recitative in church, chamber, and theatre, emphasizes that the last 'ought to be natural', expressive of the words and congruous with the action.[3] Even the notes allotted to the voice were not regarded as sacrosanct. According to C. P. E. Bach,[4] the singer is free to alter them within the harmonic

---

[1] See p. 23 ff.

[2] These two sentences are less true today than when they were written (1977), but the point still needs to be made.

[3] *Opinioni de' cantori antichi e moderni, o sieno osservazioni sopra il canto figurato*, Bologna, 1723, trans. J. E. Galliard as *Observations on the Florid Song, or Sentiments of the Ancient and Modern Singers* (London, 1742), 66 ff.

[4] *Essay on the True Art of Playing Keyboard Instruments*, trans. and ed. W. J. Mitchell (London, 1949), 423.

framework, 'especially in indifferent passages'—though it is doubtless safer to assume that these are rare in Handel. Modern productions of his operas all too often suffer from a regular, deliberate, and even sluggish pacing of the recitative; singers, influenced perhaps by traditional performances of the oratorios (themselves wrong because they treat the music as sacred rather than theatrical), tend to place too much weight on the musical articulation of every word instead of propelling the action forward. To quote Tosi again, 'it is insufferable to be any longer tormented in the Theatre with *Recitatives*, sung in the Stile of a Choir of *Capuchin* Friars'.

The continuo-player is often to blame for exceeding his function. This is not to indulge in free fantasies or extraneous flourishes, perhaps at the behest of a producer intent on finding time for stage business, but simply and solely to support the singer. There is no justification for slow lingering arpeggios at the start of a recitative, for example after another character's aria and exit. The singer, who is supposedly responding to the action, should attack his note as soon as he can, and the continuo-player must adjust himself from the outset and throughout the recitative. C. P. E. Bach puts this very clearly:[5]

When the declamation is rapid, the chords must be ready instantly, especially at pauses in the principal part where the chord precedes a following entrance. At the termination of a chord, its successor must be struck with dispatch. Thus the singer will not be hampered in his affects or their requisite fast execution, for he will always know in good time the course and construction of the harmony. Were it necessary to choose between two evils, it would be preferable to hasten rather than to delay . . . Arpeggiation must always be withheld from rapid declamation . . . Even if the score expresses tied white notes, the sharply detached execution is retained.

That was published in 1762, but Telemann said much the same thirty years earlier.[6] Both agree that, arpeggios apart, all running passages and ornaments should be kept out of recitative accompaniments. Broken chords and arpeggios are permissible on the harpsichord (not on the organ, which was not used in *opera seria*); the quicker and shorter they are, according to Telemann, the better for the singer. Quantz[7] encourages the continuo-player to help the singer where necessary by playing a quick arpeggio with his note at the top, and sometimes to anticipate in his realization the interval to be sung. He emphasizes repeatedly that he must not wait for the singer to conclude his phrases. In fact the business of both player and singer is to get on with the action, employing the flexibility that was the hallmark of Baroque performance. Above all, the player should leave the singer free to act with the voice; he may even have to compel him to do so by scaling down or pressing on with his accompaniment.

The presence of a string bass instrument in addition to the harpsichord need not impair this conception. Our only witness to Handel's practice, the French traveller Pierre-Jacques Fougeroux,[8] who heard three of his operas at the King's Theatre early

---

[5] *The True Art of Playing Keyboard Instruments*, 421–2.
[6] *Singe-, Spiel- und Generalbass-Übungen* (1733/4), ed. M. Seiffert, 4th edn. (Kassel, 1935), 39 ff.
[7] *On Playing the Flute* (1752), trans. and ed. E. R. Reilly (London, 1966), 265.
[8] See p. 41.

in 1728, says that the recitatives were accompanied by two harpsichords (one played by Handel himself), an archlute, and a cello—presumably not all at once. There is no evidence that Handel used a double bass. The chords were played *détaché*, the sound at once cut off, a method that Fougeroux's ear, accustomed to the very different treatment of French recitative, found disagreeable. The cello of course did not sustain the bass notes as written. Since his seat in the eighteenth century was next to the harpsichord, there would be no difficulty in synchronization, however free the rhythm. In modern performances, at least in small theatres, his co-operation is hardly necessary, and if it acts as a brake should be dispensed with.

Most modern editions supply vocal appoggiaturas at cadences, though the ungrammatical omission of this feature is still not unknown. But neither the extent nor the variety nor the function of the appoggiatura is understood in all quarters, despite the comprehensive pronouncements of such authorities as Robert Doning-ton.[9] A distinction must be drawn between an appoggiatura in an aria and in a recitative. In the former it is a melodic ornament, one of many options at the service of good taste, and it can be over-used: its insertion at every possible juncture, especially in the first statement of a theme or the first part of a da capo aria, becomes mannered and debilitates the melodic line. In recitative it is obligatory, especially at cadences, where it takes two common forms, the repeat of the tonic where the voice drops a fourth to the dominant, and the raising of the penultimate note by a tone where the voice drops a third to the tonic. The purpose was expressive, to articulate the sense of the verbal phrases and to modify the almost invariable female rhythmic ending (a trochaic dissyllable) of the Italian verse line, which sounds blunt if both syllables are sung to the same note. Through the ubiquitous influence of Italian opera the convention spread to other languages, such as German and English, where the line often had a masculine (monosyllabic) ending. According to Telemann,[10] the cadential appoggiatura was required here too; that is, the final monosyllable carried a falling interval of two notes. Examples given by J. F. Agricola in his translation of Tosi[11] confirm this. It is possible, however, that in this respect practice varied from place to place and according to context. Niccolo Pasquali[12] gives illustrations in which some monosyllabic cadences carry an appog-giatura and others do not. Repeated monosyllabic appoggiaturas can sound as mannered as appoggiaturas in an aria—which is never true of the dissyllabic type —and may weaken the impact if the phrase ends with a strong word. On the other hand they were not sung with a heavy stress: according to Johann Mattheson,[13] 'the appoggiatura, particularly in the throat, must be so lightly touched and slid [*gezogen und geschleiffet*] that the two sounds of which we are speaking may hang together completely and emerge almost like a single sound'. With Handel the problem only arises in English or German translations, not in the Italian original.

[9] *The Interpretation of Early Music* (London, 1963), 146 ff.; *A Performer's Guide to Baroque Music* (London, 1973), 186 ff.

[10] Preface to *Der harmonische Gottesdienst* (1725), ed. G. Fock ('Telemann: Musikalische Werke', ii), Kassel, 1953, v–vi.

[11] *Anleitung zur Singskunst* (Berlin, 1757), 154 ff.

[12] *Thorough-Bass made Easy* (1757), quoted in Donington, *Interpretation*, 530, *Performer's Guide*, 190.

[13] *Der vollkommene Capellmeister* (Hamburg, 1739; facsimile, ed. M. Reimann, Kassel, 1954), 112.

Appoggiaturas were seldom written; Tosi[14] is contemptuous of composers who put them in, considering this a reflection on singers. They were presumably omitted because they implied a tonic–dominant or other harmonic clash which was against strict rules but allowed—even encouraged—in practice. Like so many Baroque conventions they added spice to the harmony. Heinichen, Mattheson, Telemann, and Agricola among others quote examples of where unwritten appoggiaturas should be sung. One passage cited by Telemann (Ex. 1)[15] demonstrates their frequency and variety. They are by no means confined to falling phrases or to cadences; they can be upward or downward; they can leap from below the accented note and approach it from above, or vice versa; they can occur at any point of punctuation, indicated by a quaver or semiquaver rest, and in the middle of a phrase on the first of two or three repeated notes. The choice of appoggiatura depends on the expression to be given to the words. 'Expression', says Tosi, 'is the Soul of vocal Performance.'[16] Since the musical metre is free, the appoggiaturas hold the recitative together by imposing a new rhythmic pattern dependent on the words. Recitative in the theatre, unlike the aria, is as much a literary as a musical form.

Linked with the appoggiatura is the important but less frequently discussed question of the timing of the cadential chords. The normal practice is to sound both dominant and tonic after the voice has ceased—the delayed cadence. All practical editions of Handel in the last hundred years, from Franz and Chrysander to

Ex.1

Be - glück-te Stun - den,   da Mo-ses uns nicht mehr so scharf wie vor - mals

dräut!   Ja, se - gen - vol - le   Zeit,   da un-ser Heil ist   ein - ge -

- fun - den!   Zu die-sem hal - te dich mit   wah-rer Zu - ver - sicht   und lass dir

sol - ches nicht bis an   dein En - de   rau - ben,   so raubt dir gleich-falls nichts den

Schatz der   Se - lig - keit.

[14] Tosi, *Observations*, 39.
[15] Preface to *Der harmonische Gottesdienst*.
[16] Tosi, *Observations*, 71.

Coopersmith, Tobin, and Shaw, treat this as an accepted convention, although in secular music Handel and his contemporaries, both composers and authors of treatises, almost invariably wrote or printed the dominant bass note under the last accented syllable of the voice.[17] In recent years a few scholars and performers on both sides of the Atlantic have suggested, with different degrees of emphasis, that recitative cadences in late Baroque opera may have been performed as written —the foreshortened or truncated cadence.

It is necessary here to draw two firm distinctions, between music for the theatre and for the church (and perhaps the chamber) and between the practice of the first and the second half of the eighteenth century. The former is stated explicitly by Telemann,[18] who writes that in operas the cadential chords are struck immediately as the voice utters the final syllables, but in cantatas generally after them. He may be referring to church cantatas, or even church music in general; in either event the reference to opera is unequivocal. One reason for the distinction must be that other forms are not subject to the theatrical urge to hurry on the action. Another, in church music, would be the nature of the accompanying instrument: any discord arising from the foreshortened cadence is likely to be far less offensive on the harpsichord than on the organ. J. S. Bach normally wrote the delayed cadence, which according to Sven Hostrup Hansell[19] is almost invariable in contemporary manuscripts of Latin church music, whereas those of oratorios with Italian text are divided between the two types. Hansell also discusses the change of practice around the middle of the century,[20] whose origin he relates to a dispute between Leo and Durante and their followers in Naples about 1740 on whether the fourth was a consonant or dissonant interval, a matter he considers to make sense only in the context of recitative cadences. Whether or not this is historically correct—the explanation is likely to be more pragmatic[21]—statements by C. P. E. Bach, Marpurg, and others in the 1760s leave no doubt that practice had in fact changed. There is no question that the delayed cadence is correct for the age of Mozart.

So far as I know the first modern scholars to discuss the foreshortened cadence in detail were Sir Jack Westrup in 1962[22] and Hansell in the 1968 article cited above. Westrup reconnoitred the ground, quoted some of the relevant authorities, and suggested some practical solutions, not all of them necessary or even advisable. Hansell was more thorough, but his argument is badly organized and confused at the outset by long quotations from Gasparini about the acciaccatura, a different matter altogether, whose introduction may have weakened confidence in Hansell's more relevant observations. Donington in his two books slightly shifted his ground

---

[17] Chrysander adhered to this in a single work, the Italian oratorio *Il trionfo del Tempo e del Disinganno*, published in 1866, though not in the later English version of 1757, issued the previous year, or in the bulk of his edition.

[18] *Singe-, Spiel- und Generalbass-Übungen*, 40.

[19] 'The Cadence in 18th-Century Recitative', *The Musical Quarterly*, 54 (1968), 244.

[20] Ibid. 238 ff.

[21] See below, p. 86.

[22] 'The Cadence in Baroque Recitative', in B. Hjelmborg and S. Sørensen (eds.), *Natalicia Musicologica Knud Jeppesen* (Copenhagen, 1962), 243–52.

without exploring all the evidence. In 1963,[23] quoting only Marpurg,[24] he described the written foreshortened cadence as 'a conventional mis-notation in recitative' and came down decisively in favour of the delayed cadence—though Marpurg admits that 'some composers are in the habit of anticipating the penultimate note of the cadence, namely the dominant, without inserting a rest'. Ten years later,[25] after the publication of Westrup's and Hansell's articles, Donington still accepted the delayed cadence as a standard convention but admitted certain exceptions 'in operatic scenes where it is dramatically convincing for the accompanist thus to stumble across the singer's declamation in the stir and hurry of the action'. Yet the only writers he quotes, Marpurg (1762), Haydn (a letter ascribed to 1768, referring specifically to accompanied recitatives) and Macfarren (preface to the 1873 vocal score of Handel's *Belshazzar*), are very late authorities. We are not told what the generation before 1750 had to say on the subject.

Their evidence is overwhelmingly in favour of the foreshortened cadence as a regular operatic practice, though at least one of them expresses misgivings on grounds of harmonic theory. Telemann's positive statement has already been quoted. Quantz[26] stresses three times in one paragraph that the continuo-player must not wait for the singer to finish his phrase, but should enter under the penultimate or suspended (*vorhaltend*) syllable—that is, the note carrying the appoggiatura—in order to maintain constant liveliness. He applies this to all theatrical recitatives, including those with string accompaniment. In this connection Westrup[27] cites accompanied recitatives by Handel and Alessandro Scarlatti that would make nonsense if the instruments waited for the voice.

Tosi distinguishes between *cadenza tronca*, translated by Galliard as 'broken cadence', and *cadenza finale*, but gives no exact definitions or musical examples. He objects to the monotony of the 'thousand broken Cadences [*cadenze tronche*] in every Opera, which Custom has established', as 'without Taste or Art'. He admits that it would be wrong to introduce a *cadenza finale* every time, but pleads that one in ten might be so treated, adding: 'The Learned, however, do not declare themselves upon it, and from their Silence I must hold myself condemned'.[28] It is possible that *cadenza tronca* is a foreshortened cadence, as Hansell supposed;[29] Tosi, who was born about 1653, could have regarded it as a novelty introduced since his youth. More probably he was thinking of composition rather than performance, and referring to a cadence in which the voice falls from tonic to dominant at the bar-line, as opposed to one in which it closes on the tonic. Both Galliard in 1742 and Agricola in 1757 added musical examples to their translations of his book. While their

[23] *Interpretation*, 374.

[24] *Kritische Briefe über die Tonkunst* (Berlin, 1760–4; facsimile edn., Hildesheim and New York, 1974), ii. 352. The letter, one of a series on recitative, is dated 4 Sept. 1762. I do not know on what grounds Donington attributes it to Scheibe.

[25] *Performer's Guide*, 237–9.

[26] *On Playing the Flute*, 291–3.

[27] 'The Cadence in Baroque Recitative', 246, 250.

[28] *Observations*, p. 75.

[29] 'The Cadence in 18th Century Recitative', 233.

Ex.2

interpretations of *cadenza tronca* are very different, neither distinguishes it from
cadenza finale in the timing of the chords. Galliard, who almost certainly knew Tosi
in London, does indeed show the former as foreshortened, but his example of the
latter is not delayed (Ex. 2).[30] This was the commonest form of cadence for much
of the seventeenth century. For Agricola, writing fifteen years later, *cadenza tronca*
is an interrupted cadence, and both his illustrations of Tosi are delayed (Ex. 3)[31]
though this is not consistently true of all the cadence examples in his book.
Pasquali's specimens of recitative accompaniment, published in the same year (1757)
and cited above,[32] likewise show a mixture of foreshortened and delayed cadences.
What these examples suggest is that the manner of playing the chords changed some
time after 1742, and that by 1757 the tide was on the turn.

Johann David Heinichen[33] is more illuminating. His examples, quoted below,
distinguish clearly between the foreshortened and the delayed cadence. He finds the
former harmonically illogical, but calls it a licence sanctioned by long use in the
theatre, where the situation arises so often, and is prepared to defend it on the
empirical ground that the full resolution enjoined by the rules of thorough-bass,
leading to a delayed cadence, would weary the listener and unnecessarily hold up
the singer and the opera. His comments reveal a fascinating tug-of-war between the
practical man of the theatre and the pedant constrained to maintain and justify the
rule of harmonic law. He is too honest to ignore the problem; after wrestling with
it, he declares that no one has proposed a better explanation than his own.

Johann Joseph Fux[34] goes into the matter with the deliberation one might expect,
but emerges with a comment that reflects the artist rather than the schoolmaster.
His approach is similar to Tosi's, though he does not criticize current practice; he
was himself a prolific opera-composer. He quotes a number of recitative cadences,

Ex.3

[30] Tosi, *Observations*, Plate V No. 1.   [31] *Anleitung zur Singskunst*, 162.
[32] See p. 81.
[33] *Der General-Bass in der Composition* (Dresden, 1728), 673–4; summarized in G. J. Buelow,
'Heinichen's Treatment of Dissonance', *Journal of Music Theory*, 6 (1962), 249–50.
[34] *Gradus ad Parnassum* (Vienna, 1725), 277–8.

corresponding to what he calls points of punctuation (colon, full stop, and so forth), and distinguishes between the end of a sentence, of a speech, and of a recitative. In his final cadence (*clausula formalis*) voice and bass both conclude on the tonic. If however the recitative continues with another speech, the formal cadence is generally truncated (*plerumque tamen truncata*); and Fux's example exactly reproduces Galliard's interpretation of Tosi's *cadenza tronca*, the tonic of the voice coinciding with the dominant of the bass. His examples are all foreshortened; he never mentions the delayed cadence, and there is nothing to suggest that he envisaged such a thing. He does not illustrate how cadences should be accompanied by the continuo, but remarks that in recitative the aim is not so much to satisfy the strict rules of harmony (which it fails to do according to his definition—perhaps the reason why he omits to illustrate it) as to express the emotions, that being the purpose for which it was invented.

When C. P. E. Bach and Marpurg were writing in the 1760s the delayed cadence was well on the way to canonic acceptance. Bach's examples place a rest under the voice's final syllables (in accompanied recitative he allows the harpsichord to enter on the last syllable to ensure a firm entry from the orchestra when the voice has finished), and so do most of Marpurg's. The severity with which both writers censure the recitatives of their predecessors is strong evidence of a radical change. Marpurg admits not only that many players sound the dominant under the tonic but that this was the practice of very great composers. He objects to it as confusing the harmony: 'mistakes always remain mistakes, wherever they occur'.[35] That was surely the reason why Heinichen's 'licence' was withdrawn in an age that regarded its taste as less rude and more polished than that of the great Baroque masters. C. P. E. Bach complained that 'not so long ago' recitatives used to be crammed with harmonic extravagances of all kinds, and congratulated his own generation on using harmonic oddities very rarely, and then only with adequate justification.[36] He was not referring specifically to cadences, but his criticism no doubt covered them. Hansell[37] neatly illustrates the change in taste and practice by quoting a virtually identical cadence to the same words from manuscripts of Hasse's two settings of Metastasio's *Artaserse*: the first (1730) has the dominant bass note under the voice's penultimate syllable, the second (1762) places a rest there and delays both chords until the voice has finished.

We have one clue to Handel's practice. Whereas he almost invariably wrote the dominant bass note where Hasse placed it in 1730, there is one striking exception.[38] In Act II of *Hercules* (1744), at the end of Iole's warning to Dejanira 'But oh! let me conjure you, for your dear peace of mind, beware of jealousy', he specifically enjoined a delayed cadence by writing a crotchet rest under the word 'jealousy' (Ex. 4). That is the key word and central motive of the whole drama, and Handel's purpose was clearly to give it maximum emphasis by means of a double cadence,

---

[35] *Kritische Briefe*, ii. 353.   [36] *The True Art of Playing Keyboard Instruments*, 420–21.

[37] 'The Cadence in 18th-Century Recitative', 247.

[38] This is not unique. There are a few other scattered instances, chiefly in accompanied recitatives, but they are very rare.

Ex.4

first from the voice alone, then from the continuo. Here surely we have the exception that proves the rule; it strongly suggests that when Handel wrote a foreshortened cadence he meant it.

It remains to consider how the continuo-player should accompany the foreshortened cadence with its vocal appoggiatura. Here only Heinichen among contemporary writers offers detailed guidance. Approaching from the angle of the bass, he gives examples of the proper resolution (Ex. 5a), which he says is used occasionally, and of the foreshortened form in which the 6/3 on the mediant, resolving the bass d, is suppressed and the dominant bass note shifted back to the voice's last accented beat. He quotes three alternative realizations (Exx. 5b–d). Ex. 5b he regards as theoretically defensible, since the bass d can be resolved by a c in the realization of the 6/4, but not always practicable in a quick tempo. Exx. 5c and 5d, which derive from it, he accepts as legitimate licence, though they cannot be so defended. In Ex. 5d (★) he may have omitted the appoggiatura by accident, but it is more likely that he could not bring himself to indicate (and so defend theoretically) the clash with the G♯ of the continuo. An appoggiatura of some kind is certainly required; it could

Ex.5

be a descent from f′ to e′, though a repeated a′ is not impossible. Later in his book,[39] discussing a recitative cadence in a Scarlatti cantata (not an opera) where the voice drops a third to the tonic by way of the usual unwritten appoggiatura on the supertonic, Heinichen remarks that the fourth and sharpened third prepare the cadence 'which normally one would sound briefly after the voice has finished'; and George J. Buelow in his realization[40] supplies a delayed cadence with a 4–3 progression. Nothing could illustrate more clearly the pedantry of Heinichen's approach: the delayed cadence here is at once superfluous and repetitive, especially in the theatre. The progression makes perfect sense without it, and without invoking any licence.

Westrup[41] also advocates unnecessary caution. He suggests that the tonic–dominant appoggiatura, if sung in the manner described by Mattheson, 'will fit comfortably into a 5/4 or 6/4 chord before the harmony changes to the dominant, or alternatively, if delayed will serve as anticipation of the tonic chord which follows'. So it will, but there is no need for such displacement, which even Heinichen does not mention in this context. A 4–3 progression on the dominant will solve the problem, or alternatively the clash can be accepted. There is evidence that performers in the theatre at this period did not eschew 'ungrammatical' harmonic clashes. Dissonant appoggiaturas were a feature of Baroque performance. Telemann[42] states positively that if the appoggiatura introduces a progression alien to the harmony or in conflict with the bass, it should nevertheless be taken, and gives an example where the voice sings d″♮ against d♯ in the bass (Ex. 6). Roger North[43] (c.1726, but

Ex.6

thinking perhaps of an earlier period) even said that the dissonant combination of tonic and dominant harmonies was 'much used by the best organists'; on the harpsichord, lightly touched, it could scarcely offend the most fastidious ear. Moreover, as recent experience has shown, discords on Baroque instruments sound considerably less harsh than on the modern equivalents. Westrup's bowdlerization[44] of a dissonant cadence on the word 'madness' in 'Deeper and deeper still' (*Jephtha*), a string-accompanied recitative where Handel wrote g″ in the first violin part against a′♭ on the voice and undoubtedly meant it, takes all the bite out of a moment of intense poignancy.

[39] *General-Bass*, 824 n. 14.

[40] *Thorough-Bass Accompaniment according to Johann David Heinichen* (Berkeley and Los Angeles, 1966), 290.

[41] 'The Cadence in Baroque Recitative', 250.   [42] Preface to *Der harmonische Gottesdienst*.

[43] J. Wilson, *Roger North on Music* (London, 1959), quoted by Hansell, 'The Cadence in 18th-Century Recitative', p. 248 n. 57.

[44] 'The Cadence in Baroque Recitative', 251.

The 4–3 progression on the dominant was sometimes indicated in accompanied recitatives when the appoggiatura was written out. Hansell[45] notes that a 43 sign made with a single stroke of the pen is often found at cadences in Scarlatti's autographs, and suggests that it implies a single chord. More probably it is Scarlatti's shorthand for a regularly used cadential progression. This could apply equally to Francesco Gasparini's remark about cadences: 'Every time a note calls for both seventh and major third, the fourth, as an acciaccatura, is added between the major third and the fifth.'[46] It need not be struck simultaneously.

Whatever solution is adopted—and a good continuo-player will vary his procedure with the context—it is certain that the foreshortened cadence, the dominant bass note coinciding with the last stressed syllable of the voice, must be the rule in the dramatic recitative of Handel and his contemporaries.[47] Exceptions should be rare, and confined to emphasizing words that require great weight, as in the example from *Hercules*. If it be asked why such an important matter has remained unrecognized for so long, the answer must be that contemporary writers, not gifted with second sight into the taste of the next generation, saw little reason to mention what everyone accepted. If there was a convention that cadences were not performed as written, they would undoubtedly have explained it as they explained the convention about supplying unwritten appoggiaturas. As it is, we have only the rare unqualified statements of Telemann and Quantz, probable deductions to be drawn from the examples of Fux and Tosi's translators, and the testimony of those like Heinichen, who were uneasy about the theoretical basis for current practice, and of their successors like C. P. E. Bach and Marpurg, who repudiated it.

The practical lessons to be drawn are of the highest importance. Whatever may be thought of the general run of *opera seria*, Handel's greatest operas are fully articulated dramas, not concerts in costume. The recitative is an essential and functional element in the plot and its motivation. The habit of regarding it as a tedious necessity during which the audience's attention may legitimately wander before the next aria begins—even if Handel's London audience may sometimes have regarded it in that light—springs from limp and incorrect performance. If it is sung *parlando*, with the utmost flexibility of delivery, and without intrusive pauses or the repeated full stops interposed by delayed cadences, the pace of the opera, instead of becoming clogged, is accelerated and its coherence enhanced. The dramatic tension is carried forward into the next movement, whether it be an aria, a duet, or another recitative; and a cynical modern audience is not given time to laugh at the convention.

[45] 'The Cadence in 18th-Century Recitative', 246.

[46] *L'armonico pratico al cimbalo* (Venice, 1708), trans. F. S. Stillings as *The Practical Harmonist at the Harpsichord* (New Haven, 1963), 82. On the next page Gasparini quotes a foreshortened recitative cadence with 4–3 figuring.

[47] D. E. Monson, 'The Last Word: The Cadence in *recitativo semplice* of Italian opera seria', *Studi Pergolesiani* i (Florence, 1986) quotes evidence that some (mostly younger) Italian opera composers wrote delayed cadences occasionally from 1725 and rather more frequently in the 1730s. He also cites an intermediate form whereby the dominant chord coincides with the *final* note of the voice, presumably to avoid the tonic–dominant clash. This does not affect the position with Handel, who may have been conservative in indicating almost exclusive shortened cadences, as he was in other respects.

There is also a very considerable saving of time, both actual and relative. A recent production of *Giulio Cesare* at the Barber Institute of Birmingham University according to the principles advocated here[48] knocked something like half an hour off the timing of the Deutsche Grammophon recording (admittedly a heavy and stylistically anachronistic performance), largely through the activation of the recitative. The relative timing is even more important, for the whole balance of the opera is altered so that its components assume a new and more dynamic pattern. The Birmingham production, the first revival on any stage of the complete 1724 score, emphasized the remarkable tautness of Handel's dramatic craftsmanship: by common consent it seemed shorter than a cut performance, because each episode threw the listener's mind forward into the next. And of course the more time is saved in the recitative, the less pressing the demand for damaging cuts elsewhere. An authentic treatment of the recitative can make all the difference between an historical curiosity and a vivid drama capable of gripping a non-specialist modern audience.

[48] Robert Donington, after reading this article in typescript and hearing a tape-recording of the Birmingham performance, asked me to state that he is in complete agreement.

9
Gluck and the Reform of Opera

Gluck's status in operatic history has often been compared with that of Wagner; and indeed there are obvious parallels. Both reacted against the Italian policy of giving pre-eminence to the solo voice as a virtuoso instrument, and against the closed forms that established themselves as a result. Both worked for greater continuity of design, a less abrupt divorce of the action of an opera from its emotional expression. Gluck in his maturity expanded the recitative in the direction of the aria, dropping the *secco* form altogether; Wagner assimilated both types of vocal utterance into a continuous arioso, with the main musical thought concentrated in the orchestra. Both chose mythological subjects as vehicles for general truths. Moreover each drew much of his inspiration from France. Gluck's blend of Italian training with the declamatory vocal style, prominent chorus, and still more prominent ballet of the French theatre has always been recognized. A smoke-screen of his own words and the selectiveness of historical memory have concealed the fact that Wagner found the whole conception of the *Gesamtkunstwerk* (and a good deal else, including the leitmotif) in the opera of the French Revolution and Empire, which itself owed much to Gluck and the theorists of his time.

Nevertheless Gluck had neither the temperament nor the technical equipment of a Wagner. We are apt to think of artistic reformers as men with a mission, fighting their way through obstacles against the pressure of public opinion and finally attaining a goal they have pursued, in a more or less straight line, since some youthful revelation. This is a comparatively modern view; it applies to Wagner, whose precept and example have helped to nourish it, and to Schoenberg; it will not do for Monteverdi, and still less for Gluck. There never was a 'reformer' so little in advance of his age and so perfectly adapted to swimming with the current rather than against it. But if Gluck, seen in the context of history, seems to exemplify the virtues of the Duke of Plaza Toro in leading his regiment from behind, that does not diminish his achievement or his stature as an artist. Nor is he exceptional in this. As a rule the reformer who marches in front either lacks the genius to bring his ideas to full flower, in which case someone else gets the credit for them (the boldest innovators among the early Romantics were not Weber, Schubert, Schumann, Mendelssohn, or even Berlioz, but the half-forgotten composers of the previous generation, Cherubini, Méhul, Le Sueur, and Spontini); or he leads his followers into a ditch, as Wagner led his operatic successors, because they cannot see where he is going and fall into the traps he instinctively avoids.

The ideas expressed in Gluck's famous preface to *Alceste* were not new. If they had been, it is most unlikely that his reform operas would have been staged at all, much less applauded. By 1762, the year of the first production of *Orfeo* in Vienna, there was already a strong party hostile to the court poet Metastasio and the older type of *opera seria* of which he was the embodiment. The movement was largely literary in origin, deriving its ideas from Rousseau, Winckelmann, and other writers, who urged the pursuit of natural expression and antique grandeur in all the arts as opposed to the ornamental exuberance of the Baroque. Algarotti's book on opera, published in 1755, anticipated the ideas not only of Gluck but of Wagner. The leaders in Vienna were Count Durazzo, the Court Chamberlain, and the poet Calzabigi. All they needed was a composer.

Gluck was then nearly 50. For twenty years he had been purveying old-style *opera seria* in half a dozen countries, and had shown a special liking for the librettos of Metastasio himself, setting ten of them in succession between 1748 and 1756. But for Calzabigi, his collaborator in *Orfeo*, *Alceste*, and *Paride ed Elena*, he might have followed the same course to the end of his days. He himself admitted his debt to Calzabigi, adding: 'How much soever of talent a composer may have, he will never produce any but mediocre music, if the poet does not awaken in him that enthusiasm without which the productions of all the arts are but feeble and drooping'. This is scarcely revolutionary language, and we cannot imagine it on the lips of Wagner. Gluck needed a push to fire his enthusiasm. Even then it did not burn with a consistent flame. He was no implacable enemy of Italian vocalism; he wrote the part of Orfeo for a castrato, the same Guadagni who had been trained by Handel in London. (In the Paris revival of 1774 the music was recast for tenor; since Berlioz's arrangement for Pauline Viardot in 1859 it has generally been sung by a woman contralto.) Nor did Gluck abandon *opera seria*; he set three more of Metastasio's librettos in 1763–5. Moreover a good deal that we consider characteristic of his musical idiom had been anticipated in the operas of the Neapolitans Traetta and Jommelli.

Yet *Orfeo* is a genuine landmark. Calzabigi's choice of the Orpheus legend, a fertile symbol of the artist's predicament, was a deliberate return to the starting point of the early Florentines. Gone are the sub-plots, the amorous convolutions, and the dynastic rivalries of *opera seria*; everything is subordinated to the central theme in its naked simplicity. The 1762 version already shows considerable French influence, in the suppression of *secco* recitative and the organic use of choral and dance movements. Gluck, besides visiting Paris on his way to London, had composed or arranged ten French *opéras comiques* for the Viennese court; Calzabigi had spent some ten years in the French capital, which as so often was the principal source of the new aesthetic ideals. His natural, unadorned treatment of the story brought out Gluck's full potential, and enabled him to express those ideals in their most perfect operatic form.

The remarkable thing about Gluck's mature operas is not so much their place in history as the fact that most of them have held the stage ever since and can still offer a profoundly moving experience. No mere opportunist could have achieved this, as we can see from the fate of Meyerbeer. Nor is it the product of outstanding skill:

no artist ever wrought so enduringly on such a slight basis of technique. Gluck had a strong sense of the practical, both in what would come off in the theatre and —perhaps rarer and equally valuable—in what his own limitations would permit. Any challenge likely to expose them he took care to evade. We do not need to bring in Handel's cook to notice his weakness in counterpoint; but it scarcely matters, since the context seldom if ever makes demands in that direction. He stretched his gifts to the utmost, and he wasted nothing; many famous pieces, such as Orfeo's 'Che puro ciel', were salvaged from discarded early works.

Those may seem negative virtues. Gluck tells us in the preface to *Alceste* that he aimed at 'a beautiful simplicity'. Many others have done the same, and succeeded only in being flat and tedious. Gluck carried it off triumphantly, thanks to an exquisite feeling for melody and a sense of balance, both in form and texture, that enabled him to fuse drama with music and evoke a sublime vision of the world of Greek mythology. The true classical spirit may sometimes be remote, but it is never cold; the Elysian Fields are as vividly recreated as the streets of Wagner's Nuremberg. Gluck can wring our hearts by setting Orfeo's lament for the lost Euridice as a formal aria in C major with the simplest harmonic basis. We find something of the same timeless beauty in *Les Troyens* of Berlioz, the greatest work that derives from Gluck's heritage. It is the genius, not the reformer or the technical innovator, to whom posterity listens; the two are found in one body less frequently than it is now fashionable to suppose.

Iphigénie en Tauride

The first performance of *Iphigénie en Tauride* at the Paris Opéra on 18 May 1779 was the climax of Gluck's career. That this should occur in Paris was no accident. With the decline of the old *opera seria*, the French theatre of Rameau with its ballets and choruses, its classical themes and measured declamation, provided the only possible avenue for a dramatic composer in search of a valid tradition. Gluck was no stranger to French taste; it was prominent at the Viennese court, for which he had supplied ten *opéras comiques* between 1755 and 1765. The Italian *Orfeo* of 1762 already used ballet and chorus in the French manner and abandoned *secco* recitative, though it retained the castrato hero. Gluck's decision, after the production in 1779 of his last Italian opera *Paride ed Elena*, to write for Paris itself could never have brought such impressive results had it not answered the promptings of his own genius.

Of his first four French operas, two were expansions of the Italian *Orfeo* and *Alceste*; the other two, *Iphigénie en Aulide* (1774) and *Armide* (1777), though they mark a considerable dramatic advance and are full of magnificent music, do not quite reconcile the sensuous charms of *opera seria* with the stiff gestures of the heroic French style. This was the achievement of *Iphigénie en Tauride*, Gluck's masterpiece, and recognized as such by contemporaries. His last opera, *Écho et Narcisse*, produced in September the same year, was a failure. Thereupon the veteran composer (he was 65 and in poor health) returned to Vienna to rest on his laurels. He took a considerable interest in the young Mozart (a special performance of *Die Entführung* was arranged for him), and when *Iphigénie en Tauride* was given in German in 1781 Mozart attended nearly all the rehearsals. The fruit of this experience can be clearly detected in the scores of *Don Giovanni* and *Die Zauberflöte*.

The subject of Gluck's opera, based on the tragedy by Euripides, was familiar to eighteenth-century audiences. Gluck himself had conducted Traetta's *Ifigenia in Tauride* at Florence in 1767. (Piccinni's setting, chiefly remembered for the first-night inebriation of the prima donna and the comment of a spectator 'Ce n'est pas Iphigénie en Tauride, c'est Iphigénie en Champagne', though planned as a rival to Gluck's, was not produced till 1781. Goethe's tragedy in its original prose version was first heard six weeks before Gluck's opera.) Gluck collaborated closely with his librettist, Nicolas François Guillard, his letters to whom attest his care for dramatic detail. The result was an admirable text, much closer to Euripides than Traetta's. Like the libretto of Handel's *Hercules*, which Gluck probably knew (there are parallels in the music as well as in the plot, whose central character is driven mad by the Furies after killing a near relative) it is a wholly successful translation of a Greek tragedy into eighteenth-century terms.

The action takes place on the inhospitable coast of the Crimea, where Iphigenia and her Greek companions are employed as priestesses in the temple of Diana. The goddess has rescued her from the knife of her father Agamemnon, when he was about to sacrifice her at Aulis on his way to the Trojan War. Exiled from her country and family, she is further afflicted by the local Scythian chieftain Thoas, who compels her to sacrifice all strangers on the altar. Meanwhile her brother Orestes has avenged the murder of Agamemnon on his return from Troy by killing his mother Clytemnestra. Tormented by the Furies, he and his friend Pylades are wrecked on the coast of Tauris and brought before Thoas, who hands them over as victims to Iphigenia. Neither brother nor sister recognizes the other (they have not met for fifteen years, and he believes she died at Aulis); but, learning that he is a Greek, she asks after her family and learns the dreadful truth. Orestes pretends that he himself is dead and only Electra survives. Iphigenia, after pouring a libation to her brother's memory, decides to save one of the prisoners by sending him with a letter to Electra; but the other must die. Orestes, who has no desire to live, persuades Pylades to go and is himself led to the altar. When Iphigenia at last steels herself to raise the knife, he thanks her for her sympathy and cries 'Ainsi tu péris en Aulide, Iphigénie, O ma sœur!' No sooner are they in each other's arms than Thoas and his troops rush in, demanding blood; but Pylades returns with the Greek crew and kills Thoas. The opera ends with the appearance of the goddess, who lifts the curse on Orestes and orders the Greeks to return with her statue to Mycenae.

The divergences from Euripides are worth noting, since they throw light on Gluck's art. In the play Orestes and Pylades have been sent by the Delphic Oracle to steal the goddess's statue, which with the aid of Iphigenia they proceed to do; Thoas, who is quite a sympathetic character, is disillusioned by the Greeks' deceit, and only the intervention of the goddess prevents him arresting them. There is no counterpart to the storm in Act I or the fight in Act IV, and the recognition scene is differently contrived: Pylades persuades Iphigenia to read the letter aloud, thus revealing her identity to Orestes. The temper of the play is sceptical, if not positively cynical. The opera has none of this; where the rationalist Euripides is concerned to score off the Greeks, the gods, and the Delphic Oracle, Gluck's humanism exalts the spirit of man in his suffering. He seizes on Iphigenia's anguish, as evidenced by her dream at the beginning, and the madness of Orestes, and makes their relationship the focus of the opera. Neither work has any orthodox love interest; this may explain the opera's exclusion from the popular repertory. The weakest point in the libretto, the appearance of Diana as a *dea ex machina*, which has been criticized as a Gallicism, goes back to Euripides. But it seems less of an anticlimax than the final scene of *Orfeo*, for the action has already been resolved by human means. Diana's sole function is to remove the curse.

Despite the happy end, this is the most tragic in tone of Gluck's operas. Indeed from one angle it is almost a study in morbid psychology, for three of the four principal characters are convulsed by violent emotion almost throughout: Iphigenia is haunted by dreams and fears (most of them soon justified) about her family's fate, Thoas by the superstitious horrors of a primitive religion, Orestes by the Furies planted in his conscience by the murder of his mother. No dramatic composer, with the possible exception of Handel in *Hercules*, had hitherto penetrated so far into the subconscious mind. The most striking example of this, the famous air 'Le calme rentre dans mon cœur', in which the pulsating semiquavers in the orchestra, with a sforzando on the first beat of every bar, give the lie to the words sung by Orestes, adds almost a new dimension to operatic expression. And the following scene for chorus and ballet, in which the Furies return to the attack with all the more deadly effect, can be understood as a visual projection of his disordered thoughts.

This atmosphere of turbulence and guilt throws into sharp relief the friendship between Orestes and Pylades and the noble figure of Iphigenia, who alone rises above her sufferings. She is one of the most sympathetic of operatic heroines—far more so than the embittered princess of Euripides. The characteristic flavour of her music, a profound sorrow transfigured by serene acceptance, is largely due to Gluck's use of tonality. Only one of her airs—and that perhaps the least distinguished—is in a minor key.[1] At her moment of greatest trial, when she learns from Orestes that all her family except Electra have perished, Gluck repeats one of the great strokes of *Orfeo*. In the hero's lament 'Che farò senza Euridice' he had used the key of C major with scarcely any accidentals to express a grief too deep for tears. The wonderful 'O malheureuse Iphigénie', where the voice and a single oboe, joined later by female chorus, discourse in G major over a throbbing syncopated accompaniment for 112 slow bars without any repetition until the choral cadence, is one of the supreme moments in opera.[2] Only one criticism can be brought against it: the twelve-bar melody of breath-taking beauty with which the voice begins is never heard again. The next scene, in which Iphigenia and the priestesses pour libations to the shade of Orestes, is scarcely less moving. Here Gluck's tonal oscillation—C major and minor, E flat major and minor—produces an intensely emotional effect of a kind we associate rather with Schubert.

All Gluck's most powerful strokes are basically simple, but so well calculated that they never lose their freshness or their theatrical impact. The opening of the opera is a good example. There is no overture; instead we have a prelude depicting the weather, first a sunny calm and then a storm. Storms were a feature of French opera (though they seldom occur so early in the proceedings), and Gluck's, vivid as it is with the piccolo shooting forth lightnings, is not intrinsically remarkable. But the dramatic placing is superb. The curtain rises in the middle, and Iphigenia and the priestesses raise their voices in prayer against the uproar of the elements. It soon transpires that the storm is psychological as well as literal: it reflects the turmoil in Iphigenia's mind. Already torn in conscience by the Scythians' demands for human sacrifice, she has just awoken from a terrible dream, in which she saw Agamemnon's palace struck by lightning, her father flying wounded from Clytemnestra, and Orestes stabbed by her own hand. She implores Diana to end her life. Her A major

---

[1] 'D'une image, hélas! trop chérie' in Act III.

[2] Gluck adapted it from a castrato aria in his setting of Metastasio's *La clemenza di Tito* (1752); but this no more affects its aptness to the later context than do many of Handel's borrowings, from himself or others.

aria, placed between two short choruses simple in rhythm and outline but extraordinarily imaginative in their ambiguous muffled tonality, is sublime by any standards. But like everything else it gains enormously from the context. The storm has precipitated us into the middle of the action; we know the whole background of the story and are ready for the clash with Thoas in the second half of the Act. Gluck paints the blood-lust of the Scythians in a series of choruses and dances, marked by obsessive rhythms, sudden menacing unisons, and harsh scoring. The piccolos, side-drum, and cymbals of eighteenth-century 'Turkish' convention are no mere exotic adornment but a positive element in the drama.

The tension is seldom relaxed for long. Act II is mainly concerned with the mental agony of Orestes, who besides killing his mother believes that he has brought his only friend, Pylades, to his death. Pylades reassures him in a beautiful air, with a flavour of *Die Zauberflöte* (this is even more marked in the choruses of Act IV, especially the priestesses' hymn 'Chaste fille de Latone'). After 'Le calme rentre dans mon cœur' Orestes sinks to the ground, and the Furies close on their prey; their sudden change of pace at the words 'Il a tué sa mère!' has a most sinister impact. This chorus ends (on a discord) with a master-stroke of double dramatic irony. Iphigenia enters: Orestes, almost out of his mind, mistakes her for the ghost of Clytemnestra; Iphigenia, ignorant of his identity, sees only a prisoner shrinking from the sacrificial knife. The later scenes between brother and sister are handled with comparable skill, especially the final recognition at the altar. Where another composer might have expanded in a euphonious duet, Gluck hurries on. Iphigenia just has time to express her relief in a short arioso before the news arrives of Thoas's approach. The scene of violence that follows as the crazed monarch demands his pound of flesh has two links with Act I. The orchestral rhythm of his air echoes that of the Scythian choruses, and the rushing scales of the battle music balance those of the storm.

It is easy to see why Wagner and other Romantic composers were fascinated by Gluck's organic structures, his irony and symbolism (the stormy opening of *Die Walküre* owes something to this source), and his treatment of Greek myth. The continuous texture of interwoven recitative, air, and chorus links Rameau on one side with the Weber of *Euryanthe* and Wagner on the other. But Gluck's opera is much more than a historical landmark. It is a memorable fusion of music and drama, in which every detail is subordinate to the whole. Even the ballet, that most unruly element in the French theatre, has been brought to heel: the pantomime scenes for the Scythians and the Furies are strictly functional. There had always been two sides to Gluck, reflected in the subject and style of his librettos—the sensuous poet who scarcely needed a plot, and the dramatist who forgot that he was a musician (though less often than is sometimes made out). We hear a great deal about the latter, thanks to Gluck's own prefaces and the history books; but the former, the composer of *Paride ed Elena*, *Écho et Narcisse*, and a great part of *Armide*, was equally prominent. In *Iphigénie en Tauride* the two coalesce: here more than anywhere else he held a consistent balance between drama and diversion, voice and orchestra (the scoring is particularly rich), French and Italian traditions—in a word, between sense and sensibility.

Haydn's *Orfeo*

Haydn's last opera was composed for London in 1791 as part of his contract with Salomon, who paid him in advance—fortunately for Haydn, who never heard it. Designed to open the new Haymarket Theatre, rebuilt after a fire, under the management of the ex-ballet-dancer Sir John Gallini (the date was fixed for 31 May 1791), it fell victim to a dynastic quarrel. As frequently happened in the Hanoverian period, the king (George III) and the Prince of Wales were at loggerheads, and politics involved art; they supported rival opera and concert seasons. The king refused a licence to Gallini, whose patron was the Prince of Wales, after rehearsals had begun. Neither Gallini nor Haydn nor anyone else seems to have sought an alternative route to the stage, and the opera slept for a century and a half. It received an unusual première in a gramophone studio in 1950, and was first staged at Florence the following year under Erich Kleiber. There were two British productions in 1967, at Birmingham University and the Edinburgh Festival. Although Breitkopf published fragments of the score during Haydn's life (1806–7), this is its first complete edition.[1] The 1791 cancellation stopped the printing of the libretto, and there is some confusion about the opera's title and the number of acts. Haydn called it *L'anima del filosofo* in the autograph, *Orfeo ed Euridice* in his catalogue, and spoke of it as in five acts, though the last two are very short.

As a work of art it makes an odd impression. *Opera seria* was then in the doldrums. The Handelian type had died before Handel himself, and its successor, the classical *opera seria* of Metastasio and Hasse, had succumbed to the reforms of Gluck, who combined the Italian and French traditions in a compromise that only a composer of Mozart's dramatic genius could keep in repair. The Italians continued to write serious operas in profusion, but the increasing length of the arias, the expansion of accompanied recitative, and the greater use of the chorus evoked no compensating technique on the dramatic side to restore the equilibrium. Even the most successful works in this genre, such as Cimarosa's *Gli Orazi e Curiazi* (1796), are limp and episodic. *Opera seria* had to wait for the energy of Rossini and the romantic warmth of Bellini and Donizetti to renew its life.

Haydn was no operatic reformer. His experience had been confined to the Eszterháza court theatre, where most of his works were comic or mixed in style. *L'anima del filosofo* is wholly serious with a tragic end. Haydn of course, like Mozart,

---

[1] H. Wirth (ed.), *Joseph Haydn Werke Reihe XXV Band 13. L'Anima del Filosofo ossia Orfeo ed Euridice* (Munich, 1974).

commanded the technique to turn to serious ends an idiom that had more than half its roots in *opera buffa*. But he was writing for a strange land (not perhaps a major obstacle, for Italian opera was international, and he had an Italian libretto and Italian singers) and for a public opera house, not a court circle. Here his limited dramatic experience was likely to show. To make matters worse, he had a libretto of exceptional ineptitude, which Mozart would not have tolerated for a moment. We do not know if Haydn had any choice in the matter, but it seems unlikely that he could have remedied the deficiencies.

The librettist, Carlo Francesco Badini, as his title and handling of the story indicate, had been imbibing some of the more half-baked ideas of the Enlighten-ment. In choosing the Orpheus legend he was challenging history, and in particular the already classical treatment of Calzabigi and Gluck. Badini may have deliberately chosen an approach as different from theirs as possible. If so, he abandoned a theatrically viable design for an amateurish muddle, as a summary of the plot makes all too clear.

In Act I Eurydice runs distraught into the mountains to escape a forced marriage with Arideus, arranged by her father Creon. The chorus warn her against the local inhabitants, whom they describe as monsters in human shape, and advise her to go home; they are powerless to defend her. She welcomes death and in a long aria compares herself to an abandoned nightingale. The chorus summon Orpheus, who plays his lyre (the sole appearance of the harp in the score) and in an equally substantial aria describes nature's sympathy with his sufferings. This apparently melts the monsters; the chorus acclaim the power of music as the nectar of afflicted humanity. In the palace Creon, learning that Orpheus has saved his daughter from heathen sacrifice but feeling bound by his promise to Arideus, likens himself to a bird caught in a trap. The act ends with a long duet for the lovers.

By Act II they are married, but their joy is interrupted by a 'strepito ostile', and Orpheus goes off to discover the cause. In his absence a member of the chorus (*corista*) claims Eurydice for Arideus, at which point she is bitten by a snake and dies. Orpheus returns and laments his loss. In the palace another *corista* tells Creon what we have just witnessed, and he sings a vengeance aria. Act III begins with a choral tableau at Eurydice's tomb, to which Orpheus and Creon add only a few snatches of *secco* recitative. Orpheus, again in recitative, asks the Sibyl where Eurydice is. A Spirit (*Genio*) assures him that he will see her again if he seeks the nepenthe of philosophy, learns to moderate his desires, and keeps his heart armed with constancy and valour. Orpheus is prepared to face the dangers of the underworld, and the act ends with a chorus about justice.

Act IV in the underworld has choruses of Shades and Furies, but the Spirit tells Orpheus he has nothing to worry about: Charon will be happy to give him a lift over the Styx. Pluto proves equally accommodating and releases Eurydice without demur. As Orpheus travels through the Elysian Fields the chorus assure him briefly (in gavotte rhythm) that his pains are over, but he will lose Eurydice if he looks at her. In a few *secco* bars the Spirit confirms this, Eurydice quotes Gluck's 'Che farò', Orpheus immediately turns round, and the Spirit (with the equivalent of

'Now you've torn it') abruptly departs. Orpheus complains at length about the cruelty of his loss. In Act V he meets the Bacchae, who in a friendly and most un-Euripidean manner invite him to a life of pleasure and, when he refuses, offer him a drink. It is poisoned, and he dies. The Bacchae begin to feel 'insolito furore', though the jolly music shows no sign of it. However a storm rises and drowns them.

In this libretto every dramatic opportunity is squandered. Neither Arideus nor the Act I monsters ever appear (or if they do, they say nothing); the *corista's* attempt to abduct Eurydice is pointless since the serpent gets in first. There is no music for Orpheus's consultation of the Sibyl, who has not hitherto been mentioned, and the Spirit makes sure that Orpheus's journey through the underworld is as safe as a trip on the underground. He is neither tempted by the Shades nor confronted by the Furies: indeed he never confronts anybody except the monsters in Act I, who offer no opposition. The warning against looking round is casually given, and so far from struggling in his conscience he takes not the slightest notice—hardly a strong argument for philosophy. In the Greek myth Orpheus is torn to pieces by the crazed Bacchae. This could have made a superb end; but Badini's seem eminently sane —Haydn gives them music more apt for shepherdesses—and it is they who are destroyed by the storm after Orpheus's death.

In confining action to the recitative and writing vague or abstract texts for the set pieces Badini was harking back to the more incompetent librettists of Handel's day. That often misunderstood convention can be highly dramatic under competent control, but in an age when the operatic language had been totally transformed by Gluck and Mozart it made very little sense. One of the most conspicuous features of *L'anima del filosofo* is the prominence of the chorus, both as a body and as individuals in the recitative. It is not always clear whom they represent (a printed libretto might have clarified things), and their role shifts between participation and detached comment. That is not necessarily a disadvantage. It is possible that there was some influence from Handel's oratorios as well as from Greek drama; although Haydn composed the opera very early in his first London visit, either he or Badini could have been acquainted with Handel's example. But they do not seem to have thought the matter out. They make few attempts to involve the soloists with the chorus where the situation cries out for such treatment. Orpheus and Eurydice sing with the *Amorini* in the marriage sequence, but an obvious opportunity goes begging when Orpheus, and Creon too, are not musically involved in the lament at the tomb. Orpheus employs his lyre against the mute monsters in Act I, but fails to lay a finger to it in the underworld—because the Spirit has undercut the drama by making his path too smooth. Haydn's Furies are musically far more sophisticated than Gluck's nearly thirty years earlier, but they might as well be singing Christmas carols for all the effect they have on the action.

Haydn possessed dramatic vision of a kind. The sudden darkening of the harmony when Orpheus drinks the poison at the end of the Bacchae's second chorus and Orpheus's recall of the Furies' chorus towards the end of his last aria are marvellously effective. So is the sudden plunge from G major to A flat major at the words 'Ma l'adombra un sacro velo' in the Spirit's aria; and there are other examples. What he lacked was the theatrical instinct, a different thing altogether and perhaps the single major flaw in his artistic equipment. It is partly a matter of characterization, but still more of timing. He could have made more of Badini's libretto even as it stands, for example in the very perfunctory scenes where Eurydice is bitten by the serpent and Orpheus loses her for the second time. But again and again he compounds Badini's errors by expanding the most static moments, the reactions of characters after the event, which generally consist of an examination of their own feelings. The score is full of accompanied recitatives, some of them musically very fine, but the emotion they express is nearly always passive, not dynamic. One of the most arresting musical strokes, the startling interruption of the marriage celebrations in Act II, is provoked not by the entry of Arideus's followers or the serpent's bite, which go for nothing, but by a noise offstage, and it is at once devalued when Orpheus goes off to investigate. This is the opera of a great symphonist pouring new wine into dilapidated bottles. Jumping the example of Gluck and Mozart, Haydn follows that of Cimarosa and the Neapolitans. The fact that they possessed a mere fraction of his musical genius makes the total failure of *L'anima del filosofo* in the theatre all the more exasperating.

The greater part of the score shows Haydn at the height of his powers, as we should expect at this date. Gluck's influence is apparent in Creon's first aria and the choruses of the tomb scene, but it is the serene Gluck, not the master of dramatic tension. The overture is a splendid symphonic Allegro with introduction in the minor. Many of the choruses are impressive, and those of Shades and Furies in Act IV superb in their concentrated intensity. The former has a remarkable end, the voices dropping out one by one till the basses are left alone holding a bottom F pianissimo. The latter, the only movement with trombones apart from the finale (in the same key, D minor), develops immense power by a compound of ostinato, off-beat accents, chromaticism, and hollow octaves. Like so many of Haydn's greatest instrumental movements they strike one as intensely dramatic in a metaphorical, not a theatrical sense. The opera's most original stroke, which could indeed have been theatrically overwhelming had the antecedent drama been fully realized, is the stormy finale, more a symphonic movement with voices than a true chorus, which has a temper of Romantic violence prophetic of the mature Beethoven.

The solo music is brilliantly written and often very beautiful, especially the Adagios of Eurydice's and Orpheus's arias in Act I, but impersonal. Except for Eurydice's dying cavatina, a haunting piece with two English horns in a curiously high register,[2] the arias could all be concert pieces. Several of them demand spectacular coloratura and breath-control. Eurydice in her only full-scale example is required to execute enormously long divisions on the word 'crudeltà', but the music, in F major, suggests exuberance, even exhilaration, rather than suffering. She fades out completely after the middle of Act II, uttering a mere half dozen bars of recitative when restored to life. Her place as soprano is taken by the Spirit, whose single aria, composed for an unknown castrato, exploits a compass of $2\frac{1}{2}$ octaves

[2] The editor suggests that some kind of oboe d'amore may have been intended.

(b–e''') with the utmost virtuosity. Appropriately the bulk of the solo music is for Orpheus, who has three big arias and many accompanied recitatives. The part calls for a first-rate tenor. Perhaps the best of his arias is the second, an impassioned F minor Allegro con spirito in which he rails against his fate on losing Eurydice for the first time. This is one of only two pieces with clarinets, but Haydn does not write for them with Mozart's idiomatic feeling for their timbre. Creon (baritone) also has three arias, less taxing and more conventional in cut; the first contains the best music, including a beautiful and unexpected turn to the minor towards the end.

The editor seems to have done his work impeccably. Haydn's autograph in Berlin is incomplete and bound in the wrong order, and the same applies to the best early copy, now in Budapest, which was prepared in London under Haydn's supervision in 1791–2 and taken back with him to Vienna. Fortunately those two sources largely complement each other, and the only missing movement, a recitative, is available in a Paris copy of *c.* 1820–30. The editor has had to fill some minor lacunae left when rehearsals were broken off, and at one point to determine the order of movements; but there are no major textual problems. Scene headings and stage directions are more a matter of guesswork owing to the lack of a printed libretto. Here the decision to add only the essential minimum was doubtless correct. The separately published Critical Report includes a full discussion of sources and all relevant information.

Cimarosa and *Il matrimonio segreto*

Il matrimonio segreto has always been regarded—and rightly—as a masterpiece of *opera buffa*. Though by no means a musical landmark, it stands by a piquant series of coincidences upon one of the crossroads of history. After a successful career in Italy and two or three years in the service of Catherine the Great at St Petersburg, Cimarosa became court Kapellmeister in Vienna during the short reign of the Emperor Leopold II (1790–2). *Il matrimonio segreto* was the only opera he produced during that period, but it had a sensational success. Its première so pleased the emperor that he entertained the cast and orchestra to supper and then ordered them to repeat the entire opera, thus rounding off the age of formal classicism with the greatest da capo of all time. Well might he need to relax; for earlier that day (7 February 1792), impelled by the downfall of his sister Marie Antoinette, he had signed with the King of Prussia the treaty of alliance against revolutionary France which was to plunge Europe into a generation of war and destroy for ever the world of court patronage and aristocratic elegance—and incidentally land Cimarosa in prison for his political opinions. Moreover the monarch who so honoured the Italian had ignored a greater composer of *opera buffa*, and the supreme genius of his age, on his own doorstep: it was just two months since Mozart died in the same city of Vienna. Destiny took a swift and subtle revenge: three weeks after the fateful treaty and the symbolic da capo it abruptly removed Leopold from the world (thereby depriving Cimarosa of a job) and replaced him almost at the same moment, in a humble family and a foreign land, with the next lawful heir of *opera buffa*, Gioacchino Rossini.

Cimarosa's opera owes a great deal to its libretto, an admirable specimen of its kind. The play on which it is based is an equally good example of a very different kind, and—rarest of achievements in operatic history—Giovanni Bertati effected the transubstantiation with little disturbance to the plot and no sign of strain whatsoever. *The Clandestine Marriage* by George Colman the elder and David Garrick, produced at Drury Lane in 1766, is a satirical comedy that draws its point from the English social scene. Standing in the line of descent from the theatre of Vanbrugh and Congreve to that of Goldsmith and Sheridan, it seems to have exerted a strong influence on the latter. The target of the satire, which often bites deep, is the snobbery of a *nouveau riche* family: the father who relies on money to buy him everything from a country estate to a titled son-in-law, his dominating and vulgar widowed sister (one of the originals of Mrs Malaprop), and his elder daughter, the coarseness of whose mind is rivalled only by the emptiness of her head. The younger, more sympathetic, and secretly married daughter has two admirers from the genuine (but of course impecunious) aristocracy, a peer and a baronet—the former a farcical compound of vanity, shrewdness, and hypochondria. There are also three comic lawyers, who add to the hilarity of the final scene on the bedroom landing.

Bertati transplanted the story to Italy, reduced the number of characters to six, and turned them into the stock figures of *opera buffa*—two contrasted pairs of lovers, miserly father, and amorously 'flustrated' aunt (the word is one of Colman's malapropisms). He dropped the lawyers—though there could have been a place for them in the world of Don Curzio—and combined the aristocratic admirers in the single figure of Lord Robinson, whom by a happy stroke he depicted as the typical English milord of Continental tradition. This of course makes the libretto more Italian than ever. But what most distinguishes it from the play, as in the contemporary librettos based on Beaumarchais's Figaro cycle but to a still greater degree, is the virtual elimination of the satire. This was inevitable with so English an original, and is no matter for regret; we are left with an excellently constructed and very amusing plot. The skill with which Bertati has given a Mediterranean flavour to a native English dish suggests momentary comparison with Boito.

Cimarosa's music strikes the modern listener as Mozartian—a second *Così fan tutte* without the emotional light and shade, the understanding of character, the richness of orchestral detail. Although Cimarosa is said to have venerated Mozart, the resemblance is fortuitous. What we recognize is the idiom of the second Neapolitan school which Cimarosa, Salieri, Paisiello, and others made popular throughout Europe, and of which Mozart's Italian comic operas are historically an offshoot. Mozart originated nothing in the form; he simply transfigured what he found with a passionate humanity. Cimarosa's opera, a delightful flowering of comic art without this quality of genius, is for that reason more representative of the tradition that descends from Pergolesi to Rossini and Donizetti. Mozart's reputation in Italy confirms this. The Italians—at least until recent years—have been notoriously cool towards him. Even Rossini was in his day accused of writing in the German style.

But if Cimarosa lacks the penetration and pathos of Mozart and the animal gusto of Rossini, he manages the same old devices—the pattering duets and trios, the cumulative finales, the occasional pathetic air—with a very deft touch. The music sparkles with wit, melody, and rhythmic vitality. Above all, it is excellent theatre: it carries the action forward at a brisk and genial pace, like a smooth-running coach drawn by a pair of well-trained horses. Just when a situation or an idea threatens to outstay its welcome, the story takes a new twist and Cimarosa matches it with the exact musical equivalent. His modulations, changes of rhythm, and patches of orchestral colour, though never recondite or bold, are unfailingly apt for the dramatic points they have to underline: witness Robinson's attempt to drive off Elisetta in Act II by cataloguing his vices, or the scoring of the duet (a little earlier) in which the lovers plan their elopement.

The opera is in every sense a triumph of style, for it capitalizes its weaknesses.

Cimarosa had nothing of Mozart's power of differential characterization, whether in solos or ensembles. Again and again the characters repeat each other's music regardless of the opposed sentiments they are expressing. They are little more than puppets; and it is just as well. The one weak spot of the libretto is Lord Robinson's final abandonment of the more attractive daughter for the tartar, simply in order to tidy up the plot. This does not happen in the play, where it would have been unthinkable; and even in Italian opera there are limits to the eccentricity permissible in an English peer. If it had occurred in a Mozart opera—other than *Così fan tutte*, where the artificiality is miraculously preserved throughout—we might have been brought up with the sort of jolt that occasionally threatens the equilibrium of *Don Giovanni*. But with Cimarosa it does not matter, for the characters have never really engaged our sympathies. By not venturing into deep water he runs no risk of drowning.

His consistent levity may not appeal to all tastes, and some have found the opera thin and frivolous. It is true that each musical idea, like white of egg in a meringue, is made to go a very long way. But much depends on the cooking and the service. *Il matrimonio segreto* is an opera in which quality of performance counts for even more than usual. A light touch and a good ensemble are essential. It is no use complaining that if the froth is blown away there is not much substance left in the pudding. No sensible person approaches a meringue with the appetite for a beefsteak.

13

Opera under the French Revolution

There is never much danger of historians underrating the political, social, or literary importance of the French Revolution. While that cataclysmic event is acknowledged to have affected the course of musical development, as of everything else, the music composed in Paris at the time has received little attention. This neglect has distorted our view of the past. We are apt to think of the Romantic movement in music as a German development, stemming from Beethoven, who in turn built on tidy foundations laid by Haydn and Mozart. This view, fostered by German scholarship, contains an element of truth; but it is very far from being the whole story. If there was such a thing as a Romantic breakthrough, it occurred in France in the early 1790s before Beethoven had formed his style. It was largely a product of the Revolution, and like most other musical innovations during the Baroque, Classical, and Romantic periods—monody, the symphony, sonata form, the Mozartian concerto, the relaxation of tonality in Wagner—its origins must be sought in the opera house.

If we could hear the principal operas of Cherubini and Méhul today—and stranger things have happened in the Borough of Camden—I doubt if they would be received as more than historical curiosities. But I am sure that when they reminded us of other composers, it would more often be of their successors than of their predecessors. The climate in which they worked was one of turmoil, adventure, and experiment, and they laid down a stock of technical innovations that was not exhausted for another fifty years. Many of the ideas even of the mature Wagner—the leitmotif, extended if not quite endless arioso, and the whole conception of the *Gesamtkunstwerk*—are clearly present, though not of course fully exploited, in French opera before 1800.[1] So is a good deal that we associate with Berlioz, and so in outline is the dramatic rhetoric of Beethoven's symphonic style, whose main source is Cherubini, then exclusively an opera composer. There is of course far more here than can be discussed, even superficially, in a single paper.

It was natural that the revolutionary ferment should find an early outlet in opera,

---

[1] The *locus classicus* is Le Sueur's grand opera *La Mort d'Adam*, produced in 1809 but composed some ten years earlier. This must be the most comprehensive and spectacular opera ever conceived. The libretto combines a Klopstock play with substantial portions of the Book of Genesis and *Paradise Lost*. The characters embrace not only the entire human race but the total population of heaven and hell. The dying Adam prophesies much of future human history, including the coming of Christ. The leitmotif system is elaborate; at least twelve earlier passages are recalled, sometimes in combination, in the death scene.

a field in which the French have an impressive record of contention and controversy. As one would expect, the librettos were affected before the music. The
plots became ideological, at first mildly, then rabidly so. All three Paris opera houses
were soon pouring forth a stream of ephemeral pieces with a political or patriotic
message. Some gave a new twist to classical stories, others were based on contemporary events. The recapture of Toulon in 1794 and the death of the young
revolutionary hero Joseph Barra each inspired several operas, which were announced on the bills as *fait historique*. Some of these productions must have startled
the traditional eighteenth-century opera-goer. The plot of the three-act *opéra
comique Le Congrès des Rois* (February 1794) concerns a conspiracy against the
reigning kings of Europe by their mistresses, who have been won over to the
Revolution and enjoy the assistance of the adventurer Cagliosto, attending the
Congress as the representative of the Pope. (He was in fact in prison at the time.)
The opera ends with the kings dancing the Carmagnole in red bonnets. The score
employed the services of no fewer than twelve composers, including Grétry,
Dalayrac, Berton, Méhul, and Cherubini.

Another choice specimen was produced by Grétry alone at the Opéra in the same
year. *Denys le Tyran, maître d'école à Corinthe* deals with an imaginary incident in
the life of Dionysius, the dethroned tyrant of Syracuse in the fourth century BC.
As a refugee in Corinth he starts a preparatory school under an assumed name. But
he keeps his crown up his sleeve, and when no one is looking takes it out,
contemplates it 'amoureusement', and addresses it in a long air that contains the only
decent music in the opera. He canes the children for alphabetical errors and is
accused by an officious cobbler of degrading the human species—and republicans
at that. His remark in a tavern scene that there is somethng to be said for sobriety
meets the indignant retort 'Mais d'un modéré c'est là le langage!' A woman
recognizes him by comparing his large nose and thick eyebrows with his face on
a coin, whereupon the children rise in revolt, abetted by the neighbours, and hound
him out of the town. His place as headmaster is taken by a statue of liberty, and
the opera ends with the inevitable Marseillaise and Carmagnole.

This plugging of the ideological content, often in terms of the most appalling
jargon, suggests some of the less edifying products of the Russian Revolution—
socialist realism and all that. But the French leaders, though they were constantly
interfering with the theatres, laying down what could, could not, and must be
represented on the stage, went out of their way to encourage music. Instead of
denouncing opera as an exotic and irrational entertainment, the plaything of the
aristocracy, as they very well might have done, they deliberately turned it into a
vehicle for popular enlightenment and patriotic stimulus. And for a time it
flourished exceedingly.

One aspect of this official policy, though it originated outside the opera house,
deserves special mention. This was the organization of great open-air pageants in
which every section of the public was encouraged to take part, vocally, instrument-
ally, and ballistically. They were designed at first to celebrate events of the
revolutionary calendar and to commemorate or bury national heroes. Later festivals

honoured abstract virtues (liberty, equality, the sovereignty of the people, hatred of tyrants and traitors—the proclamation of slogans is not a twentieth-century invention) and such useful or inevitable functions of the community as marriage, motherhood, work, and old age. All the leading composers were urged or frightened into producing hymns and marches for these ceremonies, which sought to combine the solemn rituals of the outlawed church with the secular energies of the parade-ground and even the battlefield. While the music, being primarily functional, had a very simple basis, the forces employed—apart from participating bystanders—were often enormous. Méhul wrote a *Chant national* for three choirs and three orchestras, Le Sueur another for soloists, four choirs, four orchestras, and organ. Male voices and military bands were particularly favoured. Strings might be rejected for acoustic or moral reasons, but the brass and percussion were reinforced by many new instruments—bass drum, tamtam, *contre-clairon, tuba corva,* and *buccinus.*[2] The proclamation of the Constitution of September 1791 was celebrated by massed choirs and orchestras, the percussion department being reinforced antiphonally by 130 pieces of artillery. In the same year the overture to Vogel's opera *Démophon,* a programmatic battle piece with a victorious climax, was played on the Champ de Mars by 1,200 wind instruments and twelve tamtams. These monster performances continued into the Napoleonic period. Their influence was far-reaching: orchestras were enlarged, especially the wind and percussion sections, new sonorities explored, and operas serious and comic were invaded by male choruses, military rhythms, and patriotic and libertarian sentiments. The results appear on many levels all over Europe, in the rattling marches and military-band scoring of Rossini,[3] in Beethoven's Battle Symphony and the finale of the Ninth Symphony, in Berlioz's Requiem, Te Deum, and *Symphonie funèbre et triomphale,* and in the spectacular grand operas of Le Sueur and Spontini, whence they passed into the mainstream of Romantic opera with the works of Meyerbeer, Verdi, and Wagner.

Grétry, the leading Paris composer in 1789, was not the man to take full advantage of this or to carry a revolutionary standard, though some of his operas do anticipate later developments, especially *Guillaume Tell* (9 April 1791)—a significant choice of subject. This has a programmatic overture, full of picturesque detail, including cello harmonics, three cowhorns, and a *ranz des vaches* that may well have suggested a similar idea to Rossini. Among its many scenes of tumult and violence is a *levée en masse* of the Swiss people during a storm, which was evidently intended to make an impact not unlike the revolutionary scenes in *Boris Godunov.* Grétry tells his male chorus to sing 'avec une fureur sourde et une rage concentrée', but the music belies them. This attempt to express through the directions what

---

[2] Some of these were reconstructions of instruments depicted on Trajan's Column. The Revolution looked to Ancient Rome for inspiration, but found it more often in the Republic than in the Empire. The *buccinus* was a kind of trombone with the bell turned upwards and painted with a ferocious dragon's head, which according to Sarrette 'produced an absolutely novel and terrifying sound'.
[3] The march, along with vigorous dances like the polonaise and waltz, may be said to have taken the place of the old courtly dances.

ought to be in the music itself is characteristic of many French operas of this period, especially those of Le Sueur and later Spontini.

The new opera of the Revolution found a leading spokesman—as so often in French musical history—in a foreigner, Luigi Cherubini. After a rigorous training in counterpoint and church music under Sarti, Cherubini had produced about a dozen operas, serious and comic, in the current Neapolitan idiom. When he settled in Paris in 1786, after two years in London, he fell under the influence first of Gluck and then of Haydn's symphonies.[4] By the outbreak of the Revolution he was a mature composer without a vocation. The Revolution supplied it. All his important operas were composed during the next decade. Although he survived the turn of the century by more than forty years, he was by then a spent force. A man of austere temperament and strong idealistic principles, he was equally ill at ease in the grand opera of the Napoleonic age, with its glorification of the state and the emperor (with whom he was always on bad terms), and in the trivialities of the conventional *opéra comique*.

It was, however, the *opéra comique*, not the grand opera, that gave Cherubini and his leading French contemporaries their platform. The grand opera with its classical and mythological subjects, its sophisticated tone and contempt for the mundane, its tradition of ballet and heroic declamatory recitative, had been an idealized projection of the *ancien régime*. It was in no position to reflect the social struggles and aspirations of the common man, though it was to reclaim its own under Napoleon's Empire and again under the restored monarchy. Some of the Revolution composers did attempt grand opera, generally on classical librettos with a political slant, like Méhul's *Horatius Coclès* (1794).[5] But this proved a blind alley, and by the later 1790s the Opéra had become a quiet backwater, whose chief success, Grétry's *Anacréon chez Polycrate*, was a thoroughly reactionary work.

The *opéra comique* was a more promising vehicle for the new school, thanks to its links with real life and in particular the spoken dialogue. Recitative was all very well for Castor and Pollux; it sounded stilted and absurd in the mouth of a hero of the Revolution. *Opéra comique* in the middle years of the century had been a diversionary entertainment intended to amuse, not to elevate; the slight element of social criticism in the librettos was not pressed home. The dependence on singing actors, especially light tenors and soubrettes, kept the design simple; for the most part the airs are in strophic or other rudimentary forms, the action is confined to the dialogue, and there is an avoidance of learning or profundity, which the meagre training of the composers was in any case unfitted to supply. While these limitations persisted, the attempts of Grétry in particular to widen the genre have been too little recognized. Some of his *opéras comiques* of the late 1770s and 1780s pointed the way forward by increasing the importance of ensembles and finales and endeavouring

[4] He was in later years a passionate admirer of Mozart, though it is not clear when he first came in contact with his music.

[5] Méhul even set a version of Metastasio's *Adriano in Siria*, which was banned in 1792 and taken off on the orders of the Directory after four performances in 1799; it was doubtless too soon to represent a sympathetic emperor in the theatre.

to treat the passions and dramatic conflict on a deeper level. Works like Dalayrac's *Sargines* (1788) and Grétry's *Raoul Barbe-bleue* (1789), though technically restricted, were in some respects prophetic.[6]

The *opéra comique* of Cherubini and Méhul greatly enlarged this trend. Its intentions were almost wholly serious: the elements of comedy and parody, already dwindling in Grétry, soon disappeared. It was contemporary in spirit, if not always in setting, and contained what might be called a *verismo* element. The world of pastoral make-believe has gone; instead we may be confronted by political agitators, passport inspections, and resistance movements, and nearly always by inflamed passions and an atmosphere of violence and terror. The plots are full of spectacular catastrophes—earthquakes, avalanches, shipwrecks, volcanic eruptions, the sacking of castles, and the collapse of caverns—with a happy end supervening just in time, generally the rescue of innocence from a grisly or unjust fate by an act of heroic human courage. Hence the name 'rescue opera' by which they are commonly known. This sort of happy end is the antithesis of the old *deus ex machina*; it is produced not by chance or the gods, but by the exertions of the hero or heroine, and the object of all the violence is not so much to raise a *frisson* as to highlight the obstacles that have to be overcome. Crude political propaganda has been replaced by a glorification of the human spirit, especially when fired by some ennobling ideal. This was the wider message of the Revolution that inspired the whole Romantic age. When projected by the formidable technique of Cherubini and the restless emotionalism of Méhul, it transformed the old *opéra comique* into the model for Romantic opera.

The newly enlarged form lasted a bare ten years, not much longer than the Revolution itself, and as we shall see it carried the seeds of its own destruction; but it was immensely prolific. A spate of new works was produced in a climate of frenzied competition, not between the two traditional Paris opera houses, but between two theatres both devoted to *opéra comique*: the old Comédie Italienne, renamed the Opéra-Comique National in February 1793 and commonly known as the Théâtre Favart, and the Théâtre Feydeau, founded in 1789 as a house for Italian comic opera and reopened in 1791. The principal composers were divided between the two theatres: Cherubini, Le Sueur, and Gaveaux worked for the Feydeau (where Gaveaux was a tenor singer), Grétry, Berton, Dalayrac, Méhul, Kreutzer, and later Boïeldieu mostly for the Favart. The rivalry was so fierce that operas on the same subject were repeatedly mounted by each theatre in turn: *Lodoïska* by Cherubini and Kreutzer, *Paul et Virginie* by Kreutzer and Le Sueur, *Roméo et Juliette* by Dalayrac and Steibelt, *La Caverne* by Le Sueur and Méhul. In the end both companies became insolvent, and they amalgamated in 1801; but by that time Napoleon was in the saddle and the climate had changed. Apart from a few of Méhul's later works the *opéra comique* reverted to its former specific gravity in a more bourgeois form, as exemplified by Boïeldieu, and serious composers turned back to grand opera.

[6] See David Charlton's detailed study, *Grétry and the Growth of Opéra-comique* (Cambridge, 1986).

Cherubini may be said to have launched the new style with his first *opéra comique*, *Lodoïska*, produced at the Théâtre Feydeau on 18 July 1791. This is not the earliest rescue opera. Grétry's *Richard Cœur de Lion* (1784) is perhaps the ancestor of the type, and Berton's *Les Rigueurs du cloître* (1790) is a primitive and somewhat naïve example, in which the heroine is rescued from a convent (the symbol of spiritual death) and all the nuns are sent out into the world to rear families. But it was Cherubini in *Lodoïska* who gave the rescue opera its teeth. The plot concerns the release of the heroine by her lover Floreski from a remote castle in Poland, where she is imprisoned by the nefarious and lascivious Baron Dourlinski. Poland, recently torn apart by partitions, was a topical choice for a blast in favour of liberty, and Floreski's vote in the Polish diet is a motive in the story. The subtitle, *Comédie héroïque*, neatly sums up the two principal constituents of Romantic opera, and indeed one can almost watch the new form evolving out of the old. There is only one comic character, Floreski's servant Varbel, who has obvious links with the Figaro–Leporello tradition. But the second finale, in which Dourlinski sends three envoys (all basses) to offer Floreski and Varbel doped wine, and Varbel neatly switches the glasses so that the envoys are doped, only for Dourlinski to enter in person and turn the tables, is halfway between a *buffo* romp and a sinister conspiratorial ensemble. Floreski is very much a Romantic hero, and his ally the Tartar chief Titzikan, a noble savage with a touch of Rider Haggard's Umslopogaas, also belongs to the new age, in which operatic characters tend to be impeccable or detestable. The final conflagration is as spectacular as anything in Meyerbeer. There is one startling detail that suggests the world of Verdi or even Puccini: the first act is confined entirely to male voices until the beginning of the finale, when Lodoiska is heard singing inside the tower where she is imprisoned. She does not appear on stage till Act II.

The music may strike us today as less romantic than the story. There is not much local colour,[7] though the use of polonaise rhythm in the Act I duet for Floreski and Varbel was to be imitated in countless operas by no means confined to Polish subjects. On the other hand a powerful new leaven is at work. Cherubini has subjected the relatively simple structure of the old *opéra comique* to an enormous expansion both in weight and length. The emphasis falls not on the solo airs but on the orchestra, the ensembles, and particularly the finales, which are massive affairs in several movements held together by a tonal and architectural balance involving the repetition in the tonic of long sections first heard in the dominant and an extensive coda carrying the music to a vehement climax that sometimes subsides, very effectively, to a quiet end. Within this slow-moving harmonic framework the music is propelled by a pounding rhythmic energy, with constant sforzandos and cross-accents and extreme dynamic contrasts, not only within the bar but within the beat: for pages on end almost every note may carry a fresh dynamic mark. The orchestration too is full of contrast, huge climaxes spread over several octaves

---

[7] Cherubini was to go further in this direction in his next work, *Élisa*, the first opera to exploit the romantic attractions of Alpine scenery.

alternating with sudden pianissimos in which solo instruments, especially the woodwind, come to the fore.

This style is in essence an adaptation for serious purposes of the Neapolitan *opera buffa*, especially its cumulative finales. Since Cherubini's melodic impulse was weak, much of his thematic material also consists of *buffo* tags, whose constant motivic development in the orchestra is apt to detract from the interest of the vocal line. Although Cherubini wrote only one symphony, and that many years later, he was more like an Italian Haydn than Boccherini. Weber described *Faniska*, another Polish opera on the same lines as *Lodoïska*, as 'rather a symphony with songs than a lyric drama'. But of course the important parallel is with Beethoven, whose debt to Cherubini was very great and freely admitted. It is significant in this connection that *Lodoïska*, like most of Cherubini's operas, became far more popular in Germany than it ever was in France, where audiences preferred Kreutzer's version of the same subject.

There is little in *Fidelio*, apart from its transcendent genius and a Mozartian flavour in the musical language, that cannot be traced directly to the rescue opera of the Revolution, of which it is indeed the finest example. The fact that the libretto is translated from Gaveaux's *Léonore* of 1798[8] accounts for the general similarity, but Beethoven's model for the music and the overall design was undoubtedly the Cherubini of *Lodoïska* and *Les deux Journées*. There is the same outline—powerful overture followed by a leisurely development of the early action, with the lighter characters prominent, leading to a grimmer sort of realism as the tension develops —and the same wide range of forms, from spoken dialogue through *mélodrame* to extended solo movements and enormously weighty finales. Dourlinski seems to have served as a pattern for Pizarro, whose music is strikingly similar; moreover Dourlinski is a baritone, whereas most *opéra comique* villains of this period were tenors. The trumpet-call on the battlements is anticipated in the first finale of *Lodoïska*, where it is followed by the entry of Dourlinski's sinister henchman, Altamoras.[9] The whole texture of *Lodoïska*, as of other Cherubini operas, suggests a blueprint for Beethoven's style at a time when that composer was a young man of 20 still living at Bonn. This stands out clearly in his overtures, which like so much of Beethoven's orchestral music seem to present the kernel of a drama in symphonic form. The overture to *Élisa*, dating from 1794 and thus roughly contemporary with Haydn's last symphonies, scarcely shows Cherubini at his best; but it gives a fair idea of the rhetorical style that influenced the German Romantics. At one moment the music seems to strive for something just out of reach; at the next it falls back on a comfortable eighteenth-century commonplace. It could easily be mistaken for immature Beethoven.

Gaveaux's *Léonore* and Cherubini's *Les deux Journées* both have librettos by J. N. Bouilly founded on actual incidents during the Reign of Terror, though for prudent reasons they were transferred to another country or period. They belong to the *fait historique* class; but the climate has changed since the early days of the Revolution.

---

[8] See below, p. 129 ff.
[9] In Gaveaux the trumpet-call occurs in the dialogue, and Pizarro does not sing at all.

In both operas the persons rescued are aristocrats. Bouilly presents a moral imperative for all men to help their fellows in distress, to whatever class they may belong, and specifically underlines this in the words of the finale of *Les deux Journées* ('Le premier charme de la vie, C'est de servir l'humanité'), which Beethoven considered one of the two finest librettos ever written. In stressing this universal message he was again following Cherubini. We can perhaps see why the French Revolution proved so much more artistically fertile than its Russian successor, which in fifty years has not outgrown its restrictive and reactionary attitude to the artist.[10]

Cherubini is in some respects an odd figure to find among the leaders of a revolutionary movement. He had a fastidious distaste for emotional excess and self-indulgence, which distinguishes him sharply from many of his successors and even seems to set him apart from his subjects. He gives the impression of a Classical artist dragged willy-nilly into a Romantic age, from which, after supplying it with the technical means of expression, he retired into silence. It is perhaps not surprising that his finest opera, and the highest point reached by the *opéra comique* of the Revolution, should be quite untypical of the movement. *Médée* (1797) has no political or contemporary reference, no comedy of course, and no hopeful happy end. It is a pure classical tragedy that owes its strength to the equilibrium between the violence of the subject, all the more potent for being largely psychological, and the severe restraint of the style. But it is still formally an *opéra comique*, since it retains spoken dialogue;[11] and one of its most striking qualities is the skill with which Cherubini exploits this to widen the range of expression. In the second finale Medea, alone on the stage, listens to the decorous Gluck-like strains (chorus and wind) from the temple where her lover Jason is being married to a hated rival, and moves from spoken dialogue through *mélodrame* to recitative (supported by a small group of strings) and then to full orchestral accompaniment as she works herself into an uncontrollable passion. This subtle gradation is obliterated in most modern performances, including the Callas recording, where the dialogue has been scrapped in favour of Franz Lachner's debased recitative version of 1854.[12]

Cherubini's strong personality tended to swamp his French contemporaries. The most interesting of them, Le Sueur and Méhul, were striking innovators, but owing to defective technique they give the impression of not being in full control of their medium. Le Sueur produced three *opéras comiques* during the 1790s; he is, however, more important for his two later grand operas and their decisive influence on Berlioz, which is too big a subject to embark on here.[13] Méhul's temperament contained an element of fanaticism, reflected in the vigour with which he pursued Gluck's theories about the subjection of music to its dramatic context. He was

[10] The action of one of the more exotic rescue operas, Boïeldieu's *Béniowski* (1800), takes place in a prison camp in Kamchatka and ends with the rescue of the entire cast, not from the prison governor, who is a sympathetic character, but from the rigours of the Russian climate.

[11] It was, however, first conceived for the Opéra, presumably with recitatives.

[12] The Covent Garden revival on 6 November 1989 restored the dialogue, but distorted the opera in other respects.

[13] See my chapter 'French Opera' in G. Abraham (ed.), *The Age of Beethoven 1790–1830*, New Oxford History of Music, viii (London, 1982), 88–92.

extraordinarily rich in new ideas—far more so than Cherubini—but has received little credit for them because the most valuable were perfected by later and greater composers, often long afterwards. His experiments with operatic form sprang from an attempt to reconcile *opéra comique* convention with a more organic structure and a growing seriousness of content. This confronted him very early in his career with the rift between music that propels the action forward and intensifies it, and spoken dialogue that brings the main expressive element to a stop. Whereas Cherubini solved this problem in *Médée* through his technical skill and classical command of form, Méhul's more impulsive approach landed him in incoherence and ultimate failure, but not before it had produced some interesting results and contributed to one of the most important innovations in operatic history.

His first opera to reach the stage, *Euphrosine* in 1790, on a witty and almost Shavian libretto by F. B. Hoffman, is musically very uneven; but it contains a duet, 'Gardez-vous de la jalousie', that was singled out as a stroke of genius by both Grétry and Berlioz. Berlioz went so far as to call it a worthy musical paraphrase of Iago's 'Green-eyed monster' speech. The tyrant Coradin has fallen in love with Euphrosine. A designing Countess, who wants Coradin for herself, tells him that Euphrosine has a secret lover and deliberately inflames his jealousy under the pretence of warning him against it. The duet begins over a motif of rising and falling minor thirds in the bass, and much of the music is developed from this. Presently Coradin gives orders that Euphrosine shall be poisoned, and in Act III, believing her dead, he breaks out in an air of bitter self-reproach, 'O douleur insupportable!' Both the air and the introductory recitative make extensive use of the jealousy motif from the duet, first in its original form and later in various transformations, sometimes in the bass and sometimes as an inner ostinato. To leave the matter in no doubt Méhul used the motif in a different rhythm, 'Lent très marqué', in the introduction to the overture. Here already is a hint of the symphonic leitmotif—quite different from Grétry's use of the simple reminiscence motif in *Richard*—at a time when Méhul was still in the shadow of Gluck, Grétry, and the Neapolitans, and before the impact of Cherubini. He was no doubt influenced by certain literary ideas current in Paris just before the Revolution. Lacépède in 1785 recommended the use of motifs, whether in the voice parts or the orchestra, as a means of linking scenes or presaging future events; two years later Le Sueur noted in a pamphlet that the orchestra could express the thoughts or feelings of a character who himself says nothing.

Significantly the movements in *Euphrosine* based on the jealousy motif are far in advance of the rest of the score, in both style and quality. This happens again and again when Méhul is concerned with jealousy or remorse. We find it in the part of Simeon in *Joseph*, his best-known opera but a late work composed after the fires had begun to die down, and still more in two remarkable *opéras comiques* of the 1790s, *Mélidore et Phrosine* (1794)—which is omitted from Loewenberg's *Annals* —and *Ariodant* (1799). The plot of *Mélidore et Phrosine* is a variant of the Hero and Leander story, set in the Straits of Messina and complicated by the motive of incestuous love. Phrosine has two brothers, of whom the elder, Aimar, forbids her to marry Mélidore for family reasons, while the younger, Jule, loves her himself and is tortured by guilt and jealousy. In the first finale the nocturnal elopement of the lovers is frustrated by Aimar, who is struck down by Mélidore in the darkness. The lovers continue to meet secretly, crossing the straits by night, but Jule intercepts Phrosine's boat and casts her off to drown just as a storm rises. Mélidore dives off a cliff and rescues her. *Ariodant* is based on a well-known episode in Ariosto's *Orlando furioso* used by many composers, including Handel, Berton, and Mayr, and in part by Shakespeare in *Much Ado About Nothing*. A lover, on the night before his wedding, sees, as he thinks, his beloved admitting a rival to her bedroom. In fact the rejected rival has persuaded the lady's servant, who loves him, to dress up as her mistress in the hope that the latter will change her mind or be condemned for unchastity. He subsequently tries to have his accomplice murdered, but she is saved by the hero and reveals the deception.

In both operas a powerful and potentially tragic situation is built up, only to be dissipated in a perfunctory happy end. Jule's last-minute repentance in *Mélidore et Phrosine* is absurdly unconvincing, while Othon, the villain of *Ariodant*, who has initiated the whole action, simply fades out; we never hear what happens to him. This disproportion is greatly accentuated by the music. Méhul is obviously less interested in the humanitarian message than in individual emotions, particularly the darker passions of his villains, who have a conspicuous element of the obsessive and daemonic. (It is scarcely surprising that both operas got him into trouble with the police.) This sense of brooding evil is accompanied by a feeling for the scenic or climatic background as a governing factor in the plot, and therefore in the music. Both these qualities take us out of the world of Cherubini almost into that of *Der Freischütz*; all the distinctive spiritual ingredients of German Romantic opera are present or implicit, except the emphasis on the supernatural. The sea in its changing moods plays almost as prominent a part in *Mélidore et Phrosine* as in *Der fliegende Holländer*; the tremendous storm that rages through most of Act III, with Mélidore at its height plunging off a cliff into the waves, reminds us inevitably of Wagner's opera. Méhul is also moving towards through-composed form in this act, which contains several freely linked movements and only two patches of dialogue. In *Ariodant* the background is the world of medieval chivalry in its darker aspects, with the Gothic trappings characteristic of the period. In *Uthal*, a slightly later work of 1806, it is the impenetrable mists and forests of the Hebrides. A great part of the action of all three operas takes place at night. The music is full of nocturnes, seascapes, and picturesque scenes for peasants, sailors, bards, and so on. These are the predecessors of Weber's huntsmen and bridesmaids—there is a peasant chorus in Act II of *Mélidore et Phrosine* extraordinarily like the *Freischütz* bridesmaids; the plebeian element in the old *opéra comique* has ceased to be comic and become a vehicle for local colour.

Méhul's attempt to match these innovations in the music cannot be called a complete success, though not for want of boldness. Cherubini found the harmonic idiom of *Mélidore et Phrosine* intolerably harsh and uncouth, and it is full of abrupt modulations and progressions that are clearly evoked by the dramatic context but sound contrived rather than inevitable. Méhul was deficient in melodic and rhythmic invention and in formal organization, but his scoring is often strikingly original. When the stricken Aimar, given up for dead, is just able to identify Mélidore as his assailant, Méhul suggests his strangled voice in a passage for four horns in D, G, and F, all playing stopped notes—chords of A flat and E flat in a G major context. He uses the horns with great freedom and variety of effect in this opera—a point perhaps not lost on Weber—and omits the trumpets altogether. This was not because they were not available; in *Stratonice* he suppressed the oboes, and in *Uthal* even the violins, in order to give the opera a particular tone colour.

Méhul's overtures vary widely in form and proportions—some are brief preludes, others almost symphonic poems—but they are almost always an integral part of the opera, either leading straight into it or using some of its principal themes. The overture to *Uthal* is a piece of pure impressionism designed to evoke the atmosphere of a remote Scottish forest by the sea at midnight in the middle of a storm. After the introduction it has nothing approaching a theme and no settled tonality; and it is twice interrupted by the voice of the heroine calling the name of her lost father.[14] The overture to *Mélidore et Phrosine* epitomizes the turbulent course of the drama and the ever-present background of the sea, at first stormy in D minor, than calm in a D major barcarolle that recurs at the end of the second act, where it accompanies a chorus of sailors rowing Phrosine across the straits after she has made an assignation with Mélidore. It fades into silence with a little phrase of a rising and falling third played in imitation by the horns, first forte, then piano, then pianissimo. This is sung by Mélidore to Phrosine's name as the boat disappears and the curtain falls on Act II (Ex. 1).

Ex.1

After the dying close of the overture the curtain goes up on a fortissimo diminished seventh, and we find ourselves in the middle of an angry duet for Phrosine and her brother Aimar, who brusquely refuses her unheard request to be allowed to marry Mélidore. The last act begins with a long orchestral introduction during which Mélidore, alone on the shore at night, silently lights a beacon as a signal to Phrosine; as he does so the orchestra quotes two earlier themes, the love duet from the first finale and the Phrosine phrase (Ex. 1), which is anticipated by a solo cello and echoed in turn by three horns, one in the pit, the others in the distance behind the scenes. A little later there are two further quotations from Act II, the barcarolle as Mélidore tries to reassure himself that Phrosine is safe, and an earlier chorus in which the sailors urged Phrosine to take advantage of the favourable wind, now ironically combined in the orchestra against the storm music. Méhul is beginning to use his motifs allusively as something more than labels. The

---

[14] Méhul doubtless borrowed this idea from the overture to Grétry's *Aucassin et Nicolette* (1779), where Beaucaire twice calls the name of his son.

opera ends with another barcarolle, whose mood and texture—particularly the ostinato figure divided between the violins—is very like the mermaids' music in *Oberon*, and in the same key, E major.

The score of *Ariodant* is dominated by the jealous and vengeful character of Othon, who evidently seized Méhul's imagination much as Medea seized Cherubini's. The short overture begins with a passage for three solo cellos and string basses that left its mark on several later composers, rises in a crescendo to a violent climax, and pauses inconclusively on a dominant seventh as the curtain rises, revealing Othon alone. He makes a passionate speech—Ina, whom he loves, is even now deciding his fate—and the orchestra breaks in with the principal motif of the opera, beginning sforzando on a dominant minor ninth and leading via a single phrase of recitative into an agitated air (Ex. 2). That motif,[15] associated with the unbridled passions of Othon, torn between love for Ina and jealous hatred of the favoured Ariodant, reappears, sometimes modified and carrying ironical implications, in at least eight of the opera's fifteen numbers and actually begins five of them, each in a different key and with a different continuation. For example in No. 2 Dalinde, Othon's accomplice, tells him to calm his anger: other beautiful women will regard him with favour. After the brusque opening the mood changes suddenly from Allegro 4/4 to Adagio 3/4 for Dalinde's words 'Calmez cette colère', accompanied

Ex.2

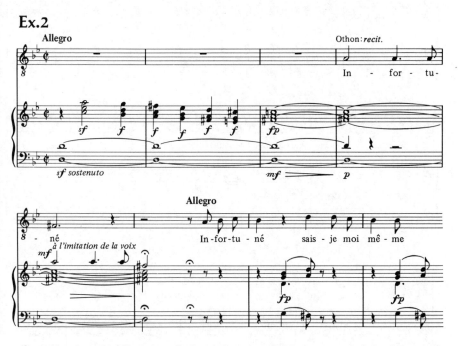

[15] Like the rising and falling minor third, it is almost a Méhul fingerprint; it had already occurred in the storm music in Act III of *Mélidore et Phrosine*. This tendency to repeat himself in later operas is a symptom of Méhul's limited powers of invention.

by strings only, before reverting to Allegro (Ex. 3). The jealousy motif returns later in the air and has again to be exorcized by the Adagio.

No. 3, a duet for Othon and Dalinde, moves in a different direction. An extended eight-bar version of the motif, fortissimo dying abruptly to pianissimo, crashes into the dialogue when Dalinde unintentionally reveals that Ariodant is Othon's rival. Othon in *mélodrame* swears to kill both Ina and Ariodant, and then—after a pause —he and the orchestra enter together with a great fortissimo cry, 'O démon de la jalousie!' (the first words of the duet) on an augmented triad (Ex. 4).

The motif is quoted again in the middle of the same duet when Ariodant walks silently along the gallery at the back and enters Ina's quarters. This is his first appearance in the opera, and the music identifies him for us—through Othon's eyes. Méhul uses this phrase constantly to throw an oblique light on character or situation and to suggest a range of dramatic irony quite unlike anything else I know in eighteenth-century opera. Ariodant's first air, a cheerful piece, looking forward to

Ex.3

Ex.4

reunion with Ina and ending with the words 'My happiness is assured', has a quiet four-bar postlude in sharp contrast as Ina enters for the first time. The allusion reminds us of the passion she has stirred in Othon, of which Ariodant as yet knows nothing; his happiness is not as assured as he thinks (Ex. 5).

Later the phrase forms a bitterly ironical pendant to the closing bars of the long and intensely dramatic finale of Act II, when Othon's deception has apparently succeeded and Ina is dragged in and charged with unchastity. In Act III, Méhul introduces it with admirable timing as the culmination of a paragraph, when Ina's father King Edgard decides that he must obey his own law against sexual transgressors and order his daughter's execution.

Some of these examples illustrate another of Méhul's experiments in trying to

Ex.5

sostenuto
(*Pendant les quatre dernières mésures de ce morceau Ina paroit.*)

improve the dramatic continuity of *opéra comique*. While preserving the set pieces, he began as early as *Mélidore et Phrosine* to link them with the dialogue before and after by means of bridge passages, sometimes purely orchestral, sometimes in the form of *mélodrame*, designed as psychological transitions.[16] The tonality of the set pieces is not disturbed—indeed it is emphasized, especially at the end, and this throws the bridge passages into stronger relief. These often modulate, the preludes leading as it were from the key of the preceding dialogue into that of the set piece and the postludes moving into the next dialogue. The former sometimes begin with a sharp dissonance (Exx. 2, 3, and 4), while the latter may end on an ambiguous or unresolved chord, the resolution being supplied metaphorically by the spoken word (Ex. 7 below). These postludes are particularly effective when they coincide with the arrival of a new character, whose impact on the drama is expressed by some harmonic twist, often pianissimo, before he speaks (Exx. 5, 6, and 7). Almost every movement in *Ariodant* ends with an effect of this kind. For instance the entry of the treacherous Dalinde after the love duet for Ina and Ariodant in Act II diverts the music from a confident and conclusive A major into a precarious F major before the dialogue begins (Ex. 6). During the closing bars of the air in Act III in which the king decides that Ina must die, Othon appears, salutes his sovereign as the tonality is wrenched abruptly from F minor on to a first inversion of E major, and offers to save Ina if she will marry him (Ex. 7).

There is one striking *coup de théâtre* in Act II of *Mélidore et Phrosine*. Jule asks a hermit to further his vengeance on Mélidore for abducting his sister. But the hermit is Mélidore in disguise, and he tells Jule in a duet that the man he wants is dead. Unknown to either of them, and to the audience, Phrosine has overheard them: she rushes on in the last bars of the duet, which momentarily becomes a trio, and faints. The music stops abruptly on a diminished seventh, and the scene continues in dialogue.

[16] The rudiments of this idea can be found in Grétry's *L'Amant jaloux* (1778). See Charlton, *Grétry and Opéra-comique*, 172.

Ex.6

(Dalinde paroit)

By this primitive form of progressive tonality Méhul was able at the same time to throw the expectation forward and to appropriate within the musical framework incidents that in earlier (and later) *opéra comique* fell into the province of the dialogue. It must surely be effective in the theatre. But of course it had no future, since Méhul's successors in Romantic opera presently took the logical step and abandoned spoken dialogue for continuous music. Only then could the leitmotif develop fully; indeed it is astonishing that its biggest leap forward before Wagner (apart perhaps from Le Sueur) should have occurred in *opéra comique*. In fact the Revolution composers had poured so much new wine into the old bottle that it burst. Neither its formal nor its human resources were adequate. The increasingly passionate and tragic temper, especially of Méhul's operas, made the happy end dramatically intolerable. The expansion of the orchestra placed a heavy strain on the singers, who were trained in correct declamation rather than virtuosity. The voice parts in these operas are strenuous and exhausting, but the absence of coloratura gives them the aspect of a skeleton, firm enough but lacking the seductive outlines of living flesh. Not till the arrival of Rossini in the 1820s did French opera, even when composed by Italians like Cherubini and Spontini, find a satisfactory solution to this problem.

Ex.7

The composers of German Romantic opera also owed more to Rossini than they were sometimes willing to admit; but the rock on which they built was the French *opéra comique* of the Revolution. Whether carried by Napoleon's armies or impelled by their content of idealism and spiritual ferment, or both, these works spread all over Europe, especially into Germany and Austria. Large numbers of them were printed in full score, and so available for study. If Cherubini supplied Beethoven with a model for *Fidelio*, and the whole German school with part of its basic technique, Méhul's affinity is with Weber and Marschner. There are obvious dramatic parallels between *Ariodant* and *Euryanthe* (not to mention *Lohengrin*), in particular the character and relationship of the two villains, the man using the woman as a tool and then discarding her. It is these two who have the finest music in both operas, and with whom the leitmotif device is principally associated. Whether Weber was directly influenced here it is impossible to say, though it is worth noting that the first performance of *Ariodant* in Berlin in June 1816 took place a week before one of his visits. He was certainly familiar with recent French opera; when he became director at Prague in 1814, ten of the first eleven operas he conducted belonged to this school, and many others followed.[17] We may be right to ignore Cherubini and Méhul in the opera house, but if we are to understand the history of opera we ought not to forget their importance.

[17] See *New Oxford History of Music*, viii. 494.

14
Beethoven and Opera

INTRODUCTION

The uniqueness of Beethoven's contribution to the operatic repertory must be ascribed to temperament rather than environment. The man who produced his single opera in three versions and equipped it with four overtures, yet complained of the same work that he found it far harder to rethink himself into an old composition than to begin a new one, was clearly not a born opera composer, least of all in the conditions obtaining at the turn of the nineteenth century. Nevertheless he was far from considering himself a one-opera man. He continued for the greater part of his life to invite librettos and plan fresh operas, only to abandon them in the early stages or allow them to lapse through inanition. His potential collaborators included such men of literary distinction and experience as Goethe, Grillparzer, Kotzebue, Collin, Rochlitz, and Rellstab. *Fidelio*, whatever its faults, is a great opera and a work of theatrical genius. Yet not even a mouse followed the birth of the mountain. One might attribute the constant search for librettos to the spur of Beethoven's environment, and its regular frustration to some hidden force in his creative personality. But only a careful study of the opera he did write can suggest an answer to the question what that force was.

The circumstances of Beethoven's life, both in Bonn and Vienna, might have been expected to encourage rather than inhibit an operatic career, or at least an attempt at it. It is true that in neither city during his residence—and especially in his impressionable years—was a composer of the first or even the second rank writing for the stage. But there was plenty of opera; old and new works, home-grown and imported, were constantly on view. In Bonn, where his father was a tenor singer, albeit a drunken one, Beethoven must have learned much of the current repertory in his childhood. In 1783 and 1784, at the age of 12 and 13, he was employed as cembalist in the Elector's theatre orchestra under the Kapellmeister Christian Gottlob Neefe. This service was interrupted by the disbandment of the orchestra on the death of the Elector in April 1784. Even so, the next four years saw a number of visiting companies in Bonn, one of which (in 1785) may have introduced Beethoven to Gluck's *Orfeo* and *Alceste*.[1] Two years later, on his first

[1] There are curiously few references to Gluck in the Beethoven literature. Czerny says Beethoven played through *Iphigénie en Tauride* for some French officers in 1805. His letters never mention Gluck's name; the only two allusions are problematical. In February 1808 he lent Collin an *Armide* that did not belong to him; about the same time he borrowed an *Iphigénie* from Zmeskall and lost it (see Emily Anderson (ed.), *The Letters of Beethoven* (London, 1961), henceforward cited as *LA*, letters 163, 263, and 264). But he must have been familiar with Gluck's music.

visit to Vienna, he had a few lessons from Mozart. In the winter of 1788 the Elector Maximilian Franz, brother of the Austrian emperor, established a new opera company at Bonn that gave regular winter seasons lasting several months. Until his departure for Vienna in November 1792—that is, for four full seasons and part of a fifth—Beethoven played the viola in the orchestra. The repertory consisted almost entirely of light works, whether Italian *opera buffa* (Cimarosa, Paisiello, Sacchini, Salieri, Sarti, Martín y Soler), French *opéra comique* (Grétry, Monsigny, Dezède, Dalayrac), or South German *Singspiel* (Dittersdorf, Benda, Schuster, Schubaur, Umlauf). But it included Gluck's *Die Pilgrime von Mecca* and three operas by Mozart, *Die Entführung aus dem Serail* in 1788–89 and 1791–92, *Don Giovanni* (three performances), and *Le nozze di Figaro* (four performances), both in 1789–90. Practical experience of these scores can scarcely have failed to make a permanent impression on the young Beethoven.

His first ten years in Vienna brought little direct contact with the stage. Although several theatres were in operation, this was not a period of Viennese operatic glory. At the Court Theatre (Kärntnertor), largely confined to Italian opera, the favourite composers were Martín y Soler, Salieri, Cimarosa, Paer, and Zingarelli. It did produce the most successful German opera between *Die Zauberflöte* and *Der Freischütz*, Winter's *Das unterbrochene Opferfest* in 1796; but this singular association of a wildly exotic plot with music of demure domesticity, packed with Mozartian echoes but deficient in structure and characterization, in which a short-winded *volkstümlich* melody may eject without warning a rocket of extravagant coloratura, had little to offer Beethoven.[2] The popular German theatres, Marinelli's Leopold-stadt and Schikaneder's Theater auf der Wieden, specialized in farces and fairy stories, often with an oriental background. These were all *Singspiele* with copious dialogue; indeed, the scenic spectacle and the coarse buffooneries of the spoken text usurped the province of the music, which seldom attempted to impose any unity of structure or atmosphere. The leading composers were Wenzel Müller, Weigl, Süssmayr, Hoffmeister, Schenk, and Kauer. Only *Die Zauberflöte*, which continued to draw audiences, can have won Beethoven's respect, and he was not tempted to emulate it, though he did compose two arias for insertion in a revival of Umlauf's *Die schöne Schusterin* in 1796. Apart from this and the ballet *Prometheus* (1801), his only tangible links with the Viennese theatre at this period are the titles of the operas from which he chose themes for variations, among them Grétry's *Richard Cœur de Lion*, Müller's *Die Schwestern von Prag*, Wranitzky's *Das Waldmädchen*, Paisiello's *La molinara*, Winter's *Das unterbrochene Opferfest*, Weigl's *L'amor marinaro*, Salieri's *Falstaff*, and Süssmayr's *Soliman II*.

In 1802 occurred an event that changed this picture decisively. On 23 March Schikaneder produced Cherubini's *Lodoïska* at the new Theater an der Wien, which had replaced the Theater auf der Wieden in the previous year. This was the first

----

[2] According to Alfred Loewenberg, *Annals of Opera*, 2nd rev. edn. (Geneva, 1955), col. 553, the last finale of Winter's *Marie von Montalban* (1800) is supposed to have influenced *Fidelio*. This claim will not bear inspection. Beyond the fact that Winter's finale contains a rescue and ends in C major there appears to be no resemblance.

major opera of the French Revolution school to reach Vienna; it was also one of the best, with a solidity of technique, a pulsating energy, and a flavour of contemporary realism that must have startled Viennese conservatives. Its success was immediate. Baron Braun, Deputy Director of the Court Theatre, went to Paris to obtain more French operas, 'all of which will be performed here most carefully according to the taste of the French.'[3] This journey led to Cherubini's commission to compose *Faniska* for Vienna. Meanwhile Schikaneder, encouraged it is said by Mozart's brother-in-law Sebastian Mayer, an actor and bass singer who was to be Beethoven's first Pizarro, decided to abandon pantomime and fairy stories for more serious fare. In the event *Les deux Journées* was produced by both managements under different titles on consecutive nights (13 and 14 August 1802). All Cherubini's other post-Revolution operas followed, *Médée* at the Kärntnertor on 6 November, *Élisa* at the Theater an der Wien on 18 December, *L'Hôtellerie portugaise* on 22 September 1803. They were the forerunners of an avalanche of French operas, many of which became more popular in Vienna than in Paris. Dalayrac (whose earlier work had long been successful in Germany), Méhul, Gaveaux, Boïeldieu, Isouard, Berton, and a little later Spontini conquered the Austrian capital as easily as the armies of Napoleon. Of the more adventurous operas, Le Sueur's *La Caverne* appeared at two theatres within ten days in June 1803, and Méhul's *Ariodant* followed on 16 February 1804.

Such was the background against which Beethoven's fitful career in the opera house began. Although its early course was inauspicious and in some respects obscure, two things are certain: the agent who established the link was Schikaneder, and the torch that fired Beethoven's imagination was the French opera—or rather *opéra comique*—of the Revolution. His opinion of Cherubini is well known. When the two composers met in July 1805, while the one was working on *Fidelio* and the other on *Faniska* (produced at the Kärntnertor on 25 February 1806), both in collaboration with Joseph Sonnleithner, Beethoven treated Cherubini with marked respect. In March 1823 he wrote to him: 'I value your works more highly than all other compositions for the theatre.' Two months later he sent Cherubini via Louis Schlösser 'all kinds of amiable messages' and an assurance that 'my most ardent longing is that we should soon have another opera composed by him'. His expressions of esteem, often repeated,[4] were not always qualified by restriction to the theatre: he regarded Cherubini as the greatest living composer. Nor was Cherubini the only member of the French school admired by the fastidious Beethoven. On 18 February 1823 he asked Moritz Schlesinger for music by Méhul and in thanking him for an unidentified score pronounced it 'so worthy of him'. Of Spontini he said in 1825: 'There is much good in him; he understands theatrical effects and the musical noises of warfare thoroughly.' He rated the French librettos as high as the music. While he constantly complained that 'the Germans cannot

---

[3] *Allgemeine Musikalische Zeitung*, quoted in E. Forbes (ed.), *Thayer's Life of Beethoven* (Princeton, 1967), henceforward cited as *TF*, 326.

[4] They were not wholly reciprocated. Cherubini said of *Fidelio* that Beethoven paid too little heed to the art of singing, and he found the modulations in the overture (*Leonore* No. 2) so confusing that he could not recognize the principal key. See *TF*, 399.

write a good libretto' and told Rellstab in 1825 that he could never compose operas on subjects like *Figaro* and *Don Giovanni*, which he found frivolous and indeed repugnant, he declared in conversation with Julius Benedict in 1823 that the best librettos he knew were those of *Les deux Journées* and *La Vestale*.

There is a certain irony in the part played by Schikaneder. No evidence appears to support Emily Anderson's statement[5] that as early as 1801 he offered Beethoven his libretto *Alexander* with which he planned to open the Theater an der Wien (Teyber's setting inaugurated it on 13 June). But he did engage him to compose an opera early in 1803, and on most favourable terms, which included free lodging in the theatre. This commission is first mentioned in a letter of 12 February from Beethoven's brother Johann to Breitkopf & Härtel and thus preceded the concert at which the oratorio *Christus am Oelberge* was first performed on 5 April. The latter may have been a by-product of the same set of circumstances (Beethoven said he wrote the music in a fortnight); it was taken as evidence of his fitness for theatrical composition. He moved into the theatre in the spring; on 2 August *Die Zeitung für die Elegante Welt* published an announcement, under the date 29 June, that 'Beethoven is composing an opera by Schikaneder'. The libretto was *Vestas Feuer*, and Beethoven worked on it for some time, though not very assiduously;[6] production was planned for March 1804. Towards the end of the year he discarded it in disgust, as he explained in an interesting letter to Rochlitz (4 January 1804), adding: 'I have quickly had an old French libretto adapted and am now beginning to work on it.'[7] This was the genesis of *Fidelio*. In the same letter he rejected the first act of a libretto by Rochlitz because its subject was connected with magic. The public were now as prejudiced against such a theme as they had formerly been enthusiastic in its favour: Schikaneder's 'empire has really been entirely eclipsed by the light of the brilliant and attractive French operas'.

That Beethoven was attracted more by the operatic idea than by Schikaneder's libretto emerges from Georg August Griesinger's report to Breitkopf & Härtel (12 November 1803) that though still at work on *Vestas Feuer* 'he told me himself that he is looking for reasonable texts'.[8] *Vestas Feuer* is not a reasonable text. It is a ponderously heroic affair set in ancient Rome (though the names of the characters suggest Parthia or India) and replete with tedious intrigue.[9] Schikaneder had lapsed from pantomime into the stagnant backwash of Metastasio while retaining (in Beethoven's words to Rochlitz) 'language and verses such as could proceed only out of the mouths of our Viennese apple-women'. Beethoven set the opening scene, in which the father of the heroine, inflamed by the dark counsels of a slave and the fact that his would-be son-in-law is the child of an old enemy, at first denounces the lovers, but is won over by their devotion and heroic bearing. The principal

[5] 'On the Road to Fidelio (1814)', in *Opera* 12 (1961), 82, and 'Beethoven's Operatic Plans', *Proceedings of the Royal Musical Association* 88 (1961–2), 62.

[6] He wrote to Alexander Macco on 2 November 'I am only now *beginning to work at my opera*.' See *LA*, letter 85.

[7] *LA*, letter 87a.   [8] Quoted in *TF*, 340.

[9] For a summary see W. Hess, *Beethovens Bühnenwerke* (Göttingen, 1962), 32–4. Hess published the complete libretto in *Beethoven-Jahrbuch*, 2nd ser., iii (1957–8), 63–106.

movements are a love duet of Mozartian grace and a trio of reconciliation for soprano, tenor, and baritone. Eighty-one pages of autograph survive, but the wind parts are incomplete.[10] The most interesting features of this fragment are the linking arioso passages (it was a grand opera, not a *Singspiel*), which have no exact equivalent elsewhere in Beethoven, the striking parallel with *Fidelio* in the progress from spiritual darkness and conspiracy to the light of joy and reconciliation,[11] and the fact that Beethoven used the material of the trio in the same key for the duet 'O namenlose Freude'.[12] Although the music is characteristic and mature in style, there are no grounds for lamenting the loss of a masterpiece. Beethoven could scarcely have transcended the slough of Schikaneder's later scenes.[13]

His contract was conveniently invalidated by the sale of the Theater an der Wien to Baron Braun on 14 February 1804. By this time he was fully committed to *Fidelio*; in March he was urging Sonnleithner to finish his task by the middle of April, so that 'the opera can be produced in June at latest.'[14] His letter to Rochlitz, already quoted, implies that he himself chose the subject, and this may well be true despite Georg Friedrich Treitschke's statement that the initiative came from Sonn-leithner.[15] Baron Braun gave Beethoven a new contract, allowing him to retain his rooms in the theatre, an event that Treitschke places at the end of 1804. This is probably an error, like his assertion that the libretto was chosen after the production of Paer's opera on the same subject (3 October 1804). It is not clear what caused the delay between the spring of 1804 and the summer of 1805, when the bulk of the work was done. The performance, planned for 15 October, was held up by the censorship, which demanded changes in the libretto (the backdating of the action to the sixteenth century dates from this time) and evoked from Sonnleithner a declaration that the empress 'found the original very beautiful and affirmed that no opera subject had ever given her so much pleasure'. The ban was soon lifted, but the delay was disastrous. On 13 November the French army occupied Vienna, which had been vacated by the nobility and most of Beethoven's friends. The opera was produced at the Theater an der Wien on 20 November before an audience full of French officers, and repeated to empty houses on the two following nights. The cast was:

[10] The score has been completed and edited by Hess (Wiesbaden, 1953; vocal score, Kassel, 1957). Gustav Nottebohm discussed the fragment in *Beethoveniana: Aufsätze und Mittheilungen* (Leipzig, 1872), henceforward cited as *NB*, 82–99, and the sketches, which are associated with those for the 'Eroica' Symphony and the opening scenes of the 1805 *Fidelio*, in P. Mies (ed.), *Zwei Skizzenbücher von Beethoven aus den Jahren 1801 bis 1803* (Leipzig, 1924), 56–7. See also Anderson, 'Beethoven's Operatic Plans', 63–6.

[11] Before the discovery of the complete libretto Nottebohm, followed by Ernest Newman in *More Opera Nights* (London, 1954), 254, and others, mistook the fragment for a final scene. They should have been alerted by the occurrence in the sketches, after the trio, of a vengeance aria for the slave, which Beethoven never completed.

[12] For parallel quotations, see below, p. 140. The second strain ('Mein Mann an meiner Brust') had been set to the words 'Gute Götter, blickt herab' in *Vestas Feuer*.

[13] *Vestas Feuer* was subsequently set by Weigl and produced at the Theater an der Wien on 10 Aug. 1805.

[14] *LA*, letter 88.

[15] Treitschke's personal knowledge was confined to the 1814 revival, and he is not always accurate about that.

Leonore	Anna Milder
Marzelline	Louise Müller
Florestan	Fritz Demmer
Pizarro	Sebastian Mayer
Jaquino	Caché
Rocco	Rothe
Don Fernando	Weinkopf

The conductor was Ignaz von Seyfried. Beethoven wished to call the opera *Leonore*, but since Paer had used this title and had close connections with the Kärntnertor Theatre the directors insisted on a change. It appeared on the bills as *Fidelio oder Die eheliche Liebe* and in the 1805 libretto simply as *Fidelio*.

The press was far from enthusiastic. The commonest complaint, not wholly without justification, was that the music, though beautiful in places, was 'ineffective and repetitious', especially in the treatment of words.[16] Beethoven's friends recognized this. In December, after he had withdrawn the opera, they organized a complete run-through with piano at Prince Lichnowsky's palace with the intention of persuading him to cut three numbers, the trio for Rocco, Marzelline, and Jaquino ('Ein Mann ist bald genommen'), the duet for Leonore and Marzelline ('Um in der Ehe'), and Pizarro's aria with chorus at the end of the original Act II. According to J. A. Röckel it took them six hours to overcome Beethoven's resistance. These pieces, though they disappeared later, were not cut in 1806. Instead, without consulting Sonnleithner, who was busy with *Faniska*, Beethoven brought in Stephan von Breuning to tighten up the libretto. When asking Sonnleithner's permission to print the result under his name (early March 1806) Beethoven added: 'To make the opera move more swiftly I have *shortened everything* as much as possible, the *prisoners'* chorus, and chiefly numbers of that kind.'[17] As will be seen, this was a misleading statement; the 1806 changes were by no means confined to cuts.

Beethoven made another attempt to restore his original title, and the new edition of the libretto appeared as *Leonore oder der Triumph der ehelichen Liebe*;[18] but the directors once more overruled him. The opera was revived on 29 March and repeated on 10 April with the original cast, except that Röckel replaced Demmer as Florestan. Although Beethoven was so late in finishing his score that only one orchestral rehearsal was possible—which no doubt explains his furious complaints in two letters to Mayer[19] that the chorus made dreadful mistakes and many of his dynamic marks were ignored—the reception was much more favourable than in 1805. There are two accounts of what followed. According to Breuning a cabal in the theatre prevented further performances; Röckel, who is more likely to be correct, said that Beethoven, fancying himself cheated of his share of the receipts, demanded his score back just when a lasting success seemed assured. In May there was talk of a private performance at Prince Lobkowitz's palace. It is not known if

---

[16] For quotations see *TF*, 387.   [17] *LA*, letter 128.

[18] The 1810 vocal score, arranged by Czerny, over which, of course, the theatre had no control, also bore the title *Leonore*. This was the 1806 version without the overture and the two finales. Three numbers had been published separately in 1807.

[19] *LA*, letters 129 and 130.

this took place; but plans to produce the opera in Berlin and later (1808) in Prague came to nothing.

Fidelio slumbered till the beginning of 1814, when Beethoven, to his evident surprise, learned that three singers[20] wished to revive it at the Kärntnertor for their benefit. He agreed on condition that he was permitted to make changes. This time the revision of the libretto was entrusted (with Sonnleithner's permission) to Treitschke, an experienced man of the theatre. Beethoven worked at the score from February until 15 May. He found it an arduous task: 'I could compose something new far more quickly than patch up the old . . . I have to think out the entire work again . . . this opera will win for me a martyr's crown' (to Treitschke, April).[21] The new overture was not ready in time for the first performance (23 May), when that to *Die Ruinen von Athen* was substituted. It made its début on the second night (26 May). The cast was:

Leonore	Anna Milder
	(Madame Hönig was the first choice)
Marzelline	Mlle Bondra
Florestan	Radichi
Pizarro	Johann Michael Vogl
	(replaced on 18 July by Anton Forti)
Jaquino	Frühwald
Rocco	Carl Friedrich Weinmüller
Don Fernando	Saal

The conductor was Michael Umlauf. The seventh performance on 18 July was for Beethoven's benefit; his advertisement stated that 'two new pieces have been added'.[22] From this revival, followed on 21 November by Weber's production in Prague, the success of the opera was assured.

GAVEAUX'S *LÉONORE*

J. N. Bouilly's libretto *Léonore ou L'amour conjugal*, set by Pierre Gaveaux and produced at the Théâtre Feydeau in Paris on 19 February 1798, was, like his *Les deux Journées* of two years later, based on a historical incident during the Reign of Terror.[23] Bouilly, serving in an official position at Tours, found himself in the role of Don Fernando; it is strange to reflect that the real-life Léonore and Florestan may have survived and even witnessed their translation to operatic fame. To prevent precise identification Bouilly moved the action to Spain, but acknowledged its authenticity by adding the words 'fait historique' to the title.[24]

The work is an *opéra comique* in two acts with thirteen musical numbers (apart

---

[20] The Pizarro, Rocco, and Don Fernando of the 1814 cast.   [21] *LA*, letter 479.

[22] See below, p. 153.

[23] Bouilly tells the story in his memoirs, *Mes Récapitulations* (Paris, 1836), ii. 81ff.

[24] This was common practice during the revolutionary period, when realism in all the arts was a matter of pride. The score has 'fait historique espagnol'.

from the overture) and much spoken dialogue. Roc, Marceline, and Jacquino talk
in dialect. The general outline of the plot remains unchanged in Bouilly's libretto
and Beethoven's three versions and is too familiar to need summarizing here; but
there are significant shifts of emphasis. While Bouilly's act-division corresponds to
that of the 1814 *Fidelio*, the course of events, the placing of the musical numbers,
and the dialogue are closer to 1805. Five of the seven numbers in Bouilly's first act
—Marceline's *couplets*, her duet with Jacquino, Roc's *chanson*, the duet for Marceline
and Léonore in which the former looks forward to the birth of their first child while
the latter dissembles, and the prisoners' chorus—were retained by Sonnleithner
with little change. The other two he combined in a single movement. Léonore has
two consecutive solos, a *romance* in which she is sustained by conjugal love and
addresses her lost husband, and an air apostrophizing hope; they are separated by
dialogue in which she learns from Roc of Pizare's orders that the prisoner is to be
killed for reasons of state and to preserve the honour of one of the noblest families
in Spain. Pizare has not revealed this to the audience; he whispers to Roc and briefs
him offstage. Léonore has an awkward moment after the duet with Marceline, who
has heard her talking in her sleep; she has to pretend she is looking for her lost father.
Although Marceline speaks of letting the prisoners out for their daily exercise, it is
Léonore who does this on Roc's orders, as a cover for their descent to dig the grave.
The prisoners' chorus contains a solo, but none of the named characters takes part
or is on the stage.

   Sonnleithner also kept the first four numbers in Bouilly's second act: a recitative
and *romance* for Florestan, the grave-digging duet for Léonore and Roc (during
which she resolves to rescue the prisoner whoever he may be), their trio with
Florestan, and the duet for husband and wife. There is no quartet in Gaveaux's
opera; the important action here, including the trumpet call, takes place in dialogue.
Pizare is heavily disguised and has to change into uniform to receive the Minister.
Roc, whose orders were to admit a masked man, is at first ignorant of his identity
as well as his motives. Léonore reveals herself before Pizare, who after unmasking
tosses Roc a second purse of gold. When Pizare's assault on Léonore has been
frustrated by her pistol and the trumpet call, Roc snatches the pistol and goes out
with Pizare, closing the door on the lovers. Léonore, her weapon gone, collapses
in despair. During the duet Florestan, still bemused, calls her, but cannot reach her
on account of his chains. She revives slowly, taking some time to grasp that he is
indeed her husband. The movement ends in mutual rapture. As Léonore explains
how she entered the prison an offstage chorus is heard demanding vengeance. This
is combined with a second duet in which the lovers, convinced that their last hour
has come, resolve to die together. The denouement reverts to dialogue. Roc after
exculpating himself restores the pistol to Léonore and throws both purses at Pizare's
feet: he is cured of his lust for gold. Dom Fernand recommends the women in the
audience to take Léonore as an example.

   Bouilly tells an intensely dramatic story in clear straightforward terms. The
compound of realism, low life, and earthy humour on the one hand (Roc is a
close-fisted French peasant with an eye to the main chance) and heroic endeavour.

a last-minute rescue, and an elevating moral on the other is typical of French opera in the revolutionary decade. So is the confined space and darkness of the setting. *Léonore* contains many premonitions of Romantic opera. It is as far as possible removed from the stagey conventions almost universal in contemporary German and Italian opera, whether serious or comic. Therein lay part of its appeal to Beethoven.

Gaveaux's *Léonore*, like many of the *opéras comiques* of Grétry and his school, is as much a play with songs as an opera. The fact that Pizare is a spoken part[25] is enough to prevent the drama permeating the score. Nevertheless the music, influenced as much by Cherubini as by Grétry, is not negligible. The introduction to Florestan's recitative and air in the dungeon has a feeling for atmosphere; the horns are directed to play the opening bars '*les Pavillons l'un contre l'autre*', a favourite device of Méhul though Gaveaux appears to have anticipated him here (Ex. 1).

Of particular interest are the strong indications that Beethoven knew Gaveaux's

Ex.1

score, which had been published in Paris.[26] Half a dozen movements seem to contain
the germs of ideas that Beethoven brought to full flower; this, not chance thematic
resemblance, is the significant debt that genius owes to the second-rate. Among such
passages are the headlong string scales in the coda of the overture, strikingly
prophetic of *Leonore* Nos. 2 and 3, though more symmetrical; the alternating minor
and major strains of Marceline's *couplets* (an interesting early experiment in local
colour marked '*Tempo di Minuetto Seguidilla*'); the cut of the melody of Roc's
chanson:

Ex.2

the use of a solo horn to introduce Léonore's *romance*; the combination of ostinato
and repeated chords in the accompaniment of the grave-digging duet; and most of
all the treatment of the prisoners' chorus. As in Beethoven, the slow-moving
harmony, long pedals and gradual climb in pitch and volume from an initial
pianissimo express the wonder of the prisoners as they creep out of their cells and
peer into the light (Ex. 3).

Ex.3

---

[26] Gaveaux's *Le petit Matelot*, a great success in Germany, had been produced at the Theater auf der
Wieden in 1801.

THE OPERAS OF PAER AND MAYR

Between the inception and the performance of *Fidelio* two other operas based on Bouilly's libretto, both in Italian, came to birth. The libretto of Paer's *Leonora ossia L'amore conjugale* (Dresden, 3 October 1804), by G. Schmidt, preserves much of the detail of the story at the expense of its spirit. The part of Marcellina is expanded, evidently for a favoured singer boasting a top D and E flat. She has two substantial arias in the first act as well as several ensembles; like Gaveaux, Paer seeks to establish the locality, setting her initial aria in bolero rhythm. Her ambitions are thrust inappropriately into the foreground not only in the first finale but in the dungeon scene, where she appears catastrophically (having stolen the key from Rocco) between Pizarro's exit and the reunion of the lovers. She brings news of the Minister's arrival and refuses to budge without specific and repeated assurances of Fedele's love. Leonora is forced to comply in an extended duet in the presence of her husband. He is the only prisoner; there is no chorus, and Pizarro (a tenor) has no solo, though he sings in ensembles. On the other hand, the librettist does attempt to construct viable musical numbers from Bouilly's dialogue. There is a *buffo*[27] trio for Marcellina, Giacchino, and Rocco (both basses) at the point corresponding to Beethoven's 'Ein Mann ist bald genommen', and another trio when Pizarro, watched by Leonora, orders Rocco to follow him to receive secret instructions. Paer has a quartet in the second act, beginning when Leonora reveals her identity, but not in the first.

His score is more ambitious than Gaveaux's, but has less character. The style might be described as sub-Mozart; the duet for Marcellina and Giacchino is heavily indebted to *Figaro*. The dramatic scenas for Leonora in Act I and Florestan in Act II are on an enormous scale, bigger indeed than those in Beethoven's opera. Each has several linked movements comprising recitative, cavatina, and cabaletta; Leonora's contains a motive used in the overture. The introduction to Florestan's, thirty-eight bars long, shows Paer at his least insipid (Ex. 4).

Richard Engländer in an emphatic article[28] has argued that Beethoven and Sonnleithner knew Paer's opera and that all three versions of *Fidelio* are considerably indebted to it. Beethoven certainly possessed a copy of the score, though there is nothing to indicate when he acquired it. Engländer conjectures that it was Paer, on a visit to Vienna early in 1803, who brought the subject to his attention, and claims his Dresden *Leonora* as a vital link between Gaveaux and *Fidelio*. It is true that Paer's and Beethoven's librettos share certain features not found in Bouilly, for example the trio for Marzelline, Jaquino, and Rocco near the beginning, Pizarro's angry return in the first finale, and the dungeon quartet; but these are predictable moves for any librettist anxious to strengthen the links between music and drama. The one unquestionable point of contact concerns the 1814 version of *Fidelio* and is mentioned below. Engländer's musical parallels are for the most part period clichés and quite unconvincing. An exception is the resemblance between the chorus 'Wer ein holdes Weib' (Ex. 5*b*) and a theme in Paer's finale (*a*).

[27] The opera belonged to the *semiseria* category, which sought to combine the old *seria* and *buffa* styles. It was an important stage in the development of Romantic opera.

[28] 'Paers "Leonora" und Beethovens "Fidelio"', *Neues Beethoven-Jahrbuch*, 4 (1930), 118.

Ex.4

Ex.5

(a)

Suon di gio - ia in si bel gior - no [etc.]

(b)

Wer ein hol - des Weib er - run- gen, stimm'in un - ser'n Ju - bel ein

This is certainly striking, and it is conceivable that some visitor from Dresden whistled—or bellowed—a little Paer outside Beethoven's window.[29] On the other hand, the sketchbook shows him hammering out his melody by the usual laborious process,[30] and the date '2 June' among the sketches for this finale probably refers to 1804 (before the production of Paer's opera) rather than 1805.[31] Paer's *Leonora* did not reach Vienna until March 1806, when it was given privately at the Lobkowitz palace. Beethoven attended its first public performance (in German) on 8 February 1809.

Simone Mayr's *L'amor conjugale*, a one-act *farsa sentimentale* (a cross between Italian *farsa* and French *opéra comique* with the *buffo* element played down), saw the light at Padua in July 1805.[32] The librettist, Gaetano Rossi, transferred the action to Poland, doubtless under the influence of *Lodoïska*, which Mayr had already set twice in Italian. His text reduces the realism and potency of Bouilly's plot to a caper with the conventions. The political content vanishes: Pizarro's motive is love for Leonora, who is rescued by the fortuitous arrival of her brother-in-law.[33] Jaquino does not appear, nor do the prisoners; Rocco patronizes the bottle (Mayr, unlike Paer, keeps the gold aria). In place of the grave-digging duet Leonora sings a strophic romance in popular French style, hoping that Florestan will recognize her voice. Unlike Gaveaux and Paer, Mayr binds together the closing scenes in continuous music, beginning with a quartet when Rocco signals to Pizarro that the grave is ready. The climax of this is delayed by a slow cantabile in E flat, typical of Mayr and his Italian successors, including Rossini, after which the pistol and the trumpet signal restore the tempo. The finale contains an angry aria for Pizarro, very like Dourlinski's in Act III of Cherubini's *Lodoïska*, which gives it a collateral relationship with Beethoven (Ex. 6). Mayr's style is not unlike Paer's; he, too, concentrates on big dramatic monologues for Leonora and Florestan. Again the introduction to the latter is as memorable as anything in the score (Ex. 7). When Florestan begins to think of his wife, two cors anglais (a favourite instrument) introduce a melody that oddly anticipates the main theme of Beethoven's 1814 overture. As usual Mayr is most individual in his treatment of the orchestra, especially the solo wind instruments. His function in the history of music was to

[29] Mosco Carner, 'Fidelio', in *Major and Minor* (London, 1980), 186–252, also believed that Beethoven used Paer's opera as a model, but curiously does not mention this parallel.

[30] Not until the last of the seven incipits quoted by Nottebohm does it begin to resemble either its eventual form or Paer's.

[31] This was Nottebohm's opinion; Douglas Johnson, Alan Tyson, and Robert Winter, *The Beethoven Sketchbooks* (Berkeley and Los Angeles, 1985), 150, opt for 1805.

[32] See L. Schiedermair, *Beiträge zur Geschichte der Oper* (Leipzig, 1907), ii. 39–50.

[33] In this summary I have retained the familiar names of the characters rather than confuse the reader with their Polish equivalents.

Ex.6

Ex.7

provide a bridge between Mozart on the one hand and Rossini and Donizetti on the other. No one has suggested that Beethoven knew his opera.[34]

THE 1805 VERSION OF BEETHOVEN'S OPERA

Beethoven's opera is by far the closest to the letter and the spirit of Bouilly. Sonnleithner's libretto is largely a translation with additional musical numbers. He divided Bouilly's first act into two, with no change of scene until the second finale,

---

[34] By a curious coincidence Mayr was invited to set a German libretto by Schikaneder in April 1803, just when Beethoven was about to take up *Vestas Feuer*. See the interesting letter from Hubert Rumpf to Mayr (Schiedermair, *Geschichte der Oper*, ii. 191) informing him, among other Viennese theatre gossip, that Schikaneder is working on an opera 'mit, und für Pethoven' (*sic*).

which he moved from the prison courtyard to another part of the fortress. Act I
has three inserted numbers, a trio ('Ein Mann ist bald genommen') in which Rocco
and Marzelline dash Jaquino's hopes of marriage, the canon quartet, and the trio for
Rocco, Leonore, and Marzelline (No. 5 of the 1814 score), after which the curtain
falls. The first three numbers in Act II, the March, Pizarro's aria with chorus, and
his duet with Rocco, are new. Pizarro posts the trumpeter before his aria and briefs
Rocco on stage in the duet, but is not overheard by Leonore. Sonnleithner retains
the long scene for Leonore and Marzelline, including the duet (without the passage,
redolent of Papageno and Papagena, in which they speculate whether their child's
first words will be 'Maman' or 'Papa') and the dialogue about Leonore talking in
her sleep. The recitative before Leonore's aria ('O brich noch nicht, du mattes
Herz!') is translated from Bouilly and very different from 1814; the apostrophe to
hope is not in the 1805 libretto, but was probably inserted before performance. The
scene changes at the end of the aria, and the finale follows at once. Marzelline lets
the prisoners out in the ordinary course of her duties. Sonnleithner extended their
chorus into a substantial finale. Rocco orders them back to the cells before telling
Leonore the outcome of his interview with Pizarro. The Governor's wrath,
warning of which is brought by Marzelline alone, is provoked not by the release
of the prisoners but by Rocco's delay in digging the grave. He hustles the jailer and
his assistants out and ends the act with a second aria, supported by male chorus, that
involves much sabre-rattling, but does not advance the plot.

Act III follows the model closely, apart from the insertion of the quartet and the
connection of Bouilly's last two numbers with the intervening dialogue in a
continuous movement. The final section of Florestan's aria, as in Bouilly, is
addressed to Leonore's portrait. Pizarro enters masked and disguised, but he reveals
himself before Leonore and does not offer Rocco a second purse. The dialogue
linking the quartet to the lovers' duet becomes a recitative. In the finale the chorus
denounce Pizarro's sentence as too lenient, and Don Fernando decides to leave the
decision to the king (was this one of the changes demanded by the censorship?).
Pizarro is silent throughout. Leonore does not mention Marzelline's dowry, and
there is no homily to the audience from Fernando or anyone else. These two details
are essentially French, the former of all time, the latter characteristic of the
Revolution period (compare Bouilly's ethical conclusion to *Les deux Journées*: 'Le
premier charme de la vie, C'est de servir l'humanité'). Perhaps in compensation
Sonnleithner (or Beethoven) introduced a slightly modified quotation from
Schiller's *Ode to Joy* in the couplet beginning 'Wer ein holdes Weib errungen',
thereby linking the opera with the finale of the Ninth Symphony. Both works carry
the same message; it is even possible that the one put the other into Beethoven's
head.

Sonnleithner's chief aim was to increase the opportunities for expressing drama
by musical means. In this he is often successful, especially in the two quartets and
the development of Pizarro's part. The finales of the second and third acts, though
not wholly satisfactory, are moves in the right direction. What is effective in Bouilly
he preserves. The obvious flaw is the enormous expansion of the first and less

dramatic half of the story. The exposition of the Marzelline subplot, leisurely in Bouilly, is further retarded by the new musical numbers. The first act merely outlines a situation; the action has yet to begin. Of the three central characters, Leonore does not appear until half-way through Act I, Pizarro until Act II, Florestan until Act III. Up to Pizarro's first exit Sonnleithner has deployed nine musical numbers (excluding the overture), several of them developed at considerable length by Beethoven, against Bouilly's three. After this the drama sags again in the superfluous scene for Leonore and Marzelline; nor does the second finale draw all the threads together. The lightweight opening in the jailer's household, whose function is to set the scene, has usurped the prominence of the main plot. When the last act begins it is too late to redress the balance.

This defect is accentuated by Beethoven's music.[35] Though never dull, its regular periods are geared to abstract musical design rather than dramatic pace; consequently it lags behind the action and seems on occasion diffuse and repetitive. This must be ascribed to lack of practical experience in the theatre. The movements are all longer—some of them much longer—than in the 1814 score,[36] and there are more of them. The trio 'Ein Mann ist bald genommen' in Act I and the duet 'Um in der Ehe' in Act II are dramatically otiose, especially the latter, which enlarges on a false situation of which we have already had more than enough and disperses the tension when it has at last begun to accumulate. The old-fashioned concertante layout with solo violin and cello, for all its charm, belongs to a more leisurely type of pre-Revolution rescue opera, that of Mozart's *Die Entführung*. In recommending the omission of these two numbers and Pizarro's second aria, the weakest music in the score, Beethoven's friends showed sound judgment, as he tacitly acknowledged when he followed their advice in 1814. The musical idiom, especially in the early

---

[35] The 1805 version, reconstructed after great labour from scattered manuscripts, many of which had been used by Beethoven for his revisions, was edited by Erich Prieger under the title *Leonore* (full score, six copies only without critical apparatus, Leipzig, 1908–10; vocal score 1905, 2nd edn., 1907; neither score contains the spoken dialogue). This material was used for the Berlin revival under Richard Strauss on 20 Nov. 1905, the centenary of the first performance. In 1967 Willy Hess brought out a new full score in two supplementary volumes (XI and XII) to the complete Beethoven edition, with a scholarly critical commentary that identifies all the sources. The basis of this score is a reproduction of Prieger's; although many corrections have been made to the text, others could not be incorporated and must be supplied from the notes. Hess's preface promises a later supplement containing the 1806 version, which has never been published in full, although as early as 1853 Otto Jahn attempted a vocal score (published by Breitkopf & Härtel), indicating the 1805 text where it differed. This was a fine achievement for its date, but later scholarship has modified some of Jahn's conclusions. Certain details remain in doubt; it is not always possible to distinguish Beethoven's changes before the first performance from those for the 1806 revival. Other disputable points are mentioned below. The best account of the various versions is Hess's *Beethovens Oper Fidelio und ihre drei Fassungen* (Zürich, 1953), which includes a line-by-line comparison of the 1805 and 1806 librettos. Adolf Sandberger, in *Ausgewählte Aufsätze zur Musikgeschichte*, ii (Munich, 1924), reprinted the Bouilly and Sonnleithner librettos and compared them in detail with Treitschke, but ignored 1806 and consequently attributed some of Breuning's work and even Sonnleithner's to Treitschke. The most reliable account in English is in Mosco Carner's 1980 study, cited above (n. 29). Ernest Newman's in *More Opera Nights*, 253ff., is misleading in several important particulars.

[36] With the single exception of the March, which (apart from a different treatment of repeats in 1814) remained unchanged throughout. Treitschke's statement that it was composed in 1814 is wrong.

scenes, is much more Mozartian in 1805 than in 1814. The 1805 overture, *Leonore* No. 2, might be criticized for its lopsided construction, especially when compared with its successor; but Beethoven's intention seems to have been to supply a graphic summary of the action rather than a formal overture. The result is a piece of programme music that ranks as a mighty forerunner of the symphonic poems of Liszt and Strauss.[37]

The original third act is a different matter. Although this, too, contains passages, especially in the finale, where the music clogs the wheels of the drama, it is less a primitive attempt at what Beethoven achieved in 1814 than a volley at a different target. This change of aim is discussed below. Meanwhile the music that did not survive 1805–6 demands comment. The *Andante un poco agitato* F minor conclusion to Florestan's aria, though it lacks the radiance of his F major vision in 1814, has a defiant stoicism that is not only most movingly expressed but enlarges our view of Florestan's character. Anyone can see his beloved in a trance; it takes a hero to look back on his past happiness and accept his fate. There is some doubt whether the *Melodram* before the grave-digging duet formed part of the 1805 score. Prieger and Hess include it; Jahn ascribes it to 1814. Certainly its surviving form cannot belong to 1805, for it quotes the F major (1814) section of Florestan's aria when he stirs in his sleep. Yet there are sketches dating from 1804 as well as 1814. The most likely solution is that it was performed in 1805 in a version since lost, and rewritten in 1814. The sketches prove that the allusions to the 6/8 section of the Leonore–Rocco duet in the previous finale ('Wir müssen gleich zum Werke schreiten') were part of Beethoven's original plan.

From the end of the quartet onwards the 1805 score (following Bouilly) has a dramatic tension and a vividness of characterization, both fully realized in musical terms, that are almost entirely absent from 1814. When Pizarro goes out, in response to the more florid trumpet call of the No. 2 overture, Leonore throws herself at Rocco's feet with a spoken appeal against the closing bars of the orchestral ritornello. Rocco snatches the pistol from her and disappears; the quartet ends with a fortissimo diminished seventh as she utters a piercing cry and falls senseless. The long recitative in which Florestan tries to reach her, she slowly recovers, and each at last grasps the truth is a superb stroke of musical drama. Based on a beautiful melody for solo oboe:

Ex.8

[37] Beethoven subsequently shortened it, but apparently not till 1814; see A. Tyson, 'Yet Another "Leonore" Overture?', *Music & Letters* 58 (1977), 192–203. For a full account of the overtures see J. Braunstein, *Beethovens Leonore-Ouvertüren* (Leipzig, 1927).

it builds up gradually over seventy-six bars to the passionate discharge of the duet
'O namenlose Freude'. The music has a quality of dawning suspense paralleled only
by that which introduces the finale of the Fifth Symphony. It launches the duet with
a tremendous impact, reinforced by the fact that both voices enter together and the
melody is carried up to the top B. This may be instrumental vocal writing (the
words are a much poorer fit than in *Vestas Feuer*), but it releases the full emotional
content of the situation. Of Beethoven's three versions of this melody the second
is by far the most exciting in its context because it has been so thoroughly prepared
(see Ex. 9).

Ex.9

Moreover the whole ambience of the duet is transformed by the fact that the lovers have no reason to believe themselves out of danger. They have lost their only weapon and naturally take the distant cries of vengeance, supported by trombones behind the scenes, as directed against them. These and the incursion of the whole tumultuous crowd into the dungeon produce another splendid theatrical climax, which may well have reminded early audiences of the storming of the Bastille. The finale contains some rather commonplace rejoicing, though Fernando's solos have a Sarastro-like nobility, and is undeniably static. The F major Andante assai, twice as long as in 1814, is a tribute to the continuity of Beethoven's development: its principal theme comes from the *Cantata on the death of the Emperor Joseph II*, composed in Bonn as early as 1790.[38] The original words are significant, and may have suggested the borrowing; but the simple dance-like accompaniment shows no sign of the later polyphonic resource (Ex. 10).

This is perhaps the point to mention the sketches and a number of drafts rejected before the first performance. The former have been studied by Nottebohm[39] and more briefly by Jahn.[40] Beethoven sketched the movements for the most part in the order in which they occur in the opera. As usual this was a prolonged labour. The first ideas are often primitive and feeble, with little or no relation to the ultimate form—for example in the prisoners' chorus and Pizarro's entrance music in the Act II finale, which suggests an elderly *buffo* rather than a tyrant. The Act I quartet was

Ex.10

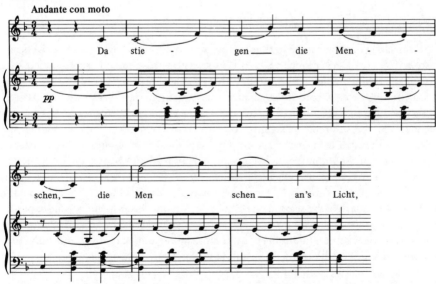

[38] Beethoven also drew on this for the first four bars of the ritornello before Florestan's monologue.

[39] Cf. *Zwei Skizzenbücher von Beethoven aus den Jahren 1801 bis 1803,* and 'Ein Skizzenbuch aus dem Jahre 1804', in *Zweite Beethoveniana: nachgelassene Aufsätze* (Leipzig, 1887), henceforward cited as *NZB*, 409.

[40] *Gesammelte Aufsätze über Musik* (Leipzig, 1867), 236 ff.

planned from the start as a canon, but it took Beethoven at least thirteen shots to evolve the melody. He drafted Florestan's aria in three sections, the second of which, Moderato in F minor with flute obbligato, was suppressed. Röckel's story that the aria originally consisted of the Adagio only, with a sustained top F for the tenor at the end, may be explained by the existence of two sketches of the Adagio running straight into the *Melodram*; but this seems to have been an abandoned later project. It is, however, possible that an early version of the aria has disappeared. The 1806 libretto has eight additional lines (of which no setting is known) after the Adagio, and no complete manuscript of the 1805 version survives.[41]

The sketches for the grave-digging duet are of particular interest; only after prolonged wrestling did Beethoven find a satisfactory accompaniment figure and a verbal declamation that distinguished the two characters. Two rejected accompaniment figures are shown in Exx. 11*a* and *b*. One sketch exhibits an almost

Ex.11

Straussian realism in tone-painting as Rocco and Leonore struggle to raise the heavy stone (Ex. 12). The minims followed by rests towards the end are explained by a stage direction in the libretto 'They draw breath' and the word 'Athemholen', which Beethoven wrote twice against the corresponding bars in another sketch. This passage is different in all three performing versions. Beethoven seems to have conceived the straining bass figure of Ex. 12 in connection with Leonore's and Rocco's attempts to move the stone. By 1805, however, he must have associated it (in place of the minims and rests) with their breathlessness after the event, for he reserved it for the pause when the voices are silent; but there is no check in the movement (Ex. 13). In 1806 he cut the voices short and added a fermata (Ex. 14). In 1814 he inserted the semiquaver figure for double bassoon and string basses (at the moment when the stone is moved) and emphasized the effort involved with two fermatas, one before (underlined by a sforzando) and one after, and only then admitted the 'breathless' figure in the bass (Ex. 15).

The fact that the sketches for Leonore's recitative and aria occur out of sequence after the Act III finale led Nottebohm to conjecture that a different aria in F was sung in 1805. This receives superficial support from the 1805 libretto, which gives two eight-line stanzas without a recitative and without the 'Komm, Hoffnung'

---

[41] See the preface and critical commentary of Hess's full score.

Ex.12

[Rocco] [Leonore] [Rocco]

Ein we-nig noch! Ge-duld! Er

[Leonore] [Rocco] [Leonore]

weicht! Nur et-was doch! Es ist nicht leicht! Es ist nicht leicht!

Ex.13

Leonore

Nur et-was noch, nur et-was noch!

Rocco

leicht! Et ist nicht leicht!

pp

Ex.14

Ex.15

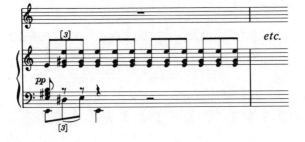

quatrain. But it seems more likely that the text was changed at a late stage in 1805 after the libretto had been printed.

There has been some debate about the date of the *Leonore* No. 1 overture, whose one point in common with its fellows is the quotation from the Adagio of Florestan's aria. Schindler's statement that it was tried out privately at Prince Lichnowsky's in 1805 and found too slight is no longer acceptable. Recent work on the sketch books points to September 1807 as the probable date.[42] This would seem to support Seyfried's statement that Beethoven composed it for a Prague production that never took place.

There are three early versions of Marzelline's aria, all related in material; probably the third was sung in 1805.[43] The first, in C major throughout, is somewhat ornate and does not convey the undercurrent of anxiety in Marzelline's mind. The second and third both adopt the C minor–major alternation with coda. The second, with a plaintive seven-bar initial ritornello, borrows the theme of the first for its sections in the major and shortens it; the third restores its full length, but reduces the ritornello to two bars. In the appendix to the complete-edition score Hess prints an earlier, slightly longer and differently scored version of the grave-digging duet with no major variants, an abandoned opening of Leonore's recitative and aria, which argues against Nottebohm's conjecture of a previous setting in F, and the rejected orchestral coda to the trio 'Euch werde Lohn'. Jahn attributed this last change to 1806.

THE 1806 VERSION[44]

The changes made in 1806 are generally dismissed as hasty cuts to serve a temporary emergency. This does less than justice to Beethoven and Breuning. Although some of the excisions are crude and were later restored, it is clear that the authors had a shrewd idea what was the matter with the opera. They reduced it to two acts by combining the original Acts I and II, but made a change of scene at the old act-break. They altered the order of movements and events in the new first act. Rocco's aria was omitted, but not before Breuning had supplied it with new words;[45] when it was eventually restored, the text was a fusion of these and Sonnleithner's. Pizarro now posts the trumpeter *after* his aria (a good touch). Leonore enters in great agitation immediately after the Rocco–Pizarro duet; she has observed their conference, but is uncertain whether Rocco has obtained permission

[42] See Johnson *et al.*, *Beethoven Sketchbooks*, 160–4.

[43] Jahn printed all three in vocal score in his edition referred to in n. 35 above; the full scores of the first two are in the second supplement to the complete Beethoven edition. Including the shortened form sung in 1814 and a further truncation without coda (see Hess, *Beethovens Oper Fidelio*, 254), there are altogether five versions of this aria.

[44] A report in *Opera* 28 (1977), 1134, stated that a hitherto unknown score of this version, with notes, corrections, and deletions by the composer, had been discovered by Oldrich Pilkert in the archives of the National Theatre, Prague. According to another account it was used as a conducting score by Weber and Smetana and carried their annotations as well as Beethoven's.

[45] Jahn prints both sets with the 1805 music.

for her to enter the dungeon. Her recitative and aria (No. 11 in 1805) follow; then the scene with Marzelline, including the duet 'Um in der Ehe' (No. 10), *preceded* by the conversation about Leonore talking in her sleep. Jaquino overhears the end of the duet. Leonore, seeking a pretext to escape, asks if it is not time to let the prisoners out for their exercise and hurries off. Jaquino flies into a jealous rage, leading to the trio with Rocco 'Ein Mann ist bald genommen' (No. 3), which like the other trio (No. 6) is followed by a change of scene. Leonore enters with keys, delighted to release the prisoners and wishing she could do the same for Florestan. But Rocco does not send the prisoners back to the cells after their chorus; they go into the garden, as in 1814, and we do not witness their return. It will be seen that several improvements usually attributed to Treitschke date from 1806.[46] Breuning also clarified a number of points in the dialogue and stage directions.

In Act II he added the direction about shifting the stone during the duet and made the words of the trio 'Euch werde Lohn' more graphic. Leonore's reference to her beating heart and Florestan's observation that the boy as well as the man seems moved are new. In the quartet Pizarro opens his cloak instead of taking off his mask. Leonore's first half-conscious words in the recitative before 'O namenlose Freude' were changed from 'Gebt ihm mir!' to 'Todt! Dahin!' There were several amendments to the finale. Just after Don Fernando raises Leonore to her feet Jaquino has a brief exchange with Marzelline. His hopes revive on the instant, and she encourages him too readily with a reference to the trio in which she refused him in Act I. This cannot be called good psychology, and it disappeared in 1814 in favour of Marzelline's single cry of distress. The long section in which Don Fernando pronounces sentence on Pizarro, Leonore and Florestan appeal for mercy, the chorus demand greater severity, and Don Fernando decides to refer the matter to the king, was replaced by a short recitative: Fernando disposes of Pizarro with a terse 'Hinweg mit diesem Bösewicht!'[47] Breuning had to supply Leonore with a new quatrain in the closing ensemble. In 1805 she was mute for the last 132 bars of the opera. Beethoven carved a top line for her out of the choral soprano part and rewrote Florestan's music here in more florid form.

Rocco's aria and the *Melodram* were the only movements to disappear entirely. But most of the others were shortened, some of them drastically.[48] Both trios in Act I suffered something approaching mutilation, and so did the opening of Florestan's scena: the recitative was rewritten, by no means for the better, and the Adagio

---

[46] The confusion is partly due to the fact that Jahn, when he prepared his score, had not seen the 1806 libretto and was unaware of the changed order of movements. Elliot Forbes falls into the same trap in *TF*: see his footnotes to p. 572. Georg Kinsky (ed. Hans Halm), *Das Werk Beethovens: thematisch-bibliographisches Verzeichnis* (Munich and Duisburg, 1955) is also wrong about the 1806 order.

[47] A mysterious (and superior) second setting of this and the three following lines was copied in a score of the 1814 version prepared for Dresden in 1823 (see Hans Volkmann, *Beethoven in seinen Beziehungen zu Dresden* (Dresden, 1942), 106). The lines belong only to 1806; but they were in the original 1814 libretto from which Beethoven worked, and he may have set them again in that year.

[48] The exceptions appear to have been Marzelline's aria, both quartets, the March, and the Pizarro-Rocco duet. Some of these were changed in detail.

deprived of its ritornello.[48] Leonore's aria lost fourteen bars in the coda, including an elaborate and taxing cadenza. An interesting change here was the insertion of the words 'O Hoffnung, O komm', marked *sprechend oder singend*, against the ritornello of the Adagio. The orchestral introduciton to the grave-digging duet was shortened by seventeen bars, but the double bassoon was added to the score.[50] Beethoven rewrote the trio 'Euch werde Lohn' in much terser form, modifying the anacrusis of the main theme, removing a long roulade for Florestan on the word 'Dank!' (bar 94 of the 1814 score), and transplanting the next section, where all three voices sing together just before the change of tempo, back into the middle of Florestan's first solo, where it replaced the earlier statement of the same material. This destroyed the balance of the movement at both points; Beethoven rectified it in 1814. He severely compressed 'O namenlose Freude' and its recitative, reducing a total of 291 bars to 185, but lengthened and improved the orchestral coda, which reached its 1814 form in 1806. Leonore's part in the duet was eased by the removal of two slow chromatic-scale passages climbing to top C, possibly at the request of Milder. Both finales were considerably shortened, the first by 122 bars, the second by 154. This affected all their principal movements. The prisoners' chorus was pruned of much repetition. In the second finale the offstage chorus lost its trombones[51] and the F major section its long opening quintet for the soloists. A more positive change was the substitution of the No. 3 overture for No. 2 and the consequent simplification of the trumpet calls in the quartet. Tempo alterations suggest that several movements were taken too slowly in 1805. The prisoners' chorus was marked up from Allegretto to Allegretto con moto, Pizarro's second aria from Allegro ma non troppo to Allegro con brio, the trio 'Euch werde Lohn' from Andante con moto (leading to Più mosso) to Allegro (leading to Un poco più allegro), the dungeon quartet from Allegro to Allegro con brio, the opening of 'Wer ein holdes Weib' from Maestoso to Maestoso vivace.

While the effect of these alterations must have been beneficial in speeding up the action, they did not go to the root of the problem, the undue prominence of Marzelline, and some of them were ill-judged. It is not surprising that Beethoven returned to the attack eight years later.

THE 1814 VERSION

Treitschke's statement that he rewrote the dialogue 'almost wholly anew, succinct and clear as possible' is disingenuous; he preserved a great deal of both Sonnleithner

---

[49] Jahn did not print the 1805 version. Hess restored the recitative and ritornello from fragmentary sources, but the 1805 Adagio, if it differed from that of 1806 (as is very likely), is lost. Hess's score diverges from Prieger's more sharply here than elsewhere because Prieger backdated to 1805 alterations made in 1814.

[50] The double bassoon in Hess's 1805 score, like the direction for scaling down the dynamics of the whole duet (also added in 1806), is an uncancelled relic of Prieger's.

[51] So did Pizarro's 'Ha! welch ein Augenblick!'—but it appears to have gained a second pair of horns, which were removed in 1814.

and Breuning, though he made cuts and a few small insertions. His changes were, however, radical in several important respects. He tackled Marzelline firmly, omitting the trio and duet shifted in 1806 and the conversation about Leonore talking in her sleep. He transposed the order of the first two numbers, obtaining a more effective launch into the drama. He abolished both changes of scene in this act. Leonore now overhears Pizarro's duet with Rocco and reacts to it in the new recitative 'Abscheulicher!' This is the one episode in *Fidelio* that undoubtedly echoes Paer's libretto, where the corresponding scene begins (in the German translation): 'Abscheulicher Pizarro! Wo gehest du hin? Was denkst du? Was hast du vor?' and the aria contains the line 'Des Meers empörte Wogen'.[52] It is at Leonore's special request that Rocco lets out the prisoners. Treitschke worked much more action into the finale. At the bass prisoner's solo 'Sprecht leise' a sentry appears on the wall and goes off to inform Pizarro. Jaquino as well as Marzelline brings warning of the Governor's wrath, which is more formidable because more strongly motivated than in 1805. Rocco takes a less abject stand. His excuses include the subtle one that since Pizarro's particular prisoner is to die the others can surely be allowed to enjoy the sunshine and celebrate the king's name-day. He has, however, to recall them from the garden and lock them up. This makes room for their second chorus and the ensemble based on it.

There are few changes in the first half of Act II, except that Florestan, instead of addressing Leonore's portrait, has a delirious vision of her as an angel summoning him to freedom in heaven. (Treitschke left a vivid account of Beethoven improvising the music of the new F major section as soon as he received the words; nevertheless it appears in its proper place among the sketches.) The quartet is interrupted after the second trumpet call by the arrival of Jaquino and soldiers, to the unconcealed delight of Rocco. This effectively circumscribes Pizarro's movements, but destroys the effect of Beethoven's modulation. At Pizarro's exit Rocco, instead of disarming Leonore, seizes her hand and Florestan's, presses them to his breast, and points to heaven before hurrying out. In the dialogue that replaces the recitative Leonore assures Florestan that all their troubles are over. Rocco returns after the duet and informs them, in dialogue, that Florestan's name is not on the official list of prisoners; his detention was therefore illegal. The scene changes to the parade-ground, where the chorus, including the prisoners, acclaim the long-awaited day of justice. Don Fernando brings from the king a pardon for all the prisoners and makes a political speech: tyranny is at an end, let brother seek the hand of brother. He is astonished when Rocco produces Florestan and Leonore (Rocco does not throw down the purse, and he tells Don Fernando a good deal that we already know). Pizarro asks permission to speak, but is refused and led off *before* the removal of Florestan's fetters.

Treitschke's treatment of Act I merits unstinted applause. The drama begins to move earlier, gathers momentum from Pizarro's first appearance, and retains a

[52] This may explain Beethoven's reference to the libretto of *Fidelio* as 'a French and Italian book' in conversation with Benedict in 1823.

tightening grip until the end. The changes in Act II produce exactly the opposite effect. Rocco's character is sentimentalized. The lovers' secure confidence saps the excitement of the duet, which in the absence of the recitative makes a standing instead of a flying start. The spoken conclusion (generally omitted today) is feeble in the extreme. The change of scene, which Treitschke regarded as the healing of 'a great fault' in Sonnleithner's libretto, fails to achieve one of the most resounding anticlimaxes in the history of opera only because Beethoven capped it with a hymn to freedom of surpassing nobility.

We must, however, recognize that this was the result of deliberate choice. Sonnleithner, like Bouilly, concentrates on the personal drama of Leonore and Florestan; the other prisoners are little more than a background. The moral is not emphasized, but allowed to emerge through the action. Treitschke and Beethoven raise it from the particular to the universal and ram it home so hard that the hollow reverberations of a thumped tub are all but discernible. (In a letter of April 1814, already cited, Beethoven told Treitschke that he was setting the text 'exactly in the way you have altered and improved everything, an achievement which every moment I am recognizing more and more',[53] but it must be assumed that they had already agreed on the main trend.) The prisoners, no longer restricted to a single chorus, play a much larger part and obviously symbolize for Beethoven the whole of suffering mankind. The finale with its general amnesty becomes a pattern of the day of judgment. Moreover the change of scene gives the opera a neatly symmetrical plan: Act I moves from light into darkness, Act II from darkness into light. But although this idealized content finds ample utterance in the music, it does not spring convincingly from the plot; the symbolism is stretched beyond its implications. We have little reason to suppose that all the prisoners had been unjustly incarcerated, or that their crime was political (though Pizarro's anonymous letter does hint that Florestan may not be the only innocent victim); they could be a set of thieves, murderers, and delinquents. In delivering this mighty paean Beethoven comes closer still to the spirit of the Ninth Symphony,[54] but he drains his characters of individuality and smudges the portrait of the hero and heroine so movingly drawn in 1805. They become personifications, and since Pizarro alone stands for evil the mottled personality of Rocco must be whitewashed into benevolent conformity.

The musical changes in 1814 nearly all bear witness to richer maturity. The splendid new E major overture supplies a more fitting introduction to the light tone of the first scene than *Leonore* No. 3, whose massive stature throws much that follows into shadow. The key may have been chosen to pick out the E major of Leonore's aria. The 1805–6 versions have a clear C major home tonic; the first and last vocal movements each move from C minor to C major, and the words of Marzelline's aria, 'O wär' ich schon mit dir vereint', announce at the outset one of

---

[53] *LA*, letter 479. This was not always his opinion. On 19 Apr. 1817 he wrote to Charles Neate that 'the book and the text left much to be desired': cf. *LA*, letter 778.

[54] The words, too, take a step nearer, especially in the two lines repeated by Don Fernando: 'Es sucht der Bruder seine Brüder, Und kann er helfen hilft er gern' ('Brother seeks out his brothers and gladly helps whom he can').

the central ideas of the story. The rearranged order and the new overture indicate a different tonal plan. Beethoven made further changes in all the numbers he retained. Many of them are small cuts, involving the elision of idle bars and florid ornamental passages, especially at cadences. Their cumulative effect is considerable, and reflects a powerful urge, typical of late Beethoven, to break down exact symmetry of phrase; at the same time they accommodate the expression and declamation of the music more strictly to the ebb and flow of the drama. Hess, though full of complaints that Beethoven destroyed the perfection of his 1805 design, rightly points out that in such movements as the duet in which Pizarro and Rocco plan the murder he took a substantial stride towards the flexible methods of Wagner. There are numerous improvements in detail. These, like the sketches,[55] throw much fascinating light on Beethoven's creative processes; only a few can be mentioned here. It is clear that he did indeed rethink the whole score from the beginning. While he accepted most of the 1806 cuts, in three movements, the two surviving trios and the recitative and ritornello of Florestan's aria, he made a partial return to the longer text of 1805, though not in identical form.

The canon quartet, slightly modified, lost a single bar. Pizarro's aria was improved by the insertion of sixteen bars with a bold new modulation and a new rhythm at the first entry of the chorus. Leonore's aria, apart from its more striking recitative, emerged in much terser and more concentrated form. The ritornello was shortened, the voice part simplified and pruned of adornments, the first twenty-two bars of the Allegro con brio with an arresting passage for horns cut altogether, thereby altering the whole balance of the aria, and the Più lento mark added at the words 'in Fesseln schlug'. Milder told Schindler that she had severe struggles with Beethoven over 'the unbeautiful, unsingable passages, unsuited to her voice' in the Adagio and finally refused to sing it in the old form. This did the trick. A comparison of the final bars indicates what she achieved (Ex. 16).

Ex.16

(a) 1805

(b) 1814

---

[55] Sketches survive for all the new music of the 1814 score except the fifty bars before the second prisoners' chorus. They are discussed in *NZB*, 293–306. At one time Beethoven thought of using the trumpet call in the new overture.

Beethoven made an interesting change—or rather two successive changes—to the tenor prisoner's solo in the chorus 'O welche Lust'. In 1805 he set the third and fourth lines as shown in Ex. 17. The pause of nearly two bars, punctuated by shy staccato arpeggios on the woodwind, gives a touching emphasis to the words 'wir werden frei', as if the singer scarcely dare utter them. In shortening the whole passage for 1806 Beethoven reduced this to a momentary hesitation, emphasizing 'frei' with a sforzando (Ex. 18). In 1814, though the accompaniment is virtually unchanged, he modified the declamation and dynamics (Ex. 19). 'Frei' carries more weight, but the pause has gone, and it is impossible not to feel that something has been lost. The later part of the finale from shortly after Pizarro's return, including the exquisite chorus 'Leb' wohl, du warmes Sonnenlicht', is all new. The formal and the tonal balance are strengthened: the 1814 finale, though it makes an impression of greater spaciousness and mass, is the shortest of the three.

Ex.17

Ex.18

Florestan's aria has many differences in addition to the restoration of the ritornello and the new F major conclusion. The introduction and recitative were refashioned for the second time, and the Adagio extended. The only musical alteration to the grave-digging duet (the words were touched up towards the end) was the new semiquaver bass figure for the shifting of the stone (Ex. 15). Beethoven again rewrote the trio 'Euch werde Lohn', bringing it much closer to 1805 than to 1806. There were many changes to the vocal lines of the quartet, especially in Pizarro's part, and to the scoring of the last section. Leonore's top note at 'Tödt erst sein *Weib*!', which had been B♮ (despite the accompanying harmony) in 1805, became B♭,[56] and her top B♭ at 'und du bist *todt*!' an octave above the trumpet

---

[56] Thus reversing the tendency of the 1804 sketches, where Beethoven began with B♭ and a mild dissonance. The 1810 vocal score has B♭. Possibly the singer found it difficult to keep the B♮ in tune.

entry fell to a low F below it. The second trumpet call was now unaccompanied, and the two introductory bars were added after the spoken interruption, perhaps to help the voices. In 'O namenlose Freude', the one movement unmistakably weakened, the voices sing the modified melody in succession instead of together. Whereas in 1805 the duet expresses the joy of reunion and the A major episode of the finale the sense of release as the spiritual light of freedom bursts into the dungeon, in 1814 the duet has to carry a double response to reunion and rescue, and the A major music (with new words) is played in full daylight after all is over. Nevertheless the new finale is musically a great improvement. The opening chorus and Don Fernando's solo are new; from the A major section onwards everything is rewritten on the old material. The F major Andante assai, now Sostenuto assai, begins not with a quintet (as in 1805) or a chorus (as in 1806), but far more movingly with solos for Leonore and Florestan expressing wonder. Beethoven had second thoughts about several of the tempos altered in 1806: the first prisoners' chorus is now Allegro ma non troppo, the trio 'Euch werde Lohn' Moderato, 'Wer ein holdes Weib' Allegro ma non troppo (Presto molto instead of Allegro con brio in the coda).

A certain mystery surrounds Beethoven's advertisement of two new pieces for his benefit on 18 July. One of them was Rocco's aria, not heard since 1805. Treitschke conflated two versions of the words; Beethoven slightly shortened the 6/8 sections, removed the trumpet and drum parts, and changed the tempos from Allegretto moderato (2/4)–Allegro non molto (6/8) to Allegro moderato–Allegro. The other insertion was a new aria for Leonore; Beethoven reported to Treitschke early in July that 'Milder got her aria a fortnight ago'.[57] Treitschke says it held up the action and 'was again omitted' (after one performance?); the *Allgemeine Musikalische Zeitung* also considered the act had 'become unnecessarily long'.[58] Despite certain inconsistencies in the press notices this was almost certainly the aria we know today. But if so, what had Milder sung at the first six performances? A dated manuscript libretto in the theatre archives, unquestionably prepared for the 1814 revival, contains a different version of the 'Abscheulicher' recitative (eight lines, the last four quite unconnected with the seven that took their place),[59] followed by the words of the Allegro con brio in the 1805–6 setting (beginning 'O du, für den ich alles trug'); no sign of 'Komm, Hoffnung'. (A later hand has inserted the familiar words, and those of Rocco's aria.) This agrees precisely with Treitschke's statement that the aria 'received a new introduction, and only the last movement, "O du, für den ich alles trug", was retained'.[60] It seems likely that an earlier 'Abscheulicher', from which the entire 'Komm, Hoffnung' section was struck out, was sung six times and subsequently lost. Some support for this conjecture may be found in another manuscript libretto[61] of very recent discovery, which also omits Rocco's aria and has the earlier form of 'Abscheulicher'. Its margins are covered with Beethoven's annotations (words, music, indications of scoring and tempo), which

[57] *LA*, letter 483.   [58] Quoted in *TF*, 588.   [59] Printed in *NZB*, 304.
[60] Much of Treitschke's account is in *TF*, 572–4.
[61] Described in Sotheby's sale catalogue, 29 Apr. 1969, lot 204A.

clearly reflect his first thoughts on receiving the text early in 1814, before sketching began. Against the last two lines of 'Abscheulicher' he wrote 'Corni $\binom{6}{8}$', an indication that corresponds with no surviving version.[62] It is true that there is no sign of a lost aria in the sketches; but those for the first finale before the chorus 'Leb' wohl, du warmes Sonnenlicht', which would have immediately followed any such aria composed in the spring of 1814, are likewise missing. The sketches for the familiar 'Abscheulicher' come very late, after those for the overture, which was not ready for the first night.

In 1925 Hans Joachim Moser suggested the construction of a fourth version of the opera, combining all that is best in the first and third. This is neither practicable nor desirable.[63] But there is no need to regard the later version as a replacement of the earlier; both are viable, and the labours of Jahn, Prieger, and Hess have made 1805 as accessible as 1814. Our preference can remain a matter of taste. It is perhaps worth commenting on the custom, introduced in the nineteenth century, popularized by Mahler, and followed by Toscanini, Klemperer, and other conductors, of interposing the No. 3 overture between the dungeon and parade-ground scenes. This cannot be defended on the score of authenticity; but neither can it be condemned as dramatically injurious, for the drama is dead. The overture repeats in summary what we have just witnessed; it scarcely affects Beethoven's paean to liberty. And it may bridge an awkward lacuna while the scenery is changed.

INFLUENCES ON *FIDELIO*

Beethoven's opera, though timeless in its appeal, is a product of the French Revolution and of the school of Cherubini in particular. The principal models were *Lodoïska* and *Les deux Journées*, especially the former, and the librettos exercised as pronounced an influence as the music. The *opéra comique* or *Singspiel* form, the background of domestic realism tinged with comedy,[64] the superimposition of a heroic or patriotic story involving violence and often a spectacular catastrophe, a happy end produced not by a *deus ex machina* but by an act of superhuman courage, a strong ethical content tending to divide the characters into sheep and goats: this

---

[62] This fascinating libretto, which has escaped notice elsewhere, has many further points of interest. Beethoven himself altered the title from *Leonore* to *Fidelio* and made changes in the words. Many of the ideas rapidly (and not always legibly) noted were subsequently adopted, but not all. He seems to have considered a new recitative before 'O namenlose Freude'. Pizarro was still to be on stage during the removal of Florestan's fetters.

[63] Moser's plan (*Neues Beethoven Jahrbuch* 2 (1925), 56) may be quoted as a morphological curiosity. It was to have three acts, Act I in the 1805 version, Act II (from the March) in that of 1814. Act III was to follow 1814 with the following exceptions: the F minor (1805) Andante un poco agitato of Florestan's aria inserted betweeen A flat and F major section of 1814; the 1805 recitative introducing the 1814 duet; the opening of the 1805 finale, accompanied by a visible scene-change after the *Parsifal* manner, leading from the revenge chorus to the 1814 finale with its orchestral introduction cut; the F major Sostenuto assai ('O Gott, O welch' ein Augenblick!') restored to its 1805 form.

[64] Ernest Newman's argument (*More Opera Nights*, 268–9) that subsidiary characters of a lower social order were required by stage convention to serve as a fill-up until the real action began misses the point. They have the vital function of emphasizing the closeness of the story to real life. This is also the artistic justification of the *Singspiel* form, at any rate in serious opera.

was the pattern of the rescue opera. That Beethoven adopted it lock, stock, and barrel (though with Bouilly he eschewed the more lurid type of denouement) can be attributed to his choice of libretto; but he imitated Cherubini's practice with remarkable assiduity. The powerful overture presenting the kernel of the drama in symphonic form, the use of *Melodram* and recitative as well as spoken dialogue, the very wide range of musical design—simple quasi-strophic airs and duets alongside others of concentrated symphonic development, trios and quartets that look now backward to Italian tradition, now forward to Romantic opera, enormous finales involving a succession of large-scale movements for chorus and principals—are the regular ingredients of Cherubini's operas. The intense energy of Cherubini's style, with its pounding rhythms, constant sforzandos, cross-accents and dynamic contrasts, massive treatment of the orchestra, and still perceptible though partly transformed influence of the Neapolitan *opera buffa*, left a palpable mark on *Fidelio*. If the duet for Pizarro and Rocco suggests *Médée*, it seems probable that Pizarro's musical character was modelled on Dourlinski in *Lodoïska*, one of the few baritone villains in French opera of the Revolution. Their vengeful outbursts are expressed in strikingly similar terms. The rhetorical vocal line and the whole orchestral layout —busy first violin figuration, tremolando second violins and violas, heavy wind chords, and contrasted dynamics—are common to several passages in both operas. Ex. 20 shows the opening of the septet in Act II of *Lodoïska*.

For the treatment of the trumpet calls there was an equally close model in Méhul's *Héléna* (on another Bouilly libretto), produced in Vienna on 22 August 1803 less than six months after its Paris première. In this opera the arrival of 'le Gouverneur' in the first finale is signalled by backstage trumpets, and the whole

Ex.20

episode is anticipated in the overture. Not only the sudden fanfare in a strange key but its repetition and the slow-moving harmony combined with pedal and string ostinato produce an effect so like the one in *Fidelio* as to rule out coincidence; Ex. 21 illustrates the appearance of this material in the overture. We can hardly condemn as maladroit the destiny that on 20 November 1805 filled the Theater an der Wien with French officers.

The other important influence on *Fidelio*, equally transmuted by Beethoven's genius, was of course Mozart. This was essentially musical rather than dramatic. It scarcely affected the design of the opera but so permeated and enriched the texture

as to render it capable of expressing an infinite variety of inflexion and emphasis. Beethoven had no use for Mozart's Italian librettos and considered *Die Zauberflöte* the best of his operas, a judgment that may explain his own willingness to collaborate with Schikaneder, though the ethical potency of the opera is due far more to Mozart's music than to the text. Edward J. Dent described *Fidelio* as 'the natural sequel to *The Magic Flute*; Florestan and Leonore are Tamino and Pamina born again as real human beings, facing as realities what they had previously seen only as symbols'.[65] This was the likeliest point at which Beethoven could make

[65] Introduction to his translation of *Fidelio* (London, 1938), xiv.

Ex.21

operatic contact with Mozart. He was interested in characters less as individuals than as standard-bearers of the human spirit. His psychological need to indulge in hero-worship (it was at this period that he gave his third symphony the title 'Bonaparte')[66] was presently dissatisfied even with the heroic end of the 1805 score: it had to be reinforced in 1814 by Don Fernando's explicit enunciation of the principles of the Revolution. The more Beethoven revised the opera, the more deeply he impregnated it with the spirit of 1789.

If any other Mozart opera left a mark on *Fidelio*, it was *Idomeneo*, which was still current in the early years of the nineteenth century, Treitschke providing a German translation for a Viennese revival on 13 May 1806, and which itself reflected an earlier French influence through Gluck. The striking rhythmic resemblance between the Allegro con brio melody of Leonore's aria (Ex. 22*b*) and a theme in Electra's first aria (*a*)[67] could be an unconscious echo, especially as both are presented over a long pedal and a similar accompaniment figure:

Ex.22

(*a*)

This rhythm, or slight variants of it, runs like a coloured thread through the score of *Idomeneo*: see, for example, the Allegro molto of Idomeneo's aria 'Vedrommi intorno' in Act I, the quartet (at the words 'morte cercando altrove'), and Electra's last aria, 'D'Oreste, d'Ajace'. Beethoven's blindness to the quality of Da Ponte's librettos was a matter of temperament and extended to other works of the Italian school. No one who has studied the vernacular German *Singspiel* of the last quarter of the eighteenth century, especially in Vienna, can be surprised that it offered no

---

[66] Alan Tyson ('Beethoven's Heroic Phase', *Musical Times* 110 (1969), 139) has associated his growing preoccupation with heroic subjects during the first years of the century, in the *Prometheus* ballet and *Christus am Oelberge* as well as the symphony and the opera, with his reactions to the onset of deafness. This may well be so; but such matters are complex, and his social and political views undoubtedly played a part.

[67] This aria made a deep impression on Beethoven in Bonn (see *Musical Times* 111 (1970), 1204).

valid alternative. If Beethoven needed a stimulus, it had to come from elsewhere. The new French operas in 1802 found something like a spiritual vacuum in Viennese operatic life, and they filled it with a sonic boom that resounded through the Romantic theatre.

ABORTIVE OPERAS

The failure of *Fidelio* in 1805–6 was far from discouraging Beethoven's new-found enthusiasm for opera. In December 1807 he submitted a memorandum to the directors of the Imperial Opera offering to compose at least one grand opera a year in return for a fixed salary, throwing in an occasional *Singspiel* gratis. He showed himself fully aware that the task would demand all his time and inhibit any other major activity. It is interesting to speculate on what would have happened if this remarkable offer had been accepted. In the event he and his friends continued earnestly to hunt for suitable librettos, a search that threw up an extraordinary profusion of suggestions during the next eighteen years. Among the projects that never left the ground were a comedy recommended by Schindler (March 1807), *Memnons Dreiklang*, on an Indian story by the orientalist Hammer-Purgstall (March 1809), *The Return of Ulysses* (Beethoven suggested this early in 1812 to the young poet Karl Theodor Körner, soon to be killed in battle), *Mathilde ou Les Croisades* (Karoline Pichler, 1814; Beethoven acknowledged that the libretto was 'very beautifully written', but rejected it), *Brutus* (Bauernfeld, winter of 1824–5), *Die Ankunft der Pennsylvanier in Amerika* (Johann Baptist Rupprecht) and *Libussa* (Grillparzer), both in January 1820, *Bacchus* (Jeitteles, 1821), *Alfred der Grosse*[68] (Marianna Neumann), *Die Apotheose im Tempel des Jupiter Ammon*[69] (Johann Sporschil), and *Wanda, die Königin der Sarmaten*. These last three (late 1823) were among proposals inspired by the successful revival of *Fidelio* at the Kärntnertor on 3 November 1822 and the offer of a commission from the theatre. Other subjects canvassed at this time were Schiller's *Fiesco*, Voltaire's tragedies, a poem by one of the Schlegels, *Macbeth* (see below), and *Romeo and Juliet*. In the spring of 1825 Rellstab sent Beethoven his libretto *Orest*. On an empty page of his letter Beethoven's brother jotted down a list of books suitable for operatic treatment, among them Scott's *Kenilworth*. Rellstab gave him another list, including Attila, Antigone, and Belisarius. The last subject mentioned, in 1826, was Goethe's *Claudine von Villa Bella*, which Friedrich August Kanne, editor of the *Allgemeine Musikalische Zeitung*, was deputed to adapt. This brings the story full circle, for Beethoven had set an aria from this work for someone else's opera in Bonn about 1790.

Few if any of the above schemes were seriously considered. Others made a little more progress, and in two or three instances Beethoven sketched some music. In 1808 Heinrich Collin embarked on a *Macbeth* libretto, about which Beethoven

---

[68] *TF*, 842. Hess (*Beethovens Bühnenwerke*, 71) gives the title as *Alexander der Grosse*.

[69] This libretto survives and has been published by Volkmann, *Neues über Beethoven* (Berlin, 1904), 67–72.

(according to Röckel) was very enthusiastic. Nottebohm[70] printed two sketches for the witches' music in the first scene, planned to follow the overture without a break. One of them, as is well known, grew into the slow movement of the D major Trio, Op. 70 No. 1. But Collin abandoned the libretto in the middle of the second act for the pusillanimous reason that 'it threatened to become too gloomy';[71] he printed the first act in 1809. Soon afterwards he produced a libretto on the Alcina story, *Bradamante*. Beethoven thought the subject too familiar and disliked the magic element 'because it has a soporific effect on feeling and reason', but promised to set it all the same.[72] Collin, however, offered it to Reichardt, whose version was produced in concert form at Lobkowitz's palace on 3 March 1809. Beethoven's manifest desire to work with Collin was frustrated by the latter's death in 1811.

Incompatibility of temperament seems to have undermined a collaboration with Goethe over *Faust*, first broached in 1808, when Cotta's *Morgenblatt* announced Beethoven's interest, and mentioned as late as 1823. When the two giants met at Teplitz in July 1812 Beethoven was repelled by the courtier in Goethe. He told Breitkopf & Härtel (24 July) that Goethe 'has promised to write something for me',[73] and two years later (29 August 1814) Count Heinrich Otto van Leoben reported that Beethoven had induced Goethe to arrange *Faust* for music.[74] But nothing came of it; at least two of Beethoven's three sketches for vocal pieces from *Faust* date from before 1800.

In the spring of 1811 Beethoven invited Treitschke to arrange a French melodrama, *Les Ruines de Babylone*, and protested vigorously when he heard that an actor intended to revive the original for his benefit. In the same letter (11 June)[75] he told Count Pálffy, a director of the Imperial Opera, that since the previous year he had turned down twelve or more librettos that he had paid for out of his own pocket. In July he asked Treitschke for 'plenty of recitatives and dances'.[76] This was the same subject as *Giafar*, which Varnhagen von Ense talked of adapting for Beethoven, only to find that he had been anticipated.[77]

On 28 January 1812 Beethoven made a direct approach to Kotzebue, offering to set anything he cared to propose. 'Whether it be romantic, quite serious, heroic, comic or sentimental, in short, whatever you like, I will gladly accept it. I must admit that I should like best of all some grand subject taken from history and especially from the dark ages, for instance, from the time of Attila or the like.' On 25 May 1813 we find Beethoven asking Ignaz Franz Castelli for 'one or two of the opera libretti you promised me'. About 1814 he told his first Leonore, Anna Milder, that when his circumstances improved 'my task will be to write an opera for our *one and only* Milder'. Her success as Leonore in Berlin revived this ambition two

---

[70] *NZB*, 225–7.   [71] Quoted in *TF*, 441.   [72] See *LA*, letters 175 and 185.
[73] Ibid., letter 379.
[74] *TF*, 602. Leoben is not mentioned in the exasperatingly inadequate index.
[75] *LA*, letter 312.
[76] Ibid., letter 317.
[77] See his letters to Rahel Levin quoted in Thayer, *Life of Beethoven*, ed. H. E. Krehbiel (New York, 1921), ii. 204–5. They are excluded from *TF*.

years later, when (6 January 1816) he asked her to obtain from Baron de la Motte Fouqué 'a subject for a grand opera which would also be suitable for *you*'.[78]

Meanwhile the 1814 revival of *Fidelio* had evoked another libretto from Treitschke. This was *Romulus*, which according to *Der Sammler* of 13 December Beethoven had 'contracted to compose'. In January 1815 he told Treitschke he was so engaged and would 'begin to write it down one of these days'.[79] Almost immediately a hitch occurred. One J. E. Fuss published a notice that he had composed a *Romulus und Remus* for the Theater an der Wien. Then the directors made difficulties about terms. Beethoven wrote to Treitschke on 24 September: 'I would have begun your Romulus long ago, but the Directors refuse to grant me for a work of this kind anything more than the *takings for one night*'.[80] He was still hopeful of having the opera ready by February or March 1816 if he could obtain decent terms. He told Cipriani Potter in the summer of 1817 that he was working on it. Sketches for a classical opera of about 1815–16 were printed by Nottebohm,[81] but they are thought to belong to *Bacchus* by Rudolph vom Berge, the libretto of which Karl Amenda sent to Beethoven on 30 March 1815. They contain references to the god Pan and the intriguing note: 'Perhaps the dissonances should not be resolved throughout the whole opera, for in those primitive times our highly developed music would not be the thing. Yet the subject must be treated in a pastoral way.'[82] Another note, 'it must be evolved out of the B.M.', led Riemann to conjecture a Bacchus motif.

The last serious candidate for collaboration, early in 1823, was the dramatist Grillparzer, a nephew of Sonnleithner. Although he was unhappy about the treatment of the voice in Beethoven's recent work and doubted if he was still capable of composing an opera, he submitted two proposals, *Drahomira*, described by Thayer as 'a semi-diabolical story drawn from Bohemian legendary history',[83] and *Melusine*, another legend. Beethoven was enthusiastic. When Grillparzer delivered the libretto of *Melusine* in the spring of 1823 he insisted on a formal contract. He had several long discussions with the poet, who offered to remove a hunting-chorus at which Beethoven seems to have jibbed and suggested the use of 'a recurrent and easily grasped melody', first heard in the overture, 'to mark every appearance of Melusine or of her influence in the action'.[84] On 17 September Beethoven wrote to Spohr that he had begun the music and hoped to return to it. Grillparzer understood that it was 'ready'. In fact, little if anything seems to have been written down, though the subject cropped up as late as 31 May 1826, when Beethoven told the publisher Adolf Martin Schlesinger that Count Brühl, the Berlin intendant, wanted him to make another choice owing to the similarity between *Melusine* and de la Motte Fouqué's *Undine*, Hoffmann's setting of which had been produced at Brühl's theatre in 1816.[85]

How seriously did Beethoven consider any of the operatic projects after *Fidelio*? His professions of enthusiasm were undoubtedly sincere. No man of his tempera-

---

[78] The letters quoted in this paragraph are in *LA*, 344, 423, and 595.
[79] Ibid., letter 525.   [80] Ibid., letter 559.   [81] In *NZB*, 329–30.
[82] Cf. Thayer, *Life of Beethoven*, ii. 315, n.1.
[83] Ibid., iii. 118.   [84] Cf. *TF*, 862.
[85] Letters referred to in this paragraph are in *LA*, 1240 and 1487.

ment would have bothered to make lightly the wide-ranging request to Kotzebue or the 1807 offer to the theatre directors. The *Macbeth* and *Bacchus* sketches are proof of more than indifference. Yet if we exclude all peripheral suggestions, the schemes that came nearest to fruition, though in many respects heterogeneous, have one thing in common. Every one of them was concerned with a distant or legendary period; all were equally remote from the climate of *Fidelio*. Beethoven expressed a preference for the dark ages; was he unaware that *Fidelio* drew its strength from its contemporary realism?

Probably his attitude was ambivalent. He was strongly attracted to opera (and his experiences with *Fidelio* could have increased rather than diminished this); yet he may half-consciously have sought reasons to avoid a final commitment. No composer was ever more certain of his strength, or more willing to stretch convention in order to give utterance to his ideas. Had his genius impelled him to tackle another opera, he would have overcome every impediment in its way. There was no inadequacy in his equipment. It is easy, in admiring the grandeur of *Fidelio*, to overlook the sheer operatic technique it enshrines. The composer who in 'Mir ist so wunderbar' could express the contrasted emotions of four characters with absolute conviction in the same music, and who could create the extraordinary dramatic intensity of the dungeon scene in the 1805 version, had few potential equals in operatic history. Yet there was something that took precedence over drama and character and ensured that the pull, when it came (and it repeatedly did), was never quite strong enough to carry the field. Humanity was of more impor-tance to Beethoven than the individual. *Fidelio* was successfully achieved because it satisfied one of the psychological needs of his existence, the search for the ideal woman. He found her in art where he failed in life, and placed her on a pedestal. No wonder he wished to call the opera *Leonore*. But in yielding to the urge to raise the height of the pedestal he partly dehumanized her. The most conclusive evidence that Beethoven was not a predestined opera composer is provided by his treatment of *Fidelio* in 1814. It is impossible to imagine Mozart or Verdi sacrificing their characters to the expediency of a moral, however elevated.

15
Beethoven in his Letters

Miss Anderson, who before the war published an excellent translation of Mozart's letters in three volumes, has now performed a like service for Beethoven.[1] Her edition, the labour of fifteen years, includes some 1,575 letters and eight other documents, of which about 450 do not appear in Shedlock's English translation of 1909, and 230 are missing from the German collected editions. Moreover her resolve to come to grips with the original manuscripts, scattered in public and private collections in all five continents, has enabled her to restore the full text of forty more. She makes no claim to finality. Letters from Beethoven are still turning up (and disappearing): his correspondence with Josephine Deym, with whom he was in love for more than two years, came to light only in 1949, and other unknown autographs were recently found lurking in the Wisbech Museum and in a brown paper parcel at the Royal College of Music. Meanwhile this edition is by far the fullest, as well as the most scholarly, that has appeared in any language.

Beethoven, unlike Mozart, was a somewhat constipated correspondent. He complained that he would rather write ten thousand notes than one letter of the alphabet, but business affairs and the urge to justify himself led to the consumption of a good deal of writing-paper. Many of his longer letters deal with the publication or proof-correction of his works, or with the several lawsuits that occupied his later years. The shorter are trivial requests or grumbles, such as today would be made by telephone (though orders to his fishmonger and enquiries about a recipe for boot-polish do help to bring the man before us). Few of them possess any literary distinction. A certain jocular humour enlivens the letters to Zmeskall and the publishers Steiner and Haslinger (until they refused to extend Beethoven's credit); but his unbuttoned mood is more convincingly expressed in notes than in words, where it is all too apt to spend itself in atrocious puns. There is a charming letter to Haslinger about a canon that Beethoven composed in his sleep in a carriage, forgot on waking, and subsequently recovered 'in accordance with the law of the association of ideas' on the return journey. Very occasionally he rises to eloquence, as in the moving letters to Wegeler and Amenda in 1801, when he was resigning himself to the permanent loss of his hearing. And in his last years, among much that is tedious and not a little that is painful, there are flashes of sudden vividness. 'Why, I feel as if I had hardly composed more than a few notes' (to Schott in 1824, after the Ninth Symphony and the *Missa solemnis*). The country round his brother's

---

[1] *The Letters of Beethoven*, collected, translated and edited by Emily Anderson (London, 1961).

estate at Gneixendorf reminds him in October 1826 of the Rhineland, 'which I so ardently desire to revisit. For I left it long ago when I was young'. Two months later, his last composition finished, he writes to Wegeler, the friend of his youth: 'I still hope to create a few great works and then like an old child to finish my earthly course somewhere among kind people.'

Two things are conspicuously absent from Beethoven's letters. Although he lived through a period of violent political and social upheaval, they contain few references to public events, apart from an occasional curse on them for disturbing his personal arrangements. He did suffer considerably from the collapse of the Austrian economy in 1811, which depreciated his income and led to several years of litigation with the heirs of his chief benefactor. And of course he was intensely susceptible to the spiritual forces released by the French Revolution. But this was a matter for his art; only what he could not digest in music was left over for his life. Secondly there is very little of musical or aesthetic interest, and for the same reason. The only contemporary composers for whom he expresses admiration (apart from a little judicious flattery of his pupil the Archduke Rudolph) are Cherubini and Méhul, both of whom shared, and indeed influenced, his serious approach to art. There is a significant reference to the abandonment of his operatic collaboration with Schikaneder (January 1804) under the influence of 'the brilliant and attractive French operas'.

Of the unrealized projects discussed in his letters, the most numerous, as well as the most interesting, sprang from his constant preoccupation with the theatre. Like Debussy, he was far from a one-opera composer by choice; he toyed with and rejected almost as many subjects as Puccini.[2] Financial considerations may have played some part in their frustration. Publishers would not take operas unless they were very successful; in 1815 Beethoven asked 60 ducats for the G major violin sonata, Op. 96, 80 for the *Schlacht bei Vittoria*, and only 30 for *Fidelio*. He did not need to discuss his non-theatrical works in letters. He was fully aware of their absolute and relative value; all that remained was to sell them—and to correct the proofs.

But if these volumes throw little direct light on Beethoven the composer, they tell us an enormous amount about Beethoven the man. And the emphasis is not always that of the biographies. One fact emerges clearly: the familiar three periods of his music do correspond with three periods in his personal life, each marked off from the next by a major crisis. Many characteristics, of the man as of the music, were prominent from the start. For example, his ill health: the first letter of all, written at the age of 16, complains of asthma and melancholia. In the fourth (1793) he quotes Schiller's *Don Carlos*: 'I am not wicked, truly not wicked. Even though wildly surging emotions may betray my heart, yet my heart is good'—a refrain echoed repeatedly in later years. These early letters show hot temper and impulsiveness, but also penitence and generosity of spirit. He quarrels with Wegeler, as later with Stephan von Breuning, but humbly begs their pardon. Publishers, who in

[2] See p. 160 ff. for Beethoven's operatic projects.

Beethoven's eyes scarcely fell within the ordinary moral code, are the target of recrimination as early as 1794. A significant new note enters in 1798, when he writes to Zmeskall: '*Power* is the moral principle of those who excel others, and it is also mine.' He made ruthless use of it, in matters small as well as great. Hopelessly impractical in daily life, Beethoven expected his friends and relations to perform all manner of menial tasks, from engaging servants and checking his laundry to supplying quill pens and advice about emetics. Most of them sooner or later were blackguarded for their pains: friendship with Beethoven was a rose with many thorns. His dependence naturally increased with his deafness; but so did his impatience. As early as 1801 he complains of having to 'associate with such miserable egoists as Zmeskall, Schuppanzigh and the like,' whom he regarded 'merely as instruments on which to play when I feel inclined.' This foreshadows the extravagant denunciations with which the faithful if unimaginative Schindler was overwhelmed in 1823–4, culminating in the fear 'lest some day through your action a great misfortune may befall me'. Surely a classical example of unconscious irony in view of the sentimental distortion of Schindler's biography and his forgery of entries in the conversation books.

Beethoven's first crisis occurred in 1801–2, when he was forced to come to terms with increasing and incurable deafness. The letters and the Heiligenstadt Testament, printed here in an appendix, tell us what this cost him. He met the challenge with a courageous defiance that did honour to his character even as it enriched his music. 'I will seize Fate by the throat; it shall certainly not bend and crush me completely' (1801). 'Well, so be it—*I shall never crawl*—my world is the universe' (1804). In 1810 he told Wegeler that if he had not read somewhere 'that a man should not voluntarily quit this life so long as he can still perform a good deed' he would have killed himself long ago. And, quite apart from his music, Beethoven did perform good deeds; his idealism was no pious window-dressing. 'Why did you conceal your need from me?' he wrote to Ries in 1803. 'Not one of my friends is to be short of money as long as I have some.' For several years he sent unpublished works to be performed at Graz in aid of the poor, refusing to take any payment; when the Ursuline nuns sent him a fee, he deducted the cost of copying and sent it back. In his first letter to Graz (1811) he wrote: 'From my earliest childhood my zeal to serve our poor suffering humanity in any way whatsoever by means of my art has made no compromise with any lower motive; or rather, the only reward I have asked for was the feeling of inward happiness which always attends such actions.'

This was the man on whom the second blow fell in 1812, the year of the 'Unsterbliche Geliebte' letter and the agonized diary entries in which he renounced the hope of marriage and apparently—for whatever cause—of any sexual relationship with women. Just at this time he wrote (to a child) perhaps his most eloquent statement about his art: 'The true artist has no pride. He sees unfortunately that art has no limit; he has a vague awareness of how far he is from reaching his goal; and while others may perhaps be admiring him, he laments the fact that he has not yet reached the point whither his better genius only lights the way for him like a distant sun.' This remained the ideal for Beethoven the artist; but the second renunciation distorted his character as the first did not. The years after 1812 saw a decline in his musical output and an enormous increase in his correspondence: three-quarters of the letters fall in this period, which has a powerful if often painful fascination for anyone interested in one of the most extraordinary series of masterpieces ever created by the mind of man.

Beethoven's conception of the artist as a being set apart, a sort of universal lawgiver, was something quite new in the history of music. The product partly of his times and partly of his character, it was indispensable to his triumph as a musician; but when the tremendous will that in defiance of destiny had created the masterpieces of his middle years was diverted into daily life, the consequences were catastrophic. We can watch the whole process at work in the letters, first over the lawsuit with Prince Kinsky's heirs, then in the far more calamitous dispute with his sister-in-law about the guardianship of his nephew Karl. Inevitably self-centred as a result of his deafness, Beethoven developed an obsession about his rights and an unquenchable capacity for moral indignation, leading to bouts of acute persecution mania. He suspected gossip everywhere—though he repeated plenty himself—and jumped to the worst conclusions about his friends: lawyers, doctors, servants, publishers, the intimates of years, all were accused of swindling him and betraying his interests.

At first the deviation was comparatively mild. 'Remember that you are acting for an unselfish artist in his dealings with a niggardly family' (the Kinskys), he wrote to the lawyer Kanka in 1814. More than once in his letters to the Archduke Rudolph, who was also a cardinal, he all but challenged the deity to keep his side of the bargain. 'Surely God will hear my prayer and will once more liberate me from so many calamities, seeing that since my childhood I have served Him trustfully and have performed good actions whenever I could.' Later he reached the limits of self-deception. Nothing is more startling about these letters than Beethoven's shrill protestations of his honour and his principles as well-known facts just when he comes closest to betraying them. He accuses Karl (aged 13) of heartless and callous hypocrisy, and Karl's mother of having sent her husband (Beethoven's brother, who died of tuberculosis) into an untimely grave, and exclaims 'Oh, may the whole miserable rabble of humanity be cursed and damned'; yet a little later he writes to his lawyer 'My well-known humane attitude, my education and my customary philanthropy guarantee that my behaviour to her will not be less noble than it is to her son'. Alas for his philanthropy! When asking Zmeskall to engage a new servant he can add: 'Even if he is a bit hunchbacked I should not mind, for then I should know at once the weak spot at which to attack him.' At the same time he became less scrupulous in his dealings with publishers, on the principle that whatever helped to pay for Karl's education was morally justified. He had always used his boasted ignorance of business affairs as a camouflage for hard bargaining. Now he played one publisher off against another, accepting an advance from A while delivering the goods to B, and set up an exculpatory howl when taxed with sharp practice. The whole tribe became 'the most barefaced blackguards'; 'it is all the same to me what hellhound licks or gnaws away my brain'.

Much must be allowed for Beethoven's ill-health, which afflicted not only his ears but many other organs and even his mind. Occasionally he showed a pathetic awareness of this: 'In my present circumstances', he wrote to Nanette Streicher, 'I can no longer *behave* as *I used to behave.*' The letters of July and August 1819 are almost insane in their tangle of thwarted love, hatred, and pride. Behind his love for Karl there are abundant signs that a warped sexual element lay at the root of the affair. He harps continually on the moral delinquencies of Karl's mother, 'that pestilential female' (the Queen of Night is his politest name for her), and makes similar charges against his servants and his other sister-in-law, the wife of his brother Johann. Letters to Johann, otherwise friendly, contain obscene references to his wife ('that loutish fat woman and her bastard . . . that former and still active whore'); when Johann would not divorce her he attempted to procure the intervention of the police, though it was no more their business than it was Beethoven's. One of his first reactions to Karl's attempted suicide, for which his own conduct must have been largely to blame, was a fresh charge of sexual depravity against the mother, this time with one of Karl's friends.

One thing preserves Beethoven from our disgust: the flagrant inconsistency between his precept and his practice never springs from hypocrisy. He was desperately sincere. The contradictions were superimposed; they did not cancel his finer feelings. On occasion he even brought himself to behave generously to the detested Queen of Night, arranging for her to meet Karl at his lodgings since 'it might hurt [her] to have to visit her child at the house of a stranger', and promising to help her when she was ill and to make his 'pigheaded brother' Johann contribute as well. (Yet within a day or two the thought that 'she has become such a strumpet' made him change his mind.) Convinced of the pure unselfishness of his motives towards Karl, he could not understand the boy's divided loyalties, his desire to see his mother, or his fear of his own explosive temper. Hence the continual nagging reproaches, the accusations of ingratitude—varied by bursts of affection and sanity ('imitate my virtues, but not my *faults*')—and the tone of neurotic selfrighteousness: 'What distresses me most of all is the thought of the consequences which *you will suffer* as a result of your behaviour. Who will believe you or trust you who has heard what has happened and how you have mortally wounded and are daily wounding me?' It may well have been the intolerable moral pressure that drove Karl to his last desperate expedient.

The moral factor too ensures that in the last resort the story is tragic rather than sordid. At the height of the quarrel in 1819 Beethoven excoriated J. K. Bernard for seeking a compromise. For Beethoven himself no compromise was possible. The very single-mindedness with which he fought and won his battle against destiny drew in all his strength and rendered him incapable of seeing any point of view but his own. To what extent these mundane quarrels influenced the content of his last works, or abridged their quantity, no one can say. But the music and the letters both exist. When they are considered together, the overriding fact is not the abasement of one human being but the ability of a brain so handicapped by bodily and mental affliction to create the Ninth Symphony, the *Missa solemnis*, and the last sonatas and quartets. This is a sufficient answer to the flabby sentimentality that wishes the letters had never been published and the frivolity that denounces the study of them as a waste of time.

As the quoted passages show, Miss Anderson's choice of 'a sort of timeless English that would reproduce the idiom of our day without its neologisms' has resulted in an admirably clear and readable text. Her notes are terse and to the point; very few references to music or persons have escaped her. It is a pity that considerations of space precluded quotation of the other side of the correspondence, where it survives; one longs for a specimen of Josephine Deym's replies to Beethoven. There are occasional slips and misprints, none of major importance. It is scarcely accurate to describe Winter's *Das unterbrochene Opferfest* as a comic opera. C. G. Breitkopf was the grandson, not the great-grandson, of the founder of Breitkopf & Härtel. If the fire that destroyed Moritz Schlesinger's premises in Paris is the 'accident' mentioned in Letter 1487 (31 May 1826), it cannot have consumed the original of Letter 1538, written in October the same year. Beethoven's reference to the ground bass of the Crucifixus of Bach's B minor Mass as a basso ostinato is surely not intended to be a joke. The illustrations, portraits of Beethoven and his correspondents, and reproductions of manuscripts, are excellent and often revealing. They include a sinister picture of Beethoven's brother Johann, who made a fortune as a war profiteer; he certainly looks the part. There is an index of persons (but not of places, subjects, or institutions) and two, differently classified, of Beethoven's published works. Projected or sketched works however are not included, and it is thus impossible to trace references to the abortive operas or the C sharp minor Mass. A map of Vienna and its surroundings in Beethoven's day would have been a welcome addition.

16

Euryanthe

Of the numerous operas in which splendid music has been strangled by an impossible libretto, *Euryanthe* is perhaps the most tantalizing. Schubert's operas were undermined by inexperience of stage technique; but Weber was a theatrical composer by profession, and *Der Freischütz* had just won a sensational success throughout Germany. Surely his next opera, on which he was known to have spent immense care, would be a masterpiece. Judged as music alone it certainly is: no other work by Weber is so replete with melodic, harmonic, and orchestral invention, so original in structure, or so rich in single strokes of overwhelming dramatic power. Yet the libretto is worse than incompetent; it is nonsensical; and it has kept the opera off the stage, except for an occasional pious revival, ever since the first production in 1823.

Its author was Helmine von Chézy, a middle-aged lady of letters; her only other contribution to history was the play for which Schubert wrote his *Rosamunde* music and whose loss it is difficult to deplore. She is said to have rewritten the libretto of *Euryanthe* nine times, with copious help from the composer; its mint state beggars conjecture. We can appreciate how the story itself, a tale of medieval chivalry of which variant forms were used by Boccaccio in the *Decameron* and Shakespeare in *Cymbeline*, must have appealed to Weber. But how could he bring himself to set the libretto as we have it, a *locus classicus* for every kind of dramatic blunder, in which two of the characters are dead and a vital part of the action completed long before the opera begins, and the survivors consistently belie their own natures in order to prevent it ending too soon? Only a serious flaw in dramatic vision can explain this. There is no doubt whatever of Weber's operatic gifts; the fact that such a libretto could evoke music not only of great beauty but of extraordinary dramatic intensity—and not least (as Tovey remarked) at the very points where the contraption creaks most painfully—proves that his imagination was fervently seized of the subject. But he saw it as a series of picturesque scenes and incidents, not as a developing whole. He never found a good libretto and never achieved a satisfying dramatic organization on a large scale. Some of Verdi's early and middle-period operas provide a parallel here; nor is it improbable that had Weber's life been prolonged to the normal span he would have attained something like Verdi's final mastery.

Euryanthe is Weber's only grand opera, and quite different in design from his other stage works, which belong to the *Singspiel* type with spoken dialogue, like Mozart's *Entführung* and *Die Zauberflöte* and Beethoven's *Fidelio*. We are accustomed to regard Weber as a purely German genius, but there was a good deal of French and Italian in his musical ancestry, and the direct forebears of *Euryanthe* are the French operas of the Revolutionary and Napoleonic period by Cherubini, Méhul, and Spontini. None of these composers had anything like Weber's creative gift, but he owed a good deal to their example in matters of orchestration and general design. Spontini's method of linking the recitatives, airs, and ensembles of *Olimpie* without intervening cadences probably provided the inspiration that carried *Euryanthe* well on the road to Wagner's endless melody. Weber did however make a radical break with his predecessors. Where they treated grand Romantic subjects in a style that preserved a good deal of the marmoreal manner of Gluck, Weber lost himself in the forests, legends, and remote realms of fairyland or medieval chivalry that encircled the stories of his operas. The early Romantics, overcome by the intoxicating sensation of entering into their experience and portraying it from the inside, were inclined to reject the detached general view, and as a result often failed to find a satisfactory form for their larger works. It is possible that Weber's consciousness of this danger was responsible for one of the most striking features of *Euryanthe*, the expansion of the reminiscence motif into something very like the Wagnerian leitmotif.

Tovey called *Euryanthe* a more advanced development of Wagnerian music-drama than *Lohengrin*, which is so plainly modelled on it that it is perhaps as well for the reputation of the later work that the earlier is so seldom performed. The resemblance is not only musical: Telramund and Ortrud are palpably drawn from Lysiart and Eglantine. The rhythmic-harmonic scheme of *Euryanthe*, built upon the contrast of a basic squareness with heavy tonic and dominant accents and a superimposed web of chromatic expressionism, the former representing the outward manifestations of chivalry and the latter the darker and more passionate elements of the plot, penetrated so deeply into Wagner's system that years of arduous and conscious effort were necessary before he could achieve the flexibility to advance from the point where Weber stopped. The leitmotif is most strongly foreshadowed in the sinuous theme associated with Eglantine (a sort of German Amneris), a brilliant stroke of dramatic psychology in itself and handled with an approach to full symphonic treatment (Ex. 1). Equally Wagnerian is the motif of the ghosts (Ex. 2), first heard in the central section of the overture (where Weber proposed to raise the curtain in a gallant attempt to elucidate the plot); its sole appearance in a major key, at the very end of the third act when the ghosts have been laid, is one of the most moving moments in the opera. *Euryanthe* lacks the

Ex.1

Moderato assai

Str. ***pp*** *lusingando dolcissimo*

Ex.2

symbolic content of *Lohengrin*; but the music has the vitality and flexibility of mature genius where Wagner is still struggling to slough off the hampering influence of his inheritance.

It is the darker side of Weber's opera that makes by far the strongest impact. His hero remains wooden, while his heroine, despite her reputation for virtue, forfeits sympathy by giving away a vital secret and then refusing to tell the truth. Furthermore the solo music of Euryanthe and Adolar is for the most part simple in content and organization, while that of Eglantine and Lysiart, especially the former's 'Bethörte! die an meine Liebe glaubt' and the latter's 'Wo berg' ich mich?', is conceived on a far grander scale and so magnificently executed that these two disagreeable characters have no difficulty in running away with the opera. Apart from them, Weber is most successful with the background: the pageantry of the court scenes, the rustic charm of the May song and the hunting chorus (so much better than that of *Der Freischütz*) in the last act, and above all the troubled mystery of the music associated with the dead Emma and her ring. It is easy to underrate Weber's power of making the paraphernalia of German Romanticism, whether natural or supernatural, dramatically convincing. This must be done by the sheer force of musical imagination; we have only to look at the operas of lesser contemporaries, even such capable composers as Marschner, to see how easily it can degenerate into the grotesque or the merely comic. Weber of course was an unrivalled interpreter of the moods of nature. The snake in Act III, that curious link between the opening of *Die Zauberflöte* and Act II of *Siegfried*, is an absurd *serpens ex machina*, but the deserted countryside and Euryanthe's loneliness are wonderfully conveyed, largely by means of harmonic adventure. So too is the darkness in which Eglantine and Lysiart operate. It was this power to express atmospheric depth and perspective, whether of time, place, or emotional experience, that was new in the music of the early Romantics. We may forget Weber's characters, but the musical environment in which he places them remains to haunt the memory.

17

Meyerbeer's Italian Operas

Historians of opera have sometimes interpreted Meyerbeer's career—two operas produced in Germany (1812–13), six in Italy (1817–24), and six in France (1831–65, the last posthumously)—as an epitome of opportunism or a paradigm of the wandering Jew. This is wisdom after the event. He *was* a Jew and an opportunist, and he wandered, but then so did many other composers of his and previous generations. Until Weber and Spohr began to establish a national school about 1816, German opera scarcely existed above the *Singspiel* level. True, this had produced three isolated masterpieces in *Die Entführung aus dem Serail*, *Die Zauberflöte*, and *Fidelio*, but they did not amount to a tradition, and there was nothing else of consequence. Most of the operas written for Germany, which, like Italy, was a divided country with many court theatres, were Italian, even when composed by Germans. Gluck, the leading opera composer of his age, never set a libretto in this own language.

The only flourishing alternative to the Italian school was the French, whose strong local tradition in the treatment of the sung text gave it a sturdy independence. Paris was the capital of a united and prosperous nation with a rich culture, especially in the theatre, and from the time of Lully and even earlier it had attracted foreign musicians. Indeed French opera seemed to require an infusion of foreign blood—especially Italian blood—before it could thrive. An astonishing proportion of its leading composers—Lully, Gluck, Piccinni, Sacchini, Salieri, Cherubini, Spontini, Rossini, and Meyerbeer himself—were either Italians or had learned their craft in Italy. Many lesser figures, including J. C. Bach, Paisiello, Reichardt, Paer, and Winter, travelled the same path. Several of them—Italians as well as Germans—set librettos in all three current languages, thereby confirming opera's status as an international art. It was through no fault of his own that Mozart did not add a French opera to his Italian and German tally.

Only the strictures of Weber, Wagner, and other German nationalists have branded Meyerbeer's career as retrograde. One of the most gifted composers of the next generation, Otto Nicolai, wrote a series of Italian operas before his single German masterpiece. Meyerbeer's sensational success in Paris has tended to eclipse his Italian period, which was its necessary prerequisite and only comparatively less of a triumph. It is worth examining his Italian operas to determine how much of the essential Meyerbeer (if we can assume that such a thing exists) antedated his arrival in Paris, at Rossini's invitation, in 1825.

These operas are generally dismissed as imitations of Rossini (his junior by six months). It is true that on reaching Venice in 1815 Meyerbeer fell at once under the spell of *Tancredi*, and that Rossini is an overwhelming influence on his Italian operas (and a palpable one on his French operas as well). That was inevitable. Rossini-fever was a germ that within a few years could be caught anywhere in Europe, and it was highly infectious. Very few composers escaped it, even the most nationally or locally orientated, such as Schubert, Weber, and Marschner. What is interesting about Meyerbeer's Italian operas is the presence of characteristic traits that he is commonly supposed to have acquired in Paris.

One of the six, *Semiramide riconosciuta* (1819), is a setting of Metastasio, whose librettos were still tempting composers even in Germany (Poissl produced operas based on *L'Olimpiade* in 1815 and *Nitteti* in 1817). In the others Meyerbeer collaborated with two of the most prolific and successful librettists of the day. Gaetano Rossi, the author of *Romilda e Costanza* (1817), *Emma di Resburgo* (1819), and *Il crociato in Egitto* (1824), worked for Mayr, Rossini (*Il cambiale di matrimonio, La scala di seta, Tancredi, Semiramide*), Mercadante (*Il giuramento, Il bravo*), Donizetti (*Maria Padilla, Linda di Chamounix*), and Nicolai (*Il proscritto*, orginally intended for Verdi). Felice Romani, who supplied the texts for *Margherita d'Anjou* (1820) and *L'esule di Granata* (1822), was the most distinguished Italian librettist between Da Ponte and Boito and scarcely needs an introduction. Several of these scores are inaccessible,[1] but the two most successful give a vivid and no doubt representative picture. *Margherita d'Anjou* was performed all over Europe for twenty years. *Il crociato in Egitto* lasted longer and travelled further, reaching places as remote as Havana, Mexico City, Corfu, Constantinople, and St Petersburg by 1841. It received a concert performance in London, said to be the first for more than a century, in January 1972.

It is hard to know how much say Meyerbeer had in the choice or treatment of his subjects at this period, but both librettos, especially *Il crociato in Egitto*, have an ominous flavour of Scribe. Rossi was always addicted to strained situations and melodramatic extravagance, with the characters dancing attendance on the plot instead of controlling it. Romani was capable of better things, as we know from his collaboration with Bellini in *Norma* and *La sonnambula*. But his libretto for *Margherita d'Anjou*, based like so many others of the period on a French *mélodrame* by Pixérécourt, does not show him at his best. Admittedly it is an *opera semiseria*, a deliberate mixing of the genres, in which the heroic postures of the old *opera seria* were modified by two strains from *opéra comique*, the *comédie larmoyante* that was part of Rousseau's legacy and the realism of the first Revolutionary decade. (*La sonnambula* is a specimen of the type at its best.) *Opera semiseria* admitted comic characters on an equal basis with their social superiors, though the comedy tended to become more and more sentimental. Some examples, including Mayr's treatment of stories set by Cherubini in *Élisa* and Beethoven in *Fidelio*, bore the title *farsa sentimentale*. It was one of the growing points of the Romantic movement in opera.

---

[1] A study in depth would require access to unpublished material, especially the full scores, which were not printed. The vocal scores (for three operas) seldom agree with each other or the librettos.

The plot of *Margherita* is nothing if not romantic.[2] The action place near Hexham during the Wars of the Roses (which had inspired Mayr's *opera seria* of seven years earlier, *La rosa rossa e la rosa bianca*, likewise by Romani out of Pixérécourt) and concerns a successful campaign by Henry VI's widowed queen against the Yorkists; the links with history are negligible. It is full of stratagems and spoils, battles, disguises, conspiracies, and tergiversations of every kind, such as might be thought not unsuited to that turbulent period. Much of it, as in many of the Revolution *opéras comiques*, takes place in darkness. The motley collection of characters includes the Grand Seneschal of Normandy (tenor), who is supposed to be in love with the queen but has no love scene with her (there is no love music in the opera); his wife Isaura, who follows him across the Channel disguised as a knight and obtains employment as his page, without being recognized, in order to watch his steps (she is then required to carry his love messages to the queen); Norcester (*sic*), a Yorkist baron disguised as a Highland chieftain, who goes over to the beaten side when his own has avenged his wrongs, presumably to prevent the opera ending an act too soon; a cowardly Gascon surgeon named Morin (originally Michele), a substantial *buffo* part designed as foil to the high-born characters and a vehicle for comic relief; and the villainous Richard of Gloucester, who does not appear till the middle of Act III. He then gets everyone else in his power, only for the tables to be turned in a most incongruously happy ending. We encounter many of the favourite ingredients of early Romantic opera—prayers, hymns, storms, an aria in polacca rhythm for the surgeon, a mute child (the young Prince Edward) threatened with death on the stage, and 'characteristic' choruses. Each act begins with one of these: French soldiers playing cards, drinking, and wenching to a bouncy tune that may have been Meyerbeer's idea of a Northumberland jig in Act I, English soldiers vowing death to the French in Act II, Highlanders addressing a hymn to the sunrise in Act III.

The music is as mixed in style as the libretto. As one might expect, the Rossini of the early comedies dominates the serious as well as the lighter scenes. The score is full of clattering march rhythms, brilliant coloratura (especially for the queen) and —a Rossini trait that Meyerbeer never outgrew—loud thumps in pianissimo passages, generally off the beat and often in the most unsuitable contexts, such as the prayer quartet in the first finale. Even the amiable hymn to the sunrise for no obvious reason sports a fortissimo penultimate chord. Yet there is a positive if fitful attempt to evoke an appropriate dramatic atmosphere and to develop the action in musical terms. A number of set pieces lead into one another without a break; Romani's design may have been a help here, as it was to Mayr in *Le due duchesse*. Meyerbeer makes rather crude efforts to differentiate the characters in duets, of which there are three in Act I: for the queen and the disguised Norcester, both praying hard for different things (and Norcester cursing in the cabaletta); for Morin

[2] There are several versions of the opera, as of so many others at this period (including *Il crociato in Egitto*), all produced within a few years and published without date. The one described here appears to be a Paris arrangement made in 1826, expanded from two to three acts with extra music borrowed from *Emma di Resburgo*. Romani should not be held responsible for every extravagance, though the essentials of the plot and the characters remain; the music all dates from Meyerbeer's Italian years.

and Isaura, she professing such devotion to her husband that she must always be with him, however badly he behaves, Morin dismissing these sentiments as obsolete (she ought to take a lover); and for Isaura in her knightly disguise and her unsuspecting husband. It is during this piece that he enlists her in his household.

More successful is the evocation of night, mystery, and shady business afoot in two trios in Acts II and III and the early part of the second finale. In the Act II trio, after a battle, Isaura is lost and frightened, the seneschal defeated and ignorant of the queen's fate, Morin thankful to the darkness for aiding his escape. Each has a long solo with its own music, but bringing in a common main theme at different points to the same words (about night); then they meet and recognize one another. Several times they think they hear Gloucester's soldiers, but decide it is the wind or the river or the echo of their own voices. The music has a light touch and an individual flavour, and culminates in a return of the main theme in augmentation. The coda leads into a substantial finale, which begins with a band of Highlanders searching for the queen and proposing to throw her in the river. Solo voices answer one another in the darkness over a creeping orchestral ostinato, first in G minor, later, as the full cast assembles, in G major. After an Andante sostenuto quintet of perplexity in A flat—the favourite key for a slow concertato in finales of this period, especially those of Mayr and Rossini—another rhythmic ostinato takes over when Norcester horrifies the defeated Lancastrians by revealing his identity, but promptly joins them and persuades his Highlanders to do the same. The resourceful treatment of ostinato is Rossinian, and so is much of the structure of the finale, but it lacks Rossini's formal balance, both between fast and slow sections and in tonality. The principal components are in G minor and major (fast), A flat major (slow), A major with excursions to D minor and F major (fast, with one short Andante), and D major (fast). The ensemble in which all thank Norcester is very Mozartian in theme and harmony, but this will never do to end an act, so the queen introduces a poor Rossinian tune with triplets and gallops away with the coda.

The Act III trio for three basses (Norcester, Morin, and Gloucester), though of clear *buffo* descent, has considerable character. Gloucester, who has not previously sung in the opera, tries to induce the other two to betray themselves by revealing their loyalties. Morin admits that he does not hate the queen, but evades the trap by saying he cannot hate anyone: he only wishes the war would go away and make life tolerable for ordinary folk like himself. Gloucester then orders Norcester to produce his wife, knowing that the woman masquerading as such is in fact the queen. Morin covers Norcester's embarrassment by saying he is a notoriously jealous husband. The situation is temporarily saved, but Gloucester's suspicions are confirmed. Meyerbeer gets a good deal of vitality and dramatic irony into the music, which is *staccato sotto voce marcato* almost throughout, and is saved from pretentiousness by the presence of the down-to-earth Gascon. Episodes of this kind —the ironical male-voice trio 'Sous votre bannière in Act III of *Le Prophète* is another—are among the most successful in Meyerbeer's operas. The more ambitious scenes of *Margherita d'Anjou* are apt to be precarious in style and hollow in sentiment.

There is nothing remotely comic about *Il crociato in Egitto*—in intention, at least. It is a very grand *opera seria* set in the period of the Crusades, with rival nationalities and religions, Christian and Islamic, at each other's throats throughout, and the usual emotional cross-currents and complications. Armando, a knight of Rhodes left for dead on the battlefield, has enlisted in the service of the Sultan Aladino under another name, conquered his new master's enemies, and had a son by his daughter Palmide. The Egyptians are prepared to regularize the union, but Armando confesses his deception to Palmide: he has betrayed everyone, including his uncle Adriano di Monfort, the Grand Master of his Order, and Felicia, his childhood companion and destined bride. When Adriano arrives with an embassy to solemnize a peace treaty, he is horrified to discover Armando in Saracen costume. He demands and breaks in two the sword he has dishonoured (the opera must have been expensive in cutlery, for the entire Christian chorus does this in Act II), and the family quarrel develops into a renewal of hostilities. Armando says Palmide will die of grief if he deserts her; Adriano says Armando's behaviour will kill his mother; Armando returns penitent to the Christian fold. Felicia arrives disguised as a knight (not an unusual situation for a mezzo at this period) in search of Armando's tomb. The two women meet in the palace garden and find a common link in a melody that turns out to be Armando's favourite song (shades of Grétry's *Richard Cœur de Lion*); Felicia recognizes his happiness with Palmide and the child, and offers to give him up, the scene culminating in a soulful trio on the melody aforesaid.

The first finale begins with a peace conference and ends with a declaration of war. In between Aladino proclaims Armando his son-in-law and heir and releases all Christian prisoners; Armando rejects Palmide and the throne; Adriano tries to stab him; Felicia, claiming to be his brother, insists on dying first; everyone says farewell to sweet dreams of love and honour (in a canonic round, predictably in A flat); each side unfurls its banners and draws up in line of battle, the infidels summoning the faithful with the aid of a 'bronzo tremendo'.

At the start of Act II all the Christians are in prison. The first two numbers are big arias for the two women, both devoted to Armando. Aladino threatens to kill his grandson, but cannot hold out against Palmide's pleas and the kneeling child, and goes to the other extreme, not only sparing the boy but releasing Armando, Adriano, and all the other Christians as well. Meanwhile the vizier Osmino is hatching a plot with the Emirs to overthrow Aladino. Palmide announces her conversion to Christianity and is hailed by Felicia as a sister and embraced by Adriano; they pray in a quartet with Armando. This goads Aladino to fury, and he despatches all the Christians back inside (quintet and chorus).

The prison scene begins with another prayer and a Hymn of Death led by Adriano, after which the Christians break their swords (it is not clear why they still have them). Armando says farewell to Palmide and his son. At this point Osmino and the Emirs take control. In a double male chorus they whisper to the knights, *sotto voce staccato, con mistero*, that all will be well; the knights reply *sotto voce e staccatissimo, con sorpresa*—as well they might. The two parties march out conspiring, and in very short order everything is sorted out to produce the statutory happy end—but not before Armando has saved Aladino from Osmino, Adriano has ordered his knights to defend the betrayed Sultan, Armando has declared himself once more Aladino's prisoner, and Osmino (whose revolt saved everyone's bacon) has been unceremoniously put to the sword. (Meyerbeer made many changes for revivals, and some versions may not agree with the above synopsis.)

Much of this reads like pure Scribe—the capitalization of religion as a stage gambit, massive confrontations brought about by the flimsiest motivation, prominent use of the chorus (all male, but often divided into four parts and two nations), and the absurdly quixotic behaviour of the central characters. Armando, a Crusader Pinkerton, cuts a contemptible figure throughout; Aladino with his alternate imprisonment and release of the Christians is a singularly inept Sultan. The two long-suffering heroines, wronged by the same man, and the mute child threatened with violence on stage are conventional Romantic tear-jerkers. Meyerbeer makes no serious attempt at characterization; he plays each scene for all it is worth and passes on to the next. Everything is pushed to extremes—in dramatic posture, vocal compass, and sheer volume of sound. This is the Rossini of *Semiramide* yoked to a high-pressure German engine. The vocal writing is of the utmost virtuosity, especially that of Armando (one of the last great parts written for a castrato—Velluti, who sang it in London in 1825) and Adriano, a freak tenor whose C major *Allegro marziale* entrance aria, with a compass of two octaves and a fifth (G to d″) and the orchestra competing against a stage band, verges on unintended parody. The ornaments and cadenzas, unlike Rossini's and Donizetti's at their best, are applied rather than organic and therefore never expressive. Like Le Sueur in France Meyerbeer plasters the voice parts with hortatory instructions designed to supply what he may have failed to convey in the music: *con impeto doloroso* and similar phrases in the first chorus, *soffocato* and *con trasportata della disperazione* in the Act I love duet, *con amara ironia* in the first scene for Armando and Adriano. He abuses the *vibrato* effect said to have been introduced by Rubini, asking for it repeatedly, and sometimes for *molto vibrato* (even in chorus parts) and *vibratissimo*. Armando at one point has *sospiro vibrato* over a fermata.

In style the music combines the attributes of Janus and a weathercock. It faces several directions, often in the same piece: back beyond Rossini to Mozart, sideways (or northwards) to Weber, forward to the pulsating energy of early Verdi. The prominence given to the castrato is incongruous, yet symptomatic. Even national influences do not derive from the same period; archaic Mozartian formulae jostle harmonic frissons derived from *Der Freischütz*. Meyerbeer possessed Puccini's knack of picking up the latest tricks, as well as his tendency to aim too low. The immensely spectacular first finale begins with echoes of Mozart, including 'Il mio tesoro'. The round (headed *Canone*) lacks the melodic inspiration of its Rossinian models, but is partly redeemed by an attractive instrumental texture with prominent flutes. The big double chorus with its brass fanfares and two stage bands, equipped with a powerful Turkish battery, reflects Spontini's *Fernand Cortez*, perhaps by way of *Semiramide*. Again Meyerbeer abjures the symmetry of Rossini's finales (the key scheme is E flat–G major and minor–A flat–C–F minor and major), but he does his best to work action into the music.

Despite extravagances the orchestration is one of the opera's stronger features. The free use of solo instruments, especially the woodwind, had been anticipated by Mayr and Rossini, not to mention Mozart; but Meyerbeer's handling is often fresh and varied, for example in the clarinet solos of Palmide's cavatina and her duet with Armando in Act I and the rich accompaniment of Felicia's rondo at the beginning of Act II.

Even the early German operas contain interesting experiments in orchestral sonority, perhaps inspired by Vogler; this was a sphere in which Meyerbeer was always a pioneer, as Berlioz recognized by many citations in his *Traité de l'instrumentation*. Harmonically too the score of *Il crociato* is enterprising for its day; here we are reminded of Weber rather than Rossini. The modulations are well prepared and often strikingly dramatic. The weaknesses are melodic and rhythmic (the ease with which the elements can be separated is itself significant). The tunes, with a few exceptions (the beautiful trio for Armando and the two women in the garden is the most conspicuous—though at the end Meyerbeer all but throws away his advantage in a vacuous multiple cadenza), tend to be short-breathed, derivative, and commonplace, the rhythms in the quicker movements to fall into a galumphing banality suggestive of a circus elephant. The occasional attempts to galvanize them—for example the heavy emphasis on the third quaver of each beat in 12/8 time in the Act I chorus of Egyptian priests and Christian knights—merely draw attention to the limitation.

Disappointment arises not from the badness of some of the score but from the startling inconsistency of nearly all of it. There is no fixative to fuse the elements together, no warning of the tumbles from the potentially sublime to the patently ridiculous. Many happy ideas are either ill executed or let down by some disastrous consequent. The opening *Pantomima ed introduzione*, in which Christian slaves labour at the fortifications under the lashes of their overseers and lament the loss of wives, children, and country, is an interesting and dramatic idea, well calculated to launch the opera, but after the Weberish chromaticism of the orchestral introduction it lapses into triviality; the conception is stronger than the invention. The Act II quintet in which the Christians are sent back to prison ends with a section (Allegro moderato 2/4 E major) almost worthy of Verdi both in its melody, introduced by each voice in turn, and its contrapuntally and harmonically arresting development, but dissolves into trashy coloratura in the coda.

Meyerbeer seems to have invented that special brand of conspiracy music, evolved from the *buffo* ensemble but treated with a straight face, that Sullivan parodied so hilariously in *The Pirates of Penzance*. There are two sterling specimens in *Il crociato*, the four-part chorus of Egyptian conspirators near the beginning of Act II and the double chorus of Emirs and knights towards the end. The former begins impressively with drums alone and much harmonic suspense, including a splendid plunge from E flat to G flat followed by a gradual and well-managed return, but the entire effect is destroyed when the voices enter with an absurdly jaunty tune. Here, and in the double chorus with its comic flourishes between the vocal phrases, a posse of policemen seems to emerge from the wings.

The finest music in the opera occurs in the prison scene. The long orchestral introduction and Adriano's arioso conjure up the grim atmosphere most impressively; the sudden chord of A flat after C major at the mention of death is a thrilling moment. The F minor Hymn of Death, with harp accompaniment and longer than usual phrases, sustains the tension, and the F major section at the end, again faintly Verdian, would be a not unworthy companion to the famous prayers in *Mosé* and *Nabucco* but for the otiose scales and cadenzas.

There are enough flashes of imagination to suggest that a potential operatic genius was lost in Meyerbeer. But tantalizing lapses of taste were characteristic of his whole career. He was to achieve—had already achieved in fair measure—an easily recognizable manner, but never a coherent style. In a few later scenes—the blessing of the daggers and the love duet in Act IV of *Les Huguenots*, the coronation scene in *Le Prophète*, the finales of Acts II, IV, and V and the opening of Act III of *L'Africaine*—he was to surpass anything in *Il crociato*. But he never rid himself of its faults. He never outgrew the short square melodic phrases (Wagner had a similar weakness to overcome), the Rossinian thumps, the tendency to spoil an eloquent vocal movement with extraneous flummery, the debasement of religion and politics to the level of stage carpentry (so unlike their treatment by Verdi or Musorgsky), above all the subordination of character to intrigue and dramatic emotion to hollow rhetoric.

The explanation lies in his character. He was constitutionally a timid man, afraid of failure, afraid of his public (whom he attempted to bribe, both by giving them what he knew they liked and, in his Paris days, more literally by lavish payments to the claque and other influential persons), afraid of trusting his own real gifts, afraid to let go of the past and advance into the unknown. Rossini too had a touch of this; it is the most likely explanation of his early retirement from the theatre. Meyerbeer's insecurity was more basic. It made him afraid to be sincere. He mortgaged his future fame to enjoy the plaudits of contemporaries. By no means a negligible composer, he remained a hopelessly flawed one—and the central flaw has exposed itself to posterity in the most damning form, as a want of artistic integrity.

His arrival in Paris in 1825, to supervise a production of *Il crociato*, did not elicit anything new. One of the most enjoyable features of his French operas, the gift for ballet music and attractive diversions, is adumbrated in the Chorus of Disembarcation in Act I of *Il crociato*, as the ship carrying the Christian embassy is wafted by gentle breezes down the Nile. Besides the task of mastering French declamation, Paris merely gave him a larger theatre of operations—literally and figuratively, for it was still the Mecca of opera composers. And it introduced him to a librettist, Scribe, whose stockbroker attitude to theatrical enterprise coincided all too precisely with his own. Scribe's vast cenotaphs were to chill the bones of Donizetti and Verdi; they must have appeared to Meyerbeer the perfect habitation for his muse.

18

Donizetti and Queen Elizabeth

One of the colourful by-products of the Romantic movement was the sudden popularity of the British Isles as a station for opera, and of English or Scottish history as a foundation—however remote—for the details of the plot. It is true that the scene of Handel's *Ariodante* had been laid in Edinburgh, but for the most part eighteenth-century *opera seria* had confined itself to classical and mythological subjects, or to historical events as open to fable as the early crusades. With the nineteenth century, however, we find continental librettists laying and hatching opera plots all over Britain, Donizetti at grips with *Emilia di Liverpool,* and Verdi dividing *Aroldo* between 'Kenth' and the banks of Loch Lomond. One cause of this was the popularity of Scott's novels; another was the discovery of Queen Elizabeth I as a born coloratura soprano. The two things are connected, of course, through Scott's *Kenilworth,* published in 1821. But Queen Elizabeth came first. Rossini's *Elisabetta, regina d'Inghilterra* had been produced in 1815, with an overture written for *Aureliano in Palmira* and since indissolubly attached to *Il barbiere di Siviglia.* In 1818 there followed *Elisabetta in Derbyshire* by that singular Neapolitan, Michele Enrico Francesco Vincenzo Aloisio Paolo Carafa di Colobrano, who began life as an aristocratic soldier of fortune and ended it as a Paris crony of Rossini, accompanying his walks in the Bois de Boulogne on a horse said to have been acquired from the profits of a long-forgotten operatic success. At least nine operas have been based on *Kenilworth,* including Auber's *Leycester* (1823) and Donizetti's *Il castello di Kenilworth* (1829). But other authors continued to swell the Elizabethan stream. Mercadante's *Il conte d'Essex,* to a libretto by Romani based on Thomas Corneille, was produced at the Scala in March 1833, and Donizetti's opera *Roberto Devereux, conte d'Essex,* taken from a forgotten tragedy by Jacques Ancelot called *Elisabeth d'Angleterre,* followed at the San Carlo, Naples, on 28 October 1837, twenty-two years almost to the day since Rossini's initial grapple with Gloriana.

Donizetti must by this time have been fairly familiar with the love life of our early sovereigns; he had already dealt with King Alfred, Fair Rosamond, Ann Boleyn, and the Earl of Leicester—not to mention Mary Queen of Scots. He is credited with between sixty and seventy operas, of which *Roberto Devereux,* according to the Ricordi vocal score, is the fifty-first. The libretto was the work of Salvatore Cammarano,[1] later to supply Verdi with four operas remarkable for

---

[1] According to W. Ashbrook, *Donizetti and his Operas* (Cambridge, 1982), 401, Cammarano borrowed from Romani's libretto for Mercadante.

the spotlessness of their heroines and the depth of their intrigue, of which the best known are *Luisa Miller* and *Il trovatore*. It would be too much to expect accurate or even plausible history in an Italian libretto of this period, and Cammarano presented Donizetti with the usual quadrangular love drama, complete with compromising tokens of devotion in the form of jewellery and clothing, and characters who either leap to impossible conclusions or fail to notice what has been lying all evening under their noses. Nevertheless, historically absurd as it may be, it is not bad melodrama; and Cammarano, while eschewing political for amorous emotion, made some attempt to portray Elizabeth as a queen as well as a woman.

Furthermore the story, for Italian opera, is relatively unencumbered. The four central characters are Elizabeth, Essex, and the Duke and Duchess of Nottingham (baritone and mezzo soprano). Beside them stand Lord Cecil, a vengeful Parliamentary tenor, and Sir Gualtiero Raleigh, a monosyllabic bass who has little to do but arrest Essex and conduct him to the scaffold. Essex has committed political and amorous treason before the opera begins; he is in (undeclared) love with Sara, Duchess of Nottingham, and she with him. But neither the queen nor Nottingham knows this, though the queen suspects the existence of a rival. In fact, Sara is as close a confidante of hers as Nottingham is a staunch friend of Essex. The latter's open enemies are the Parliamentary party, led by Cecil and Raleigh, who spend a great part of the opera deliberating in the wings and endeavouring to gain the queen's consent to Essex's condemnation. But she still loves him, and in the first act gives him a ring with the guarantee that it will always procure him a pardon in emergency. Being an honest tenor, he refuses her love, whereupon she denounces him and her unknown rival most trenchantly. The act ends with a passionate duet for Essex and Sara, in which, while admitting their love, they agree to part. She gives him as a last pledge a scarf she has been embroidering, and he leaves Elizabeth's ring on her table.

In Act II Raleigh reports the capture of the fleeing Essex and gives the queen the scarf found on him. She is now resolved to condemn Essex, despite the renewed pleas of Nottingham. Essex is brought in and confronted with the scarf, to the stupefaction of Nottingham, who in a manner hallowed by baritone tradition (compare Carlo in *La forza del destino* and Renato in *Un ballo in maschera*) is instantly transformed from friend into fiend. The queen offers Essex the choice of revealing the woman's name or dying on the block; he chooses the latter.

Act III has three scenes. In the first, Sara resolves to take the ring to the queen, humiliating herself in the process, but is locked up by her fuming husband as Essex is dragged past the window to the Tower. Scene ii discovers Essex in the condemned cell, waiting for the ring to work his release. He is thunderstruck when Raleigh tells him the verdict is death, but discharges a cabaletta before being led off. In Scene iii Elizabeth, her anger cooled and her confidante missing, is also pinning her hopes on the ring. When Sara brings it, having broken her captivity, it is too late. No sooner has the queen ordered Essex to be brought back alive than a cannon shot from the Tower announces that all is over. She turns and rends the Nottinghams, and abruptly abdicates in favour of James VI of Scotland, whose sole mention in the opera comes in the very last line. As the curtain falls, Elizabeth is seen lying on a sofa kissing Essex's ring.

It is all too easy to laugh at Italian opera of this period; but there is also a danger, illustrated by the recent reception of Bellini's *Norma*, in allowing the pendulum to swing too far the other way. Indeed it is difficult to decide which is the more pointless, the complaint in some quarters that Bellini's score is not embroidered with ethics and counterpoint, or the claim that skilfully executed bel canto will conceal unlimited deficiencies. A production of *Lucia di Lammermoor* at Covent Garden might make it clear that Donizetti, while by no means a Verdi, is a considerably more interesting composer than Bellini.[2] His melody is more varied and energetic, his harmony and orchestration rather more resourceful, and his dramatic sense, though unreliable, very much stronger. Yet he too lapses often into the tinsel of vocal display and the vulgar march rhythms derived from the military band music of the Napoleonic Wars. *Roberto Devereux* contains examples of all these things, from the absurdly chirpy and undignified cabaletta sung by Elizabeth in Act I at the prospect of seeing Essex again, and the even more ludicrous performance of Essex in the condemned cell (which sounds like a debased and galvanized version of the slow movement of Weber's E minor piano sonata), to the superb ensemble that opens Act II. The court is anxiously awaiting the verdict on Essex: the grand sweep of the melody, first in the orchestra and later in the voices as well, jostled by a reiterated ostinato in an inner part, produces a tension almost worthy of the Verdi of *Simon Boccanegra*. And when in time the courtiers depart we find Donizetti using the same material in a different key over a pedal, much as Bizet uses the habanera at the end of the first act of *Carmen*.

The concerted numbers are nearly all superior to the solos. The two big duets in Act I are both excellent. The scene for Elizabeth and Essex is admirably contrived, both vocally and dramatically, from the top G of Essex's first entry to the fiery conclusion. There is a charmingly tender passage in A flat as the two are left alone. The Andante in 3/8 time leads by a nicely graded increase of tension to a cabaletta for once fully justified by the context: when Essex, unaccompanied, denies his love for Elizabeth, she vents her fury in a tune of splendid energy that Verdi employed almost verbatim at the climax of the trio that ends Act I of *Il trovatore*.[3] (Donizetti wrote two versions of this cabaletta, the second a good deal weaker than the first.) The duet for Sara and Essex at the end of the act is scarcely less good, and here again a Verdi parallel at once leaps to mind—the wonderful duet under the gibbet in *Un ballo in maschera*. Anyone who compares Donizetti's *Dacchè tornasti* (6/8 time, D flat major) with Verdi's *Non sai tu*, together with the striding Allegro in common time introduced by the tenor in each scene, and who further reflects on the similarity of the dramatic situation (lovers meeting secretly at night with the baritone friend-husband lurking in the background, ripe for disillusionment), may be pardoned for

---

[2] *Lucia* was revived at Covent Garden on 17 Feb. 1959, for the first time in 50 years, apart from a single performance in 1925.

[3] See p. 200, Ex. 7.

supposing that Verdi had heard this opera.[4] There is of course no question of conscious borrowing, and no doubt about Verdi's superior artistry. Another fine concerted piece ends Act II, with a moment of great solemnity when the queen signs Essex's death sentence. The final section is an ensemble in F sharp minor, initiated by the queen with a stirring sixteen-bar theme ranging over nearly two octaves.

The duet for Sara and Nottingham in Act III gives the latter his best music in the opera. He is a wooden, though characteristic figure. His Act I cabaletta about friendship with its preposterous military-band bass is from the same stable as the friendship theme in Verdi's *Don Carlos*, and there are points in common with another Verdi Don Carlos, the implacable avenger of *La forza del destino*. But even Donizetti's poor tune is momentarily redeemed in the coda by unprepared modulations from F major first into A flat and then into A natural. In the duet his big tune in E flat is well contrasted with Sara's agitated and syncopated imprecations in the tonic minor. After the weak Tower scene the finale returns to full dramatic vigour. The queen's anxiety is portrayed through a sensitive chromaticism, the rising excitement at Sara's entry by a powerfully rhythmic theme with low trills. The fatal cannon shot is followed by a remarkable scene for Elizabeth: first a sultry Larghetto in B minor, to which a repeated figure of two detached quavers in the bass gives a most sinister flavour, and then a magnificent Maestoso melody in D major with leaping sevenths and tenths in the vocal line that would not be out of place in the mouth of Lady Macbeth.[5] The wandering sequences in which the melody falls from its climax, only to recover suddenly and mount yet higher, are very moving in the context. There is a sudden modulation from D to B flat for the abdication, after which Donizetti brings down the curtain with commendable promptitude.

The opera has two points of historical interest. One is the prognostication of Verdi, of which two more examples may be given: Sara's 'All'afflitto' in the first scene begins exactly like 'Va, pensiero' in *Nabucco*, and—even more striking—the opening of the scene in the condemned cell reappears (with slight but significant changes and in the same key) in the introduction to Ulrica's Invocation (*Un ballo in maschera*).[6] The second point is Donizetti's use of reminiscence motifs to emphasize the drama. This was not new, but although there are instances in Rossini it was much more characteristic of the French Revolution composers[7] and the German Romantics, especially Weber, than the Italians. The march-like theme that accompanies Cecil's first mention of Essex's treason in Act I comes back in the minor when Essex is haled past Nottingham's window to the Tower (Act III, Scene i); and a figure of similar cut associated with Raleigh and the guards in the prison scene returns when Cecil tells the queen that the execution is in progress. Two earlier themes are recalled at the outset of Act III (Sara's duet with Nottingham)—that of Nottingham's friendship aria in Act I and, when the servant brings Sara a letter

---

[4] As he certainly had: it was enjoying a long and very successful run at the Scala while *Oberto* was in rehearsal in Nov. 1839.

[5] See p. 192, Ex. 1.   [6] See p. 201, Ex. 10.   [7] See pp. 114–19.

from Essex, the last section of her duet with him at the end of the same act. Unfortunately the themes, except the last, are not very distinctive, nor are they handled with particular skill. But the fact that the attempt was made shows Donizetti's concern with dramatic problems as well as with prima donnas.

Could *Roberto Devereux* stand revival? This examination, inspired by curiosity as to how Benjamin Britten's coronation theme had been handled by his predecessors, had no such hope in view. But odder things occur in the operatic world, and London has seen sillier revivals, even in the last few months. *Devereux* was a great success in its own day, not only in Italy: within six years of its first production it had reached fifteen countries in three continents and been heard as far afield as Havana, Odessa, Mexico, and Smyrna. The last revival recorded by Loewenberg was at Pavia in 1882; but, if some of the weaker arias were pruned and the abdication cancelled (as it easily could be), there might well be life in the old Don yet. The real difficulty would not be aesthetic but practical: the discovery of suitable singers, in particular a soprano able to discharge the vocal rockets and Roman candles set down for Queen Elizabeth. If this could be done—well, *Norma* is by no means the best opera of its period.[8]

[8] This essay was written just after the Covent Garden production of *Norma* with Callas (Nov. 1952), but some years before the first signs of renewed interest in Donizetti's serious operas. *Roberto Devereux* was revived for the first time since 1882 at Naples on 2 May 1964. It has since been staged in seven countries, but has had only a concert performance in Britain.

19
Donizetti's Serious Operas

Until recently Donizetti was not respectable enough for musicology. He was remembered for two or three comedies; yet he and Rossini both devoted their mature years almost entirely to serious opera. Of Donizetti's seventy stage works, a few of which are lost, exactly half belong to the *opera seria* class (that includes two French grand operas); three are early works on classical subjects, nine are *opere semiserie*, and twenty-three are comedies or farces. But those figures do not give a true picture. In the first place, twelve of the comic operas but only one of the serious are in a single act. Second, if we take the end of 1828 as a dividing line—which ·is roughly when Donizetti reached maturity—we find that before that date he composed twenty-nine operas, of which only six are serious, whereas after it he produced eight comedies (five in one act), four *semiseria* (one in one act), and twenty-nine full-length serious operas. Clearly he regarded Romantic tragedy as his main line.

Traditional opinion assures us that, because Donizetti composed very rapidly, 'even allowing for the thinness and conventional character of the accompaniments, it is clear that such work can be no more than successful improvisation'. (Exactly the same could be said of *Messiah*.) '. . . Facile, sentimental melodies can no longer sustain the interest or be supposed to represent adequately dramatic action, and Donizetti seldom rises above that standard.'[1] That view was almost universal in England until perhaps the last ten years, and is still heard today despite the enterprising revivals of so many of Donizetti's forgotten operas—though at least half of the best have not yet been staged in this country. The prejudice derives partly from our peculiar brand of philistinism that regards music written gratefully for the singing voice as *per se* trivial, if not immoral, and partly from the increasing reputation of German opera, especially Wagner. Donizetti was of course not the only casualty: Bellini, nearly all Rossini, and a great deal of Verdi were likewise consigned to the garbage heap.

Before considering Donizetti's achievement it is worth glancing at the origins of his style. His teacher, Simone Mayr, was a very important influence on Italian nineteenth-century opera. Mayr was a Bavarian, a younger contemporary of Mozart, who studied in Italy and soon decided to settle there, italianizing his name. Between 1794 and 1824 he composed more than sixty operas, all in Italian; like Donizetti he tended to concentrate on comic operas in youth and serious in

[1] *Grove's Dictionary of Music and Musicians*, 5th edn. (London, 1954), art. 'Donizetti'.

maturity, and he had many successes in both forms. In 1802 he established himself
at Bergamo, Donizetti's birthplace, from which he refused to budge, despite
invitations to London, Paris, Lisbon, and Dresden. His operas, like those of Peter
von Winter and Ferdinando Paer, give a very good idea of what may be called the
routine style during the period of Beethoven's early maturity, the generation before
Weber, Schubert, and Rossini. They are thoroughly competent, but suffer from a
bland tone and a lack of creative heat. They look back rather than forward, to
Gluck, Cimarosa, Cherubini, and above all Mozart; the demonic D minor element
in *Don Giovanni*, which influenced so many composers of this period, brought out
the best in Mayr, notably in *Medea in Corinto*, perhaps his most successful opera,
which was produced at Naples in 1813. The novel feature of his music, from an
Italian point of view, was his varied and subtle treatment of the orchestra, especially
the woodwind instruments. He probably learned this from Mozart; he certainly
bequeathed it to Rossini, who was much more his direct heir than Donizetti. There
is very little Romantic feeling in Mayr. In his Leonora opera, *L'amor conjugale*,[2] one
is never aware of the darkness of the dungeon as a dramatic force, as one is in
Beethoven and in earlier French Revolution composers like Méhul and Dalayrac.
Nor was Rossini in this sense a Romantic composer, though the powers of nature
do make themselves discreetly felt in his later operas, *William Tell* in particular.
Romanticism in Italy was always a matter of pathos and politics rather than the
supernatural that obsessed the Germans. The negative side of this emerges from
Verdi's treatment of Joan of Arc's voices and the witches in *Macbeth*.

From Mayr, an excellent teacher, Donizetti acquired a sound operatic technique,
a feeling for instrumental colour, and a firm control of harmonic movement,
especially in big concerted pieces. He was more profoundly and lastingly influenced
by Rossini, whose bouncy rhythms, clattering orchestration, irrepressible crescendos, resounding thumps off the beat before the voice enters, and rare but decisive
and cunningly judged modulations haunt Donizetti's early operas and reappear
from time to time in the later ones, serious as well as comic. It was the digestion
of the Rossini influence more than anything else that delayed Donizetti's maturity
till beyond the age of 30. What seems to have turned him from a follower of Rossini
into a Romantic composer was his contact with Bellini, his junior by four years
—'seems' because the matter requires more detailed investigation. The two were
composing at the same time, often for the same theatres and with the same
collaborators, and they were constantly in direct competition. Temperamentally
they were very different. Donizetti was the most generous and open-handed of
men; he admired Bellini and said so repeatedly. Bellini on the other hand was
consumed by suspicion and envy, convinced that every other composer's hand was
against him; Donizetti, as the most successful of his rivals, was most frequently
accused of trying to damage his interests and his reputation. Bellini's character was
as unlike his music as could be imagined; but it is his music that matters, and it can
hardly be coincidental that Donizetti's sudden emergence as a composer of

[2] See pp. 135–6.

Romantic opera came soon after his encounter with Bellini. He wrote most enthusiastically of *Bianca e Fernando*, Bellini's second opera, at Naples in May 1826; but the decisive work was probably the very successful *Il pirata*, produced at La Scala in October 1827. Bellini's individual brand of long-breathed elegiac lyricism was conspicuous here for the first time (along with much that was trivial and still immature), and Donizetti soon began to reflect it, combining it with his own stronger feeling for harmonic structure, orchestration, and rhythmic energy. His later operas, especially those written for Paris and Vienna, show many signs that he studied Beethoven, Meyerbeer, and Weber among others; and it is amusing to find him echoing 'Va, pensiero' from *Nabucco* in *Dom Sébastien*.

Before staking any claims for Donizetti one must allow some weight to the case against him. It is true that his work is uneven. He did write, if not too rapidly, at least without always exercising a due measure of self-criticism. Even his best operas are liable to regress without warning into footling little tunes more appropriate to a municipal bandstand than an imperial or renaissance court. The young Verdi was an even more glaring offender here, if only because he put more vim into them. It is also true that Donizetti's plots sometimes throw up dramatic absurdities. Two flagrant examples are the happy ends of *Adelia* and *Maria Padilla*; in the latter, after a splendid tragic build-up, all logic is suddenly abandoned: the heroine recovers her lover while he is in process of marrying someone else, fires off a brilliant rondo-finale, and dies of joy—or perhaps sheer surprise. This was due not to cynicism on Donizetti's part—he was thoroughly disgusted with what he had to do—but to the censorship's refusal to permit a suicide on stage. Librettists at this period could be slapdash and inconsequent, but some of their worst excesses were imposed on them by the censors. Everyone knows the trouble Verdi had over *Rigoletto* and *Un ballo in maschera* a decade or two later, and he was a tougher character than Donizetti.

There are three main reasons for looking closely at Donizetti's serious operas. First, though none is a flawless work of art, a great many are—or could be—extremely moving in the theatre. Second—though this may come as a surprise—Donizetti was not just content to accept things as they were; he was from the first a conscious innovator, eager to expand the range of operatic form, though hampered at every stage by factors over which he had little or no control. Third, he exercised a more decisive and fruitful influence on Verdi than is commonly recognized. These points of course are connected. Marco Bonesi, a fellow-student under Mayr, said that as early as 1820 Donizetti 'had many ideas how to reform the predictable situations, the sequences of introduction, cavatina, duet, trio, finale, always fashioned the same way. "But", he added sadly, "what to do with the blessed theatrical conventions? Impresarios, singers, and the public as well, would hurl me into the farthest pit." '[3] He told Mayr in a letter of February 1828 that he wanted to break the yoke of the finales, an ambition he achieved with striking success. In 1832, long before Verdi, he was demanding brevity from his librettists. In 1839, when preparing *Poliuto* for production in Paris, he rejoiced in the chance

³ Quoted by W. Ashbrook, *Donizetti* (London, 1965), 42, and *Donizetti and his Operas*, 19.

to get rid of crescendos and cadenzas and in the emphasis laid by French taste on motivation between verses of cabalettas, so that they do not become mere repetitions. His letters are full of care for dramatic detail; again and again they refute E. J. Dent's suggestion[4] that he took little trouble to read the libretto he was setting.

It was not so easy to put this into practice, and Donizetti had to proceed cautiously; but proceed he did, loosening the forms by degrees from the inside. One characteristic feature was his treatment of recitative, in particular the relaxation and expansion of dialogue sections by means of short lyrical ariosos, often only a few bars long but intensely expressive of the emotion behind the words. Besides varying the design this helped to deepen the characterization. It is rare in Bellini and almost unknown in Rossini, even in *William Tell*, but common in Donizetti's operas from *Il paria* (January 1829) and *Anna Bolena* (December 1830). The final scene of *Anna Bolena*, his first great international success, is a masterpiece of dramatic pathos of a type personal to Donizetti, but quite unlike Bellini or for that matter Verdi (though it haunted Verdi's memory). The unhappy queen languishes in prison, her mind wandering, after being condemned to death by her brutal husband, whose marriage procession with her supplanter Jane Seymour is heard backstage. Instead of the conventional and far inferior mad scene he was to write in *Lucia di Lammermoor*, and which we meet in Bellini, Meyerbeer, and elsewhere, Donizetti gives the queen a series of ariosos of varying length, interspersed with comments from the chorus (her ladies in waiting) and other characters. By expanding the recitative and at the same time breaking up the cavatina sections he produced a fluid texture that reflects the quickly changing moods—until the final cabaletta, which is more conventional. The last scene of *Maria Stuarda* is similar, though not quite on the same level; and so is much of Act IV of *La Favorite*. Vivid little ariosos that never return occur throughout Donizetti's serious operas. Sometimes, as with the first phrase uttered by Lucrezia Borgia or Tasso's 'Poco dunque ti pare' in Act II of *Torquato Tasso*, he seems to toss away material that could have formed a whole movement. There are beautiful ariosos for Emma in Act I of *Ugo, conte di Parigi*, both Parisina and Duke Azzo in the bedroom scene of *Parisina*, Nello in Act II of *Pia de' Tolomei*, Pedro the Cruel at his first entry in *Maria Padilla* (and for Maria herself near the beginning of Act III), and countless others. Most of them are mere fragments, yet they haunt the memory and carry the individual stamp of the composer.

One of the notorious stumbling-blocks to appreciation of Italian opera of this period is the regularity of the aria plan. All too often an expressive cantabile is followed by a bouncy cabaletta over a standardized accompaniment that may bring applause to the singer (which of course was one of its intentions) but causes the fastidious listener's heart to sink. It is not easy to vary them, as Verdi complained later. Donizetti wrote quite enough of the regular pattern, which he eventually discarded; but he also evolved a new type—the slow cabaletta, generally marked Andante or Moderato or Maestoso, which pays more attention to the dramatic requirements than to the pyrotechnical demands of the singer. If there is coloratura,

'Donizetti: an Italian Romantic', in H. van Thal (ed.), *Fanfare for Ernest Newman* (London, 1955), 92. The reference is to the early operas, but the implication is extended to the later.

it is expressive rather than spectacular; and that applies to Donizetti's coloratura in general, much more than to Rossini's. Perhaps the most familiar example of the slow cabaletta is Edgar's 'Tu che a Dio spiegasti l'ali' at the end of *Lucia di Lammermoor*. Quite a few other operas, including *Parisina, Pia de' Tolomei, Torquato Tasso*, and *Roberto Devereux*, end with a movement of this kind. There are no fewer than five in the score of *Pia de' Tolomei*, and almost as many in *Maria di Rohan* and *Gemma di Vergy*. The cabaletta of Chevreuse's aria in Act I of *Maria di Rohan* is actually slower than the cantabile before it. These are all dark tragic operas, in which the hero or heroine is betrayed, condemned, or killed by someone he or she loves; more often than not it is a wife despatched by her jealous husband. One response to this threat is to hurl defiance in the face of destiny, as Anna Bolena does; but other solutions can be more moving and revealing of character, quite apart from the variety they introduce into the musical design. Pia's final aria begins with a Larghetto expressing love for her husband, who has already poisoned her out of groundless jealously, though she does not know it; in the Andante cabaletta she forgives him, and prays for peace between the warring factions. During the second stanza the drooping vocal line and the accompaniment gradually disintegrate as she grows weaker. Parisina is suddenly confronted with the corpse of her lover, who has been executed by her husband; her cabaletta is a lament over his body, and at the end she collapses. One of the most striking examples is Queen Elizabeth's 'Quel sangue versato' at the end of *Roberto Devereux*. If we can forget the historical absurdity of her abdication in favour of James I, this makes a superb end to a very impressive opera.[5] Her plans for rescuing Essex, whose execution she had ordered but intended to circumvent, have been frustrated by the jealous Duke of Nottingham, with whose wife Essex has been having an affair. The cannon from the Tower announces the execution, and the queen gives vent to a vision of blood and horror in a superb Maestoso melody nearly thirty bars long (Ex. 1). This is not at all like Bellini's long tunes, but it is very similar in mood and outline to Lady Macbeth's 'Vieni t'affretta', in which another formidable queen has the smell of blood in her nostrils.

These slow cabalettas not only underline a tragic denouement. They can set up a situation rich in dramatic irony at the first entrance of the principal character. The heroine of *Gemma di Vergy* sits at home longing for her husband's return from the wars. In the first scene of the opera we learn that he intends to divorce her and marry again. When she makes her entry she does not know this, but everyone else on stage does, though each views the prospect differently. Her cantabile expresses her horror of war, which has been disturbing her dreams. She is then told that her husband is returning that very day, and cries out in joy. By setting this cabaletta in slow tempo, while the chorus remarks that her happiness is doomed, Donizetti exploits the irony of Gemma's predicament to the full.

So far as I know, Donizetti was not anticipated in this type of cabaletta. More surprisingly it was not seized upon by Verdi, perhaps because in his cabaletta days he was more concerned to release energy than express pathos. What is in no doubt

⁵ See preceding essay.

Ex.1

is the contribution the slow cabaletta made to the flavour of Romantic melancholy, founded not in sentimentality but in dramatic irony, that pervades all the best of Donizetti's serious operas and is perhaps his most personal contribution to the form.

Other factors operated to the same end: choice of subject, vocal layout, harmony, orchestration, and the shaping of individual scenes and movements. Donizetti was not interested only in swooning heroines. At least three operas, *Sancia di Castiglia*, *Lucrezia Borgia*, and *Belisario*, have no love interest at all in the usual sense. They are concerned partly with politics and partly with relationships inside the family, especially between parents and children. The mutual love of father and daughter that is one of the central themes of *Belisario* was not lost on Verdi; the duet in which they set out for their lonely exile is paralleled and directly echoed in the last act of *Luisa Miller*, even down to the slow cabaletta (one of the very rare examples in Verdi[6]). Both operas incidentally have librettos by Cammarano. There is another

[6] Another, surely the greatest of all slow cabalettas, is 'O terra, addio!' in Act IV of *Aida*.

fine father-daughter duet in Act III of *Maria Padilla*. In *Torquato Tasso* Donizetti tried to combine a tragic theme, the love of the poet for a woman above his station, with a *buffo* element represented by a comic bass and a male chorus of courtiers who make fun of him and also comment on the action. It is perhaps not a complete success, but it shows enterprise, and one can almost sense the courtiers in *Rigoletto*. This is even more evident in Act III of *La Favorite*, where the courtiers mock Fernando when he finds he has married the king's discarded mistress; we think too of the laughter of Samuel and Tom in *Ballo*. *Torquato Tasso* is not an *opera semiseria*, a type descending from the French Revolution *opéra comique* with a bourgeois domestic background, as in *Emilia di Liverpool* and *Linda di Chamounix*, or for that matter *La sonnambula*, but an attempt to enlarge the scope of Romantic opera by bringing together two things much further apart, heroic tragedy on the one hand and broad comedy on the other, as Verdi was to do in *La forza del destino*.

The fact that Tasso, the lover-hero, is a baritone considerably darkens the vocal colour. This is very characteristic of Donizetti's serious operas, especially the later ones. In *Belisario*, *Maria Padilla*, and *Caterina Cornaro*, as well as *Tasso*, the tenor is almost a peripheral figure; in *Maria Padilla* he is the heroine's father, who goes mad, thereby poaching the conventional prerogatives of both baritone and soprano. Again and again the soprano and baritone carry the main burden of the plot, and there is often a prominent bass as well. *Marino Faliero* has four basses and baritones, all important in the action, two of them very substantial parts composed for Tamburini and Lablache. In *Gemma di Vergy*, *Parisina*, *Pia de' Tolomei*, and *Maria di Rohan* the powerful figure of the jealous baritone husband dominates the opera, vocally and dramatically. The magnificent scene in Act II of *Parisina*, where the duke is maddened by jealousy on hearing his sleeping wife murmur her lover's name, inevitably suggests Othello—and the grim concentration of the music is closer to Verdi's opera than to Rossini's. *La Favorite* has a mezzo-soprano heroine, another dominant baritone in the king, and a Grand-Inquisitorial bass in the prior of the monastery. It was Donizetti who established the type of dramatic baritone that Verdi was to put to such splendid use.

As early as *Anna Bolena*, and much more later, Donizetti's operas show a growing preoccupation with the darker emotions of guilt, jealousy, and remorse. They inspired some of his finest music and, especially in the late works written for Paris and Vienna, are reflected in a greatly enriched harmony and orchestration, the result no doubt of contact with French Grand Opera. The bold, restless harmonic style of parts of *Dom Sébastien*, his last opera (1843), is closer to middle-period Verdi, even the Verdi of the Requiem, than to Bellini or Donizetti's own operas of a few years earlier. *La Favorite* shows how little justification there is for criticizing Donizetti's accompaniments for their 'thinness and conventionality'. Not that the Italian operas lack either fullness or individuality in scoring: witness the trio in *Maria Padilla* accompanied by cor anglais alone, the long introduction for bass clarinet and harp to Act II of *Maria di Rudenz*, and the original obbligato for glass harmonica in the *Lucia* mad scene.

The sombre orchestral introductions with which Donizetti liked to begin an act or important scene are often memorable in themselves and very effective in creating an atmosphere. The introduction to Act II of *Lucia* is a familiar example, and *Poliuto* and *Maria Padilla* each have more than one of outstanding quality. There is a hint of Florestan's dungeon in the C minor Andantino that begins Act III of *Torquato Tasso*. Some of these introductions suggest other Romantic composers, and not always earlier ones: for example the extended Schumannesque syncopations that begin Act II of *Sancia di Castiglia* or the startling anticipation of Mahler's First Symphony in the prelude to *Dom Sébastien*, which recurs as a funeral procession in Act III of the opera. The opening bars of Essex's scene in the Tower in *Roberto Devereux* were actually borrowed by Verdi; they might equally be early Wagner. One theme in the introduction to Act IV of *La Favorite* has a strong flavour of *Tannhäuser*; it may or may not be a coincidence that the first edition of the vocal score was arranged by Wagner. Donizetti's use of the horns, generally four of them, to evoke a sinister or Romantic atmosphere has not a little in common with *Der Freischütz*, for example in the prelude to *Maria Padilla*; it is worlds apart from *William Tell*, where Gessler's horns—an important element in the drama since for two acts they are all we hear of the tyrant—sound neither sinister nor Romantic but merely jolly.

One feature in which Donizetti is nearly always at his best, and consistently superior to Bellini, is the construction of ensembles, especially the slow pieces that concentrate the action at the beginning of a finale. Everyone knows the sextet in *Lucia*, but there are plenty of others of equal quality, sextets in Act I of *Belisario* and Act III of *Maria Padilla*, the quartet in Act III of *La Favorite*, a magnificent septet in Act IV of *Dom Sébastien*, and a complex trio-cum-quartet in Act II of *Gemma di Vergy*. If a headlong stretta follows, which is not always the case, it is sometimes arrested at the climax, by a recitative in which the hero surrenders his sword in Act I of *Ugo, conte di Parigi*, by a death sentence and a drop from Vivace to Maestoso in Act III of *Dom Sébastien*. Towards the end of his life Donizetti tended to abandon the stretta and adopt unorthodox ends to acts and whole operas. In *Dom Sébastien* again, an opera whose principal feature is its uncompromising dramatic honesty, he concludes Act II with a romance without cabaletta, its second stanza enriched by new chromatic harmony, and the whole opera with a free recitative such as Verdi employed at the end of *Simon Boccanegra*. The lovers are shot just when they think they are safe; instead of giving them a duet of hope or farewell Donizetti cuts them off before they can open their mouths, and the opera ends with a defiant cry from the loyal poet Camoens. The whole scene occupies three pages in the vocal score. This is nearly twice as long as the astonishing last scene of *Maria di Rohan*. After B flat has been established as the key, there is a violent plunge into D major for the climactic recitative; B flat is regained for a single bar, whereupon the tonality collapses into E flat minor during the quick nine-bar coda, and only just gets back in time for the curtain. An earlier and weaker opera, *Marino Faliero*, also ends with a dramatic recitative, punctuated by the fall of an executioner's axe. The finale of *Belisario* is on the face of it a big solo scene for the soprano, the commonest type of conclusion in Rossini and Bellini. But the cantabile is separated from the cabaletta

—another slow one—by a beautifully managed episode, a conflation of funeral march, ensemble, and recitative during which Belisario is carried in mortally wounded; the voices are superimposed conversationally on the march rhythm without interrupting it, and Belisario's death triggers off the cabaletta, sung by his treacherous but now penitent wife. The opera also contains a prime example of the patriotic Risorgimento-type aria, 'Trema, Bisanzio', which has the same accompaniment figure as 'Di quella pira' in *Il trovatore*.

The big double arias and duets by no means always adhere to the conventional plan of a cantabile followed by a two-stanza cabaletta; in the late operas they very seldom do. Almost all the set pieces in *Caterina Cornaro*, *Maria di Rohan*, and *Dom Sébastien* and many in earlier operas (the father-daughter duet in *Maria Padilla* is an outstanding example) are free and unpredictable in design, abandoning symmetry to follow the dictates of the plot. This is far too complex a matter to explore here, but Donizetti's duets and trios in particular, and a comparison of his methods with those of Verdi, would make a rewarding study. A very effective stroke that Donizetti made his own, though it was not peculiar to him, is the introduction of the second voice in a duet with a change of mode as well as new material. There are two beautiful examples in *Poliuto*. In Act II the baritone Severo has a regular sixteen-bar stanza in E minor with short agitated phrases, at the end of which Paolina (who formerly loved him but is now married to Poliuto) enters with a much broader melody in E major beginning on a long-held top E. The fact that her words are sad ('Ei non vegga il pianto mio') enhances the impact. A similar stroke, in the same key, distinguishes the duet for Paolina and Poliuto in the last act: she urges him, in the minor, to escape a horrible death by renouncing his Christian faith; he proclaims his belief in a happier afterlife in the major, again entering on the top E. One thinks inevitably of 'Ah! che la morte ognora' in *Il trovatore*, especially as the accompaniment changes to triplets at the same time. There is a similar moment in the duet for the two sisters in Act II of *Maria Padilla*. Other personal traits—again not unique—are Donizetti's habit of vacillating between major and tonic minor in the course of a melody, to produce an effect of plaintiveness or pathos, and of modulating unexpectedly just before the end of a paragraph. In Camoens's cavatina in Act I of *Dom Sébastien* he goes from F to A in the third bar of a nine-bar tune, regains F in the fifth and is in G flat by the seventh. In the same character's Act III romance, a much longer melody, he suddenly moves from E flat to G flat two bars before the cadence, and then after regaining the tonic adds a second paragraph in E flat minor. Neither of these arias has anything approaching a cabaletta.

Donizetti makes happy use of Rossini's trick of a running tune in the orchestra, sometimes repeated in different keys, while the voices carry on independently, but he invests it with a more powerful irony, for example in Act II of *Lucia*, where the almost flippant A major melody during the recitative before the signing of the marriage contract returns with mocking effect when Edgar learns of the wedding. There is a very striking instance of this sort of texture in the little duet for two spies in Act I of *Lucrezia Borgia*, where a sinuous tune winds its ironical way through the orchestra, punctuated by pairs of staccato quaver chords, while the voices hatch a plot in free parlando. This was almost certainly the inspiration for the colloquy between Rigoletto and Sparafucile, which is identical in layout and dramatic context and conveys the same impression of dirty business afoot, and more remotely for the entry of the Grand Inquisitor in *Don Carlos*.

Anyone who considers Donizetti's choruses may at once recoil from the tiresome jauntiness of the wedding guests in *Lucia*, one of the most prehensile tunes ever written. But he can do much better than this. *Belisario* contains choruses of puzzled senators in the first act and exiles in the second that are not only impressive in themselves but go a long way towards establishing these bodies as living characters in the drama instead of a mere background. The scene in Act II of *Roberto Devereux* where the courtiers await the outcome of Essex's trial, based on an ostinato figure and a long winding melody in the orchestra, is a marvellous compound of lyricism and suspense. The unison prayer for male voices, 'Divo spirto', in Act II of *Pia de' Tolomei* is fully the equal of the famous prayers in *Mosé* and *Nabucco*. *Lucrezia Borgia* has three vivid choruses of ruffians, at once swashbuckling, furtive, and sinister, that play an important part in the plot, and *Caterina Cornaro* a chorus of assassins so fraught with menace that it reduces Banquo's murderers in *Macbeth* to the status of a child's puppets.

The many direct anticipations of Verdi to be found in Donizetti's operas are not confined to the chance resemblances one would expect between two near-contemporaries using the same idiom and writing for the same audience.[7] Of course Verdi was influenced by Rossini, Bellini, and Donizetti—it could hardly be otherwise —and sometimes used them as models. But I suggest that Donizetti was easily the most important of the three, for two principal reasons. First, when Verdi echoes him either literally (which is not to say deliberately) or in more generalized fashion, one constantly finds quite intricate parallels, not only in mood and material but in key and dramatic situation. Second, these echoes are far less common in Verdi's early operas than in those of his growing and complete maturity. There are very few before the first version of *Macbeth* (1847) but a great many in the operas from then on, up to and including *La forza del destino*. It was when Verdi began to individualize his characters and explore their more complex emotions that he became most susceptible to Donizetti's influence. This is not as surprising a conclusion as it may sound. We are apt to look at the early Verdi with hindsight, knowing what he was to achieve later, and scarcely knowing Donizetti at all. But whereas the Verdi of the 1840s was a composer of immense energy and spasmodic insight, the Donizetti of the later serious operas was a more experienced and in many ways a more subtle artist. The early Verdi was simply not ready for him.

Direct echoes in the same keys are sometimes very striking, as between the last scene of *Anna Bolena*, where the queen's mind wanders into the past (Ex. 2*a*), and another queen in the same situation, Lady Macbeth sleep-walking (Ex. 2*b*). The virtually identical melody, harmony, rhythm, and key in Exx. 3*a* and 3*b* correspond

[7] For a fuller account see my paper 'Some Echoes of Donizetti in Verdi's Operas', *Atti del IIIᵉ congresso internazionale di studi verdiani* (Parma, 1974), 122–47.

Ex.2

Ex.3

to their virtually identical dramatic situations and even their position in the operas. Both are ariosos of the characteristic Donizettian type, mentioned earlier, the first sung by Percy in *Anna Bolena* after he knows he has lost Anna for ever, the second by the duke in *Rigoletto* when he thinks he has lost Gilda. Another pregnant arioso is sung by Ghino in the first scene of *Pia de' Tolomei* when he thinks Pia has betrayed his love (Ex. 4). It is scarcely necessary to quote the parallel in *La traviata*. The duets in *Belisario* and *Luisa Miller* in which father and daughter decide to spend the rest of their lives in exile are similar all through in mood and layout, and built around the same keys, F major and minor and A flat major, though Donizetti's cabaletta

Ex.4

is in F, Verdi's in A flat. Each begins with a falling seventh; Belisario sings it to the words 'O figlia!' (Ex. 5a), Verdi leaves it to the orchestra (Ex. 5b). Or again, two tenors cursing, both (as in the last pair of examples) to words by Cammarano; Edgar in *Lucia di Lammermoor*, on Lucia's betrayal (Ex. 6a), and Rodolfo in the last act of *Luisa Miller*, cursing the day he was born (Ex. 6b), may sing in different keys, but rhythm, accompaniment, and general shape are the same.

Il trovatore echoes at least five Donizetti operas—six if we count one melody that occurs in two works—of which three deserve particular mention. First, the duet for Elizabeth and Essex in Act I of *Roberto Devereux* (Ex. 7) is mirrored in the trio that

Ex.5

Ex.6

(a)

(b)

Ex.7

ends Act I of *Trovatore*. Second, a prominent theme from the finale of Act II of *Poliuto* (Ex. 8), which also occurs in *Maria di Rudenz*, may have suggested part of the Count di Luna's 'Il balen'. And third, Riccardo's aria 'Alma soave e cara' in Act II of *Maria de Rohan* (Ex. 9), a late opera consistently prophetic of Verdi in mood, especially in the last two acts, has a parallel in Leonora's 'Mira, di acerbe lagrime',

Ex.8

which has the same accompaniment figure and the same harmony, including the soulful diminished seventh in the third bar.

There are two remarkable reminiscences of *Roberto Devereux* in *Un ballo in maschera*. In key, harmony, and both its principal phrases the introduction to Essex's scene in the Tower (Ex. 10*a*) was virtually taken over by Verdi for the opening of Ulrica's incantation (Ex. 10*b*). There is a more subtle relationship between the two big love duets, whose dramatic situation is identical: the tenor is keeping a secret assignation with the wife of his closest friend, and this leads directly to the catastrophe. The nearest thematic resemblance is between a secondary idea—not the main theme—in the slow 6/8 sections near the beginning, bars 5–8 in Donizetti, 13–16 in Verdi. Each composer repeats the phrase, but Verdi—now in full maturity more than ten years after Donizetti's death—makes more of it. There is an interesting tonal link here. Donizetti's movement is in D flat, Verdi's in F; but when Amelia takes the phrase over from Riccardo she steers it into Donizetti's key with the harmony it had on its first appearance in his opera but not in Verdi's.

Ex.10

One might suppose that by 1862, the year of *La forza del destino*, Verdi would have outgrown Donizetti. Far from it, though he does of course enrich him. There are three surprisingly close parallels. One is the scene which occurs in both *Forza* and *La Favorite* where the heroine (Leonora in each case) comes to a monastery, hears monks praying accompanied by an organ, and longs for sanctuary and forgiveness. The whole treatment of voices and accompaniment, as well as one phrase sung by the soprano, is remarkably similar. When Verdi's Leonora thanks the Father Superior for giving her sanctuary and calls on the angelic choir to welcome her, the music echoes the duet from *Poliuto* in which hero and heroine claim the blessing of the Church in their martyrdom (Ex. 11). The tune is not the same, but almost everything else is; key, rhythm in the voice parts (steady 4/4 crotchets), accompaniment with triplet arpeggios on the harp, and even some of the words (a few bars later Verdi's Leonora sings 'Plaudite, o cori angelici, mi perdonò

Ex.11

(a)   [Allegro vivace]

(b)   [Moderato] Più mosso

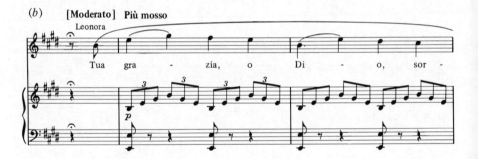

il Signor' to a variant of the same melody). And the overture to *La Favorite*, produced in 1840, must surely have been at the back of Verdi's mind when he wrote the overture to *Forza* more than twenty years later. There are resemblances between all three themes in both works, but the most notable feature is the similarity of atmosphere and design: an agitated nervous main theme in the minor, then a soaring melody with a climax in the major, starting quietly against tremolo accompaniment and rising higher at the second statement before falling back to a recall of the opening. The climax of both overtures is a fortissimo statement of the major melody at the end.

There is one significant point about these examples. None of them is musically trivial. They tend to show both composers at their best and most characteristic, taking into consideration the period when they were written. The conclusion to be drawn is that there was a quality in Donizetti's imagination that appealed to the maturing Verdi, who responded in much the same way to similar dramatic stimuli. His unconscious memory did the rest. From *Rigoletto* on of course he far outstripped Donizetti. But the man who inspired Verdi in this way was a considerable artist in his own right.

20

La Damnation de Faust

Berlioz presents the curious phenomenon of a composer long-breathed in individual movements yet fragmentary over whole works. While he could prolong a melody or a musical paragraph with unrivalled eloquence, his larger structures are apt to fall into a series of adjacent blocks, with the connections either clumsily handled or omitted altogether. These blocks, often perfectly shaped in themselves, seem to have been conceived without reference to each other. When placed in succession they resemble a string of pearls threaded haphazard, or a window of exquisite stained glass incompetently leaded. It is as if his inspiration were effective only over a certain distance; when it ran dry he could only begin again from scratch.

In *La Damnation de Faust* this tendency is reinforced by special circumstances. Berlioz's first published work of any consequence, composed in 1828 two years before the *Symphonie fantastique*, was *Huit Scènes de Faust*. Eighteen years later these scenes became the framework of *La Damnation*. It is a tribute to the early maturity of Berlioz's genius that many of the most famous episodes—Marguerite's two songs, Mephistopheles' Song of the Flea and Serenade, the Concert of Sylphs— occur in the early version, although they were modified later. But his re-use of old material was governed less by suitability of context than by dislike of waste: the 'Tristesse' of Romeo was originally that of the moribund Sardanapalus, and the monodrama *Lélio* might have been the composer's answer to an urgent appeal for salvage. He placed the first scene of *La Damnation* in Hungary simply because he wished to use his recent version of the Rakoczy March, and introduced the 'Amen' fugue on the theme of Brander's song about the rat in order to parody a favourite device of his enemies the Conservatoire professors—and very amusingly he does it. The parable about new wine and old bottles does not quite apply, since the old material may be newly thought out; but this method of composition hardly makes for a unified conception.

Berlioz called the work first a concert opera and later a dramatic legend. As these titles suggest, it falls between two stools (had he possessed the structural power of a Wagner he might have welded them into a substantial bench), being too spiritually disjunct for oratorio and too inconsequent for opera. Although it is intensely dramatic in many of its details, and whole scenes appear to yearn for the stage (especially in Part III, whose opening is barely tolerable without it, and whose finale closely resembles the conventional operatic type against which Berlioz the critic was never tired of inveighing), attempts to stage it have always failed owing to the jerkiness of the action, which is alternately immobile and elliptical to the point of incomprehensibility. The story is handled in a very casual manner. While unimportant details are expanded, essentials are often abbreviated into obscurity; Faust only signs the deed committing himself to Mephistopheles' power the moment before starting for the Abyss. In these circumstances any comparison with Goethe would be absurd. We are not much interested in whether Faust is damned or not; nor perhaps was Berlioz. What we have is a series of vignettes—pictures from a *Faust* exhibition.

The score is so full of music of the most profound beauty and originality that despite all its faults we cannot afford to leave it on the shelf for even a short period. The great things are so great that custom never stales them. Here is the full variety of Berlioz's genius, the compound of Romantic sensuousness and exuberance with the purest Classical detachment that seems to sum up the very best in both lobes of the artistic temperament. It is in this sense that Berlioz has been compared with Shakespeare. He enters for the moment into the soul of a situation, while at the same time observing it with the tense objectivity of a great Classical artist. His musical language has defied the analysts from his own day to this. One of the supreme melodists in all music, his congenital habit of thinking in phrases of irregular length and rhythmic stress perplexed his contemporaries and has made fools of many worthy persons since. Musical history has nothing to compare with the almost unbearable beauty of Marguerite's song about the King of Thule (which was not even composed for these words), or with the rhythmic vitality of Mephistopheles' and Brander's songs. Berlioz has been accused of contrapuntal ineptitude; yet this one score yields things as varied as the Amen parody, the almost Bachian chromatic polyphony of the first scene in Part II (Faust in his study), and the admirably contrived double chorus of soldiers and students. Only as an orchestrator has he never suffered a slump in reputation—and that may be partly due to the fact that he achieved respectability by writing a treatise on the subject. The Dance of the Will o' the Wisps is an astonishing *tour de force* that no later experiment has outshone. Perhaps the loveliest scene of all, though not the most original, is the famous episode on the banks of the Elbe, where Berlioz weaves every kind of musical enchantment, sometimes by the most unlikely means (he conjures a wonderful effect of remote poetry by accompanying an air with four trombones and draws measureless magic from a few bare octaves), while binding the whole scene together with subtle anticipations of the Dance of the Sylphs that forms its climax.

If the greatness of a work of art consisted in the sum of the beauty of its parts, there would be a case for ranking *La Damnation de Faust* above anything else in nineteenth-century music. But there is no denying the tepid matter and the dross. The awkwardness of the joins is often desolating, and the recitatives seem all the more perfunctory for the polished brilliance of the blocks they are required to cement. Faust's remarkable invocation to Nature in Part IV is followed by a chaotic and scrambled recitative, penetrated by unexplained hunting horns, during which the action suddenly jumps several steps. Before we know what has happened we are on the way to the Abyss. This latter episode is a highly imaginative tone picture; but it is difficult not to smile at the princes of darkness (twelve basses) talking their infernal language in Pandemonium, but breaking into French to address Mephistopheles. What are we to say of creatures who make remarks like 'Diff, diff' and 'Fory my Dinkorlitz'—the last word surely a perfect name for the latest diabolical cocktail? As for the angels of the Epilogue, they have been described with admirable succinctness as 'of the stonemason's yard, stony'.[1]

Berlioz was inspired by the peaks only; he did not see that the valleys between cannot be neglected if the whole terrain is to be seen in proportion. This partly accounts for the impression of strenuous grandiosity received by many listeners, an impression belied by the music itself, which even when it employs huge forces handles them with restraint. But, with the notable exception of his epic opera *Les Troyens*, he could not present a comprehensive vision on a grand scale since he had no such vision himself. There was at his centre a philosophical void; as he said himself, he acted as if he believed in everything when in fact he believed in nothing. This negative philosophy, for which a vague pantheism (it appears in Faust's monologues) is no valid substitute, is unlikely to create a masterpiece on a theme like *Faust*. Berlioz resembles not so much Bach or Mozart or Beethoven as a defective Shakespeare, a potential universal genius with faults to scale. A contemporary whose career displays many of the same personal and artistic qualities, the same calm classicism apparently at variance with an extreme Romantic exuberance, uttered the profound epigram: 'Great men too often have greater faults than little men can find room for.' It has been applied to its author, Landor; it could equally be applied to Berlioz.

[1] J. H. Elliot, *Berlioz* (London, 1938), 184.

Les Troyens

Berlioz regarded *Les Troyens* as the climax of his artistic life, and with reason. His last major work except for the comic opera *Béatrice et Bénédict*, it was the fruit of an enduring love for Virgil and in lesser degree of Gluck and Shakespeare. He composed words and music—like Wagner he was his own librettist—during the years 1856–8, but was never destined to hear the opera in full. After long and fruitless wire-pulling at the Paris Opéra, then at a particularly stagnant period of its not very edifying history, he finally allowed Carvalho, the manager of the Théâtre-Lyrique, to detach the last three of the original five acts and perform them separately under the title *Les Troyens à Carthage* in 1863. Even so the score was clumsily cut, and the work fell flat. The first two acts (*La Prise de Troie*) were not performed till 1890 (after Berlioz had been more than twenty years in his grave), when Felix Mottl conducted the entire work, spread over two evenings, at Karlsruhe. Paris still awaits a complete stage performance; and until this month the opera has never been given professionally in Britain,[1] though Erik Chisholm in Glasgow (1935) and J. A. Westrup in Oxford (1950) conducted enterprising performances with largely amateur companies.

Most good judges who know the opera—and this knowledge cannot be gained from the vocal score, which offers little more than a caricature—are agreed that for grandeur of conception, nobility of tone, and imaginative range it has scarcely a rival in operatic history. How is it then that we so seldom hear it, even a century after its composition, when Wagner has accustomed us to great length, and his successors to almost every other kind of operatic excess? There are several answers to this question, apart from the natural conservatism of audiences. In the first place, *Les Troyens* is a very long opera, and the licence allowed to *Götterdämmerung* and *Die Meistersinger* has not been extended to any other composer. Secondly, unless we count the ballet, it is completely lacking in those concessions to popular taste (however justifiable) which are an important ingredient in all the most successful operas of the French and Italian repertory. Berlioz writes exacting parts for the singers without ever allowing them to show off; he is never sentimental; he never aims at a cheap heart-throb. On the contrary, he demands an unusual degree of co-operation from the audience, in the absence of which he withholds his charms. Thirdly, the organization of the opera is of a most unusual kind. This is due partly

[1] This essay was written to introduce the first professional production in Britain, at Covent Garden on 6 June 1957.

to the nature and source of the subject, and partly to Berlioz's peculiar make-up as an artist.

His imagination is quite unlike that of any other composer. Apart from the occasional strangeness of his musical idiom (the silly charge of incompetence, revived as recently as the article in *Grove 5*, can be dismissed with the contempt it deserves), he had a strong literary bent, which showed itself not only in the quality of his critical and autobiographical writings—he was by far the best writer among the great composers—but in his choice of subjects for musical treatment, and still more in the treatment itself. He was apt to assume in the listener a grasp of the literary background akin to his own, and so to hurry over or suppress altogether the links necessary to a self-sufficient work of art. All his earlier dramatic or quasi-dramatic works—*Benvenuto Cellini*, *Roméo et Juliette*, *La Damnation de Faust*, *L'Enfance du Christ*—contain scenes of overpowering beauty and originality. Yet each in the last resort makes a disjointed and uneven impression, because Berlioz worked in terms of a series of tableaux rather than a unified whole. It is like a film in which time and again the camera lingers over a beautiful shot and then shifts to another of perhaps equal beauty without supplying an adequate connection. In a dramatic composer this is a serious weakness. The success of an opera in the theatre depends quite as much on timing as on quality of vision (we can see this in Puccini); a miscalculation can waste the most splendid music. It is this defect that has fatally handicapped an opera so musically rich as *Benvenuto Cellini*: Berlioz could not resist putting in scenes because they appealed to him rather than because they contributed to the unity of the whole. We would not be without them when we hear the opera; but their presence, by destroying its coherence, ensures that we very seldom do. The same fate would probably have overtaken the other works mentioned above had Berlioz written them for the stage.

In *Les Troyens* we find the same tendency to proceed in a series of jerks; but there is a new factor. It has an overriding, unifying theme. The first two acts deal with the fall of Troy (by means of the Greek horse) and the fate of Cassandra, blessed with the gift of prophecy but cursed by the attached condition that she shall never be believed, the last three acts with the love story of Dido and Aeneas at Carthage, likewise doomed to a tragic issue. The whole is braced together by the idea of the continuity of Troy and the city's refoundation at Rome; the gods have imposed this duty on Aeneas, and to it all personal happiness must bow.[2]

Berlioz took over this theme intact from Virgil's *Aeneid*, on which the libretto is very closely based, and thereby imported into a drama much of the framework of an epic. The two methods are radically different. *Les Troyens* is therefore likely to disconcert an audience that expects a traditional opera and is not prepared for new sensations. The same factor makes the opera difficult to stage, since an epic point may not be easily enforceable by dramatic means. (But it should not be impossible: Wagner's music dramas present equal if not greater scenic difficulties,

---

[2] Those who would study the plot in detail—and in few operas is this so rewarding—should consult the excellent synopses in Ernest Newman's *Opera Nights* (London, 1943) and recent editions of *Kobbé's Complete Opera Book*, edited by the Earl of Harewood.

and Berlioz did not require Laocoon to be devoured by serpents on stage, a demand well within the capacity of Wagner.) It also means that the work is subject to peculiar internal strains. It is never easy to give theatrical validity to a political idea, least of all in a musical work, especially if it runs against the natural sympathies roused by the story. Berlioz lacked Wagner's ability to turn his characters into symbols and manœuvre them like chessmen on a board. Their sufferings as human creatures were intensely real to him, and we cannot be surprised that Cassandra and Dido became to a great extent the heroines of two separate, loosely linked tragedies. The bisection of the opera, though it was imposed on Berlioz and though it obscures his theme, does correspond to something deep in the nature of the work. It also of course appeals to managers who wish to spread it over two evenings, since it does away with certain difficulties of casting, such as the demand in the first two acts for great dramatic singers who never appear again.

If *Les Troyens* were a traditional opera, this dichotomy would break its back. But Berlioz does not proceed in ordinary dramatic terms. In the Trojan acts the Greeks, except for a few anonymous soldiers at the very end, do not appear at all, so that one vital element of conflict is missing. At Carthage we do not see Aeneas confronted with the gods' decree or making the decision to leave Dido: Mercury simply enters after the lovers have left the stage at the end of their great duet, utters the magic word 'Italie!' and the curtain falls. Berlioz relies on the audience to supply the connection. The main epic theme does not arise from the drama at all; it is superimposed from without, as it is in Virgil, who shaped the whole *Aeneid* as a tribute to Augustus, the supposed heir of Aeneas. Again and again, Berlioz appeals over the heads of the characters directly to the audience and its acquaintance with literature and history. The marvellous scene in which Hector's widow and little son kneel in mourning before Priam is one of the most profoundly moving in all opera. Yet Priam is not established as a character, and neither Andromache nor Astyanax utters a single word. Berlioz enlists our prior knowledge of the emotional and historical significance of Hector's death, of all that it means to Troy, and of the terrible fate in store for the survivors. This epic irony, so to speak, is in its context overwhelming. The appearance of Mercury (the only glimpse we have of the gods who supply the main motive power of the action) has a somewhat similar effect; and the very end of the opera, when Dido on her deathbed foresees the rise of Hannibal while a vision of Rome and the Capitol appears like Valhalla on the backcloth, is an extension of the same idea.

Berlioz is able to get away with this because the double epic-dramatic vision exactly suits the nature of his genius, and in particular his tendency to project the action in isolated episodes, like friezes on the pediments of a Greek temple. Thus, whereas the dramatic symphony *Roméo et Juliette* disintegrates into incoherence, the epic opera *Les Troyens* does achieve a possible new synthesis. It may be precarious and even fortuitous, and it is certainly unique; but it is valid, provided the audience will co-operate. Here the subject itself is an advantage. By taking one of the great classical legends, whose story and its overtones are familiar to all, Berlioz can jump from scene to scene with comparatively little risk of disaster; and his overall theme, however loosely superimposed, does help to keep the episodes in focus. Further-more, a story that combined the fatalism of Roman-Greek mythology with the pathos of Cassandra's and Dido's sufferings and the violence of the Trojan cata-strophe was perfectly calculated to inspire that rare compound of the classical and the Romantic that we find in Berlioz. The notion of Berlioz the arch-Romantic, striking extravagant and farouche attitudes, which derives some justification from his life as a young man, never was supported by his music. Of all the composers who have treated dramatic subjects from the ancient world, only Handel, Gluck, and Berlioz recreate anything like the authentic blend of intense feeling, clear vision, and moral detachment that underlies the pure classical spirit. But whereas Handel and Gluck worked in sympathy with their period, Berlioz was born out of time, a Classic in a Romantic age, who necessarily reflected this conflict in his art. Hence perhaps the element of profound melancholy that haunts all his greatest work. If we seek a parallel, we can perhaps find one in Landor, who likewise combined a Romantic turbulence in private life with a serene Classicism in the best of his art, whose attempts at the larger forms were frustrated by a similar broken vision, who also wrote an epic (*Gebir*) rooted in Virgil, and whose final quasi-dramatic synthesis in the *Imaginary Conversations* is perhaps the nearest approach in literature to Berlioz's method.

The balance between the component forces and the level of musical inspiration varies considerably in the course of *Les Troyens*. After the striking first scene, in which the Trojans, exploring the deserted Greek camp, recoil in horror from the very name of the dead Achilles (another appeal to the audience's associations), the duet for Cassandra and Coroebus approaches conventional grand opera and is disproportionately long for its place in the scheme. Berlioz could not resist allowing Cassandra to dwarf everyone else in these two acts; Aeneas does not come to life till he reaches Carthage, where however Berlioz makes him a much more sym-pathetic character than he is in Virgil—or Purcell. Nevertheless the Trojan acts contain several scenes with a tremendous dramatic impact. In the great ensemble of horror that follows the news of Laocoon's death Berlioz beats Meyerbeer at his own game. The scene in which Hector's ghost, stalking down the scale by semitones, warns Aeneas to leave Troy for Italy derives strength from its dramatic and its epic connotations. Both finales rank among Berlioz's most exciting set pieces. In the first, where the Trojans, ignoring Cassandra's cries of warning, drag the gigantic horse across the back of the stage into the city—and it should be visible to the audience—Berlioz uses subsidiary brass bands and choral groups offstage to represent the gradual approach of the procession. Here the Trojan March, so important later, appears for the first time. The second finale depicts the mass suicide of Cassandra and the Trojan women in the temple of Vesta. Berlioz has presented the fall of Troy in a series of historical vignettes; he has not established any of the characters except Cassandra and to a lesser extent Coroebus, and he has not given us the causal links between the episodes. But when we have adjusted ourselves to the epic scale this ceases to be disturbing.

The Carthaginian acts begin at a lower emotional temperature. Some of the set pieces—the civic prize-giving in Act III, the ballet celebrating the victory over Iarbas in Act IV—are stiffly conceived. The greatest of them all of course is the famous Royal Hunt and Storm, for which Berlioz prescribes a most elaborate stage action; Ernest Newman, not without reason, called it 'the finest and most sustained piece of nature painting in all music . . . like some noble landscape of Claude come to life in sound'.[3] This is pure epic, from its heightened descriptive style to the nymphs' cries of 'Italie!'. And it is typical of Berlioz that, although it also represents the climax of the love of Dido and Aeneas, he should have conceived it as a detached incident, without a predetermined position in the opera. He placed it after Act III (the march against Iarbas); in some modern scores it comes after Act IV (the love duet), its place in the dramatic sequence. It can be fitted into either context, but belongs inevitably to neither.

From the song of the poet Iopas in the middle of Act IV to the end of the opera Berlioz never falls below the highest level of inspiration. The epic and dramatic elements are perfectly fused; only Gluck at his finest has approached this compound of the statuesque with the intensely emotional. The sequence of movements at the end of Act IV—quintet, septet, love duet—has no rival anywhere for sustained nobility and a serenity trembling on the edge of tears; moreover it is full of subtle dramatic psychology. In the quintet Berlioz hints at the idea, explicit in Virgil, that Venus—Aeneas's mother—has substituted her son Cupid for Ascanius. In the duet he takes another form of epic licence. The words are based on the dialogue in *The Merchant of Venice*, Act V Scene i, in which Lorenzo and Jessica compare their situation with that of the great lovers of the past ('The moon shines bright: in such a night as this', etc.), among them Dido and Aeneas. The manipulation of the conceit, with Aeneas adapting Lorenzo's final words to his own situation, is strangely moving to those who catch the reference.

Berlioz's dramatic craftsmanship in Act V is superb. The song of the home-sick sailor Hylas has a lingering nostalgic quality utterly free from sentimentality and unlike the music of any other composer. Its placing here, followed presently by the duet of the two sentries who have no wish to leave the fleshpots of Carthage for a risky journey to an unknown Italy, throws into relief the tragedy that follows. Berlioz takes pains to emphasize the humanity of his characters, whether they be queen or commoner; with the entry of the Trojan ghosts to dispel any weakness in Aeneas he restores the balance and reunites epic with drama. Later, during Aeneas's duet with Dido, the Trojan March in the distance once more recalls him to duty, while the disconsolate queen is haunted by reminiscences of the love duet. Berlioz's very effective use of these motifs of course has nothing to do with Wagner's leitmotif; his characters never represent anything but themselves.

It would be a fatal mistake to condemn Berlioz's methods because they do not conform to our ideas of what an opera should be. After all, nor did Wagner's in their time. Berlioz's way of filling five hours with music, though very different, is quite as rewarding; this would have been recognized long ago had he ever, during

---

[3] *Opera Nights*, 311.

his life or since, enjoyed the advantages of a Bayreuth. His virtues and defects, each on the grand scale, are inextricably intermingled (as are Wagner's), and must be accepted in their totality. If a small effort of understanding is required in the first instance, it will be repaid by one of the most profoundly moving experiences in the musical theatre.

22

Berlioz and the Comic Muse

It is remarkable that two of the greatest nineteenth-century masters should each have ended a long and adventurous career with a Shakespearian comedy. Berlioz and Verdi were lifelong admirers of Shakespeare; both had concentrated on tragic subjects, including some based on their favourite dramatist (between them they touched the entire cycle of tragedies apart from the Roman plays and *Timon*); in each case the single comedy came at the very end, and disclosed a new burgeoning of youth in age. *Béatrice et Bénédict* and *Falstaff* share that mixture of ironic detachment with an undercurrent of deeper emotion that marks the finest exploits of the comic muse.

Berlioz had contemplated a 'lively opera' on *Much Ado About Nothing* as early as 1833, but did not begin it till 1860, on a commission from Bénazet, the impresario at Baden-Baden. He treated it as a holiday task after *Les Troyens*, and the work at first went so easily that he did not wait to finish one piece before beginning the next; it was later interrupted by illness and not completed till early in 1862. The opera was well received at Baden-Baden in August that year, and at Weimar in 1863, but did not reach Paris till 1890. This would not have surprised Berlioz, who described it as 'not Parisian music' and, with equal truth, as 'a caprice written with the point of a needle' and 'one of the most spirited and original' of his works. It is however astonishing that an opera of such quality on such a subject should have waited ninety-eight years for its first stage performance in London[1]—although Bernard Shaw did recommend it to D'Oyly Carte in 1892.

Berlioz wrote his own libretto, using a French translation of Shakespeare's dialogue. He drastically shortened the play, omitting Don John's intrigue against Hero's honour and the constabulary humours of Dogberry and Verges, and thereby leaving too little plot—a rare fault in a libretto based on a literary original. In their place he added a characteristic figure of his own, the court musician Somarone (meaning great donkey), who rehearses and performs an academic fugue in honour of the Sicilian victory. Berlioz could never resist a hit at the pedants, including certain teachers at the Conservatoire who had vexed him in youth. In life we can scarcely blame him, for few great artists have been so despitefully used in their own country; unhappily he allowed it to impair his art. The Amen fugue in *La Damnation de Faust* scores a fair hit on the same target, but Somarone is an intrusive irrelevance and his music is by far the weakest in the score. It is tempting to suppose

[1] By University College Opera Society on 10 Feb. 1960.

that without him *Béatrice et Bénédict* might have made a satisfactory one-act opera (which was the original plan), or that if Berlioz had developed the Hero-Claudio side of the story he might have written a comic masterpiece. But his congenital weakness would probably have found him out.

He could never shape his larger works as structural unities; instead he built them up as a series of tableaux, loosely connected or entirely detached, hoping that the total would be greater than the sum of the parts. Of course it never is, though the episodes are often as original and dynamic in design as they are penetrating in content: witness the first duet for Béatrice and Bénédict and the male trio in Act I. The *opéra comique* form, with the musical numbers separated by spoken dialogue, favoured Berlioz's method; but he nearly squandered this advantage by concentrating at the wrong points. The trio in Act I of *Benvenuto Cellini* shows what a brilliant musical *tour de force* he might have made of the crucial scene in which Benedick overhears Claudio and Don Pedro discussing Beatrice's love for him; yet he leaves it in dialogue. Hero and Claudio are reduced to mere foils; the unfortunate Claudio, though his wedding is the mainstay of the plot, has no love music and no solo of any kind. Even the exquisite duet for Hero and Ursula at the end of Act I, which recreates the magic world of Act IV of *Les Troyens* (and which Berlioz claimed to have sketched during a speech by one of his colleagues at the Institute), is strictly irrelevant. It should have been a love-duet, with Claudio replacing Ursula; but Berlioz was fascinated by the blend of female voices, which he further exploited in the Act II trio, another lovely movement in slow 6/8 time. The coda of the duet (*ppp*), for clarinets and strings in twelve parts (four of them solo), is one of the most magical passages of orchestral sound that even Berlioz conceived.

The outstanding feature of the opera is the comic genius revealed in the music for the two principals. The theme of a love affair based on mutual irritation might have attracted Rossini or Offenbach. The former would doubtless have graced riotous fancy with a coating of sentiment, the latter whipped up a soufflé of frivolity. Berlioz does neither; his tone of conversational banter masks a deep underlying melancholy. In the glittering orchestration, which combines virtuosity with the texture of chamber music, he provides a perfect counterpart for the verbal wit of the play. The mid nineteenth century was no age for classical comedy; life (and love) was either too serious or too absurd. Berlioz treated it as real but not earnest; he both felt and mocked, and he made no allowance for self-deception. The duet-finale in which Béatrice and Bénédict (trippingly accompanied by the main theme of the overture) sign a matrimonial truce but look forward to resuming hostilities on the morrow is—despite its brevity—as original, witty, and satisfying as the climactic fugue in *Falstaff*. But Berlioz's style was too dry for the sweet tooth of the period; it was scarcely safe for Verdi thirty years later to mock the sacred cow of Romanticism.

Berlioz's whole career was out of step with the times. This fact, together with the Teutonic conception of musical history as an orderly progress towards higher things, accounts for much of the disparagement he has received. Here was a composer who, from early prominence among the avant-garde, moved ever backwards towards the classical world of Gluck, just when the giant saurians of German Romanticism were beginning to wallow in the swamps created by the expansion and imminent explosion of tonality. It is easy to find links with Gluck in *Béatrice et Bénédict*, for instance the first section of Hero's air 'Je vais le voir' and the Marche nuptiale in Act II. It is also easy to stumble over the peculiar chromaticism that stamps even this exuberant and extrovert score with Berlioz's characteristic melancholy, notably in Béatrice's air 'Il m'en souvient' (used in the overture) and the Sicilienne. Preconceived standards condemn this as ungrammatical and haphazard, just as ears hide-bound by the symmetrical phrase and the orthodox cadence are deaf to Berlioz's stature as a superlative melodist. Wagner's chromaticism, always securely founded in tonality, links Beethoven with Schoenberg, and each step can be logically demonstrated. Berlioz's, being non-structural, leads nowhere (his direct influence, except in orchestration, was confined to minor figures like Cornelius); it is justified only by the context.

Most of the old charges against Berlioz, which reflect nothing but the inadequacy of their authors and propagators, are conclusively disproved by the score of *Béatrice et Bénédict*. If, like so much he wrote, it is a work of flawed genius, the genius is infinitely more conspicuous than the flaws. Now that the old battles are over we can appreciate its unique flavour to the full. It is never safe to estimate a work of art by its progeny.

23

Cornelius and *Der Barbier von Bagdad*

Peter Cornelius is one of the most attractive figures in German nineteenth-century music. He was a poet as well as a composer—he wrote his own librettos and the words of many of his songs—the nephew of a painter, and in his youth (like his parents) an actor. Although he served Liszt as secretary for some years and later became a friend of Wagner, his personality was not submerged; he refused (in his own words) to be the nought after Wagner's one, and even allowed himself, in Act II of *Der Barbier von Bagdad,* a parody of the clotted diction of *Der Ring.* He had wider sympathies and a less ponderous touch, in life and art, than most of the New German School; the flavour of his humour is that of wine rather than beer. In this respect at least he had nothing to fear from the rivalry of Wagner.

Although he seems to have realized from the first that his gifts lay in the direction of comic opera, *Der Barbier von Bagdad,* composed in 1855–8, is his only essay in this form. Its failure after a single performance at Weimar (15 December 1858) seems to have been due to a cabal aimed at Liszt (or his mistress the Princess Sayn-Wittgenstein) rather than Cornelius. But the composer, a retiring man, took it so much to heart that he abandoned the genre altogether (a disaster for German music as well as for his own career) and made two still-born attempts at grand opera. His colleagues can hardly have helped him. Liszt, even less endowed with humour than Wagner, had at first thought little of *Der Barbier,* and tried to divert Cornelius in the direction of church music. We may see here a parallel with Chabrier, who after finding his feet in an admirable comic opera allowed himself to pursue the same false gods with the same sad results. But the ill luck of *Der Barbier* persisted long after the composer's death at the age of 49. Like the operas of Musorgsky and (in different circumstances) the symphonies of Bruckner, it fell into the hands of 'improvers'. Mottl (1884) and Levi (1885) both exercised their talents at its expense; the latter said that the original form was impossible on the stage and, if published, would remain a historical curiosity. It is Levi who is now the historical curiosity. *Der Barbier von Bagdad* received its second authentic performance in 1904 and, although never a repertory piece, has been revived at intervals and won many admirers.

The story is a typical Arabian Nights entertainment, fashioned with exceptional wit and skill. In choosing for his central figure an old man whose garrulity bores the other characters to distraction, Cornelius was perhaps raking a risk. There are indeed moments in Act I when the old Barber, a *buffo* with an enviable compass, and the tenor hero Nureddin threaten to grow tedious. But unlike many comic operas *Der Barbier von Bagdad* improves as it goes on. Act I has some excellent scenes; Act II (there are only two acts) is rich in invention and all but flawless in construction. Cornelius is conspicuously successful in the difficult task, which floored many greater composers and taxed even Mozart, of bringing a comic opera to a musically satisfactory conclusion. Where as a rule we are reaching for our hats some minutes before the end, Cornelius leaves us asking for more.

The weakness of the opera lies in its solo music; this alone would account for its failure to win a more universal suffrage. Cornelius's lyrical gift, never strong, is at its best in his songs, which have their own niche in the history of the German Lied. In the operas it appears derivative and is liable to be clogged in a morass of rich harmony. Nureddin's first air is little more than stale Schumann, and the Barber's patter song 'Bin Akademiker' is a pale echo of Rossini without the buoyancy of Donizetti or Sullivan. Cornelius was evidently aware of this weakness, which he sought to counteract by using irregular metres, at a period when this practice was not the commonplace it has become since. It is only the rhythm—alternate bars of quadruple and triple time, a scheme that recurs in the beautiful carol *Die Könige* —that saves the love duet in Act II from stagnation. The delightful canonic duet for Bostana and Nureddin near the beginning of the opera gains considerably from the interpolation of an occasional 9/8 bar into the 6/8 pattern.

If Cornelius's models—Schumann, Rossini, Liszt, early Wagner (in the love music), Weber's *Abu Hassan,* and the Berlioz of *Benvenuto Cellini* (whose libretto he translated)—obtrude in the solos and the orchestral writing, he is quite himself in the concerted pieces, especially when he gets things moving on the stage. The singular virtue of this opera is the unusually close blend of music and drama; Cornelius, as the author of both, knew just how to make each play into the other's hands. A delicate irony moves continually over the surface of the score. Nureddin's love for Margiana reminds the old Barber of another Margiana whom he loved in youth, so that whenever the name or its characteristic musical theme recurs it is apt to set up a double train of association. In the trio that opens Act II each voice begins joyfully with the same words ('Er kommt! Er kommt!') to the same phrase; but whereas Margiana and Bostana are thinking of the former's lover Nureddin, her father the Cadi is expecting his chosen son-in-law who has just sent a chest full of treasure. Later, when Nureddin has been hidden in the chest, there is a similar double play on the word 'Schatz'—'treasure' in both senses. Cornelius, unlike some of his German successors, has sufficient restraint not to overelaborate the joke.

There is plenty of straightforward fun into the bargain, for instance in the duet where the Barber, reminded of his Margiana in the act of exercising his profession, indulges in an endless cadenza with his lathered and half-shaved victim helpless in the chair. In Act II Cornelius piles up an intricate series of misunderstandings until he has the whole cast at cross purposes—surely the true end of comic opera. The strangely poetical scene of the muezzins, anticipated in the entr'acte, makes an effective contrast. The later ensembles are most amusingly characterized, especially that which follows the extraction of the insensible Nureddin from the chest; the men mock the bamboozled Cadi Mustapha, while the women in honeyed thirds try to revive the 'corpse'. This is achieved at last by the Barber with the aid of the Margiana motive—a gentle parody, perhaps, of one of the favourite tricks of Romantic opera. Cornelius builds his finale on a musical device which he has employed several times in earlier scenes. In the Barber's first song ('Mein Sohn, sei Allahs Frieden hier'), and again in his reflections on the fatal effect of love on his numerous brothers near the end of Act I, each vocal phrase ends with an emphatic cadence, identical in rhythm but ingeniously varied in its tonal and harmonic implications. This may have been intended to suggest the old man's repetitive garrulity. In the finale it is carried to a fitting apotheosis. Every line of the Barber's song of obeisance to the Calif culminates in a cadence of this kind on the word 'Salamaleikum', accompanied by a deep bow; and each cadence in turn is taken up and varied by the entire company, also bowing—to the Calif and perhaps in anticipation to the audience.

24

Verdi's *Otello*: A Shakespearian Masterpiece

Verdi's *Otello* is commonly considered not only the greatest opera based on Shakespeare but one of the supreme masterpieces of the art. There is no reason to dispute this judgment. It is however interesting, and possibly instructive, to examine the premises on which it rests. How has the unique quality of the play been translated into operatic terms? What demands does Shakespeare make on the librettist and composer? How did Boito and Verdi come to succeed where so many others have failed?

Opera is a highly complex and baffling art-form, since it pulls in so many directions at once. It must reach a compromise between several means of artistic expression—music, drama, spectacle, scenic design, perhaps ballet—each with its own demands and disciplines and liable to assert its own supremacy. The balance has varied at different periods, but it is always precarious. When the opera is based on a literary masterpiece, the difficulties are multiplied. Music can illumine words, but it can easily obscure, distort, or clog them; the richer their content, the more they defy musical setting (the history of music is littered with the debris of literary lilies snapped off by presumptuous gilding). This is true on the small scale of a song or cantata; in a full-length opera, apart from the sheer size of the undertaking, the odds against success are lengthened by the fact that the pace of music is not only slower than that of a spoken play; it is different in kind.

A mature Shakespeare tragedy confronts the librettist and composer with the most formidable challenge it is possible to imagine. It is no accident that *Hamlet*, *King Lear,* and *Antony and Cleopatra* have never inspired an opera of even the second rank, and that the few great composers who have considered these plays have prudently retired from the contest. Each play is a complete work of art, packed with vitality and meaning and already so long that it is generally shortened for a modern audience. What can music possibly add to a texture so complex, a plot and characters so many-sided, a poetry so infinitely rich in suggestion? Strictly speaking, the answer is: nothing. All that the librettist and composer can do is to construct a parallel work, a kind of translation, that conveys in different terms the artistic stature and spiritual integrity of the play.

We are concerned here with late nineteenth-century opera. It is possible that another age may one day evolve a different compromise; but hitherto all the most successful Shakespeare operas (with the single exception of Benjamin Britten's *A Midsummer Night's Dream*, which wisely does not scorn the tradition of Verdi) have been produced in the half century after 1845. There are good reasons for this. The age found Shakespeare particularly congenial, and there was something in his technique of developing a character and laying out a scene that lent itself to the methods of Romantic opera with it dependence on set numbers—airs, duets, choruses, and ensembles—linked by flexible recitative. These methods exploited to the highest degree the one important dramatic advantage that opera enjoys over a spoken play, its capacity to develop the action on two or more planes simultaneously. If the characters in a play declaim their lines at the same time, the result is chaos. In opera, especially Romantic opera, this is not only possible; it is a source of immense strength, for (apart from any retrenchment in time) it enables the composer to present conflict in a form at once expansive and concentrated, so that the audience, while grasping the individual strands, can comprehend a whole that is more than the sum of the parts. This facility is not confined to the voices. The orchestra is no mere accompaniment; it can comment with the detachment of the composer, or tell us the hidden thoughts of a character, or suggest those of one who is not present. Opera is the richest of all the arts in its command of dramatic irony.

The first requirement of the Shakespeare librettist is compression, readiness to cut ruthlessly. He must take the plot to pieces and reassemble it in operatic terms. He will probably have to sacrifice many incidents, some whole characters, and perhaps a subplot. He will certainly—if he is wise—make short work of the poetry, not merely because its load of association and overtone might cripple the composer's creative powers, as well as tempting him to sesquipedalian discursiveness, but because it encroaches directly upon his prerogative. The poetry of opera resides in the music, not in the words. Of course, the more he can retain of Shakespeare's spirit, his characterization, and his dialogue, the more satisfying the result is likely to be. But a good libretto is a scaffold, not an independent structure. To compare it with the play is irrelevant and unfair; if there is to be a comparison, it must be between the play and the whole opera, music and words together.

In tackling *Othello* Verdi and his librettist, Arrigo Boito, had one advantage that may seem at first of dubious value. Neither of them could read the play in the original. They received the poetry at one remove; the verbal associations it carries for the English reader would have been set at a distance, like those of Goethe's *Faust* for readers unfamiliar with German. It may be noted in passing that *Faust* has never inspired a great German opera, but was already the subject of Boito's most important work, *Mefistofele,* an experience that left its mark on his conception of Iago. The resemblance to Mephistopheles, especially in the Credo aria in Act II, has often been remarked. This does not imply any contradiction with Shakespeare; indeed Boito seems to have built this scene from hints in other Shakespeare plays besides *Othello,* notably *Timon of Athens* and *Titus Andronicus.*[1] Mephistopheles and Iago have common roots in the tradition of European thought; each is the attempt of a great dramatist to create an incarnation of evil.

The collaboration between Boito and Verdi rested on shared gifts as well as

---

[1] James A. Hepokoski, *Giuseppe Verdi: Otello* (Cambridge, 1987), 182, has shown that Boito was following the analysis of Iago's character in the French translation of the play by François-Victor Hugo which was his principal source.

complementary qualities of character. Both were composers familiar with the problems of opera. Both were lifelong admirers of Shakespeare. The most prophetic of Verdi's early operas, the one he loved best and over which he took most trouble, was *Macbeth*, produced in its original form in 1847, exactly forty years before *Otello*. Soon after this he had discussed a *King Lear* with Cammarano, his collaborator in four operas, including *Il trovatore*, and he commissioned a libretto on the same subject from Somma, author of *Un ballo in maschera*. Much later, after *Falstaff*, Boito himself was to do some work for him on *Lear*. Boito had also written (for Franco Faccio in 1865) a libretto on *Hamlet* so excellent that we can only regret that it was not available to Verdi. But his partnership with Verdi would have come to nothing had he not possessed a quality of tact and selflessness rare at any time among creative artists. The story of his dealings with Verdi, a notoriously touchy and suspicious man, from the estrangement caused by a youthful indiscretion in 1863 to the mutual trust and admiration of twenty years later, is one of the most moving in the annals of opera.

The genesis of *Otello* can be traced to a dinner party in the summer of 1879, when Faccio and the publisher Giulio Ricordi, apparently by prearrangement, suggested the subject to Verdi (by way of Rossini's opera on the same story) and put forward Boito as a possible librettist. Within three days Boito produced a scenario, which was favourably received by Verdi, and in November he sent the first version of the complete libretto. Verdi at once bought it and (in the words of his wife) 'put it beside Somma's *Re Lear*, which has slept profoundly and without disturbance for thirty years in its portfolio'. He was in no hurry to commit himself to 'this chocolate project', as he called it, but he continued to correspond with Boito, and the librettist made a number of changes, especially in the finale of Act III, which he rewrote several times. One of these revisions offers a striking example of his tact. In 1880 Verdi suggested that the act should end with an attack by the Turks, at which Othello (who has just thrown Desdemona to the ground) 'shakes himself like a lion' and prepares to lead the Venetians to victory, while Desdemona prays for his success. Boito without comment rewrote the finale in this form, and only when Verdi pressed him about its effect on the drama and characterization did he point out that it would destroy the whole carefully built fabric of the tragedy and force them to reconstitute it in the last act.[2]

Verdi's confidence, which must have been strengthened by this incident, was further reinforced by Boito's helpful collaboration over the revision of *Simon Boccanegra* in 1881. Even so, he did not begin to compose the music of *Otello* till early in 1884, and then the whole project was nearly ruined by gossip in the press: Boito was reported as saying that he had finished the libretto unwillingly and regretted not being able to set it himself. Verdi promptly offered to return it as a gift. Boito replied that the libretto was Verdi's 'by right of conquest' and sent him the words of Iago's Credo. After that all went well; Verdi finished the rough score in October 1885, the orchestration by the end of the following year, and the opera

[2] This letter was suppressed in Verdi's published correspondence. Nardi printed it in his life of Boito (1942), followed by Frank Walker in *The Man Verdi* (London, 1962), 478–9.

was produced with spectacular success at La Scala, Milan, on 5 February 1887. As Boito wrote to Verdi when he heard that he had resumed work in December 1884, 'One can't escape one's destiny, and by a law of intellectual affinity that tragedy of Shakespeare's is predestined for you'.

The opera begins just before Othello's arrival in Cyprus at the height of the storm (about II. i. 94); a large crowd, including Montano, Iago, Cassio, and Roderigo (but not Desdemona or Emilia), is waiting anxiously for his ship to reach harbour. By suppressing the Venetian act Boito achieved a double dramatic advantage; he saved valuable time for the later development of the story, and he launched the opera on a tremendous climax in which the physical uproar prepares the climate for the psychological turmoil to come, as if the elements are in league with human passions. But he did not ignore Shakespeare's first act; at least five passages from it are worked into the libretto. The first scene is largely choral; each of the four men utters a few words, but not enough to establish character. This helps to throw all the more emphasis on Othello when he lands and reports the destruction of the Turkish fleet (II. i. 204); his greeting of Desdemona is reserved for later, but the few bars he sings establish him at once as a heroic leader. After a brief chorus of acclamation as the storm dies down Iago begins to work on Roderigo's jealousy, using motives from both their scenes in Act I of the play. Roderigo's 'I will incontinently drown myself' (I. iii. 306) comes most appositely in the context of the storm. Iago assures him that he shall enjoy Desdemona (I. iii. 365) and expresses his own hatred of Othello for promoting Cassio above him (I. i. 16 ff.) Another chorus as the people light bonfires in celebration of the victory leads to the drinking scene. Iago urges the reluctant Cassio to drink the health of Othello and Desdemona (II. iii. 30), at the same time bidding Roderigo keep his eyes open and in due course setting him to provoke Cassio (II. i. 270 ff.). Boito neatly combines two episodes here. Iago's *brindisi* (drinking song), in which Cassio and Roderigo join, springs naturally from 'And let me the canakin clink'. Cassio's intoxication, his provocation by Roderigo, the wounding of Montano, and Iago's despatch of Roderigo to cry mutiny follow as in the play. The scene culminates in the return of Othello (II. iii. 162); before his 'What is the matter here?' Boito slips in the words with which he quelled an earlier disturbance in the play, 'Keep up your bright swords' (I. ii. 59). What follows is much condensed, but all the essential lines—notably Othello's 'Honest Iago ... on thy love, I charge thee' (II. iii. 177)—are preserved as far as the general exit (II. iii. 258). Instead of Iago remaining behind with Cassio, Othello stays with Desdemona.

The love duet that ends the act has no exact parallel in the play. Its position in the opera is crucial, quite apart from its sublime musical beauty, for it has to assume the function of Shakespeare's first act in revealing the background of this strange marriage, its origins, and the purity of its emotional substance. It does so without ever seeming to inform the audience. This is Desdemona's first scene in the opera, and Othello has appeared only as a general; yet by the end of the act their whole relationship is clear and the scene is set for the tragedy to come. The cue is Othello's

'All's well now, sweeting; come away to bed' (II. iii. 242), but most of the material comes from his speech to the council in Venice (I. iii. 128 ff.), with a climax on the lines 'She lov'd me for the dangers I had passed, And I lov'd her that she did pity them' (167–8). Desdemona in the first words she sings ('Mio superbo guerrier!') has borrowed Othello's greeting as he lands in Cyprus, 'O my fair warrior' (II. i. 184). Boito returns to that scene with Othello's 'If it were now to die' (II. i. 191–200) and ends the act with the kiss.

Act II (a ground floor room in the castle) takes up the story at the point in II. iii where Iago hypocritically comforts Cassio's wounded pride, beginning with an assurance that he will soon regain his position with Bianca (a necessary insertion to clarify later developments, since Bianca never appears in the opera). Let Cassio beg Desdemona to intercede with Othello ('Our general's wife is now the general', II. iii. 318 ff.). As Cassio goes out Iago throws gibes after him. His Credo is partly based on the soliloquy at this point ('When devils will their blackest sins put on', 357 ff.). He watches from the veranda as Cassio appeals to Desdemona in the garden. The conversation equivalent to the opening of III. iii takes place in dumb show, but from Iago's 'Ha! I like not that' (35) the scene in which he begins to fan Othello's suspicions follows the play closely, except that Boito postpones Desdemona's intercession with Othello (41–92). He retains all the crucial stages of the deception, Iago's enquiry whether Cassio knew Desdemona before her marriage, his warning against the green-eyed monster (165), and his 'Look to your wife; observe her well with Cassio'. At this point (189–200), while Iago is still talking, choral voices are heard in the distance. A group of country people enter, serenading Desdemona and offering her flowers and jewels. As she happily echoes the last line of the chorus (a wonderfully revealing touch of character), Othello's suspicions are disarmed, as well they might be, and Iago's malignity redoubled. Now Desdemona comes forward with Emilia and pleads for Cassio (42–55); Othello repulses her much more roughly than in the play (he can hardly reply 'I will deny thee nothing' *after* Iago's warning). A moving detail here is Desdemona's (no doubt unconscious) echo of a haunting phrase from the Agnus Dei of Verdi's Requiem at the words 'Tu gli perdona'.

Boito's treatment of the handkerchief episode differs significantly from Shakespeare's. Othello snatches it angrily from Desdemona and throws it down; Emilia picks it up and Iago takes it from her while Othello and Desdemona are still on the stage. The scene is laid out as a quartet, which allows the action to unfold on several dramatic and psychological levels at the same time: while Iago disputes with Emilia over the handkerchief (313–19), Desdemona begs Othello's forgiveness if she has offended (suggested by 289, 'I am very sorry that you are not well', and 89, 'Whate'er you be, I am obedient'), and Othello voices his fears that she may be tired of him because he is black or ageing (from his soliloquy, 263–6). Verdi expresses every strand of meaning in a beautifully poised and unified musical design. When the women have gone, Iago (aside) plans to lose the handkerchief in Cassio's lodging (321–2). The scene for Iago and Othello is resumed from 'Ha! ha! false to me?' (333) to 469, with a few contractions. Its moments of climax are the magnificent setting of Othello's 'O! now, for ever Farewell the tranquil mind' ('Ora e per sempre addio'), his demand for 'ocular proof', Iago's narrative of Cassio's dream, his claim to have seen the handkerchief in Cassio's hand, and the oath 'Now, by yond marble heaven', expanded into a sinister and ironical duet as both kneel to demand vengeance.

Act III (the Great Hall of the Castle) begins with a herald announcing the arrival of the ship with envoys from Venice. Iago continues to plot Othello's downfall with his victim's co-operation. He will engage Cassio in conversation about Desdemona; let Othello watch his gestures (IV. i. 75 ff.) and remember the handkerchief (IV. i. 10). Next comes the conflation of three passages between Othello and Desdemona: III. iv. 33–98 (his ironical comments on her hand, her renewed plea for Cassio, his ever more importunate demand for the handkerchief), IV. ii. 25–43 ('Let me see your eyes'... 'Swear thou art honest'... 'Am I the motive of these tears, my lord?'), and 70–90 ('Alas! what ignorant sin have I committed?'—'I took you for that cunning whore of Venice That married with Othello'). Again the developing action gains concentration and unity from the music: Othello denounces her in a distortion of the lovely phrase with which she greeted him at the beginning. He drives her out, and his speech 'Had it pleas'd heaven To try me with afflicton' (IV. ii. 47–64) becomes a soliloquy ('Dio! mi potevi scagliar'). Iago returns, places Othello in hiding, and questions Cassio about Bianca, taking care to mention Desdemona while Othello is still in earshot. From 'How do you now, lieutenant?' (IV. i. 104) the scene follows the play in essentials, but with certain changes designed to increase its operatic impact. Othello is maddened by Cassio's laughter at Iago's remarks about Bianca, which he takes as referring to Desdemona, and still more when Cassio produces the handkerchief (an inevitable change in Bianca's absence). The latter part of the scene is worked up into a brilliant trio, which projects the complex ironies and cross-currents with a biting economy impossible in a play.

Trumpets announce the arrival of the embassy (IV. i. 225), and against distant fanfares and greetings from the chorus Iago continues his plotting (179–83), countering Othello's suggestion of poison with advice to 'strangle her in her bed, even the bed she hath contaminated' (216–27). Ludovico enters, followed by the whole cast, and the chorus salute the lion of Venice. The first part of the finale follows IV. i. 218–79 (with some rearrangement), except that Emilia and Roderigo are present, Cassio is summoned to hear his appointment as Othello's successor, and Desdemona and Othello do not leave the stage. The climax, when Othello strikes Desdemona to the ground, leads to a big concerted movement in which the seven soloists and the male and female chorus each sing a different set of words—nine in all. But this is no static ensemble; the action continues; while each character or group reacts variously to the outrage, Iago advises Othello to accomplish his vengeance quickly while he himself deals with Cassio, and then invites Roderigo to kill Cassio before morning to prevent Desdemona's departure (IV. ii. 230 ff.). At the end Othello sends everyone away. Desdemona tries to comfort him, but he curses her, raves about the handkerchief, and falls into a trance (IV. i. 46–8, with Iago's 'Work on, My medicine, work!'). As the chorus in the distance renew their salute to the lion of Venice, Iago with a gesture of triumph spurns the unconscious

Othello with his foot: 'Ecco il Leone!' This contribution from Boito is one of the most devastating *coups de théâtre* in any opera.

Act IV takes place in Desdemona's bedroom and again fuses several scenes. The opening dialogue between Desdemona and Emilia comes from IV. iii. 11–13; IV. ii. 104–5 (Desdemona's request for her wedding sheets); IV. iii. 24–33('If I do die before thee, prithee, shroud me In one of those same sheets'), and 41–59. Boito changed the sense of the Willow Song, omitting the bitter irony of the last line. He also cut out Emilia's raillery and her defence of cuckoldry, and made some telling additions. Desdemona gives Emilia a ring, calls her back for a final embrace just she is leaving (a wonderful moment), and sings a prayer to the Virgin, suggested perhaps by the prayer at the corresponding point in Rossini's opera. Othello enters and kisses her, to the music that accompanied the kiss at the end of Act I. The scene of the murder (V. ii. 23–84) scarcely deviates from the play; that which follows (Emilia's return and Othello's discovery of the truth, 85–228, with a few later phrases) is much abbreviated. Iago does not stab Emilia, and does not return after his first exit. We hear nothing of his fate, and Roderigo's is passed over very rapidly. There remains Othello's dying speech, which is compounded of 267–76 ('Here is my journey's end'), 281 ('O Desdemona! Desdemona! dead!'), and 358–9 ('I kiss'd thee ere I kill'd thee; no end but this, Killing myself to die upon a kiss'). The opera ends with another recall of the exquisite kiss motif in the orchestra.

It does not take more than a cursory glance to see that a great deal of the play has been sacrificed. Bianca and the Clown disappear in addition to the characters who are confined to Act I; Cassio's role is appreciably, and Roderigo's and Emilia's drastically reduced. They fulfil their functions in the plot and are at once cast aside. Not enough remains for Verdi to draw any of them in the round. Even Iago fades out in Act IV. Shakespeare's rich tapestry of characters is reduced to three full-length figures. This was probably inevitable if the central conflict was to retain its proportions in an opera lasting less than three hours, though it is arguable that Boito cut a little too much in the last scene[3] and threw away a valuable detail in Iago's deadly insinuation 'She did deceive her father, marrying you'. He was right to concentrate on Othello and Desdemona. Although we lose one or two facets in such scenes as her appeal to Iago (IV. ii. 148 ff.) and Othello's questioning of Emilia before the murder (opening of IV. ii), their stature is not a whit abridged. Since the tragedy depends on the extent of Othello's fall, it is essential that his basic nobility and her innocence should be established so firmly at the outset that we never question them, and this is beautifully managed. Boito's hero and heroine, as interpreted by Verdi, are as great as Shakespeare's.

So is his villain, though here there is a shift of emphasis. He is less consistently the smooth dealer, the 'honest Iago' whom everyone trusts (though this aspect is not neglected), and more explicitly satanic, obliged by his own nature to pit his

[3] His first version included much more, translated literally from the play (see Hepokoski, *Otello*, 34–5).

strength against virtue. But if his nihilism is more self-conscious, it does not deny the play; Boito brings out what is implicit in Shakespeare, the almost limitless power of evil to corrupt good. And he reaches the same conclusion; although Iago's villainy prospers, his triumph is brief, for Othello recovers his nobility and our sympathy at the last. Iago is defeated in the moment of victory by the spiritual quality of his victims. This is sufficient justification for Boito's curt despatch of him in the last act.

The most conspicuous difference between libretto and play, the excision of so much of the poetry, has already been accounted for. While Boito retains many striking phrases from Shakespeare's dialogue, most of them are either concrete statements or brief metaphors like the 'green-eyed monster'; he goes for the dramatically telling detail rather than the flight of fancy. Nearly all the passages that haunt the memory of the reader or play-goer—'Not poppy nor mandragora', 'The pity of it, Iago', 'Thou hast not half the power to do me harm', the whole of Othello's marvellous last speech except its final couplet—are swept away. Boito was unquestionably right here. Unlike too many Shakespearian librettists, he took care never to obstruct the music by overloading the text.

His insertions are few, and mostly concern the chorus. Verdi at first wished to write the opera without chorus, but he soon came to see its advantages. When Boito in June 1881 sent him the words of the country people's serenade to Desdemona in Act II, he answered: 'What a splash of light amid so much gloom!' That is indeed its effect, but it is a splash of light with a functional purpose; it illuminates Desdemona's character and assists the drama at a vital moment by suggesting the passage of time between the sowing of Othello's suspicions and their growth to maturity, a process that Boito (unlike Shakespeare) has to accomplish within a single act. The chorus is of value in launching the first scene of the opera, and in Act III it is twice the vehicle of powerful dramatic irony, when its jubilations on the arrival of the embassy form the background first to the plotting of Desdemona's death and later to Iago's savage moment of triumph.

The intense concentration to which Boito subjects the material raises one or two difficulties. Othello's jealousy, as we have seen, develops more rapidly than in the play, and Desdemona's tactlessness in pleading for Cassio seems to receive too much prominence. Shakespeare makes both points convincing by a careful manipulation of the time scheme. Boito is more restricted in this respect; indeed the trouble is largely due to the different pace of opera and the inevitable suppression of intervening matter. He was certainly aware of the problem, and he goes a good way towards remedying the first point by the introduction of the serenade and by placing Desdemona's first appeal for Cassio *after* Iago has begun to work on Othello's suspicions, which are therefore more liable to rapid inflammation. But this brings Desdemona's appeals rather close together, and the last of them in particular, after the entry of Ludovico and the ambassadors, does appear gratuitous. At this point in the play Othello has not yet denounced her as 'that cunning whore of Venice'. Is it credible that after this crowning insult she should still take his demands for the handkerchief as 'a trick to put me from my suit'? If the discrepancy is less disturbing in performance than a reading of the libretto might lead us to expect, this is due to the surpassing beauty and tenderness of the music Verdi puts into her mouth.

Boito's work may not be faultless, but his compression and rearrangement of Shakespeare's text is astonishingly skilful, as the above analysis demonstrates. Almost every scene is a conflation of two or more episodes in the play, and often details from one context have been smoothly accommodated to another. Above all, he has reshaped the material in operatic terms, while retaining as much as possible of the language and spirit of the drama. Sometimes this involves a change in the order of events. The most striking instance is the postponement of Othello's trance to the end of Act III, where it crowns the big ensemble after Othello strikes Desdemona. A move in the other direction is the setting back of the trumpets announcing the arrival of the ambassadors before, instead of just after, Iago and Othello plan the details of the murder. This heightens the suspense with the suggestion that they are plotting against time. The clattering antiphony of the trumpets, joined later by the chorus, punctuates their hasty colloquy. Here, as in their earlier dialogue against the opening bars of the serenade in Act II, Boito exploits opera's power of simultaneous development. Innuendo and innocence, conspiracy and festivity are presented at one and the same moment, and each throws the other into the sharpest relief.

It is here that Boito's adherence to the traditional layout of Italian Romantic opera, with its sequence of arias and ensembles linked by recitative, pays most dividends. There is some blurring of the edges, but each act contains formal movements that can be paralleled in Verdi's earlier operas or those of Donizetti: the storm and bonfire choruses, Iago's *brindisi*, and the love duet in Act I, the Credo, the serenade, the handkerchief quartet, Othello's 'Ore e per sempre addio', and the vengeance duet in Act II, the duet for Othello and Desdemona, Othello's 'Dio mi potevi scagliar', the trio for the three men, and the final ensemble in Act III, the Willow Song, Desdemona's prayer, and Othello's death scene in Act IV. Nearly all of these, apart from Othello's monologues and the Willow Song, were grafted on to the story by Boito or spun from a few hints, an achievement the more remarkable since *Othello* lends itself to such treatment less readily than most of Shakespeare's plays.

This framework enabled Verdi to make the best of two worlds, to carry the action forward in an unbroken flow while allowing the music to fulfil itself in its own terms. His style had by now attained such a degree of flexibility that we are scarcely conscious of the seams; indeed some commentators have missed the point and talked of him imitating the endless melody of Wagner. The entire fabric of the opera depends on the underlying tension between freedom and strict design. The *brindisi* sets the whole drama in motion, paints Iago's character in indelible colours, and touches in Cassio and Roderigo as well. It is flexible and dynamic, yet at the same time a linear descendant of the similarly titled movement in Act II of *Macbeth*. The handkerchief quartet and the Act III trio exhibit a kaleidoscopic complexity of dramatic development while retaining a perfect—almost a traditional—musical shape. In *Otello* Boito and Verdi solved one of the most intractable problems of opera: how to adjust the pace of the music to that of the drama without sacrificing the advantages of either, and without painful gear-changes between the narrative-expository sections and the more expansive flights of lyrical expression.

Verdi's score is as remarkable for economy as for emotional intensity. It is never overloaded. Some of the profoundest effects are obtained by the simplest means; at several moments of tension—the opening words of the murder scene, part of the following conversation between Othello and Emilia, Othello's 'Come sei pallida, e stanca, e muta' ('Cold, cold, my girl!')—Verdi leaves the voice entirely unsupported, as if responding to the daring simplicity of Shakespeare's language. The contrasts are often extreme (one of the most electrifying, though the marking is pianissimo, is the drop of more than five octaves, from the high A flat of the violins to the low E of the double bass, when Othello enters Desdemona's bedroom), but they are never meretricious. Every detail is subservient to the whole. As in *Falstaff*, the action sometimes moves so fast that we may have to strain to catch all its implications; the first scene can leave the listener breathless, and it is difficult to grasp all the detail in the third finale.[4] But the closer we look, the more we find.

This concentration is not achieved by the use of leitmotifs, of which there are none in the strict sense, though the orchestral prelude to Act III is based on Iago's 'green-eyed monster' phrase and the two returns of the kiss motif in the last scene are musically and dramatically overwhelming. The characterization rests on the consistent and subtle use of certain specific turns of phrase. Iago, who fascinated Verdi from the start (his first intention was to call the opera *Iago*, and he exchanged some interesting letters with the painter Morelli on his physical appearance), is depicted by means of sinister trills, appoggiaturas, and chromatic cadences, which recur again and again in the voice part and the orchestra, most conspicuously in the *brindisi*, the Credo, and at 'Ecco il Leone!' Yet his music, far from being ugly, is often surpassingly beautiful. (Verdi employed some of the same means, though with very different implications, for his portrait of Falstaff.) Desdemona's part has a tender lyricism that would melt a heart of stone, not only in her pleas for Cassio but in the phrases with which she initiates the handkerchief quartet, the duet with Othello in Act III, and the final ensemble of that act. Othello has many noble gestures, from his first utterance in the opera ('Esultate!') to the thrilling 'O gloria!' in the last scene. His corruption is suggested in a tendency to borrow (and distort) the music of other characters: the triplet figure in the accompaniment of 'Dio! mi potevi scagliar' recalls Iago's Credo and his plotting with Cassio at the beginning of Act II, his denunciation of Desdemona as a whore is based on her own lovely phrase ('Dio ti giocondi, o sposo'), and his final monologue begins with the heavy accented chords associated with her 'Buona notte'.

It is curious in a composer as dependent as Verdi on vocal melody that most of the solo and duet movements in an opera by no means deficient in that quality —the Credo, the Ave Maria, Othello's monologues in the last two acts, the love and vengeance duets—should begin with the repetition of a single note by the voice, while the emotional shading is left to the orchestra. This is one aspect of that

---

[4] Perhaps for that reason Verdi wrote a shortened and simplified version for Paris in 1894.

perfect balance between the vocal and the symphonic, between free arioso and formal strictness, and between dramatic clarity and musical intensification, that distinguishes the whole opera. Another is the extraordinarily subtle placing of cadences, often combined (as in the *brindisi,* the Willow Song, and the Ave Maria) with irregularity of rhythm or phrase-length. Again and again a simple cadential formula produces an overwhelming effect. The tripping cadence that punctuates the conversation between Iago and Cassio at the start of Act II is beautiful in itself (and profoundly ironical in its context), and enhanced beyond measure by the fact that we never quite know when it is coming. The same technique—also characteristic of *Falstaff*—appears in the Act III duet for Othello and Desdemona and the scene for Desdemona and Emilia in Act IV, where the cadences, perfect or interrupted, at Desdemona's 'Son mesta tanto, tanto', 'Povera Barbara!', and (most of all) 'Ah! Emilia, addio!' have a beauty that makes the heart ache. Equally potent, on a different scale, are the enormously extended cadence at the end of the Ave Maria and the mighty harmonic gestures that interrupt the closing bars of all four acts.

This is a matter of impeccable timing. Everything turns on a needle-point between expectation and surprise; the implication is constantly overtaken and surpassed by the event. Verdi either teases the ear by postponing or veering away from the projected moment of repose, or he leaves the form fluid and suddenly reins it in to emphasize a particular sentiment. As with all great artists at the height of their powers, his sense of context is masterly. It embraces an astonishing range of orchestral colour, from the electric frenzy of the storm (based on an organ pedal of three adjacent semitones) to the ethereal refinement of the love duet and the spare accompaniment of the last act with its haunting woodwind solos. (One detail, the clarinet's grim low E when Otello tells the astonished Desdemona that Cassio is dead, may have been suggested by a similar effect in Act II of *Carmen*.) The occasional patches of very bold harmony, for example at Iago's warning against jealousy and his description of Cassio's dream, which at first glance seem so alien to Verdi's style, are perfectly in place. The element that binds all together is his unfailing sense of rhythm. This had supplied the driving pulse of his early operas and keeps them fresh today. In *Otello* it has acquired an almost infinite flexibility and subtlety of nuance that permeates every bar of the score.

Otello is the only opera to challenge a Shakespeare tragedy and emerge undimmed by the comparison. With the exception of Handel's *Hercules* (which at a climactic moment draws on the same play) and possibly *Carmen,* it has no rival as a depiction of jealousy in musical terms. Like all supreme works of art it remains untouched by time, reflecting new facets of truth in each generation. Dyneley Hussey, happening to discuss the credibility of Iago's baseness in the autumn of 1939, pointed inevitably to 'the intellectual sadist's passion for the destruction of other people's happiness' then rampant in Europe.[5] Today we may be reminded more sharply of racial prejudice. This universal quality is the property of play and opera alike.

[5] *Verdi* (London, 1940), 250.

25

The Man Verdi

The tragic death of Frank Walker removed one of the most talented of musical scholars. The appearance of this posthumous book,[1] the fruit of many years' work, sharply accentuates our loss, for it shows that Walker's powers were still expanding. His biography of Hugo Wolf, published in 1951, remains the best in any language. Its handling of documentary material is impeccable, but it suffers slightly in balance from a too close identification of author with subject and from occasional awkwardness of style. *The Man Verdi* has all the virtues of its predecessor and neither of these blemishes; it is conspicuously well written, and preserves a well-nigh perfect balance through a whole series of psychological quicksands. There is scarcely a judgment that can be queried, much less faulted. Moreover it is a book of a very original kind.

It is neither a straight biography nor, like *Hugo Wolf,* a 'Life and Works'—a scheme that Walker regarded as having failed—nor a study of Verdi's musical mind. Little of it has any explicit bearing on Verdi as a composer, and much is concerned (on the surface at least) with his background and contacts rather than his character. There is no discussion of his music. It might be described as a series of oblique but minutely detailed impressions of Verdi's life, each treated from a specific angle involving his relationship with one or more individuals. Its climaxes, except in the final chapter on the collaboration with Boito, do not coincide with the creative peaks of his career, but rather with the psychological and personal crises that certainly underlay them but can seldom be specifically related to the art they fostered.

This 'biographical experiment', as the author called it, would not work with many artists; with Verdi it is quite exceptionally rewarding. It is an effective method of circumventing the difficulties raised by his secretive nature and unrivalled capacity for covering his tracks. Such a situation is notoriously calculated to divide biographers into sheep and goats; either they follow each other's tails along the same old path, or if they make an unexpected (and all too often incomplete) discovery the obstinacy of their prejudices leads them to distort its significance. Verdi has suffered severely from both these failings, though his clamlike defensiveness and his habit of remembering his youth inaccurately have not aided enquiry. Walker proves himself a tireless sheep-dog, subjecting his predecessors to the closest inspection, chivying them along, and administering a sharp nip in their flanks when they go

[1] *The Man Verdi* (London, 1962).

astray. The sheep are separated from the goats, and more than one wolf is unmasked in sheep's clothing and expelled from the fold: there are numerous instances of deliberate falsification, and some of downright forgery, such as the letters designed to prove that Verdi lived and died a sincere Catholic.

It is possible that the book owes its novel design to the impulse to straighten the record. If so, the end justifies the means: so far from degenerating into a discharge of brickbats or a bombardment of Aunt Sallies, as could easily have happened with an author endowed with a less imperturbable sense of proportion, it makes a very positive contribution to history. The occasional *cris de cœur* of the scholar ('The Italian authorities never seem to bother to check anything', 'The careless inaccuracy of reputable Italian writers is almost incredible') are more than justified by the wholesale malversation of the truth of which many earlier biographers are convicted. Walker establishes his right to speak, not only by his meticulous treatment of the evidence but by the admirable reflections on the biographer's task with which he begins his eighth chapter. These paragraphs on the credibility of eyewitnesses and the endless possibilities of self-deception and unwitting misrepresentation should be studied by every would-be biographer.

Like *Hugo Wolf*, this book is based on first-hand examination of documents, especially letters and obscure theatrical periodicals. A great part of it consists of extensive quotations from these sources, many of them hitherto untapped. Walker had an exceptional flair for unearthing fresh material; few scholars have been so gifted with serendipity, the faculty of making happy discoveries by accident— though he had of course a shrewd idea where such accidents were likely to occur. He also possessed a mind clear of fog and prejudice, and was constantly able to draw fresh conclusions from old facts. A simple instance of his practical common sense occurs early in the first chapter, where he demolishes the sentimental reflections of one biographer on the boy Verdi's Sunday walk to fulfil his duties as organist ('*Three or four hours* just for the journey there and back!') with the dry comment: 'I have myself walked from Busseto to Le Roncole in forty-three mintues.' Equally conclusive is his demonstration that the common view of Verdi's first wife as a pathetic shrinking creature, far less worthy than Giuseppina to share his throne, is based on nothing better than a lack of documents: the little available evidence points the other way.

Walker's method involves a certain amount of overlapping and repetition, for the standpoint changes with each chapter (the presentation of views of the same circumstances from different angles can however be revealing). It also entails the omission of a good deal that would find a place in a normal musical biography: there is almost nothing about Verdi's dealings with librettists other than Boito, or about his ideas on the production of his operas, a subject that Walker treated elsewhere.[2] But the long sections devoted to elucidating the careers of people who played a vital part in his life—the impresario Merelli, the singers Napoleone

[2] 'Verdi's Ideas on the Production of his Shakespeare Operas', *Proceedings of the Royal Musical Association*, 76 (1949–50), 11–21.

Moriani and Teresa Stolz, the conductor Angelo Mariani, and above all Giuseppina Strepponi, who became the composer's second wife—are by no means irrelevant. Apart from their contribution to building up a portrait in depth of the inscrutable central figure, they illuminate the circles in which he moved and the whole background of Italian operatic life throughout the nineteenth century. Not only the student of Verdi will be rewarded here.

Moreover the material itself is fascinating. An extraordinary series of picturesque and bizarre figures flits across these pages. There is the Countess Samoyloff, who 'was a passionate collector of cats, dogs, parrots, monkeys and operas singers', and whose admirers made ice-cream from the asses' milk in which she bathed every morning; Merelli's grand-daughter, who committed suicide with her father, leaving a note 'Please leave me dressed as I am and bury me like this, because my underclothes are clean; I changed them last Saturday'; the harpist Bochsa, professor of his instrument at the Royal Academy of Music, who made a fortune by forging the signatures of Méhul, Boïeldieu, and the Duke of Wellington (among others) and composed a 'Grand Military Concerto for the harp, with accompaniments for an orchestra'; Solera, the librettist of *Nabucco,* who recited improvised poetry to piano accompaniment on themes drawn from an urn, including 'The Nineteenth Century' and 'The Eclipse of 1842'; and the opera composer Luigi Ricci, who fell in love with identical twins (sisters of Teresa Stolz), married one, and lived with both simultaneously, producing a family tree singularly encrusted with mistletoe.

The long second chapter, devoted to the early career of Giuseppina Strepponi, represents a feat of historical detection worthy of Sherlock Holmes. It has generally been supposed that Giuseppina, when she met Verdi at the period of *Nabucco,* was living with Merelli, by whom she had a child, and that Verdi's opera gave her one of her greatest triumphs as a singer. Walker's reconstruction of her career, a brief but very successful one, in both tragic and comic roles, of which she herself destroyed all her personal records, includes a list (with exact dates) of every opera in which she sang. By a brilliant synthesis of journalistic, epistolary, medical, and chronological evidence he not only fits in two illegitimate children, a miscarriage, and an attack of German measles, but decisively acquits Merelli (for all his irresponsibility in other directions) of the taint of paternity and brings home the charge against the celebrated tenor Napoleone Moriani, a married man with a family. Far from enjoying a triumph in *Nabucco,* she sang so badly that none of the reviews mentioned her and, in the words of Donizetti five days later, 'her Verdi did not want her in his own opera, and the management imposed her on him'. She was ill, threatened with consumption, and worried by the search for a protector who would keep her and her children; it is difficult to resist the conclusion that *La traviata* was inspired by events and emotions very near home.

Such an investigation not only exposes legends and illuminates character; it reveals a great deal about the harsh and sometimes macabre conditions in which operas were born and the formidable grip that impresarios held over all concerned, especially the singers. It helps to explain Verdi's life-long repugnance to a theatrical career (as early as 1845 he talked of retiring within three years)—and perhaps

Rossini's as well—and may account for the chronic stomach and throat troubles of nervous origin which the act of composition regularly induced in Verdi. For all his affected indifference to what people said about his operas, he was so touchy on the subject that Walker can ask 'Was there ever a composer so sensitive to criticism, so tenacious in rancour?'

Among those who emerge with enhanced credit are Verdi's early benefactor Antonio Barezzi, Donizetti, and Boito. Gatti's biography misrepresents Verdi's relations with Donizetti in every respect, professional and personal. Walker has no difficulty in proving that Donizetti, whose attitude to other composers was un-failingly generous—unlike Bellini and Nicolai, who regarded Verdi as 'a pitiable, contemptible composer' and the libretto of *Nabucco* as 'utterly impossible to set to music'—was an unswerving admirer of Verdi. And he comprehensively demolishes Gatti's theory that both composers were rival lovers of Giuseppina Appiani, pointing out by the way that the lady was middle-aged, the mother of at least six children, and probably a grandmother to boot.

Nearly a third of the book is devoted to Verdi's breach with Mariani and his relations with Teresa Stolz, the first Aida at La Scala and previously Mariani's fiancée and mistress. Here the new documents and their interpretation throw a completely fresh light on the character of all the principals, and are likely to modify our view of Verdi as a man. Ever since a scurrilous article in a Florentine paper in the autumn of 1875 accused Stolz of having a clandestine love affair with Verdi, there have been two views on these matters, which caused a prolonged crisis in the lives of all concerned. One party believed that Verdi stole Mariani's mistress and the conductor avenged himself by going back on his promise to conduct the first performance of *Aida* in Cairo, espousing the cause of Wagner and importing *Lohengrin* into Italy as a sort of Trojan horse. The other denied the existence of any affair between Verdi and Stolz and ascribed the quarrel with Mariani to other matters, among them Verdi's dissatisfaction with Mariani's attitude to the compo-site Requiem planned to commemorate Rossini in 1869 and his disapproval of Mariani's embezzlement of a substantial loan from Stolz. Walker's examination of Mariani's unpublished correspondence and Giuseppina'a letter-books reveals an extraordinary state of affairs.

Mariani emerges as a vain, unstable, and masochistic character, with a positively canine devotion to Verdi ('Such an attitude of intense respect and devotion', Walker remarks, 'was a prerequisite for any close friendship with Verdi'), whom he treated —and feared—as 'a veritable father-figure'. The language of his letters is flowery and hyperbolical, their tone full of grovelling flattery. For years Verdi made use of him for menial tasks, such as the purchase of magnolias, shotguns, and a steam engine. Gatti's theory that Mariani was offended by Verdi as early as 1857 and thenceforward sought every means of opposing him, including the establishment of Meyerbeer as a rival deity, is seen to be ludicrously remote from the facts. But so are many other common assumptions. The charge that Mariani was responsible for the fiasco over the Requiem for Rossini is 'grossly unfair'; Verdi had only himself to blame. Moreover, having abused Mariani to his face and behind his back for failing in his duty as a friend and an artist, he calmly appropriated Mariani's rejected suggestions and recommended them to Ricordi as his own. If Mariani broke a promise to conduct *Aida* in Cairo, he had every excuse in view of Verdi's insulting letter of a few months earlier ('If I had thought fit to send you in my place I should have asked you; if I did not do so that is proof that I did not think fit and that I had entrusted the task to someone else'). Mariani's engagement to conduct *Lohengrin* sprang from a commercial rivalry between the publishers Ricordi and Lucca and was certainly not planned as an act of revenge. Nor was the quarrel occasioned by Mariani's mishandling of Stolz's money, for he paid it back. In fact 'the revulsion of feeling, the failure to comprehend, the harshness, were all on Verdi's side,' and the conduct of both the Verdis leaves the nastiest taste in the reader's mouth. It combined sanctimoniousness (who were they to make insinuations about Mariani living in sin?) with gratuitous brutality. In July 1870 Mariani, dying of cancer of the bowel—an illness whose authenticity the Verdis preferred not to credit—announced his intention of seeking a cure at the shrine of Loreto. This was apparently taken at Sant' Agata as an ostentatious attempt to make a fool of Verdi: the vulgarly abusive reply, stigmatized without exaggeration by Walker as 'this truly odious letter' and 'this atrocious document', was signed by Verdi's bailiff Corticelli but drafted, as the letter-book shows, by Giuseppina.

What is the explanation of all this? Two suggestions present themselves. Verdi, like other dictators before and since (Walker's evidence disposes finally of the idyllic picture of life at Sant' Agata and convicts Verdi of 'domestic tyranny of a truly monstrous order' towards his wife and his servants), had lost touch with reality behind his 'iron curtain'. He imagined insults where none was intended and could brook only servile submission, even from his wife. The second explanation concerns Teresa Stolz, whose letters reveal her as 'garrulous, sometimes rather malicious, and not particularly intelligent'. She broke off her liaison with Mariani immediately after a visit to Sant' Agata in the autumn of 1871. Rumours of an affair with Verdi were circulating early the following year and are mentioned in the letters of Mariani, now desperately ill. As early as February 1869, when Verdi first spent any length of time in Stolz's company, Giuseppina's letter-books contain a draft letter to Verdi complaining about 'the strange and bitter consequence with which I am faced, *of being repudiated*' and 'the most acute and humiliating wound you have dealt me'. During the early performances of *Aida,* and again in later years, Verdi paid so many flying visits to Milan—quite contrary to his usual habit—that Giuseppina suggested it would be worth his while to buy a season ticket. Some of Stolz's numerous letters to Verdi, themselves quite innocent, bear jealous annotations in Giuseppina's hand. In 1874 she complained of being disgusted with life and losing faith in man and God. A draft letter to Verdi in April 1876 objects to his private visits to Stolz and excessive attentions to her for the past four years, and begs him to tell the truth. Another in October the same year begins: 'Since fate had willed that that which was my whole happiness in this life should now be irreparably lost'. (All these documents were either suppressed or camouflaged 'with tendentious commentary' in Luzio's *Carteggi Verdiani*). Walker considers it 'beyond all doubt that he was in love with Teresa Stolz', but scrupulously hesitates before the natural conclusion, apparently because it would convict Stolz of being 'about the biggest hypocrite that ever lived' (she and Giuseppina kept up a superficially friendly correspondence throughout the whole period). Yet that conclusion is surely inescapable. And if Verdi could torture Giuseppina by keeping her in the dark for years, is it not overwhelmingly probable that his treatment of Mariani, for which Walker can find no motive, was the product of a guilty conscience?

This book destroys for ever the sentimentalised Verdi of legend. He emerges as hard, suspicious, and vindictive, a man who never forgot and seldom forgave an injury, even a fancied one (there is new material on his unedifying quarrels with the Busseto authorities during the 1860s, as a result of which he severed all relations with the Barezzi family). He could also be disingenuous, maintaining one set of moral standards for himself and another for the rest of the world. If we are to have biographies of men of genius, it is best that they should tell the truth. In Verdi's case this has the effect of spotlighting the more humane virtues of others. Giuseppina's character in particular, except in the quarrel with Mariani where she took her cue from Verdi, shines with peculiar brightness. Her position required an almost superhuman degree of tact and tolerance. She had no illusions about his 'stern, decided and very reserved' character, yet she was content to subordinate her entire life to him. When he was about to embark on *La forza del destino*, she wrote to Corticelli: 'For my part, to avoid all storms, I intend to agree with everything he says from mid October to the end of January, foreseeing that during the hard labour of composition and rehearsal it will by no manner of means be possible to persuade him that he is wrong about any single thing!' She was a delightful letter-writer as well as a woman of selfless devotion. Her letter-books reveal not only that she drafted many letters in Verdi's name, but that others, in which she specifically claims to be writing without his knowledge, appear first in his writing. No wonder we are given repeated warnings about the need for care in the use of documents.

Another who appears in a most sympathetic light is Boito, who had to overcome Verdi's early and lasting resentment for a supposed insult, and was moreover marked by the stigma of admiration for Meyerbeer and Wagner. (It was not enough to admire Verdi, as the critic Filippi found when his request for a portrait met with a harsh snub; one must abjure independent judgment and respect for other living composers, especially Germans—the complement of Wagner's own attitude.) Boito's magnanimity when Ricordi tried to secure for Verdi his libretto of *Nerone,* on which all his future hopes as a composer were founded, is as remarkable as the self-effacing tact with which he 'played' Verdi, like some great salmon, in the interests of art. When Verdi wished to introduce a battle and a victory for Othello as the climax to Act III of the opera, thereby debasing Shakespeare to the conventions of his earlier librettos, Boito gave him exactly what he asked for. Only later, in response to a direct enquiry, did he demonstrate its falsity and win the day. This remarkable letter, one of the most penetrating in the history of operatic creation, was suppressed by Luzio out of a desire to give Verdi all the credit. Boito himself found an admirable biographer in Piero Nardi, a fact that limits Walker's scope for fresh discovery. Even so he detects one or two errors and produces a new chronology for the composition of *Otello*. If Verdi appears at his most relaxed and urbane in his correspondence with Boito, much of the credit must go to his 'incomparable librettist'.

Those are the last two words of Walker's book, which in its own sphere too may be hailed as incomparable. It puts every other Verdi biography out of date. There is no attempt at psychological analysis in the manner of Mosco Carner's study of Puccini, and to that extent Verdi's character remains veiled. But the materials are all there, and they cannot fail to challenge every reader for whom the alloy of gold and clay in creative genius is a subject of endless fascination.

26
Shakespeare in the Opera House[1]

There have been so many operas founded on Shakespeare's plays— I know of more than 200—and the question of what constitutes a good opera, and why, raises so many complex considerations, that I cannot hope to do much more than scratch the surface of the subject. Admittedly the average artistic level is not high. With the exception of a few masterpieces, which can be counted on the fingers of one hand, and a scarcely larger group, mostly based on the comedies, that are good for an occasional airing, you are never likely to hear them in performance. Any interest they possess is historical, and it concerns the history of opera rather than of Shakespeare. Sometimes too they have a certain entertainment value of a type not envisaged by their authors.

The scarcity of masterpieces is hardly surprising. A great opera, depending on a balance between several arts—music, drama, scenery, spectacle, ballet—of which the two most important, music and drama, are notoriously unaccommodating bedfellows, is rare in any circumstances. When one half of the partnership is based on a literary classic, the chances are slenderer still. It is not just a matter of the librettist being faithful to the play and the composer writing agreeable music. A whole series of compromises is necessary if the different time-scales imposed by music and the spoken word are to be reconciled; and the opera, if it is to be worthy of the occasion, must not only rise to the play, musically and dramatically; it must add something of its own. Otherwise there is no point in its existence.

This has not deterred scores of composers of all periods and nationalities from trying conclusions with Shakespeare. They include many of the greatest, though not all of them managed to finish their task. Among the abandoned projects are Beethoven's *Macbeth*, Tchaikovsky's *Romeo and Juliet,* and the *King Lear* operas of Debussy, Puccini, and Verdi—the last of which was on the stocks for something like half a century. Mendelssohn at various times planned an opera on *The Tempest* with three different librettists, one German, one French, and one Italian. Sometimes bad luck seems to have taken a hand. Mozart died immediately after accepting a libretto on the same play, though such a peculiar one that it is difficult to imagine him setting it as it stood. Smetana went mad while composing an opera on *Twelfth Night*. Against these disappointments we have Verdi's three Shakespeare operas and

[1] This essay was given as a lecture at the Eleventh International Shakespeare Conference, Stratford-upon-Avon, 2 Sept. 1964. The list of operas has been updated. For a fuller account, see my chapter in P. Hartnoll (ed.), *Shakespeare in Music* (London, 1964), 89–175.

others by Purcell, Rossini, Bellini, Nicolai, Berlioz, Bloch, Holst, and Britten. They are not all of equal merit, but none of them deserves to be forgotten.

Before returning to them it may be of interest to take a glance at the whole field and then consider the approach of different periods and countries to Shakespeare as an operatic source. Of the twenty-seven tragedies and comedies, all but one, *Titus Andronicus,* have inspired at least one opera. There are a few on *Henry IV* and *Richard III,* but for obvious reasons the histories have proved less popular. At the other extreme *Romeo and Juliet* is almost an operatic cliché; it has everything— star-crossed lovers against a background of family feud, duels, dancing, crowd scenes, a wedding, and a pathetic finale among the tombs. This was the perfect subject for Romantic composers, especially in France and Italy, but its appeal has not been confined to them: *Romeo and Juliet* operas have first seen the light in places as operatically remote as Minorca, Middlesbrough, and Mexico City. Quite a number of them enjoyed considerable success in their time, though not many are heard today.

The chief attraction of *The Tempest,* especially for German composers, has been the opening it gives for symbolism and allegory. This is reinforced by the striking resemblance between the characters and those of Mozart's *Zauberflöte.* Prospero offers a parallel to Sarastro, Miranda to Pamina, Ferdinand to Tamino, Caliban to Monostatos; Trinculo or Stephano will do at a pinch for Papageno, and Ariel— who moreover plays a magic pipe—for the Three Genii. There is even a potential Queen of Night in Sycorax, who though she is only mentioned in the play appears as a character in several *Tempest* operas. It is no accident that this play sired a whole brood of German operas in the decade after *Die Zauberflöte,* and quite a lot more during the nineteenth century. Nor is it surprising that they are nearly all very bad —generally because the librettist has deposited such a weight of symbolism on the plot that the characters emerge as caricatures or abstractions or a mixture of the two. This has been an unlucky play in the opera house. No composer has managed to translate its essentially lyrical quality into music, and most of them make Prospero preach like a cross between Wagner's Gurnemanz and a Presbyterian divine.

It is a very odd fact that the Germans, who have probably the best translations of Shakespeare, have achieved almost no success in turning him into opera. Of nearly fifty attempts, the only one that comes near to hitting the mark is Nicolai's *Die lustigen Weiber von Windsor*—and Nicolai spent an important part of his career in Italy. If I may now plunge into rash generalization, German opera composers have tended to make Shakespeare sententious or sentimental, the French have often made him just sentimental, the English have made him dull, while the Italians have turned him into roaring melodrama. There are of course exceptions in each case. For reasons to which I shall return, the Italian method, when refined, has produced the most satisfactory results.

It has also produced plenty of failures, especially with the great tragedies, which the Italians have set repeatedly, whereas the Germans, wisely, have left them alone. There are no German operas on *Hamlet, Lear,* or *Othello,*[2] and only one—a

[2] This was true up to 1978; German operas on *Lear* and *Hamlet* have appeared since.

singularly tame work—on *Macbeth*. It is the comedies that have inspired the most varied treatment—operas of every conceivable type from a Handelian *opera seria* on *As You Like It* to a modern American musical, from Purcell's Restoration Masques to a German serial setting of *Troilus and Cressida* with overt reference to the last war, from Fibich's portentous Wagnerian music drama on the *The Tempest* to sexy French operettas on *Cymbeline* and *All's Well that Ends Well*. Audran's *Gillette de Narbonne,* based remotely on this last play, consists almost entirely of waltzes and polkas in the manner of Offenbach. Of the libretto I will only say that the character corresponding to Shakespeare's Diana, that virtuous Florentine, becomes a promiscuous gipsy who declares that a man has only to whisper the word 'Turlututu' in her ear for her virtue instantly to collapse.

Every age is inclined to see its own reflexion in Shakespeare, to take what it wants from him and leave the rest. This is as true inside the opera house as outside. The idea that a libretto ought to preserve as much as possible of the spirit, plot, and characters of the play is comparatively modern. Until about the middle of the nineteenth century, and in some countries much later, the composer and his librettist simply converted the play into the type of opera then in fashion. Shakespeare was no more treated with the respect due to a classic than is the grist that goes into the Hollywood mill today. This was not so very different from the treatment he received in the straight theatre, even in England, where the 'improved' versions of Dryden, Tate, Cibber, Garrick, and others were still acted in the nineteenth century. People who first made their acquaintance in the theatre, whether here or abroad, probably did not know what was Shakespeare and what was not. It has recently been shown that even such a fanatical Shakespeare-lover as Berlioz based his dramatic symphony *Roméo et Juliette* not on the original text but on Garrick's perversion of it.

There is another reason why we cannot expect to find satisfactory Shakespeare operas before the nineteenth century. Until the time of Mozart's maturity the art of opera was not sufficiently developed to cope with a drama of such complexity and sophistication. Serious opera, an entertainment devised for courtiers and aristocrats whose principal interest was in the singers (and the ballet dancers, if there were any), consisted almost entirely of recitatives and solo arias. Composers of comic opera in Italy were beginning to develop the ensemble, but it was not till Mozart adapted these methods to higher artistic purposes, and the French Revolution altered the whole social basis of opera, that an adequate instrument was available.

There had been Shakespeare operas long before this. The earliest, those of Purcell,[3] are scarcely operas at all in the modern sense. What mattered to the Restoration audience was not the play or the music but the spectacle—the stage machinery and the dancing. To make openings for this, elaborate masques were introduced with mythological characters who had nothing to do with the story; and it was in these scenes that the music was concentrated. Hence there were two

---

[3] Only one song in *The Tempest* is certainly by Purcell. The rest of the music has been attributed to John Weldon.

separate casts, one for acting and one for singing, and the composer scarcely came into contact with the dramatist at all. In *The Fairy Queen,* based on *A Midsummer Night's Dream,* Purcell never set a line of Shakespeare, even where the poetry seems to cry out for it. The final scene for instance was replaced by an entertainment in a Chinese garden, complete with a chorus of 'Chineses'. In *The Tempest* Shakespeare himself supplied a masque in the scene for the three goddesses; but this was not good enough for the Restoration writers, who substituted a much more spectacular affair for Triton, Amphritrite, and other marine deities, and also adorned the play with a whole range of new characters.

In the 1750s J.C. Smith, a pupil of Handel, turned the same two plays into operas, basing himself partly on the Restoration versions. The spectacle has gone, but there is no real attempt to combine music and drama. All that remains is an emasculated play interspersed with songs which are often irrelevant. In his version of *A Midsummer Night's Dream,* called *The Fairies,* Smith omitted Bottom and the rustics altogether. Lysander has a very large part, sung by the famous castrato Guadagni, the creator of Orfeo in Gluck's opera, but Demetrius does not sing at all, probably because only a straight actor was available. Act II of Smith's *Tempest* ends with a bibulous trio for three tenors, and a glance at the score—which names the singers, not the characters—suggests that Prospero has joined the drunken sailors at the bar. It appears however that the same singer doubled the parts of Prospero and Trinculo.

Garrick wrote a prologue to Smith's *Fairies* in which he made a time-honoured point about English opera by apologizing for a work in a language comprehensible to the audience, and went on:

> This awkward Drama—(I confess th' Offence)
> Is guilty too of Poetry and Sense.

That can scarcely be said of Veracini's Italian opera on *As You Like It,* produced in London in 1744. This too is a succession of arias, but the plot diverges more and more from Shakespeare into the more stylized world of Handel's operas. Its climax is a spectacular siege in which Rosalind is rescued from a tyrant's castle. The male parts were mostly sung by sopranos—two of them (including the usurping duke) by women, and Orlando by a castrato. Veracini based one aria on a Scottish folksong, which the historian Burney regarded as a tactical error, since no self-respecting Scotsman would waste half a guinea on what he could hear better sung by his cook-maid Peggy in his own kitchen. One of the few later operas based on *As You Like It* was composed by an American contralto who died in 1962; she must be the only opera-composer in history whose legs have been insured for 10,000 dollars.

The earliest Shakespeare opera on the continent seems to have been a setting of *Timon of Athens* by the Holy Roman Emperor Leopold I in 1696. Since this monarch's sole delight, we are told, was 'to compose doleful melodies', the subject at least was a good choice. It was in the last thirty years of the eighteenth century that Shakespeare operas began to appear all over Europe, most of them on *Romeo and Juliet, The Merry Wives of Windsor,* or *The Tempest.* By far the best of these librettos was a version of *The Comedy of Errors* by Mozart's famous collaborator Lorenzo da Ponte. He wrote it for Vienna in 1786, the same year as *Le nozze di Figaro*, for Mozart's English pupil Stephen Storace, who set it with a good deal of skill in a fluent style clearly learned from his master. The libretto of Salieri's *Falstaff* (1799) keeps closer to the play than might be expected at this date, adding a scene in which Mrs Ford visits Falstaff disguised as a German maid, but the music remains strictly within the *buffo* convention.

The first *Romeo and Juliet* operas reflect the spirit of the Age of Enlightenment, with sweet reason prevailing at the end. Friar Lawrence or his equivalent—he is often not a priest but a doctor, a chemist, or a family friend—always reaches the tomb in time to explain things to Romeo and so ensure a love duet and a happy conclusion. The earliest libretto, set by Schwanenberger in 1773, has only three characters. The third is Benvolio, who supplies the potion and manipulates almost the entire plot offstage. This is another Italian aria-and-recitative opera, with a trio as finale. Georg Benda's German opera of three years later is a *Singspiel;* that is, like all German operas before about 1820, it has spoken dialogue—and far too much of it. The end is again happy, and excruciatingly sentimental: when Romeo proposes to die in the tomb, he weeps copiously over the childless old age of his and Juliet's parents, and looks forward with a certain relish to haunting the place when tourists come to lay flowers on his grave.

This play continued to be a popular operatic subject during the French Revolution and its aftermath, when a priest on the stage would probably have provoked a shower of rotten vegetables. In Zingarelli's opera of 1796 Friar Lawrence becomes one Gilberto, a sort of best man who is entrusted with the wedding arrangements and gets them hopelessly mixed up. At the end Romeo dies but not Juliet. Instead of killing herself she soundly rates Gilberto for his imcompetence. This is a poor opera, but it was very successful, perhaps because it was a great favourite of Napoleon, whose musical taste was elementary.

A much more interesting opera on this play was produced in Paris in the middle of the Revolution (1793). The composer was Daniel Steibelt, a German pianist whose morals gave such offence in Paris that he had hastily to remove himself to London. This is an *opéra-comique,* with spoken dialogue, but the music has a great deal of energy and makes far more use of choruses and ensembles than any previous Shakespeare opera. It is also richly scored, and is the first opera to employ the gong in the orchestra. But it is the art of opera that is growing up, not the understanding of Shakespeare. Capulet swears that anyone who avenges Tybalt's death by killing Romeo can have Juliet. A Spaniard called Don Fernand undertakes this task; but when all the Capulets have cornered the unarmed Romeo in the tomb, he decides that the odds are too great to satisfy his honour and changes sides—thus affording a classical example of the quixotry expected from operatic Spaniards. The enraged Capulets rush in for the kill, but the noise made by three choruses and all the principals singing at once wakes up Juliet, and all ends happily.

The German *Tempest* operas of this period are almost a study in themselves. There were about a dozen of them, including eight in the two years 1798–9. Four of these were settings of the libretto that had been intended for Mozart, though it was altered later. It presents the play as a struggle between white and black magic. Prospero rules by day, Sycorax by night, and it is Sycorax who invokes the storm. Ferdinand's only companion is a skittish and amorous page, played by a woman, like his obvious model Cherubino in *Le nozze di Figaro*. In order to prevent the lovers from falling asleep and so into Sycorax's power, Prospero keeps them up all night counting corals. The action is a weird compound of spectacle—including a volcanic eruption engineered by Prospero—ballet, ethical humanism, and buffoonery. Sycorax and the good spirit Maja are played by dancers, but Ariel is both voluble and sententious and is continually giving Prospero advice, especially on how to control his daughter. The opera ends with Caliban taking refuge in the sea, after which the entire company sing a hymn in praise of the fatherland. Perhaps the oddest thing about it is that Goethe called the libretto a masterpiece—but he was a friend of Gotter, its author.

The mixture of magic transformation scenes, a high ethical tone in the serious parts, and coarse Viennese farce in the rest is typical of German opera at this period, as indeed we can see from *Die Zauberflöte* itself. All these *Tempest* operas belong to the *Singspiel* type, with fragments of Shakespeare's original dialogue cropping up in the oddest contexts. In Wenzel Müller's opera Stephano has a sister called Rosine, who gets the better of Caliban's improper advances by what can only be called a superior knowledge of judo, and eventually marries Trinculo in order to keep the court supplied with jesters. Miranda—here called Bianka—is so excited by her father's promise of a young man that she throws herself into the arms first of Rosine and then of Trinculo; when she eventually meets Ferdinand she upsets his sense of propriety by doing all the wooing. Ariel teases the comics by conjuring up three seductive female shapes, which at the decisive moment change into three bears. In Ritter's opera Ariel himself masquerades in female shape and changes into a tree when embraced. Trinculo has the biggest part here, rather after the manner of Papageno. He steals Prospero's magic robe and convinces Caliban that he is a great magician called Magnus Pumphius Karpunkulus, a descendant of Dr Faust, and that Prospero is an incompetent pupil whom he was compelled to dismiss. Another composer, Hensel, wrote his own libretto and published it with a sour preface denouncing the affectations of Mozart and his school, of which he considered the public were heartily sick.

By the early nineteenth century the literary Romantic movement on the Continent had welcomed Shakespeare as an exciting if unruly predecessor of its own revolt against the age of reason. His plays were often translated, and like Scott's novels became an increasingly popular operatic source. Hands were laid for the first time on the great tragedies. Rossini's *Otello* of 1816 was the first Shakespeare opera to be acclaimed as a European masterpiece. We are apt today to remember Rossini only as a composer of farcical comedies. In fact he wrote many more serious operas, and virtually abandoned comedy before he was 25. His *Otello* is a landmark, and not only because it was the first Italian opera in which the recitatives were accompanied throughout by the full orchestra instead of the keyboard. In the first two acts the librettist followed the conventions of his day. Iago is a rejected suitor of Desdemona, Roderigo a typical scorned lover who fights a duel with Othello; Othello himself—who never leaves Venice—is little more than an irritable tenor. The handkerchief is replaced by an intercepted love-letter containing a lock of hair; since Desdemona has omitted to address it properly, Iago has no difficulty in convincing Othello that it was intended for Roderigo. But when he reached the last act, the librettist suddenly adhered to the play, including not only the Willow Song and the scene that follows, but the final murder. This was an innovation, and shocked people so much that in some revivals Rossini felt compelled to alter it. But the interesting thing is that most of this last act is musically on a far higher level than the rest of the score. Something of Shakespeare's dramatic truth seems to have penetrated to Rossini. Here, perhaps for the first time, we can detect the influence of Shakespeare on a great composer: Rossini's Willow Song and prayer (which probably suggested the Ave Maria in Verdi's opera) are fully worthy of their context.

The most distinguished Italian librettist of the Romantic period, Felice Romani, wrote four Shakespeare librettos. His *Hamlet,* set by Mercadante in 1822, has an interesting preface in which Romani calls the play the *Oresteia* of the north and says that he has deliberately emphasized the resemblance between the three chief characters and Orestes, Clytemnestra, and Aegisthus, since the English original is too fantastic for the opera house. Thus Hamlet enters for the first time pursued by the Furies, uncertain whether the Ghost is a product of his own imagination. The melodramatic events that follow seem to us far more fantastic than the play. Ophelia is the daughter not of Polonius but of Claudius, who wants to make a diplomatic marriage between her and the Prince of Norway, and Hamlet survives the denouement to mount the throne. Both these refinements occur in other nineteenth-century operas on this play. The part of Hamlet, like that of Romeo in several early Romantic operas, was sung by a woman. This was a survival of the castrato hero, before his place had been taken by a tenor.

Romani's libretto on *Henry IV,* again for Mercadante, includes two of the most famous Falstaff scenes, but involves the young Prince Henry in a complicated web of amorous and political intrigue. This is very funny, but I am afraid there is not time to describe it. Both Romani's *Romeo and Juliet* librettos preserve at least the outline of the play, since the tragic end was now acceptable—though of course there had to be a love duet first. Unfortunately the better libretto was set by the lesser composer. In Vaccai's opera of 1825 all the characters are remarkably well drawn, including Juliet's parents and Tybalt, who is in love with Juliet. Vaccai's music is quite pretty, but no one would think of reviving it today. Bellini's opera, on the other hand, five years later, is full of exquisite melody, and I think Covent Garden might have revived it this year instead of Bellini's later opera *I Puritani*.[4] The characters are more the cardboard figures of melodrama, but Bellini does recreate the youth and ardour of the lovers. In this sense the opera takes Shakespeare's point, even if there is a wide difference in the details.

[4] It was revived at Covent Garden on 26 Mar. 1984.

By this time *Macbeth* had made its operatic bow, at the Paris Opéra in 1827. The composer was Hippolyte Chélard, the librettist Rouget de Lisle, otherwise known to fame as the author of the 'Marseillaise.' It is difficult today to take this work as seriously as the authors evidently intended. To begin with, the first Witch rejoices in the good Scots name of Elsie. Banquo, Macduff, and Malcolm are left out. Duncan's sole heir is a daughter, Moïna, and Macbeth has a son; but for some reason the librettist does *not* draw the expected conclusion. He gives Moïna a love scene with Douglas, Prince of Cumberland, and a brilliant air in praise of Highland scenery. The murder occurs in the finale of Act II and is not discovered till the very end of the opera, after the sleep-walking scene, which in fact gives the show away since the listeners put two and two together. Among the incidentals—always an important feature of French grand opera—are a chorus of Ossianic bards and an extended ballet. Here Chélard attempted a little local colour by quoting 'Auld Lang Syne'—in a somewhat corrupt text. His score is a strange compound of early German Romanticism and the skittish coloratura of Rossini's comedies.

Another curiosity is Wagner's early opera *Das Liebesverbot* (1836), to a libretto of his own based on *Measure for Measure*. Except that one theme reappears later in *Tannhäuser*, it is fairly safe to say that no one would recognize the composer. Wagner does all the things he was later to denounce with particular fury in other people's operas. The score is full of French and Italian tricks and ornaments, many of them again borrowed from Rossini, and sounds rather like the sort of thing Sullivan parodies in *The Pirates of Penzance*. Wagner interpreted the play as an outright attack on Puritanism and a glorification of free love. Angelo becomes the German Viceroy of Sicily, and may, like Beckmesser, have been meant as a caricature of one of Wagner's enemies. All the characters are more or less unpleasant, including Isabella, who is prepared to flirt with Lucio almost before she is out of the convent. Pompey is translated into a *buffo* tenor called Pontius Pilate, whose chief aim in life is to redeem the name his parents so tactlessly bestowed upon him.

Towards the middle of the century the attitude of librettists to Shakespeare began to change. Instead of manhandling his plots to fit the convention in the same way as they adapted the latest French or Spanish melodrama, they paid him a certain respect. In 1838 the librettist of Balfe's *Falstaff* apologized for his deviations from *The Merry Wives*, although the fact that the opera was written for London—albeit in Italian—may have had something to do with this. Apart from the omission of some characters the libretto does not deviate very much—though Falstaff writes *three* identical love letters, one of them to Anne Page—and the opera, which is full of sparkling Rossini-like tunes, might merit revival if Balfe had any feeling for character. Unfortunately in the scene between Falstaff and the disguised Ford he makes no distinction in mood between their music, which is virtually interchangeable. Ford's jealousy aria is a cheerful and bouncy polacca.

Nicolai's attitude is typical of the changing climate. He first of all said that no composer but Mozart was a fit companion for Shakespeare. Then he himself made a preliminary prose sketch. The finished libretto, by S. H. Mosenthal, borrows hints from three other Shakespeare plays besides *The Merry Wives*. Moreover, where it alters the plot, which is not very often, it preserves its spirit. Although Nicolai's fat knight smacks of the German beer cellar, and is of course overshadowed by Verdi's wonderful creation, the opera successfully combines the sparkle of the comedy with the atmosphere of dawning Romanticism that we find in Mendelssohn's *Midsummer Night's Dream* music—clearly one of Nicolai's models. This is particularly true of the Windsor Forest scene, which begins with a real inspiration, a chorus to the rising moon. There is nothing about this in the play, but it sets the mood perfectly for what follows and is a most beautiful piece in its own right. The music is familiar, since Nicolai used it for the first section of his overture.

Almost contemporary with Nicolai's *Lustigen Weiber* is the first version of Verdi's *Macbeth* (1847); and Verdi too began by giving his librettist a prose synopsis. The form in which we usually hear the opera today is the result of a partial revision in 1865, and presents rather a mixture of styles. Had Verdi first approached the play in his maturity he might have made a superb thing of the Porter's scene, which he left out altogether; on the other hand he would hardly have written the comic-opera choruses of Witches and Murderers, which for some reason he allowed to survive the revision. Yet the sleep-walking scene, also part of the original score, is not only the finest thing in the opera: it is a masterpiece by any standards. And it is an almost literal setting of Shakespeare's words.

Here, as in Act III of Rossini's *Otello*, and all through Verdi's last two operas, we find the contact between Shakespeare and a composer of genius producing great opera. Obviously this could not have happened if Verdi had not been an assiduous student and a passionate admirer of Shakespeare, and in some way peculiarly in tune with him. But another important factor is at work here. There is something about the design of many scenes in Shakespeare that corresponds to the operatic forms current in Verdi's day—to what is called the number opera: that is to say, solo arias, duets, and ensembles in closed forms, linked by recitative. The sleep-walking scene, with its watching doctor and gentlewoman, is an example. It does not need to be manipulated for operatic purposes; it can be set as it stands. There is an even more striking instance in Lady Macbeth's first soliloquy, beginning with the reading of the letter and interrupted by the Messenger with the news of Duncan's approach. First she reacts to Macbeth's letter

> Hie thee hither,
> That I may pour my spirits in thine ear,

then—much more violently—to the Messenger's news

> Come, you spirits
> That tend on mortal thoughts, unsex me here.

All this exactly corresponds to the almost invariable form of the operatic aria in the first half of the nineteenth century: first a recitative, then a cavatina, then—after some interruption has changed the mood—a rapid and brilliant cabaletta. Shakespeare might have been writing for the opera house.

Of course some plays and some scenes lend themselves to this more than others. *Macbeth* has further operatic advantages in that it is reasonably short, has no subplot, and tells a straightforward story of human passions. *King Lear* is far more difficult, and has defeated every composer who has attempted it. *Hamlet* presents a fascinating problem, which has likewise not been solved but is perhaps not insoluble. The most successful opera on this play is by the French composer Ambroise Thomas (1868). Here we have another libretto that veers between adherence to the play and grotesque travesty of it, and again this proves a touchstone for the composer. Thomas's music is never first-rate, but in the passages that fall easily into operatic shape and reflect the action and the language of the play fairly closely—the appearance of the Ghost on the battlements, the ensemble of the play scene, much of the closet scene, and the 'To be or not to be' soliloquy—he reaches a standard far above the rest of the score, and indeed above the rest of his operatic output. A curious point about the play scene is that it includes, in an ironic recitative, the first operatic appearance of the saxophone.

There is one first-rate libretto on *Hamlet*. It was written in 1865 by a young man of 23, Arrigo Boito, and set to music—unfortunately—not by his later collaborator Verdi, but by Franco Faccio. The remarkable thing about Boito's *Hamlet* libretto is how very little he modified the plot or the stature of the characters. Of course the action is contracted, but its spirit is there, waiting for the composer to recreate in terms of his own art. This is equally true of his *Otello* and *Falstaff,* which in Verdi's settings are generally recognized as the greatest of Shakespeare operas—if not the greatest of all operas. They are the only two that rank as works of art with the plays themselves; many people indeed would place *Falstaff* considerably above *The Merry Wives of Windsor.*

To justify this claim in detail would occupy too much time. I can only point to various features that render the collaboration between Verdi, Boito, and Shakespeare unique. For it *is* a triple collaboration: on the level of dramatic sympathy, which is what matters most in opera, both librettist and composer had a profound understanding of Shakespeare. But they had to be masters of compression, since music needs so much more time to make its points than the spoken word. Conciseness was always a prominent feature of Verdi's style, so much so that in his early operas he often cut his corners too fine and left out essential links in the story or the dramatic motivation. This is what happens in *Macbeth,* where he reaches the murder too soon without having established the character of Duncan, who comes on but never sings.

Here Boito's double qualifications helped; he was at once a brilliant and sensitive writer and a distinguished opera composer in his own right. Although he used a great deal of Shakespeare's language, as well as his ideas, characters, and situations, he was not afraid to modify the original in the interests of operatic form. The astonishing tautness of design in these two librettos results not merely from cutting things out but from putting things in, and still more from fusing two or three strains into one. In *Falstaff* Boito reconstituted the fat knight of the *Henry IV* plays within the framework of *The Merry Wives,* by means which I think have never been fully analysed.[5] The libretto includes at least eight passages from *Henry IV,* five from the first part, three from the second, and twice combines lines from both parts in a single sentence. Invariably the insertion fits its new context with marvellous aptness. To give an example: Boito attaches the famous speech about honour in *1 Henry IV* to Falstaff's dismissal of Bardolph and Pistol for refusing to play the pander (*Merry Wives,* I. iii); and his link is a line taken from a later scene (II. ii), Falstaff's rebuke to Pistol 'You stand upon your honour!' Some very happy details were invented by Boito, generally with the idea of tightening up the plot: for instance the identification of the 'great lubberly boy' whom Dr Caius marries with his enemy Bardolph, and the brilliant moment in the linen-basket scene when the jealous Ford and his henchmen, after ransacking the house, hear the sound of a kiss behind a screen. Thinking they have caught Falstaff and Mrs Ford in the act, they stalk the screen and after a conspiratorial ensemble throw it down, only to reveal Fenton and Anne. This dovetailing of the various strands of the plot, which goes on all through the opera, has a double advantage; it performs the essential function of saving time, and it opens fresh opportunities for the composer, whose one great advantage over the dramatist is that he can develop two or more ideas simultaneously.

In *Otello*[6] Boito had an infinitely harder task owing to the much greater richness of the play in character, incident, and overtone—not to mention the poetry. His bold decision to omit Shakespeare's first act and start the opera with Othello's arrival in Cyprus at the height of the storm was a masterpiece of economy; for the storm, a thrilling opening in itself, presents a physical parallel to the violent psychological upheaval that is soon to follow. But this left very little space in which to establish Othello's stature as a soldier and a man, and the quality, as well as the facts, of his relationship with Desdemona. On these two points of course the proportions of the tragedy depend; and I do not think anyone familiar with the opera would deny that they come across quite as convincingly as in the play. One of Boito's means is the time-honoured convention of a love-duet. But this is like no other love-duet in operatic history. So far from being an unfunctional point of repose, it tells us everything about the past and present relationship of the lovers. Here, as elsewhere in the opera, Boito worked in passages from Act I of the play.

In the short second act he had to demonstrate convincingly the growth of Othello's jealousy from nothing to the savagery of his vow, 'Now, by yond marble heaven', in a fraction of the space available to Shakespeare. To do this he made two small changes; he put in a charming scene in which the Cypriots serenade Desdemona, which at once marks the passage of time and adds a tremendously potent dramatic irony, and he placed Desdemona's first plea for Cassio *after,* instead of before, Iago has roused Othello's jealousy, so that it naturally bursts into more rapid flame. A striking feature of this opera is the way in which the drama and the music play continually into each other's hands, and on several levels at the same time. In Act I Iago sings a *brindisi* or drinking-song, interrupted by comments from other characters and the chorus—another convention of Romantic opera. It corresponds of course to the scene in the play where Iago makes Cassio drunk and provokes the

    [5] But see J. Budden, *The Operas of Verdi,* iii (London, 1981), 417 ff.   [6] See p. 220 ff.

fight leading to his disgrace; but besides doing all this it has to introduce the characters themselves for the first time and set the whole plot in motion while retaining a coherent musical shape.

One of the most pregnant episodes in any opera is the famous quartet in which Desdemona tries to soothe Othello's first outbursts of jealousy while Iago through Emilia gets possession of her handkerchief. Here we have events and characters and their motives, whether explicit or concealed, all developed simultaneously with an economy and a multiplication of irony that is not possible in a play, where there is no orchestra and the characters cannot all speak at once. It is at the same time a piece of music of marvellous beauty and shapeliness. If you read Boito's libretto without the music, you find a good deal of the play missing; but that is rather like reading a prose synopsis of the play instead of seeing it in the theatre. Verdi's music completes the dramatic connection, and supplies an equivalent for the poetry. The result is a great opera, which is not just a cobbling together of two arts, or a compromise between them; it is a new experience in its own right, and an extraordinarily complex and profound one.

There are I think two special and interlinked reasons why Shakespearian opera reached its climax in late nineteenth-century Italy. The first concerns operatic history. I have mentioned the way in which certain scenes in *Macbeth* lend themselves to the aria-ensemble forms of Romantic opera. But in 1847 these forms were too stiff to take all the situations in a Shakespeare play without detracting from its stature. Forty years later the position was different. *Otello* and *Falstaff* represent the historical climax of the number opera, in its tragic and comic forms, just when it was giving way to a more fluid method of construction. Boito and Verdi contrived to get the best of both worlds. Both operas, while giving an impression of effortless flow, depend on the old fixed forms of aria, duet, and ensemble. They possess the structural strength of the set piece without its drawback of holding up the action, and the freedom of continuous arioso without its shapelessness. Everything is in perfect balance—the forward thrust of the plot against the lyrical expansion demanded by the music. This would not have been possible, however great the genius of librettist and composer, had the time itself not been ripe.

The second reason is a quality in Shakespeare himself. Everyone knows that he found many of his plots in Italy and that Elizabethan drama owed a considerable debt to the Italian Renaissance; but the similarity in approach, temper, and design between his plays and the Italian opera of two and three centuries later is not merely superficial. Nor is it confined to plays on Italian subjects. *The Merry Wives of Windsor* itself has the flavour of an *opera buffa* by Cimarosa or Rossini, for example in the linen-basket scene, an absolute gift for a comic opera finale. Boito seems to have been the first to perceive and exploit this affinity. He wrote after the first performance of *Falstaff*: 'Shakespeare's sparkling farce is led back by the miracle of sound to its clear Tuscan source'—in Boccaccio. Undoubtedly the same Italian roots nourished Shakespeare and his clowns on the one hand and the *commedia dell'arte* and *opera buffa* on the other. If we remember this, and the dramatic detachment characteristic of Italian opera until the late nineteenth century—by which I mean its willingness to allow the story to emerge without smothering it in sentimental, ethical, or symbolic encrustations—I think we have the explanation why nearly all good Shakespeare operas have either been written by Italians or have followed Italian methods.

One other nineteenth-century opera might have turned out a masterpiece of the same order. This is Berlioz's *Béatrice et Bénédict* (1862).[7] Berlioz, who was his own librettist, was in most respects as good a writer as Boito and as good a composer as Verdi. But he lacked one essential, the ability to subordinate the part to the whole. Like Boito, he cut away much of the play he worked on and added material of his own; and some of this—again like Boito—is not only excellent but Shakespearian. But the rest, instead of binding together what remains of the plot, does the opposite. In place of Dogberry and Verges, Don John's conspiracy, and the church scene, we have a character of Berlioz's invention, a musical pedant called Somarone, in whom, at quite disproportionate length, he caricatured his enemies at the Paris Conservatoire. This ruined his opera as a work of art. But nothing can dim the beauty of the rest of the score, in which he depicts the sex-war between Beatrice and Benedick with a brilliant wit, an ironic detachment, and an underlying sense of the impermanence of human life unlike the music of any other composer. Perhaps the play calls for this last mood less than some others; but it *is* a quality in Shakespeare, and one that Berlioz particularly associated with him. He was very soon to end his memoirs with the lines from *Macbeth* beginning 'Life's but a walking shadow'.

During the last century Shakespeare operas have continued to appear at the rate of at least one a year, and the flow shows no sign of diminishing. With a few exceptions I think the standard has declined rather than improved. For one thing the sharpness—tartness even—of Shakespeare's characters was soon lost when the sugar-content of late Romantic opera began to rise. Gounod's *Roméo et Juliette* is a succulent morsel for those with a sweet tooth, but it is idle to pretend that it comes closer to Shakespeare than his *Faust* does to Goethe. Goetz's version of *The Taming of the Shrew* (1874), which contains some charming lyrical music, suffers from the almost painful domesticity of Katharina before the taming even begins. Three German operas on the *The Winter's Tale* all omit Autolycus and turn the play into a sentimental romance.

There was a tendency to introduce all the favourite devices of Romantic opera whether the context called for them or not. Taubert's *Cesario* (1873), on *Twelfth Night,* has a hunting chorus in Olivia's garden and a naval wedding with a ballet of tritons and sea-spirits. Urspruch's *Tempest* opera (1888) goes one better with a chorus of huntresses seductively dressed (or undressed) who claim equal prowess in the pursuit of beasts and men. Ariel explains that they are only phantoms, but they enable the composer to offer the attractions of the huntsmen of *Der Freischütz* and the flower-maidens of *Parsifal* at one and the same time. The most eccentric opera of this type is Salvayre's *Richard III,* produced at St Petersburg in 1883. This begins with a funeral march followed by a drunken orgy, and ends with Richard interrupt-

[7] See pp. 213–15.

ing Henry VII's coronation by whipping the crown off his head and falling dead on the steps of Leicester Cathedral. The numerous choruses include large formations of gipsies, huntsmen, clergymen, Welshmen, and ghosts. Richard has a court jester called Puck, who sings a song about Queen Mab but is sacked when he breaks down in the middle. A passing minstrel is called in and given his job, and turns out to be the future Henry VII in disguise. Later we meet a band of gipsies living in 'a forest of druidic aspect' near Leicester under the government of a professional soothsayer called 'Madgy', who I need hardly say is Queen Margaret of Anjou. Perhaps the most startling episode is Richard's attempted marriage to his own niece, which begins with a grand wedding march led by Cardinal Bourchier and four bishops to the tune of 'Rule Britannia'.

The decline of the ensemble-opera at the end of the nineteenth century led to types of design less suited to Shakespeare. The Wagnerian music-drama, with its slow-moving action carried chiefly by the orchestra, tends to turn Shakespeare's mercurial and Italianate characters into ponderous abstractions. The results cannot be described as happy. At one point in Fibich's *Tempest* opera Prospero rides in on a chariot drawn by Caliban and three dragons, gives the courtiers a long moral lecture, and indicates the posture of Caliban as a proof of the triumph of mind over matter. The chess game between Miranda and Ferdinand becomes an elaborate and obscure allegory of married life, with the spirits whispering suggestions into their ears. When they are on the point of kissing, Ariel appears behind and knocks their heads together, whereupon the spirits burst out laughing. A complicated leitmotif system does not make this any easier to swallow.

Leitmotif of course can be an asset. By far the best Shakespeare opera that owes any considerable debt to Wagner is Bloch's *Macbeth* (1910), where the leitmotif system is employed with great skill and subtlety to illuminate the drama. For example, when Macbeth takes the lead after the banquet ('It will have blood, they say; blood will have blood'), he appropriates the cruelty motif of his wife; and in the sleep-walking scene ('What's done cannot be undone') she borrows one of his motifs, associated hitherto with his guilty conscience. Bloch's motifs are musically distinctive (especially in rhythm), which is the first essential; he treats the characters as human beings, not as symbols; and he takes care to retain many features of the number opera. Some of the set pieces, the finales in particular, are very impressive.

The Italian *verismo* method with its emphasis on sensational plots and naked emotion, as in *Tosca* or *Cavalleria rusticana,* is even less appropiate to Shakespeare and has produced one or two deplorable operas on which there is no need to dwell. A more common cause of failure in the twentieth century is the antithesis of this, a scrupulous respect for Shakespeare's text and a refusal to tamper with it except for a few cuts. This sounds admirable, but it makes the task of the composer very much harder, especially if he sets it in English. The language is so rich in associations and overtones that he may be tempted to bend the music to fit it instead of the other way round. If the music adds little or nothing to the total experience it might just as well not have been written; there is no point in gilding what is already complete. Perhaps the only successful full-length opera of this type is Britten's *Midsummer*

Night's Dream; and one of the reasons is that the music, instead of slavishly following the verbal rhythms, does not hesitate to impose its own. Another reason is that Britten has grasped the point about the number-opera; although the libretto contains scarcely a word not taken from the play, its design falls constantly into airs and ensembles. Of course this would not be enough without the intense concentration of Britten's style. It has a sinewy quality, a refusal to luxuriate in emotion, which I think is essential for a Shakespearian subject.

Holst's one-act opera *At the Boar's Head,* on the Falstaff scenes in *Henry IV,* has this spareness; Vaughan Williams's *Sir John in Love,* on *The Merry Wives,* has not. Both these operas are built on folksongs and the folk idiom; but where Holst is nimble and preserves the pace and sparkle (if not the style) of *opera buffa,* Vaughan Williams seems to accommodate his music to the mental processes of a country bumpkin. That surely is to mistake the flavour of the play.

Many continental composers of recent times have set the plays in translation, more or less cut: among them Malipiero and Castelnuovo-Tedesco in Italian, Orff, Klebe, Blacher, and Frank Martin in German. All seem to me to fail, some completely, some more narrowly, either because the music does not add enough of its own or because it adds the wrong thing. A more successful opera, based on an adaptation rather than a translation, is *The Taming of the Shrew* by the Russian Shebalin. Though produced as recently as 1957, this uses a thoroughly old-fashioned traditional idiom; but at least it hitches on to an appropriate tradition, that of *opera buffa,* and it translates into music a good deal of the high spirits of the play.

There seems no valid reason why good Shakespeare operas should not be written in the future, though the composition of any opera is an arduous task and the mortality rate is and always has been enormous. But the modern composer has very definitely to meet a challenge. Audiences today are more sophisticated than in the past, and will inevitably judge the opera, consciously or not, on how it measures up to the play on which it is based. The final criterion is not the literal fidelity of the libretto, or even the originality of the music, but the creation of a new unity out of the constituent elements. A unity of appropriate stature, needless to say. With the great tragedies this will require an act of rare genius. But I find it surprising that there has never yet been an opera of even the second rank on *As You Like It* or *Twelfth Night.* And there are plenty of opportunities in other Shakespeare plays if the composer and his librettist can discover how to exploit them.

TABLE 1. Operas based on *the plays*

Composer	Title	Librettist	First Performance
ALL'S WELL THAT ENDS WELL			
E. Audran	Gillette de Narbonne (operetta)	H. C. Chivot and A. Duru	1882, Paris
M. Castelnuovo-Tedesco	Tutto e bene quello che finisce bene	Composer	1958 (comp.)
ANTONY AND CLEOPATRA			
J. C. Kaffka	Antonius und Kleopatra (duodrama)	—	1779, Berlin
E. F. von Sayn-Wittgenstein-Berleburg	Antonius und Kleopatra	J. Mosenthal	1883, Graz
S. V. Yuferov	Antony i Kleopatra	Composer	1900 (pub.)
G. F. Malipiero	Antonio e Cleopatra	Composer	1938, Florence
S. Barber	Antony and Cleopatra	F. Zeffirelli	1966, New York
E. Bondeville	Antoine et Cléopâtre	—	1974, Rouen
AS YOU LIKE IT			
F. M. Veracini	Rosalinda	P. A. Rolli	1744, London
Florence Wickham	Rosalind (operetta)	—	1938, Dresden
I. Jirko	[As You Like It]	—	c.1968, Liberec
P. Hasquenoph	Comme il vous plaira	F. Didelot	1982, Strasbourg
THE COMEDY OF ERRORS			
S. Storace	Gli equivoci	Lorenzo da Ponte	1786, Vienna
A. Lorenz	Die Komödie der Irrungen		c.1890
I. Krejčí	Pozdvižení v Efesu	J. Bachtík	1946, Prague
A. Wilson-Dickson	Errors	R. Warren	1980, Leicester
CORIOLANUS			
A. Baeyens	Coriolanus	—	1940, Antwerp
S. Sulek	Koriolan	Composer	1958, Zagreb
J. Cikker	Coriolanus	Composer	1974, Prague

Composer	Title	Librettist	Date, Place
R. Kreutzer	Imogène, ou la gageure indiscrète	J. E. B. Dejaure	1796, Paris
E. Sobolewski	Imogene	—	1833, Königsberg
E. J. L. Missa	Dinah (operetta)	M. Carré and P. de Choudens	1894, Paris
CYMBELINE			
A. Eggen	Cymbelin	Composer	1951, Oslo
HAMLET			
L. Caruso	Amleto	G. M. Foppa	1789, Florence
G. Andreozzi	Amleto	F. Romani	1792, Padua
S. Mercadante	Amleto		1822, Milan
M. Mareczek	Hamlet		1840, Brno
A. Buzzolla	Amleto	G. Peruzzini	1847, Venice
A. Zanardini	Amleto	Composer	1854, Venice
A. Stadtfeld	Hamlet	J. Guillaume	1857, Darmstadt
L. Moroni	Amleto		1860, Rome
F. Faccio	Amleto	A. Boito	1865, Genoa
C. L. A. Thomas	Hamlet	J. Barbier and M. Carré	1868, Paris
J. L. A. Hignard	Hamlet	P. de Garal	1888, Nantes, (pub. 1868)
L. H. Heward	Hamlet		1916 (comp., unfinished)
J. Kalniņš	Hamlets	Composer	1936, Riga
M. Zafred	Amleto	Composer and L. Zafred	1961, Rome
S. Kagen	Hamlet	—	1962, Baltimore
A. Machavariani	Hamlet		1965 (comp.)
H. Searle	Hamlet	Composer	1968, Hamburg
S. Szokolay	Hamlet	Composer	1968, Budapest
P. Bentiou	Hamlet	Composer	1974, Marseilles
Chervinski	Hamlet	—	c.1977, Dortmund
H. Reutter	Hamlet		1980, Stuttgart
R. Kelterborn	Ophelia	H. Meier	1984, Schwetzingen

TABLE 1. Cont.

Composer	Title	Librettist	First Performance
W. Rihm	Hamletmaschine	H. Müller	1987, Mannheim
HENRY IV			
S. Mercadante	La gioventù di Enrico V	F. Romani	1834, Milan
G. Holst	At the Boar's Head (1 act)	Composer	1925, Manchester
G. Getty	Plump Jack	—	1987, San Francisco
JULIUS CAESAR			
J. García Roblez (1839–1910)	Julio César	Composer	—
G.F. Malipiero	Giulio Cesare	Composer	1936, Genoa
G. Klebe	Die Ermordung Cäsars (1 act)	Composer	1959, Essen
KING LEAR			
M. Séméladis	Cordélia	E. Pacini and E. Deschamps	1854, Versailles
A. Cagnoni (1828–96)	Re Lear	—	—
A. Reynaud	Le Roi Lear	—	1888, Toulouse
G. Cottrau	Cordelia	Composer	1913, Padua
Alberto Ghislanzoni	Re Lear	Composer	1937, Rome
V. Frazzi	Re Lear	G. Papini	1939, Florence
A. Reimann	Lear	C. H. Henneberg	1978, Munich
LOVE'S LABOUR'S LOST			
Z. Folprecht	Lásky hra osudná	Čapek brothers	1926, Bratislava
A. Beecham	Love's Labour's Lost	—	1936 (pub.)
N. Nabokov	Love's Labour's Lost	W. H. Auden and C. Kallman	1973, Brussels
MACBETH			
F. Asplmayr	Leben und Tod des Königs Macbeth (pantomime)	Moll	1777, Vienna
H. Chélard	Macbeth	C. J. Rouget de Lisle	1827, Paris
G. Verdi	Macbeth	F. M. Piave and A. Maffei	1847, Florence
	Macbeth	C. Nuitter and A. Beaumont	1865, Paris

W. Taubert	*Macbeth*	F. Eggers	1857, Berlin
Lauro Rossi	*Biorn*	F. Marshall	1877, London
E. Bloch	*Macbeth*	E. Fleg	1910, Paris
N. C. Gatty (1874–1946)	*Macbeth*		—
L. Collingwood	*Macbeth*	Composer	1934, London
H. D. Koppel	*Macbeth*	Composer and A. Koppel	1970, Copenhagen

MEASURE FOR MEASURE

R. Wagner	*Das Liebesverbot, oder die Novize von Palermo*	Composer	1836, Magdeburg

THE MERCHANT OF VENICE

C. Pinsuti	*Il mercante di Venezia*	G. T. Cimino	1873, Bologna
L. P. Deffès	*Jessica*	J. Adenis and H. Boisseaux	1898, Toulouse
J. B. Foerster	*Jessika*	J. Vrchlický	1905, Prague
F. Alpaerts	*Shylock*	H. Melis	1913, Antwerp
A. Radó	*Shylock*	—	1913–14 (comp., unfinished)
O. Taubmann	*Porzia*	—	1916, Frankfurt/Main
A. Beecham	*The Merchant of Venice*	—	1922, London
F. Brumagne (1887–1939)	*Le Marchand de Venise*	—	Brussels
Beatrice Laufer	*Shylock*	—	1929
R. Hahn	*Le Marchand de Venise*	M. Zamaçoïs	1935, Paris
M. Castelnuovo-Tedesco	*Il mercante di Venezia*	Composer	1961, Florence

THE MERRY WIVES OF WINDSOR

Papavoine	*Le Vieux Coquet, ou les deux amies*	Douin	1761, Paris
F. A. D. Philidor	*Herne le chasseur*		1773 (comp.)
P. Ritter	*Die lustigen Weiber*	G. C. Roemer	1794, Mannheim
K. Ditters von Dittersdorf	*Die lustigen Weiber von Windsor und der dicke Hans*	G. C. Roemer (altered)	1796, Öls
A. Salieri	*Falstaff osia le tre burle*	C. P. Defranceschi	1799, Vienna
M. W. Balfe	*Falstaff*	S. M. Maggioni	1838, London
O. Nicolai	*Die lustigen Weiber von Windsor*	S. H. Mosenthal	1849, Berlin

TABLE 1. *Cont.*

Composer	Title	Librettist	First Performance
A. Adam	*Falstaff* (1 act)	J. H. Vernoy de Saint-Georges and A. de Leuven	1856, Paris
G. Verdi	*Falstaff*	A. Boito	1893, Milan
R. Vaughan Williams	*Sir John in Love*	Composer	1929, London
A MIDSUMMER NIGHT'S DREAM			
H. Purcell	*The Fairy Queen*	?T. Betterton	1692, London
R. Leveridge	*The Comick masque of Pyramus and Thisbe* (1 act)	Composer	1716, London
J. F. Lampe	*Pyramus and Thisbe* (mock-opera, 1 act)	Partly based on Leveridge	1745, London
J. C. Smith	*The Fairies*	Composer	1755, London
E. W. Wolf	*Die Zauberirrungen*	F. H. von Einsiedel	1785, Weimar
C. Manusardi	*Un sogno di primavera*	—	1842, Milan
F. von Suppé	*Der Sommernachtstraum*	—	1844, Vienna
L. Mancinelli	*Sogno di una notte d'estate*	F. Salvatori	1917 (comp.)
V. Vreuls	*Un Songe d'une nuit d'été*	P. Spaak	1925, Brussels
D. Arundell (1898–1988)	*A Midsummer Night's Dream*		
M. Delannoy	*Puck*	A. Boll	1949, Strasbourg
C. Orff	*Ein Sommernachtstraum*	Composer	1952
B. Britten	*A Midsummer Night's Dream*	Composer and Peter Pears	1960, Aldeburgh
J. Doubrava	*Sen noci svatojanské*	R. Vonášek	1969, Opava (comp. 1945)
MUCH ADO ABOUT NOTHING			
H. Berlioz	*Béatrice et Bénédict*	Composer	1862, Baden-Baden
A. Doppler	*Viel Lärm um Nichts*	—	1896, Leipzig
P. Puget	*Beaucoup de bruit pour rien*	—	1899, Paris
C. Podestà	*Ero*	—	1900, Cremona
C. V. Stanford	*Much Ado About Nothing*	J. R. Sturgis	1901, London

Composer	Title	Librettist	Date, Place
R. von Mojsisovics	*Viel Lärm um Nichts*	—	c.1930, Graz
R. Hahn	*Beaucoup de bruit pour rien*	J. Sarment	1936, Paris
H. Heinrich	*Viel Lärm um Nichts*	—	1956, Frankfurt/Oder
OTHELLO			
G. Rossini	*Otello osia il Moro di Venezia*	F. Berio di Salsa	1816, Naples
G. Verdi	*Otello*	A. Boito	1887, Milan
PERICLES, PRINCE OF TYRE			
G. Cottrau	*Pericle re di Tiro*		c.1915 (comp.)
RICHARD III			
L. Canepa	*Riccardo III*	Fulgonio	1879, Milan
G. Salvayre	*Riccardo III*	E. R. Blavet	1883, St Petersburg
F. Testi	*Riccardo III*	Composer	1987, Milan
ROMEO AND JULIET			
J. G. Schwanenberger	*Romeo e Giulia*	C. Sanseverino	1776, Leipzig[a]
G. Benda	*Romeo und Julie*	F. W. Gotter	1776, Gotha
L. Monescalchi	*Romeo e Giulietta*	G. M. Foppa	1789, Rome
S. von Rumling	*Roméo et Juliette*	—	1790, Munich
N. Dalayrac	*Tout pour l'amour, ou Roméo et Juliette*	J. M. Boutet de Monvel	1792, Paris
D. Steibelt	*Roméo et Juliette*	J. A. P. de Ségur	1793, Paris
N. A. Zingarelli	*Giulietta e Romeo*	G. M. Foppa	1796, Milan
B. Porta		—	1806, Paris
P. C. Guglielmi	*Romeo e Giulietta*	S. Buonaiuti	1810, London
N. Vaccai	*Giulietta e Romeo*	F. Romani	1825, Milan
V. Bellini	*I Capuleti e i Montecchi*	F. Romani	1830, Venice
A. M. Storch	*Romeo und Julie* ('Komisch-tragische Oper', 1 act)	I. Forst	1862, Vienna
M. Morales	*Romeo y Julieta*	F. Romani	1863, Mexico City
F. Marchetti	*Romeo e Giulietta*	M. M. Marcello	1865, Trieste
C. Gounod	*Roméo et Juliette*	J. Barbier and M. Carré	1867, Paris

TABLE I. *Cont.*

Composer	Title	Librettist	First Performance
A. Mercadal	*Romeo e Giulietta*	—	1873, Mahon (Minorca)
P. X. D. (Marquis) d'Ivry	*Les Amants de Vérone*	Composer	1878, Paris
H. R. Shelley	*Romeo and Juliet*	?Composer	1901 (pub.)
C. del Campo	*Los amantes de Verona*		1909
J. E. Barkworth	*Romeo and Juliet*	Composer	1916, Middlesbrough
R. Zandonai	*Giulietta e Romeo*	A. Rossato	1922, Rome
H. Sutermeister	*Romeo und Julia*	Composer	1940, Dresden
G. F. Malipiero	*Romeo e Giulietta*^b	Composer	1950, Italian radio
B. Blacher	*Romeo und Julia* (scenic oratorio)	Composer	1950, Salzburg
E. Gaujac	*Les Amants de Vérone*		1955, Toulouse
A. B. Zanon	*La leggenda di Giulietta*	M. Spiritini	1969, Bergamo
THE TAMING OF THE SHREW			
T. S. Cooke and J. Braham	*The Taming of the Shrew*		1828, London
H. Goetz	*Der Widerspänstigen Zähmung*	J. V. Widmann	1874, Mannheim
S. Samara	*La furia domata*		1895, Milan
C. Silver	*La Mégère apprivoisée*	H. Cain and E. Adenis	1922, Paris
R. Bossi	*Volpino il calderaio* (1 act)	L. Orsini	1925, Milan
M. Persico	*La bisbetica domata*	A. Rossato	1931, Rome
R. Karel	*The Taming of the Shrew*	—	1942–3 (comp., unfinished)
P. G. Clapp	*The Taming of the Shrew*		1948, New York
V. Giannini	*The Taming of the Shrew*	Composer and D. Fee	1953, Cincinnati
V. Y. Shebalin	*Ukroshchenie stroptivoi*	A. A. Gozenpud	1957, Kuibyshev
THE TEMPEST			
?H. Purcell (?J. Weldon)	*The Tempest; or, the Enchanted Island*	J. Dryden, W. Davenant, and T. Shadwell	1695, London
J. C. Smith	*The Tempest*	?D. Garrick	1756, London

Composer	Title	Librettist / based on	Date, Place
F. Asplmayr	Der Sturm	Patzke	1781, Vienna
J. H. Rolle	Der Sturm (Die Bezauberte Insel) (1 act)		1784, Berlin
V. Fabrizi	La tempesta	—	1788, Rome
P. von Winter	Der Sturm	—	1793, Munich
F. Fleischmann	Die Geisterinsel	F. W. Gotter and F. H. von Einsiedel	1798, Weimar
J. F. Reichardt	Die Geisterinsel	F. W. Gotter and F. H. von Einsiedel	1798, Berlin
J. R. Zumsteeg	Die Geisterinsel	F. W. Gotter and F. H. von Einsiedel	1798, Stuttgart
F. Haack	Die Geisterinsel	F. W. Gotter and F. H. von Einsiedel	1798, Stettin
W. Müller	Der Sturm	F. W. Gotter and F. H. von Einsiedel	1798, Vienna
P. Ritter	Der Sturm, oder die bezauberte Insel	K. F. Hensler	1799, Aurich
J. D. Hensel	Die Geisterinsel	J. W. Doering	1799, Hirschberg
L. Caruso	La tempesta	Composer, based on Gotter and Doering	1799, Naples
F. L. A. Kunzen (1761–1817)	Stormen	—	—
A. J. Emmert	Der Sturm	—	1806, Salzburg
P. J. Riotte	Der Sturm	—	1833, Brno
E. Raymond	Der Sturm	—	c.1840 (comp.)
E. Rung	Der Sturm	—	1847, Copenhagen
F. Halévy	La tempesta	E. Scribe, tr. P. Giannone	1850, London
E. Nápravník	Der Sturm	—	1860, Prague
E. Frank	Der Sturm	J. V. Widmann	1887, Hanover
A. Urspruch	Der Sturm	E. Pirazzi	1888, Frankfurt
Z. Fibich	Bouře	J. Vrchlický	1895, Prague
A. Farwell	Caliban (Masque)		1916
A. M. Hale	The Tempest	? Composer	1917 (pub.)
N. C. Gatty	The Tempest	R. Gatty and composer	1920, London

TABLE 1. Cont.

Composer	Title	Librettist	First Performance
F. Lattuada	La tempesta	A. Rosato	1922, Milan
H. Sutermeister	Die Zauberinsel	Composer	1942, Dresden
K. Atterberg	Stormen	—	1948, Stockholm
F. Martin	Der Sturm	Composer	1956, Vienna
J. Eaton	The Tempest	A. Porter	1985, Santa Fe
L. Hoiby	The Tempest	M. Shulgasser	1986, Indianola (Iowa)
TIMON OF ATHENS			
Leopold I, Holy Roman Emperor	Timone misantropo	—	1696, Vienna
TROILUS AND CRESSIDA			
W. Zillig	Troilus und Cressida	Composer	1951, Düsseldorf
TWELFTH NIGHT			
E. Steinkühler	Cäsario, oder die Verwechslung	—	1848, Düsseldorf
W. Rintel	Was ihr wöllt	—	1872, Berlin
W. Taubert	Cesario	E. Taubert	1874, Berlin
K. Weis	Viola (Die Zwillinge)	B. Adler, R. Šubert, and V. Novohradský	1892, Prague
F. B. Hart	Malvolio	—	1913 (? comp.)
B. Smetana	Viola	E. Krásnohorská	1924, Prague (comp. 1874–84, unfinished)
G. Farina	La dodicesima notte	—	1929, Milan
A. Kusterer	Was ihr wöllt	—	1932, Dresden
H. Holenia	Viola	O. Widowitz	1934, Graz
A. de Filippi	Malvolio	—	1937 (? comp.)
C. A. Gibbs	Twelfth Night	Composer	1947 (comp.)
I. Jirko	Večer tříkrálový	—	1967, Liberec
D. Amram	Twelfth Night	J. Papp	1968, Glenn Falls, N.Y.
J. Wilson	Twelfth Night	H. Moulton	1969, Wexford

THE TWO GENTLEMEN OF VERONA

J. L. Seymour	The Two Gentlemen of Verona (operetta)	—	1937, Berkeley

THE WINTER'S TALE

C. E. di Barbieri	Perdita oder ein Wintermärchen	K. Gross	1865, Prague
M. Bruch	Hermione	E. Hopffer	1872, Berlin
J. Nešvera	Perdita	J. Kvapil	1897, Prague
H. Bereny	Das Wintermärchen	—	1898
C. Goldmark	Ein Wintermärchen	A. M. Willner	1908, Vienna
J. Harbison	A Winter's Tale	Composer	1979, San Francisco

[a] A printed edition of Sanseverino's libretto dated 1773 (?Berlin) may refer to this or an earlier setting.
[b] One section of a composite drama, *Monde celesti e infernali*.

27

Bizet's *Ivan IV*

On 12 October 1951 the Grand Théâtre in Bordeaux gave the first public performance of *Ivan* IV, an opera in four (originally five) acts by Georges Bizet. About the same time the Paris firm of Choudens published a vocal score, and on 6 April 1952 the opera was produced with considerable success at Cologne. The event, as usual with such exhumations, caused a certain stir in musical circles and much conjecture and inaccuracy in the press. This was nothing new with Bizet, who has suffered more than most composers of his period from the misrepresentations of posterity, and who has the curious distinction, along with Berlioz, of having been consistently undervalued in his own country. It is now possible to throw a good deal of fresh light on this opera, and although it is no masterpiece there are several widely divergent reasons for examining it in detail. (1) Both libretto and music have a strange and interesting history. (2) It has hitherto escaped thorough scrutiny. The autograph has been in the Paris Conservatoire Library since 1929, but few scholars have availed themselves of their opportunity.[1] (3) The facts as given by Bizet's biographers are meagre and contradictory, and the circumstances of the publication are calculated in some respects to obscure rather than clarify them. (4) The score, though uneven, contains some charming and characteristic music. (5) It may help us to understand a composer of genius whose development has always appeared somewhat baffling. (6) It suggests a new chronology for Bizet's work at an obscure period of his career. (7) Recent research has added appreciably to our knowledge.

The first edition (1886) of Charles Pigot's life of Bizet attributes the libretto of *Ivan le Terrible* (as the opera has generally been called) to Louis Gallet and Édouard Blau. This couple supplied Bizet with the texts of two other operas, *La Coupe du roi de Thulé* (1868) and *Don Rodrigue* (1873), which by mischance have not been preserved in complete form, but neither had anything to do with *Ivan*. In his second edition (1911) Pigot named another pair of librettists, Arthur Leroy and Henri Trianon.[2] According to Jean-Paul Changeur, the resident producer at the Bordeaux theatre and author of an interesting series of six articles on the opera in *La Vie Bordelaise* (12 October to 16 November 1951),[3] the more active partner was Trianon, and his

[1] See, however, J. Chantavoine, *Quelques Inédits de Georges Bizet* in *Le Ménestrel*, 4 Aug.–22 Sept. 1933, and W. Dean, *Bizet*, 3rd edn. (London, 1975). See also n. 11 below.

[2] This has not prevented some later writers from adhering to Gallet and Blau. Gallet had denied his authorship in *Notes d'un librettiste* (Paris, 1891).

[3] These articles contain important new information on the history of the libretto and describe the events leading up to the 1951 production. A manuscript of the libretto, said to have been used by Bizet, is still in the possession of the Trianon family.

colleague was not Arthur but François Hippolyte Leroy, who worked in various Paris theatres from 1837 and in 1849 became stage-manager at the Opéra under Nestor Roqueplan. Trianon (1811–96) was a critic of art and letters, translator of Xenophon and the pseudo-Homeric *Batrachomyomachia,* under-librarian (1842) and librarian (1849) of Sainte Geneviève, and from 1852 an inveterate compiler of librettos and ballet scenarios for all three Paris opera houses. One of his labours was a translation of *Don Giovanni,* produced at the Théâtre-Lyrique in 1866. Unfortunately for his fame, his librettos were all associated with minor composers whose names are today scarcely known even to specialists. The one exception was *Ivan le Terrible;* with this he hooked two of France's leading opera composers, but he lost them both before he could bring them to land.

The libretto was written in 1855, and in the following January François Louis Crosnier, general administrator at the Opéra, offered it to Gounod. It was accepted with enthusiasm, and the press announced that rehearsals of the opera would begin in November 1856. But in the meantime Crosnier was succeeded by Alphonse Royer, who was less favourably disposed towards Gounod. Changeur says that Gounod finished his opera by the end of the summer of 1858; this may be a mistake for 1857. At any rate, despite periodical elbow-jogging by the press, Royer repeatedly postponed the production. We catch an echo of this in a letter of September 1858 from Bizet (in Rome) to Gounod; he has heard that a work of Gounod's is announced for production at the Opéra, and enquires if this is *Yvan* (*sic*). Gounod is said to have been ill satisfied with his score and to have withdrawn it; but it is possible that, like Bizet later, he abandoned it only when he failed to get it produced. Not all the music was wasted: the Soldiers' Chorus in *Faust* (produced at the Théâtre-Lyrique, 19 March 1859), the March in *La Reine de Saba,* and the air 'Le jour se lève' in *Mireille* were all composed for *Ivan le Terrible.* The Soldiers' Chorus, which replaced an air in which Valentine boasted of his sister's beauty, was incorporated in *Faust* at the pressing suggestion of the painter Ingres, Carvalho (director of the Théâtre-Lyrique), and Gounod's brother-in-law, Dubufe.

On 6 June 1863, in a letter to Leroy, Gounod renounced his rights in the libretto, and on 10 March 1864 *Le Figaro* announced that Bizet's *Ivan le Terrible* would follow *Mirieille* (*sic*)—'already christened *Mirieleison* by the artists'—at the Théâtre-Lyrique. Since the first performance of *Mireille* took place only nine days later (five years to the day after that of *Faust*), this suggests that Bizet's opera was virtually finished, a point that will require consideration presently. The history of Bizet's setting now begins to ape Gounod's in a remarkably sedulous manner. The press continued at intervals to announce its expected production; in June 1865 *La France musicale* named it among the operas scheduled for the forthcoming autumn season. Bizet's correspondence with Edmond Galabert began about this time, and the earlier letters contain several references to the opera. In the late summer '*Iwan* (*sic*) is at the copyist's' and Bizet expects it to come on at the Lyrique about the end of January or beginning of February 1866. But nothing happened. In fact Carvalho, whose set policy was to produce the work of the younger French composers (he had already commissioned *Les Pêcheurs de perles*), had six new full-length operas on his hands and very little money with which to mount them. Only one of the six, *La Fiancée d'Abydos* by Barthe, whom readers of Bizet's Rome letters will remember as the winner of the Prix Rodriques for which Bizet submitted his Te Deum, reached the stage during this season; *Don Giovanni* in Trianon's version and Nicolai's *Lustigen Weiber von Windsor* had to be put on as money-raisers. According to Changeur, Bizet had no contract with Carvalho and therefore no legal remedy;[4] but this is contradicted by Bizet's own testimony. In a letter[5] to an unknown Belgian correspondent, to whom he gives a summary of his career up to the end of 1866, he says that after *Les Pêcheurs de perles* (September 1863) 'Carvalho m'a immédiatement commandé un *Ivan IV* en 5 actes qui n'a pu, pour une foule de raisons, être représenté'. He certainly regarded Carvalho as committed to the production: an unpublished letter to his publisher, Choudens, written about December 1865, gives unbridled expression to his bitterness at Carvalho's behaviour.

The outcome is not in doubt. Early in December Bizet withdrew the score from the Lyrique and submitted it to Perrin, director of the Opéra, with a rather wry covering letter. Pigot's explanation of Bizet's withdrawal from the Lyrique—that he had deliberately sought in *Ivan* to combine the traditional French style with that of Verdi, thought better of it, withdrew the score in an access of artistic conscience, and a few years later burned it—is certainly insufficient, but it may, as will appear, contain a few more grains of truth than is generally allowed. Bizet must or should have known that the elaborate sets and costumes, choruses and ballets demanded by *Ivan* were not likely to recommend it to a director who, as he admitted to Galabert at this very moment, 'n'a pas le sou!'[6] But there is no doubt that the frame of mind in which he sent it to the Opéra was one of high dudgeon. Here, too, he was destined to be disappointed. There has survived a departmental memorandum[7] to the Minister of Fine Arts, dated 11 December 1865 and signed by Camille Doucet,[8] in which note is taken of Bizet's intention to submit *Ivan* to the Opéra. Doucet states that the Opéra is already fully committed, and Bizet would be better advised to stick to the Lyrique, where his work may come on before the end of the season (June 1866), and await a more favourable opportunity of courting the heavier risks of the larger house. Doucet adds that the subject of the opera renders it more suitable to the Lyrique, a statement it is difficult to take seriously. The libretto, it will be remembered, had been written for the Opéra in the first place. It seems clear that neither Doucet nor Perrin, whom he associates with his opinion, had then any acquaintance with the score (Doucet was not sure of the number of acts); and both must have known the financial condition of the Lyrique.

The Opéra, of course, did nothing. In January or February Bizet wrote to

---

[4] In any case the remedy was dubious. Litolff, another of the disappointed five, who had a contract, brought an action against Carvalho and lost it.

[5] Quoted by H. Malherbe, *Carmen* (Paris, 1951), 50.

[6] Fifth letter to Galabert, early Dec. 1865.

[7] For this and other unpublished documents summarized here I am indebted to Mina Curtiss.

[8] Directeur des Théâtres at the Ministry since 1863 and a close friend of Bizet's teacher and future father-in-law, Halévy.

Galabert: 'Nothing new at the Opéra. One must wait still and intrigue always.'[9] After this *Ivan* disappears from the records, except for two or three references in letters of February 1869, when there appears to have been some question of Bizet submitting the score to Pasdeloup, who had succeeded Carvalho at the Lyrique the previous year.[10] Galabert says that Bizet never spoke of the opera in later years. In July 1866 he signed with Carvalho the contract for *La Jolie Fille de Perth,* which in its turn was delayed for a full year. The score of *Ivan* became a quarry, to the advantage of *La Jolie Fille de Perth* and *Jeux d'enfants* among other works. The parallel with Gounod was complete.

The posthumous history of the opera is also chequered. For more than sixty years it remained a mystery and a legend. Bizet's only legitimate son died by his own hand in 1922, his widow in 1926, and her second husband, Émile Straus, in 1929, none of them leaving descendants. Most of Bizet's musical manuscripts—though not his private papers—passed to the Paris Conservatoire. Among them was an autograph score of *Ivan* without title page or list of characters and with the orchestration of the last act incomplete.[11] This was sumptuously bound and placed on view in the Bizet Centenary Exhibition at the Opéra in 1938. During the war one Guillaume de Van, described by Changeur as an intellectual adventurer of dubious nationality, became keeper of the music at the Bibliothèque Nationale and organized a private performance of *Ivan,* without orchestra or action, at the Théâtre des Capucines in the winter of 1943. An intended performance with orchestra at the Galerie Mazarine never took place owing to the liberation, when de Van apparently vanished. Meanwhile the Germans, who have always held Bizet in high respect, had microfilmed the manuscript and were preparing their own performance. According to reports current at the time, they supplied the opera with a new libretto, entitled *König Turpin,* with the scene laid at the Merovingian court in the sixth century, and planned to produce it at Dresden. In the event, the first stage performance (presumably private) took place at Mühringen Castle near Tübingen during 1946 under the title *Ivan le Terrible.*

In connection with one or other of the projected German performances Schott of Mainz commissioned a German translation and prepared a vocal score. A legal dispute followed between Schott and Choudens, as a result of which the latter obtained publication rights, while agreeing to publish Schott's German translation. It is characteristic of the neglect of Bizet scholarship that, although the score had been publicly exhibited in 1938 and described, together with quotations, by Chantavoine in 1933, neither Choudens nor the society to which Émile Straus left the Bizet copyrights had ever heard of the opera, while Malherbe in 1951 ascribed

[9] Bizet had first approached the Opéra through the good offices of Benoit-Champy, Président du Tribunal-Civil de la Seine, to whom *La Jollie Fille de Perth* is dedicated.

[10] It is most unlikely that Pasdeloup would have produced *Ivan*; his short regime (1868–70) was financially even less happy than Carvalho's.

[11] It was one of the manuscripts offered to the Conservatoire by Réne Sibilat, Straus's nephew and heir, in 1929. Mme Straus had bequeathed the autographs of *Carmen* and *L'Arlésienne.* All have since been transferred to the Bibliothèque Nationale.

its discovery to Choudens and Schott, and a German writer, Richard Kraus, in 1952 to his compatriot Ernst Hartmann during the war. Choudens and Schott were also at loggerheads about the manner in which the opera should be completed and 'revised'. The legal victors entrusted this task to the veteran composer and conductor Henri Busser, and it was his version that reached print and performance in 1951. Paris, not for the first time in Bizet's story, was less interested than the provinces.

A final touch of irony concerns the title under which the opera at last met the public—*Ivan IV*. Pigot calls it *Ivan le Terrible,* and so do the press announcements of the 1860s; *Ivan le Terrible* it has always been. But those concerned with the 1951 revival were troubled by the association of this title with Rimsky-Korsakov's *Pskovitianka* and with an opera by Raoul Gunsbourg (1910), which, moreover, had been published by Choudens. They therefore decided to change it, and after consulting many eminent persons, including no less a figure than the statesman Édouard Herriot, they hit on *Ivan IV,* although this title, too, had been used twice before, for an opera by Brion d'Orgueval (Marseilles, 1876) and for the Prix de Rome cantata of 1860, won by Paladilhe. By a singular fluke they restored the correct title. Bizet generally spoke of the opera as '*Ivan*' or '*Iwan*'—each number in the autograph is headed 'Ivan'—but in his more formal letter to a Belgian correspondent, quoted above, and in Camille Doucet's memorandum to the Minister of Fine Arts it appears as *Ivan IV.* Nowhere does Bizet call it *Ivan le Terrible.* This may have been Gounod's[12] title, or the librettists' original, which the press would naturally apply to Bizet's setting of the same libretto.

Before comparing the printed score with the autograph and drawing certain fresh conclusions about the period when Bizet was at work on the opera, it may be as well to describe it in the form in which it is available to the public. For theatrical convenience Busser reduced the number of acts from five to four by running the first two into one. In this analysis Bizet's original form will be preserved.

The scene of Act I is laid in the Caucasus in the sixteenth century. A number of Caucasian women, among them Marie (soprano), daughter of the local king Temrouk, are drawing water from a spring. After a charming chorus of Gounod-esque cut a stranger appears, a young Bulgarian (soprano or mezzo),[13] who explains that he has been separated from his master in a mist. The girls promise to put him on his way, and he and Marie sing a duet which contains the most distinguished music in the act; Bizet perhaps recognised this when he transferred most of it verbatim to *La Jolie Fille de Perth,* where it appears as the flute melody at bar 28 of the Prelude. A second stranger now enters, introduced by a striking figure that reappears frequently in the course of the opera:

[12] But Gounod, inscribing a photograph for Madame Halévy in May 1860, added a musical quotation with the words, '(Ivan IV) 1855—'. This suggests that he had still not finally abandoned his opera. The music is an earlier version, in 2/4 time and with different words, of the theme of the air 'Le jour se lève' in *Mireille.*

[13] Busser changed this to tenor.

Ex.1

This is the Tsar Ivan (baritone), the master of the young Bulgarian, who at once explains that he has not given away his identity to the Caucasians. Marie bids the stranger drink from the spring, and as he does so we hear a characteristic melody (*espressivo*) on the clarinet, in which the Bizet of José's Flower Song is clearly recognizable:

Ex.2

Ivan, in an arioso based on the same ostinato figure as the Prelude to *Les Pêcheurs de perles,* offers her a rare flower he has found in the mountains. He then goes out with the young Bulgarian to the strains of Ex. 1, and another characteristic billowing melody, this time on the flute,

Ex.3

leads to a reprise of the opening chorus, during which Marie reflects on the new exaltation that has suddenly come over her.

Temrouk (bass) enters, looking very worried; almost at once an offstage voice calls the Caucasians to arms against a Russian attack. But the Caucasian menfolk are not at hand, and a Russian officer, striding in unopposed, demands the surrender of Marie at the command of the Tsar, as Ex. 1 growls menacingly in the orchestra. Temrouk indignantly refuses, and when the officer threatens to kill every Caucasian child within reach leads a concerted appeal *avec beaucoup d'expression:*

Ex.4

This theme, again redolent of Gounod, served Bizet later when he came to patch up Halévy's unfinished opera *Noé*. To prevent bloodshed Marie surrenders herself to the Russian officer and is led away. Her capture appears to be the sole exploit of Ivan's army in the Caucasus; we are never told their purpose there.

A cornet or trumpet is heard fanfaring off, and the Caucasian males, led by Marie's brother Igor (tenor), proclaim a victory—over wolves and bears. They swear vengeance on Marie's ravishers in a 6/8 Allegro whose jogtrot rhythm suggests not so much implacability as the nursery warfare of 'Chevaux de bois' in *Jeux d'enfants*. Temrouk stops them: he feels the breath of Allah, and as usual when Bizet tries to sound a religious note the music lapses into the portentously sanctimonious. Temrouk bids the young men cast lots to decide who shall avenge Marie: as we should expect in opera, the lot falls on Igor. The 6/8 episode returns to crown a rather weak finale, in the coda of which Bizet suddenly and unsuitably remembers *Lohengrin*:

Ex.5

Act II takes us to the banqueting hall in the Kremlin, where the Boyars are celebrating Ivan's victory over the Tartars. Here for the first time Bizet attempts local colour. The music is hardly Russian, but it has vigour and character, and as usual in his early operas attains greater distinction than the more straightforward material:

Ex.6

Suddenly a distant side-drum reduces the company to superstitious muttering. Ivan, accompanied by the bass element from Ex. 1 presented in a formidable barrage of Puccini octaves (a device Bizet uses effectively elsewhere, notably in the great Act IV duet in *Carmen*), explains that it is only a procession of his victims on their way to the scaffold, and bids the company resume their drinking. This is one of the most impressive scenes in the opera. Ivan, after congratulating his henchman Yorloff (bass)[14] on his assistance in unmasking his enemies, bids the young Bulgarian give them a song from his homeland. He obliges with the admirable Serenade in bolero rhythm, spiced (like the chorus of Boyars) with a little exoticism in the scoring, which Bizet had written in Rome for his symphonic ode *Vasco de Gama:*

Ex.7

Since Bizet's local colour was never meant to be taken literally, the transmigration from Portugal to Bulgaria is easily accomplished. Ivan caps this love song with something more suited to a warrior, a Cossack Song of which three complete settings survive.

The Tsar explains that he has been seeking a consort who shall supply him with worthy sons (another of Bizet's *espressivo* melodies rises from the orchestra). Yorloff is certain the honour will go to his daughter—and woe betide the Tsar if it does not! A throng of veiled female captives is brought in, lamenting their expatriation in thirds to a fair specimen of a Mendelssohn gondola song. This is not allowed in the Kremlin, and Ivan orders them to unveil. Marie, who is of the party, at first electrifies the company by refusing, but presently complies rather than submit to force. The melody of Ex. 2 is heard when she recognizes in the Tsar the stranger who gave her the flower, and again when he sees her face. Despite her love, she begs, in an F sharp minor Andantino that hardly shows Bizet at his best, to be restored to her family and country. Instead Ivan offers her his hand, which she defiantly refuses; whereupon he orders her forcible removal. Now comes a fresh intervention. A contingent of nuns, commanded by Ivan's sister Olga and accompanied by the organ in a fruitily harmonized prayer to the Virgin, takes Marie providentially under its protection. 'Cette fille est à moi!' bellows the Tsar. 'Cette fille est à Dieu!' replies Olga *avec autorité*, and dares Ivan to defy the crucifix she holds aloft. The act ends with a stout ensemble, reinforced by bass drum, harps, and organ, on the theme of the nuns' prayer (which closely resembles the hymn to Brahma in *Les Pêcheurs de perles*), with Ivan and Yorloff adding a frustrated counterpoint in jerky double-dotted rhythm. Bizet seldom sank to this level of emotional flatulence.

As the curtain rises on Act III public festivities are in full swing in a courtyard of the Kremlin. The orchestral introduction again has a faintly 'Russian' tinge, due to the repetition of sharply rhythmic phrases over a pedal, but this soon yields to a commonplace Second Empire waltz. The E flat central section of this chorus

---

[14] Busser cut the first appearance of Yorloff's motif (Ex. 8 below) at his entrance (p. 72 of the vocal score). The pagination of the autograph suggests that Bizet first wrote it in full, then reduced it to the equivalent of the first two bars.

anticipates the trio of the *Arlésienne* Minuet in its compound of a trochaic theme in the voice parts with a running quaver countersubject in the orchestra over a double (tonic and dominant) pedal, but there is little here of the savour of the later piece. A herald, with a truculent fanfare of cornets and trombones, announces the approach of the Tsar to celebrate his wedding. The procession, headed by a stage band of three saxhorns (soprano, bass, and contrabass), two cornets, two trumpets, and three trombones, marches across the court into the cathedral. Here the bourgeois element in Bizet supplies music less worthy of an imperial marriage than of a municipal brass band on a Bank Holiday outing.[15]

As the organ strikes up in the cathedral, Igor, on his mission of assassination, complains of the difficulty of disposing of so popular a monarch. Providence now produces Temrouk, who has heard nothing for eight months and come to Moscow in disguise, unable to bear the suspense any longer. Father and son encourage one another in a duet whose complacent jauntiness suggests one of the weaker pages of *La Jolie Fille de Perth,* the duet 'Moi, Smith, simple artisan'. The B flat major episode ('Fatigué de l'incertitude') owes a clear debt to Schumann's song 'Er, der Herrlichste von allen'. Yorloff enters, ascertains their grievance, and proclaims his own, which is, of course, the slight to his daughter (we are left to assume that Ivan's bride is Marie, a fact unknown to Igor and Temrouk). The earlier part of this scene is handled by Bizet with rare dramatic skill. As the three conspirators jockey for position, violas and cellos unwind the sinuous, wheedling theme associated with the traitor Yorloff:

Ex.8

Andante moderato (quasi lento)

This tune and Bizet's use of it as a background to the hatching of the murder plot may have been suggested by the scene between Rigoletto and Sparafucile. When Igor reveals that his enemy is the Tsar we hear a variant of Ex. 1—its upper component this time—and, as all three plan the murder of Tsar and Tsarina, Bizet employs the compound of pedals and chromatic scales in contrary motion that became a prominent fingerprint of his dramatic style:

Ex.9

Un peu animé

[15] It is only fair to add that the German writer of the programme note for the Cologne performances detected in this march a fusion of Russian folksong with the spirit of Handel's oratorios.

Unfortunately the formal trio is much weaker, and the finale, despite the possibilities of the stage situation, is ruined by the return of the irretrievably vulgar wedding march with full chorus and organ.

The opening scene of Act IV (a room outside the Tsar's nuptial chamber), though extraneous to the drama, is one of the most charming and characteristic in the score. The young Bulgarian, accompanied by a predominantly wordless chorus, is heard behind the scenes summoning Marie to embark in the state barge which is to convey her round the city waterways on her wedding evening. We might wonder what induced the librettists to include this Venetian exploit did we not know that the music exists as a detached barcarolle, both for chorus and for piano solo, under the title *Le Golfe de Baïa*. The lay-out of the introduction and coda (the voices are accompanied in the autograph) with the basses thrumming rhythmically in fifths, the light scoring, woodwind trills, and long pedals, as well as the placing (offstage at the beginning of an act), is reminiscent of the chorus 'L'ombre descend' in *Les Pêcheurs de perles*.

There follows a long scene for Marie, in which she explains (none too soon) how she has come to marry Ivan after all. It appears that the Tsar, deprived of her love, wanted only to die; whereupon the practical Olga took her to see him and all discord was resolved, God giving her up in favour of Ivan. The music is very unequal;[16] the finest section has a ritornello for four woodwind soloists in A flat minor revealing the miniaturist of *L'Arlésienne*:

Ex.10

At the end she proclaims her love for Ivan in a cabaletta with vocal *fioreture* after the manner of early Verdi, while the unseen chorus repeat fragments of the barcarolle. (At this point Busser inserted a love duet for Marie and Ivan.) As Marie embarks, the orchestra plays another *espressivo* theme:

Ex.11

Meanwhile Ivan has found on his bed a paper containing a brief account of how Judith beheaded the sleeping Holofernes. This had been placed there by Yorloff

---

[16] The first two bars of the 12/8 theme, 'Quand la sainte Olga', reproduce the melodic line of bars 47–50 of the piano piece *Chasse fantastique* (published 1865). This is probably accidental; there is no similarity of mood.

with the idea (only feasible in opera) of suggesting that Marie might have similar
intentions. Ivan merely bids Yorloff keep watch, and goes out with his suite. Yorloff
makes final arrangements for the murder with Igor, who still does not know the
identity of the Tsarina he is to slay. This scene makes effective use (though without
development) of three earlier motifs, Ex. 1 at Ivan's exit, the theme of the trio near
the end of Act III, and Ex. 8 at Yorloff's exit. It is now time for a tenor air, and
Igor conveniently recalls the old happy days with his sister in the Caucasus. The
theme has a characteristic melodic fingerprint that was to become prominent in *La
Coupe du roi de Thulé* and *Carmen*:

Ex.12

A snatch of the barcarolle, without orchestra, announces the return of the state
barge, and as Marie enters to Ex. 11 brother and sister embrace with joy. But Igor
is horrified to learn that she is Ivan's wife. He will not renounce his vow; she bids
him kill her in Ivan's place. This outcome is naturally precluded when both think
of their mother, and the vow goes by the board. Nearly all the music of this long
duet—it runs to sixty-three pages in the autograph, but Busser made cuts—later
came to rest in the even longer duet for Saraï and Ituriel in Act II of *Noé*.

Ivan, Yorloff, and the court burst in. Yorloff, changing sides for the second time,
denounces Igor; Ivan is broken-hearted at the thought that Marie is in league with
the assassins. An officer reports that Temrouk's party have started an insurrection
and set fire to the Kremlin. At the climax of the consequent ensemble of hatred and
recrimination Ivan collapses in an apoplectic fit. Marie[17] bids all kneel and pray for
him; the final return of Ex. 11, which after much B minor storm and stress brings
the act to a quiet end in the dominant, is an insertion by Busser, but wholly in
Bizet's manner. This is the best of the finales in *Ivan,* even if it is indebted to the
big ensembles of Verdi, and particularly to the gaming scene in *La traviata*.

Act V has two scenes. The first, on the walls of the Kremlin in early dawn, begins
with a quiet march which will surprise all lovers of Bizet and indeed of French
music. It is the 'Trompette et Tambour' march from *Jeux d'enfants,* in the same key
and essentially unaltered, though many refinements of detail were added later. In
the opera it forms the core of one of those admirable little vignettes so characteristic
of Bizet's operas; the closest parallels are the Chorus of the Watch in *La Jolie Fille
de Perth* and the boys' march in Act I of *Carmen*. An officer challenges the sentry
on guard, the password is exchanged, we hear that Ivan is dead and Yorloff in
control of the Kremlin, the sentry mutters a prayer: only a few snatches of recitative
before the march is resumed (the whole episode amounts to a mere twenty-two
bars), but the dramatic effect is brilliant. Temrouk appears, gloomily reflecting that

---

[17] Yorloff in the autograph.

Marie and Igor would have done better to remember their father and country. Cries are heard in the distance[18] as Ivan enters, having recovered consciousness, broken his fetters, and killed his guards. He has to explain himself in a fiery B minor air before Temrouk recognizes him. The news that Marie is to be executed produces vocal exuberance rather than action: baritone and bass indulge in a duet full of threats against persons unknown. It is not till Ivan hears the bell that sounds only for a Tsar's death that he leads Temrouk into action against his enemies within. The whole episode is weakly handled by librettists and composer. Busser shortens it considerably.

The last scene has the same setting as Act III. Yorloff informs the court that he has assumed the throne with the title of regent, since Marie's treachery has driven Ivan out of his mind; the chorus clamour for her execution. She and Igor sing a short duet of farewell to their Caucasian fatherland; the melody—which has appeared earlier in the opera, although not in the published score—is a variant of the original duet-finale of *Les Pêcheurs de perles*. As Yorloff orders the royal diadem to be torn from Marie's brow Ivan strides in and consigns Yorloff to the scaffold prepared for Marie and Igor. The opera ends with a brief return of the wedding march and chorus. It must be admitted that after the first number Bizet's inspiration flags badly in this act, even though the instrumental parts are not his.

The defects of the libretto need no emphasis and might have smothered a more mature talent than Bizet's. It is a typical product of the Scribe school, which was concerned not with character but with the manipulation of a number of stock dramatic situations, generally involving a head-on clash between dynastic politics and sex and often wildly improbable on the human level. Bizet's genius was the reverse of dynastic; when offered a libretto on the story of Vercingetorix he complained that the difficulty would be Caesar, since musical emperors were the very devil. So it proves in *Ivan*. There was little in the libretto to evoke that gift for musical characterization on the human level which must have been latent in him from the first. None of the characters comes to life throughout, though several of them, notably Yorloff and Marie, have their moments. Significantly much of the best music is associated with secondary figures like the young Bulgarian and the sentries of Act V, who are little more than vehicles for local colour. We may note, too, that while all five acts begin well—the second, fourth, and fifth outstandingly so—all but the fourth are let down by their finales, where Bizet, called on to sum up a situation and bring it to a musical climax, too often took refuge in a grandiosity foreign to his nature. He never really mastered this difficulty till *Carmen,* though he achieved one admirable and original finale in Act II of *La Jolie Fille de Perth,* and there are signs that another may have been lost in Act I of *La Coupe du roi de Thulé.*

The strongest influences are those of Meyerbeer, Gounod, and Verdi. Meyerbeer, the Michelangelo of his age (as Bizet among others called him), was an inevitable model for an opera of this kind in the France of the 1860s—even Verdi could not

---

[18] From this point only the voice parts are by Bizet.

escape him—but can never have been a good one for Bizet, except, perhaps, in orchestration, where he was an innovator. But *Ivan,* except in some of the exotic and incidental pieces, hardly shows Bizet's orchestration at its best. Much of it is overpoweringly massive, with batteries of brass and percussion employed to inflate rather commonplace music. He had not yet learned Berlioz's lesson that the effectiveness of large forces depends on their sparing use. Gounod's influence went deeper and proved harder to shake off; Bizet was equally susceptible to the lyrical and the pretentious accents of his master's voice. His music for the nuns and the wedding, with its square rhythms, sugary harmony, and absence of counterpoint, is typical of a great deal of quasi-religious music written for church, stage, and concert hall in the middle years of the century, and not only in France. Although it owed a good deal to the homelier aspects of Schumann and Mendelssohn, its major prophet, from whom Bizet certainly imbibed it, was Gounod. A more beneficial influence was Verdi, whose vulgarity—when he was vulgar, which was far less frequently than his contemporary detractors supposed—sprang from animal energy and not from a complacent sense of moral mission. But if *Ivan IV* is a palpably immature opera, there is enough authentic Bizet to justify its exhumation, especially for those interested in the painful and laborious process by which genius shakes itself free from the conventions and commonplaces of its period.

At this point the enquirer finds his way blocked by a matter of editorial ethics. When posterity disinters an immature work of art which for one reason or another has been suppressed during the author's life, to what extent is it entitled to trim and alter its discovery to render it more palatable to later taste? In Bizet's autograph of *Ivan* the scoring is complete only as far as Temrouk's 'Pourquoi ces cris?' near the beginning of Act V (p. 303 of vocal score). Clearly it was necessary to fill this lacuna, and to make a choice from the three versions of the Cossack Song in Act II. Changeur says that Schott wished to confine revision to these points, but that Choudens and his advisers insisted on considerable cuts and other changes in order to exclude inferior matter and speed up the action; it was thought unsafe to leave this to individual opera houses. Changeur justifies this procedure on the disingenuous ground that Bizet would undoubtedly have made changes during rehearsal, and reaches the remarkable conclusion: ' "Reviser" le manuscrit, c'était simplement remplacer Bizet.' Busser was thus given a free hand. What this was likely to mean may be guessed from Malherbe's statement that among his tasks was to 'modify certain passages that are too dated'—as if the whole opera would not date by 1951.

It is true that no opera house today would want to produce this very long and uneven opera as it stands in the autograph. It is also true that anyone dissatisfied with the published score can go to the Bibliothèque Nationale and put himself to considerable expense of time and money on collation and copying. But there is a vital distinction between performing a modified text in the theatre and publishing a doctored score without acknowledging that extensive facial surgery has been practised. A published score assumes, if not a definitive, at least a dominant status;

and historians, not to mention laymen, will not have time to check every printed score by the original, so that in course of time the composer will be known and judged by a corrupt text. Every musical scholar could quote examples of this, even from the greatest classics; and Bizet himself furnishes several of a portentous nature. All the vocal scores of his operas issued by Choudens since his death, with the exception of *Djamileh* and the 1975 edition of *Les Pêcheurs de perles,* not only mutilate or suppress some of his music but contain music which he did not write.[19] Nor is there anything in the scores to indicate this.

Busser's score of *Ivan IV* reproduces this situation with ominous fidelity. His short introductory *Notice* mentions as his own work only the completion of the scoring, and it contains several inaccuracies. It is not true that the opera was put into rehearsal at the Lyrique in 1866 (when Bizet had already withdrawn it), and virtually certain that it was never rehearsed at all. Still less was there any question of a performance in 1867: Bizet's contract for *La Jolie Fille de Perth* was signed in July 1866, and he worked on that opera, using material from *Ivan,* for the rest of the year. Therefore the visit of the Tsar Alexander II to Paris in April 1867 can have had nothing to do with the withdrawal of *Ivan*. Pigot never said that Bizet destroyed his vocal score; as Busser correctly states, he wrote his operas in full orchestral score, using only rough preliminary sketches.

Busser's revisions, apart from the completion of the scoring, fall under the following heads:

1. *Cuts.* These are very extensive and include two big pieces in Act I, an air for Marie with female chorus ('Quand il fait jour sur le Caucase')[20] and an air for Temrouk with male chorus ('Sort fatal!'). The former, a languid Mendelssohnian affair in F minor, 9/8 time, is certainly superfluous, but it contains a theme in A flat major that recurs in the duet for Marie and Igor in the final scene, and its excision to some extent distorts the design. Temrouk's air, C sharp minor, 12/8 time, is a lament for the abduction of his daughter; Bizet re-used some of it in the first finale of *Don Rodrigue*. Act II[21] suffered seven smaller cuts, the most important of which removed the first appearance of Yorloff's motif (Ex. 8). The duet for Igor and Temrouk in Act III has lost a 6/8 Andante, 'Ah! de nos hirondelles', very much in Gounod's manner, which occurs twice, and 44 bars have gone from the following men's trio. In Act IV Marie's big air has been shortened and deprived of its more extravagant vocal cadenzas; Igor's cavatina and his duet with Marie are likewise considerably abridged, especially the latter, and there are several cuts in the finale. In Act V the principal cut occurs in the duet for Ivan and Temrouk in the first scene.

[19] A comparison of the scores published in Bizet's lifetime with later editions of the same works is instructive in this connection. Guiraud (and perhaps others) tinkered with *La Jolie Fille de Perth* and *Carmen*, Godard with *Les Pêcheurs de perles;* the trio at the end of the latter opera in most scores, including the only full score, was added in the eighties. *Don Procopio* has been shockingly rehashed; since there was no publication during Bizet's life it must be compared with the autograph. For the fate of *Carmen,* see following essay.

[20] It is possible that Bizet intended to suppress this in favour of the duet for Marie and the Young Bulgarian, which is not included in the original pagination.

[21] Busser's Act I, Scene 2.

It is only fair to say that there is both musical and dramatic justification for many of Busser's cuts.

2. *Additions*. These are another matter. There are five in all, differing widely in nature, scale, and purpose. Having decided to run Bizet's first two acts into one, Busser composed as interval music a so-called *Prélude Dramatique*, printed as an appendix to the score. This piece, though said to be based on unpublished themes by Bizet, bears no approximation to his style, but suggests rather a Franck pupil of the 1880s. The themes, if they are Bizet's, are quite uncharacteristic. Secondly, a 17-bar interlude is added between the two scenes of Act V (p. 320). Something was doubtless needed here; Bizet had ruled twenty-eight bars but written no music. Changeur pokes fun at Schott's German arranger for proposing an interlude precisely twenty-eight bars long. This seems ungracious; better German pedantry than slovenly scholarship. The other three additions were inspired by a desire to improve the plot. In Act IV, on the ground that the opera lacked love interest, Busser inserted a duet for Marie and Ivan (pp. 224–8), thirty-nine bars long, based on the theme of Bizet's song 'Rêve de la bien-aimée'[22] but differently treated. Another reference to this theme occurs in an addendum to the last scene, the six bars from the signature of five sharps on p. 333. Changeur claims that the addition of a tender elegiac side to Ivan's complex character makes him more sympathetic and endows him with greater psychological profundity. It might be objected that when so much genuine Bizet is suppressed there seems little reason to add pseudo-Bizet, even if it were a dramatic improvement, which is questionable. Finally Busser supplied a new character in Yorloff's daughter Sophia (originally nameless and mute). Since she has only a few phrases of recitative and a part in the concerted finale of Act II, she does little violence to Bizet's music.

3. *Other Changes*. Under this head come the octave transposition of the Young Bulgarian from soprano to tenor, the addition of the orchestra to the vocal sections of the Act IV barcarolle, the altered end of the Act IV finale, and many verbal changes to the libretto. Some of these were evidently designed to modify the stiffness of its phraseology and improve the prosody. Others alter the sense and even the plot. After Ivan's collapse in the Act IV finale it is Yorloff (not Marie) who sycophantically bids the people pray for him. At several points in the first scene of Act V the original words are both clearer and stronger.

Finally Busser had to decide between the three versions of the Cossack Song (p. 80). The first of these is in E flat major, the second and third in C minor. He chose the first, a generalized summons to pillage set strophically with choral refrain, which seems the weakest. The second (Allegro feroce) describes the effect of a Cossack charge much as Escamillo describes a bullfight, and is musically the most fully developed. Schott wished to print the third, which—apart from being presumably Bizet's latest thought—treats the text of the second more succinctly and is the most characteristic. It begins as shown in Ex. 13.

---

[22] The same song had already been used, with equal lack of authority, to 'improve' *La Jolie Fille de Perth:* see the current vocal score, p. 253.

Ex.13

Allegro deciso

Hur-rah! Hur-rah! Vi-ve la guer - re! Co-

- sak, en - tends –tu le sig - nal? Vi - ve la guer - re!

Finally we come to a chronological puzzle of considerable importance for plotting the course of Bizet's development. When was *Ivan* composed? The surviving autograph raises two questions which have never been answered and were apparently not asked by those who promoted the revival. In the first place, why is the last act incomplete? It will be remembered that the voice parts are perfect to the end of the opera (it was always Bizet's practice to write them out first)[23] but the orchestration stops abruptly in the penultimate scene. This is not a mutilated full score, like the later and finer *La Coupe du roi de Thulé*, but a score that Bizet never finished writing out. Yet there must once have been a complete autograph and a complete copy as well. 'Iwan is at the copyist's', he told Galabert in the autumn of 1865; and later that year he submitted the score to two opera houses. The surviving autograph would be useless either to a copyist or a director. What is the explanation? No sane composer goes through the appalling labour of writing out an operatic full score a second time—least of all a work like *Ivan*, which is not only immensely long but scored with an elaboration beyond anything else ever attempted by Bizet—unless he cannot help it; in other words, unless he has meanwhile rewritten the music. The inference is that the surviving score is not the *Ivan* that Bizet sent to Carvalho and Perrin in 1865,[24] but an earlier abandoned version. At once we remember Pigot's positive statement—and Pigot, though he made

[23] The autograph of *Don Rodrigue* has the voice parts complete—688 pages of them—with only a few pencilled indications of the scoring, except in one number: that, ironically, is the wedding march from *Ivan IV*, saxhorns and all.

[24] We know that he actually sent it, for his letter to Perrin refers to 'mon gros rouleau.'

mistakes, had many good sources of information denied to his successors [25]—that Bizet burned the score of *Ivan*. It seems quite possible that he did—and overlooked his first draft.

This brings us to the second question. Bizet, as is well known, habitually re-used music written for earlier works which he had abandoned. There are numerous and sometimes very surprising examples in all his operas,[26] and not a few (as already noted) in *Ivan* itself. Other composers have followed the same procedure, which for obvious reasons has one almost invariable feature: since the sources are unpublished the borrowing cannot be detected by contemporaries. Is it conceivable that Bizet would have composed and submitted to two opera houses a score making use, not once but in four places, of material from his latest, biggest, and only publicly familiar work, which had been performed eighteen times and published less than two years earlier? For that is the relationship between *Ivan* and *Les Pêcheurs de perles* on the usual supposition that *Ivan* was composed in 1864–5; and there is no other instance of Bizet using published material a second time.

Here we meet one of the unhappy results of defective publication; for two of the four parallel passages are omitted by Busser and a third was removed from all scores of *Les Pêcheurs de perles* before 1975. As for the remaining parallel, should the reader observe that on pp. 22–3 of *Ivan* Bizet has used the striking ostinato figure of the Prelude to *Les Pêcheurs de perles*, which reappears later as Leila's entrance music, he might well put it down to chance—especially as a variant of this figure recurs in *Djamileh*. Even so it is surprising to find Ivan, soon after his first entrance, supported by the same key (A major) at the same pace (Andante) and for almost the same number of bars (21 against 19) as Leila at *her* first entrance, even though the melody above is different. That is not all. The suppressed portion of the duet for Marie and Igor in Act IV contains a section beginning 'Ah! si ma voix encore', of which the vocal line of bars 5–8 reappears in Act I of *Les Pêcheurs de perles* (p. 45 of 1885 and 1975 vocal scores) at Zurga's 'Et nul ne doit la voir, nul ne doit l'approcher'— words on which the entire plot depends. Finally, two passages in *Ivan,* the short duet for Marie and Igor in Act V (p. 328) and part of Marie's air in Act I which it dramatically recalls, use the theme of the duet 'O lumière sainte' at the very end of *Les Pêcheurs de perles:*[27]

Ex.14

Ivan IV

Pêcheurs de perles

[25] When his book was published Bizet's widow, all his closest friends, and even his father were still living.

[26] It is more than a little startling, for instance, to find among the sketches for *Grisélidis* (1870–71) not only the famous saxophone theme of the *Arlésienne* Prelude, virtually unchanged, but the greater part of José's Flower Song, sung by a baritone in C major.

[27] This was later suppressed and turned into a *Regina Coeli:* Bizet had nothing to do with either event.

Furthermore, the dramatic situation in both operas is identical: soprano and tenor, condemned to death, sing a valedictory duet just before being rescued by the baritone on the final curtain. It is impossible to believe that Bizet would have used the same theme, with only a slight rhythmic variant, at the same point in two consecutive operas, unless the earlier of the two had been withdrawn—in other words, unless the score of *Ivan* as we have it was written before, not after, *Les Pêcheurs de perles*.

This fresh chronology would, if accepted, clear up a number of minor mysteries in the score of *Ivan* and in Bizet's life. In August 1862 he attended the music festival at Baden together with Berlioz, Gounod, and Reyer, each of whom had an opera produced there.[28] It is clear from an unpublished letter from Reyer to Bizet (10 July 1863) that Bénazet, the Baden impresario, had agreed to put on a Bizet opera at the 1863 festival, and Reyer implies that Bizet had one ready. We also know that earlier the same year Marmontel, Bizet's old piano teacher, submitted the score of an unperformed opera supposedly by Bizet to Berlioz, who was still music critic of the *Journal des Débats;* Berlioz's reply, dated 28 March 1863, is quoted by Maurice Emmanuel in the November 1938 issue of the *Revue de musicologie*. It has been assumed hitherto that this opera was *Les Pêcheurs de perles,* as stated by Emmanuel,[29] but closer examination of the evidence proves this to be impossible. In a letter precisely dated Tuesday 7 April 1863,[30] 8 p.m., Gounod congratulates Bizet on 'ta commande en trois actes pur le Théâtre-Lyrique' and offers him advice on the frame of mind in which to approach a task for which he has very little time ('l'époque très rapprochée que tu m'indiques comme assignée à la représentation de ton oeuvre....'). This must mean that Bizet had only just received the contract for *Les Pêcheurs de perles,* and since the first night was fixed for 14 September the same year (it was postponed till the 30th on account of the illness of the soprano) he certainly had to hurry, and may well have found it necessary to make use of music already composed. (He told Gounod that the subject was Mexican: were the 'Indians' of Ceylon originally redskins?)

What, then, was the score submitted to Berlioz and perhaps written for Baden? We know nothing of any opera composed between Bizet's return from Rome in 1860 and *Les Pêcheurs de perles* except the last *envoi* of his Rome pension, the one-act *La Guzla de l'Émir,*[31] and no work of any kind can be certainly assigned to 1862. Two considerations might be urged against the supposition that it was *Ivan*. (1) Berlioz referred to the manuscript as 'ces trois actes'. But it is clear that he had not yet looked at it; and *La France musicale* of 2 July 1865 also refers to *Ivan* as in three acts, which, except at the Opéra, was a commoner number than five. (2) Gounod

---

[28] *Béatrice et Bénédict* and *Érostrate* (Reyer) in that year; *La Colombe* (Gounod) in 1860. Bizet at different times assisted all three composers with rehearsals of their works.

[29] Despite Emmanuel's positive statement there remains some doubt whether the opera in question was by Bizet. Berlioz's letter mentions only 'un jeune artiste cher à votre brave cœur'.

[30] There can be no mistake about the date: 7 Apr. 1863 was indeed a Tuesday.

[31] This has disappeared. The music may well have gone into *Les Pêcheurs de perles*. Its exact date of composition is not known, but it must have been some time before 1862, the date of the report by the Académie des Beaux-Arts (Mina Curtiss, *Bizet and his World* (New York, 1958), 123, 446).

did not renounce his rights in the libretto till June 1863. He might, however, have handed on a libretto he had long abandoned to a much-loved disciple some time earlier and omitted to formalize the position. The most probable date for such an event would be August 1862, when Bizet and Gounod were both in Baden and Bénazet suggested a Bizet opera for the following year.[32] From the absence of references in Gounod's letters of January-June 1862 it is fairly clear the Bizet was not then working on *Ivan*—and also that Pigot's statement that *La Guzla de l'Émir* was rehearsed at that time is probably wrong. These rehearsals, abandoned when Carvalho offered Bizet the libretto of *Les Pêcheurs de perles,* should be put forward to early 1863.

If Bizet wrote *Ivan* in the first place for Baden, it explains the incongruity, on the accepted chronology, of his apparently setting for the Lyrique a libretto written for the Opéra and emphasizing rather than toning down the elements that must have made it a formidable and expensive proposition for the poorer theatre. He may have had his eye on the Opéra at the same time (there is an obvious context for a ballet at the beginning of Act III); he told Lacombe in June 1872, in reference to *Don Rodrigue,* that it had taken him ten years to break open the doors of the Opéra, which he is not otherwise known to have assaulted before December 1865. It is risky to make deductions from stylistic evidence, especially with a composer like Bizet, but *Ivan* seems in many ways less assured than *Les Pêcheurs de perles*. Its weak passages are more frequent and more conspicuous, and it has nothing so memorable as the opening choruses of the first two acts, or so firm in sustained dramatic tension as the second finale, of that similarly unequal opera.

Until further evidence comes to light the matter must be regarded as unproven. But it does seem possible that the *Ivan* of the surviving autograph reached its present form early in 1863, when Bizet dropped it for *Les Pêcheurs de perles,* leaving the last act incomplete.[33] Here we may note the announcement in *Le Figaro* of 10 March 1864, that *Ivan* would follow *Mireille* (first performed on the 19th of the same month) at the Théâtre-Lyrique, and Bizet's statement that Carvalho commissioned it immediately after *Les Pêcheurs de perles*. In this year or the next, if the conjecture stands, he rewrote the opera, presumably removing the passages used in *Les Pêcheurs de perles* and perhaps adapting it to the more limited resources of the Lyrique, submitted this new version to Carvalho and Perrin, and eventually destroyed it, leaving the forgotten earlier score to turn up sixty years after and puzzle posterity. It is even possible that Verdi left a heavier imprint on the later score, as Pigot said; but that we shall never know.

[32] A paragraph in *Le Ménestrel* of 8 Mar. 1863 quotes the German press to the effect that 'Gounod is at present working on a new opera whose libretto has for hero and title *Ivan le Terrible*. The German papers . . . do not tell us for what theatre this work is intended.' It is most unlikely that Gounod was working on his *Ivan* as late as this. Could the Germans have caught a rumour of his passing the libretto to the then unknown Bizet and misinterpreted it? Octave Séré's statement in *Musiciens français d'aujourd'hui* that Bizet had an opera produced at Baden in 1854 is perhaps a confused echo of the same episode.

[33] Would he have let Berlioz see it in this condition? It is not impossible, especially if he wanted Berlioz's advice on what was suitable for Baden. The two were on friendly though never intimate terms. Berlioz, alone of the critics, wrote a conspicuously fair notice of *Les Pêcheurs de perles,* and a few months later asked Bizet to play for rehearsals of *L'Enfance du Christ* at the Conservatoire.

28
The True *Carmen?*

========

French musicologists have shown so little interest in Bizet, and his operas have been so regularly and progressively corrupted in Paris, whether in print or performance, that the prospect of the *grande machine* of German scholarship getting to work on his masterpiece is bound to whet the appetite. Hitherto there have been two full scores of *Carmen,* one French, published by Choudens, and one German, edited by Kurt Soldan and published by Peters (re-issued later by Kalmus and International). Both contain Guiraud's recitatives in place of the original spoken dialogue, but both are based principally on the autograph (as it exists today, not as Bizet left it) and there are few material differences between them. Soldan replaces Bizet's cornets with trumpets, a solecism repeated in Fritz Oeser's new edition.[1] It is surprising too to find a 'kritische Neuausgabe' giving Bizet's French tempo indications only in Italian and German.

The aims and the execution of this edition raise so many points of cardinal importance for the whole realm of musical scholarship that it demands examination in detail. Oeser lists seven major sources: Bizet's autograph score (*A*); the manuscript conducting copy used in 1875 (and later) (*B*); incomplete manuscript orchestral parts, also used in 1875 and later (*C*); the manuscript copy prepared in the summer of 1875 for the first Vienna performances in October (*D*); the first edition of the Choudens vocal score (*E*); the first edition of the printed libretto (*F*); and the manuscript rehearsal schedule of the Opéra-Comique during the winter of 1874–5 (*G*).

Of these sources, *B*, *C*, and *D* are drawn on for the first time. *D* is not of primary importance since it was prepared after Bizet's death; but it yields one curiosity in a new end to the opera, supplied by some Viennese conductor, in which the melody of Escamillo's *couplets* rises to a final apotheosis after the manner of a Palm Court or military band selection. *B* and *C* are of great interest for the early history of the opera's composition. In several important movements Oeser has been able to reconstruct the various stages of the text in fuller detail than the present condition of the autograph allows. By the same token he has established the approximate date of certain cuts, insertions, or alterations according to whether they appear in the conducting copy or the parts. Pigot's statement that the entr'acte before Act III was composed for *L'Arlésienne* receives some support from the fact that it antedates the

---

[1] *Carmen. Kritische Neuausgabe nach den Quellen von Fritz Oeser* (Alkor-Edition/Bärenreiter), 2 vols, score and critical report; also vocal score.

other entr'actes, which were not ready in time to be copied with the main body of the score. Oeser prints (not quite accurately) the *Grisélidis* sketch for baritone in C major that later became José's Flower Song; but the even more interesting origin of 'Dût-il m'en coûter la vie' (Act III finale) in *La Coupe du roi de Thulé* receives only a casual mention in the chapter on Felsenstein's German translation.

The steps by which a work of genius came into existence have a perennial fascination, particularly when we can watch a great dramatic composer reconciling the demands of words, music, and action. In *Carmen* this process can be observed in all its stages from the first writing down of the full score (Bizet habitually made few preliminary sketches). Oeser's examination of *B* and *C* brings out two points of outstanding interest; both have been noted before, but the new evidence clarifies the picture. One is the great care Bizet expended on the finales, all four of which were repeatedly revised, the first, third, and fourth as many as four times. The other is the much more lavish use of *mélodrame* in the original score. Bizet was clearly following up his very successful harnessing of this device in *Djamileh* and *L'Arlésienne*.

We already knew that the scene of the changing of the guard in Act I, instead of being broken in two by dialogue (or recitative in the Guiraud version), originally comprised a single long movement with an orchestral middle section based on a canonic treatment of the street urchins' melody, against which Moralès informed José of Micaëla's arrival.[2] It was also known that the *mélodrame* in which Carmen makes insolent fun of Zuniga later in the act had been much longer. Oeser has discovered two further instances of this treatment. The arrival of Escamillo's torchlight procession in Act II consisted of three sections, an unaccompanied offstage chorus, an orchestral march (much expanded from its earliest version) with dialogue against it, and a short final chorus; of these only the third section and a fragment of the first were hitherto available.

Similarly José's offstage 'Dragon d'Alcala' song in Act II, two unaccompanied stanzas separated by dialogue, was originally set to a different melody with light orchestral accompaniment and linked by a *mélodrame* quoting Carmen's motif. This version survives incomplete in the parts. Oeser makes the valid point that the diminuendo instrumental codas to several movements (some of them a good deal longer as first written) were intended to ease the transition from full musical treatment to spoken dialogue. Bizet was here following the example of Méhul's serious *opéras comiques* composed before the end of the eighteenth century, notably *Mélidore et Phrosine*,[3] of which he possessed a full score.

Another discovery is the refrain of the original 6/8 habanera, rejected early in the rehearsals in favour of the modified Yradier melody. No trace of it remains in the autograph, but it survives pasted down in the conducting copy at the point where the female chorus repeat it after Carmen has thrown the flower. It is an undistinguished and jaunty little tune; if it is true that Galli-Marié asked Bizet for something better, she deserves our gratitude (Ex. 1). Oeser reconstructs with some plausibility the melody of the verse sections by piecing together incomplete orchestral parts in

---

[2] First quoted, from the autograph, in my *Bizet* (London, 1948).   [3] See pp. 120–1.

Ex.1

the cancelled finale of the act; for, as with the Yradier habanera later, Bizet brought it back just before Carmen trips José. This too is poor stuff.

The passages cut by Bizet at the earliest stage, before the score and parts were copied, include the ineffective return of Escamillo's refrain accompanied by a single cello towards the end of Act III and Carmen's two references to the card scene in the third and fourth finales, which struck such a false note in the Sadler's Wells revival of 1961.[4] Oeser is right to condemn Bizet's first idea here as unworthy of the heroine and the opera. His detective work on the early changes further establishes that the air with pantomime for Moralès and chorus near the beginning of the opera (previously printed only in the 1875 vocal score), of which Bizet wrote three versions, was composed during rehearsals late in 1874. This happened when the baritone Duvernoy was cast as Moralès; and at the same time the small part of an anonymous tenor officer (Andrès in the first draft of the libretto) in Acts II and IV was transposed for him.

Thus far all is well. Oeser's new material, mostly derived from cancelled passages in the conducting score, is clearly of the highest interest. Before examining it we should remind ourselves of the textual history of *Carmen* as given in most opera houses since 1875 and reflected in pre-Oeser scores. The first performance took place at the Opéra-Comique on 3 March 1875; the first edition of the vocal score appeared a week or so later; Bizet died on 3 June in the same year; Choudens published the full score about 1877 and numerous further editions of the vocal score from that year on. It is widely known that every pre-Oeser score except that of March 1875 contains recitatives composed by Ernest Guiraud after Bizet's death. They were written to replace the original spoken dialogue at the Vienna production in October 1875, a task Bizet himself had undertaken to perform, though no doubt he would have carried it out differently. Guiraud's recitatives, which until recent years were used in nearly all performances outside France,[5] apart from transforming

---

[4] This version, based on suppressed passages and what could be deduced from fragmentary incipits and endings in the autograph, was the work of Maurits Sillem and Arthur Hammond, who had no access to Oeser's *B* and *C*.

[5] Even at the Opéra-Comique, which otherwise retains the dialogue, one of Guiraud's recitatives (before Micaëla's Act III air) is—or was—regularly performed, and at least one French writer damned Bizet for it.

Carmen from an *opéra comique* into a grand opera, inevitably destroyed one of the subtlest features of Bizet's score, his use of *mélodrame*.

It is also known, but sometimes forgotten, that the 1875 vocal score contains three passages, two long and one short, omitted from all other pre-Oeser scores. The short passage, fourteen additional bars of coda to the opening chorus of Act IV, was cut by Guiraud when, also for Vienna, he inserted a ballet on music from *La Jolie Fille de Perth* and *L'Arlésienne* and altered the words of the chorus. The other two, the pantomime for Moralès and chorus early in Act I and the much longer duel between Escamillo and José in Act III, also disappeared in 1875. They were almost certainly removed during the original run,[6] when the opera, very long by Opéra-Comique standards, was playing to poor houses. This must have been done with Bizet's knowledge, perhaps at his instigation: the pantomime, though a lively and characteristic piece of music, holds up the action when it has barely started, and the longer duel is musically undistinguished. Guiraud probably supplied the upper (soprano) alternative notes in Carmen's part, which are not by Bizet, and introduced a few slight modifications, mostly in tempo and metronome marks and dynamics, in the full score.[7]

How should an editor approach the mass of cancelled material recovered from the conducting score and parts? Now that *Carmen* is a classic he must surely print or describe it all; but he needs to bear in mind at least five considerations. (1) He should take pains to find out everything that is known about the composer's background and that of the work he is editing. (2) His text should clearly distinguish what was performed while the composer was alive to oversee it from what was not. (3) He should endeavour as far as possible, with the aid of all available evidence, to determine the composer's wishes and intentions on every debatable point. (4) He should separate fact from conjecture and avoid a priori assumptions about the motives of everyone concerned in the production of the opera. (5) Having adopted a policy on what to include in the main text, the appendices, and the notes respectively, he should stick to it.

On all five points this edition goes disastrously off the rails. The differences between its main text and that of the traditional score can be roughly summarized under three heads: (1) the restitution of a large number of cuts, some of considerable length, made before performance; (2) the restoration to their original or an earlier form of passages subsequently altered (Oeser describes this as the removal of 'retouches', which for the most part appear in the autograph but which he attributes to various alien hands); (3) the insertion of extraneous or composite material,

---

[6] Both are missing from the score prepared for Vienna, from a piano arrangement by Antony Choudens, of which the copy in the Biblothèque Nationale is back-stamped 1875, and from vocal scores dated 1877 and 1879 as well as the full score. *Carmen* was not performed in Paris between 1875–6 and 1883. An unreported second impression of the 1875 vocal score, discovered by Lesley Wright in Harvard University Library, has a footnote to the pantomime, 'Au théâtre on passe ce numéro', engraved on the original plate.

[7] According to Minnie Hauk, who sang Carmen's part frequently from early in 1878, the tempos indicated in the full score for the ensembles in the second and third acts, and especially for the quintet, are too fast.

affecting both the libretto and the music, where Oeser, as a result of preconceptions about the nature of the opera, scraps or confuses Bizet's and the librettists' readings and supplies new ones of his own. All three groups involve numerous changes from the very great to the very small.

A little study of published work on the composer could have saved Oeser from some of his more egregious errors; it is symptomatic that he regularly misspells the names of Pigot and Mina Curtiss and cites the latter's book only in its mutilated French translation. It is most unlikely that Bizet had the scenario of *Carmen* as early as June 1872, and inconceivable that Offenbach's soubrette Zulma Bouffar was his first choice for the heroine. Possibly, as Mina Curtiss suggested, the conception of Carmen owed something to Céleste Mogador, but to trace the habanera directly to her because she was singing another song by Yradier in 1865 is far-fetched in the extreme (Bizet had several of Yradier's songs in his library); and the picture of Bizet at that date as a paragon of morality tied to the apron-strings of his mother (who had been dead for four years), and to whom Céleste would appear a being from an alien world, is ludicrous to anyone acquainted with his personal life.

But his character as an artist matters more. Oeser's attitude to this emerges from his conclusion that the quotation of the card scene at Carmen's death must have vanished before Galli-Marié caught a glimpse of the score, since she would never have allowed Bizet to cut it. This patronising view of a most fiery and self-willed composer as a weakling unable or unwilling to stand up for his rights or take decisions on his own account underlies Oeser's whole approach. He has assumed that all the rehearsal cuts (which number more than thirty), and hundreds of other changes to be mentioned later, were made against Bizet's wish or better judgment. He claims to be able to distinguish firmly between changes made by Bizet for artistic reasons and those to which he assented grudgingly if at all, and he places an overwhelming preponderance in the latter category. He says that Bizet made a distinction between important and permanent corrections to the autograph, which he entered in ink, and changes to serve temporary needs, which he wrote in pencil. There is no evidence for this supposition, which is more than once controverted by Oeser's own notes.

In seeking a definition of his editorial principles, we are confronted by the remarkable statement with which he begins his general introduction (*Allgemeines zur Neuausgabe*): that a critical edition of *Carmen* 'must restore all those alterations that owe their origin to the dissensions of the first stage rehearsal, and present the authentic form of the work by opening the cuts'. This is to beg every question. In the first place, though there may have been such dissensions at the first stage rehearsal (there frequently are with new operas—and old ones, for that matter), we know nothing about them, and no changes can be positively attributed to them. Secondly, Oeser does not draw the important distinction between the cuts and other alterations. Thirdly, he implies that the score before the first stage rehearsal was 'the authentic form of the work'. He is so wedded to his preconceived theory, that virtually all suppressed and subsequently altered passages are essential to the integrity of the opera, that he waves aside every explanation except the stupidity

of the producer, the inexperience of the chorus, the inadequacies of the Opéra-
Comique stage, the hostility of du Locle (the director), and the general bafflement
caused by an unfamiliar and shocking subject.

Now it is quite possible, but not susceptible of proof, that these considerations,
or some of them, did play a part. They *could* account for some of the cuts and
changes, though certainly not for all. Again we lack specific evidence. What we do
know is that Bizet ferociously resisted every change. He may not always have been
successful; but Oeser's assumptions not only contradict all we know of his personality and temperament but—though Oeser does not appear to notice this—reflect
on his integrity as an artist. Oeser's whole method of argument is perilous and
unscholarly. Having assumed his premisses, he constantly asserts as facts, qualified
now and then by words like 'sicherlich' or 'zweifellos', what are no more than
guesses, some of them possible or even probable, but a great many unlikely or quite
impossible. And, as we shall see with the retouches, he repeatedly denounces as sins
against Bizet's style and dramatic vision changes that can be conclusively proved to
originate with the composer himself. Indeed it is very lucky this is so; otherwise the
score of *Carmen* might be permanently corrupted.

This elasticity of principle extends to every feature of the score. One whole
character (Andrès), whom Bizet removed before the end of 1874, is put back
throughout the opera. The choral repeat of Escamillo's refrain at his exit in Act II
is included, though it was cut before the beginning of orchestral rehearsals; but the
pantomime for Moralès and chorus, sung and printed in 1875, is banished to an
appendix. We are given the rejected first form of Carmen's humming *mélodrame* in
Act I, and Guiraud's rehash with recitatives, but not the version performed in 1875,
which on any reckoning deserves priority. There are many changes to the words,
early discarded versions being preferred to Bizet's improvements (for example in
the seguidilla), and even more to the stage directions, some of which have no
authority whatever. Oeser makes a great fuss about the shortening of instrumental
codas, which he attributes to the first producer's *horror vacui* and other nameless sins,
yet he marks as an optional cut one such passage (at the exit of the smugglers in
Act III) that Bizet never shortened.

A high proportion of the commentary is devoted to special pleading that can
only be called tendentious, a frame of mind that predisposes an editor to mistakes
both of omission and commission. The text of the Alkor score teems with both.
This might be less damaging if the sources were clearly distinguished. But they are
not. It would take many hours—perhaps days—even with the aid of the commentary (which sometimes omits the most important evidence), to discover from this
edition what was performed in 1875 and what readings have Bizet's final authority.
A busy conductor would never have time for this. Yet if he performed the score
as printed, he would in hundreds of places be resurrecting what Bizet, often for the
clearest artistic reasons, specifically rejected.

CUTS

The many cuts in the autograph, conducting score, and parts are of several kinds, and were made at different periods. Some passages, such as the later references to the card scene in the third and fourth finales, were removed before the autograph was copied. Oeser generally and rightly relegates these to an appendix, though he is none too scrupulous about reinstating certain details in the text when he approves of them. It has been known for some time that extensive cuts were introduced during the prolonged rehearsals, which began in October 1874. The most notable of these are the string *mélodrame* during the changing of the guard, substantial extra sections in the cigarette girls' chorus and the quarrel ensemble—in which Carmen entered not at the end but in the middle against a combination of two motifs in the orchestra—a much longer *mélodrame* when Carmen hums insolently to Zuniga, sixteen bars of bustle linkng the seguidilla to the first finale, a very extended approach, including *mélodrame*, for Escamillo's torchlight procession, additional sections in the Act II duet for Carmen and José and the finale that follows, and several shorter passages in Act IV.

Why were these removed? There are several likelier reasons than the crude explanations postulated by Oeser. He admits that the longer introduction to the cigarette girls' chorus is difficult to bring off in the theatre, but does not consider the possibility that Bizet may have cut it for that reason. It is likely that the *mélodrame* during the changing of the guard, with its canon for solo violin and cello, was suppressed because the superimposed speech, shouted orders, and noisy stage business rendered it inaudible in a large theatre (this is a point where a gramophone or radio performance gains). The Act IV cuts, to which I shall return, so far from weakening the drama, make it immeasurably stronger. Bizet was a great dramatic composer, and an immensely practical one, as his letters reveal. The implication that he never willingly modified a bar as a result of stage rehearsals is absurd. He is not likely to have shared Oeser's compulsive attachment to *Bogen* form, or bothered about the 'formally indispensible' elaboration of codas, if there was any question of interference with the dramatic action. Indeed he removed the 'Dragon d'Alcala' *Bogen* before rehearsals began. If, as is possible, the size of the Opéra-Comique stage or the difficulty of timing choral entrances and exits led to cuts, they are just as likely to have brought musical improvements in their train, as in some instances they palpably did. One of the most striking features of Bizet's style is the care for dramatic concentration emphasized by his frequent revisions, especially in finales. The tendency is always towards brevity, economy, and sharp contrast. Oeser rightly points to the first finale as an example of the superiority of such reworkings, yet elsewhere (as we shall see) he misses few opportunities to reverse the trend.

The obvious explanation of the major cuts, especially in Act I, where most of them occur, is the great length of the opera. On the first night, *as shortened, Carmen* played for 174 minutes excluding intervals. Act I alone, without the Prelude, took 58 minutes. Act IV did not begin till after midnight. The Sadler's Wells revival in 1961, which restored some but by no means all of the cuts and considerably abridged the dialogue, demonstrated that Bizet had good reasons for retrenchment. There is no need for Oeser's guess that the producer used what he calls the revolt of the chorus (who are known to have had difficulty with their parts) an an excuse for simplifying his own task. Oeser dismisses the idea that the object was to save time, on the ground that only seven minutes would be involved (which is more than doubtful, and in any case no answer since all depends on the context), and that this could have been made up by shortening the intervals—an argument that additionally ignores the habits and preferences of Paris audiences. He therefore prints the opera in three acts and opines that Bizet's conception can be understood only if it is played with a single interval after Act II. This is to put the composer in his place with a vengeance. His definitive version was in four acts, with three intervals; and it had reached this form before the last entr'acte was composed.

It is certainly arguable that some of the cuts, including most of those listed above, deprived us of good things, and there is everything to be said for having all the material in print, so that conductors and producers can test it in the theatre and make their choice of what to restore. Now that Bizet is at last recognized as a great master, the more of his music we have available the better. Had Oeser confined himself to printing the rehearsal cuts, and properly distinguishing them, he would deserve nothing but gratitude.

RETOUCHES

Oeser's second declared purpose, after restoring the cuts, is to seek out and expunge all textual alterations attributable to alien hands. It seems likely that his point of departure was the discovery that the autograph had been tampered with, by Guiraud and others, after Bizet's death. This is true, and most reprehensible; the manuscript has been defaced by the removal of most of the rehearsal cuts, together with the three passages printed only in the 1875 vocal score; and the insertion of Guiraud's recitatives has obliterated Bizet's *mélodrames*. The object seems to have been to prepare the manuscript as copy for the Choudens full score.

Guiraud's treatment of Bizet's posthumous works certainly leaves him with a good deal to answer for, and Oeser evidently found him a ready-made scapegoat. He proceeds to lay on Guiraud's shoulders a mass of misdemeanours of which he was quite innocent. Guiraud is accused of shortening the Act III duel for Vienna in 1875, though Oeser tells us twice elsewhere that this was not done till the 1883 revival. As we have seen, this is wrong on both counts. Guiraud and the 1883 producer are held responsible for beginning Act III with a tableau and a full stage, whereas Bizet, we are told, had the curtain raised before the end of the entr'acte on an empty stage, where the smugglers gradually assemble at the summons of one of their number sounding a horn. This was Bizet's first idea, but it was altered before performance, as the 1875 score proves. (This is one of the changes that could have been made for reasons of theatrical convenience, such as the difficulty of getting the chorus on stage in time; there is even a case for rejecting it in performance, since it leaves an inconsistency in the text.)

What Oeser failed to notice, though the proof lay under his nose, is that, especially where the retouches are concerned, Guiraud's hand in the autograph was endeavouring to carry out Bizet's wishes. Composers frequently modify or retouch their work during rehearsal—often witholding publication till after performance for that very reason—and this is particularly common in opera, where they have to accommodate themselves to dramatic as well as musical demands, sometimes of an unpredictable nature. We should expect Bizet to make changes at this stage, when the conducting score and parts were in use and the autograph in temporary retirement, especially in a bold opera like *Carmen,* which had an exceptionally long and arduous period of rehearsal. He would not need to insert them in the autograph once the score and parts had been copied; it would be the responsiblity of the conductor to see that these were correct. But he would be quite certain to incorporate all such improvements in a printed score. There could be no question here, as there might be in the matter of cuts, of pressure from the theatre authorities. Only the publisher stood between the composer and the public.

That is precisely what occurred. As we have seen, the vocal score (Oeser's Source *E*) was published early in March 1875, almost concurrently with the first performance; it was advertised ('vient de paraître') in the weekly paper *Le Ménestrel* of 14 March, and Choudens made the legal deposit at the Bibliothèque Nationale on the 18th. Bizet himself arranged the score, as the title page proclaims, and personally corrected the proofs, of which twenty pages (from his own library) survive. Oeser mentions them once, quite casually, and only to express a doubt whether the corrections are in Bizet's hand. They unquestionably are; but even if they were not, *E* is *ipso facto* an absolute guarantee of authenticity on all matters that can be expressed in a vocal score—that is to say, everything except details of orchestration and perhaps some dynamics. In a critical edition its reading should be cited at every point where the text is in question, and only rejected for the very weightiest reasons. If the autograph has two readings, X changed to Y, and the vocal score (*E*) has only Y, it is obvious that Y must be correct.

No retouch to the autograph, whether it is in the hand of Bizet, Guiraud, Antony Choudens, General de Gaulle, or the Archbishop of Canterbury, can by any human possibility have got into the 1875 vocal score after Bizet's death or (barring misprints) without his approval. All such modifications to the autograph must have been made in conformity with Bizet's wishes as expressed in the vocal score.

In fact Guiraud and others made too few rather than too many changes of this kind. Bizet added certain refinements to *E*, especially in matters of tempo, that (if Oeser is correct) do not appear even in the conducting score and parts; nevertheless they are not to be rejected. *E* also contains his metronome marks, some of them modified or inserted in his hand in the proofs—a point nowhere mentioned by Oeser, who prints them in editorial square brackets when he approves of them and silently omits them when he does not.

How does Oeser treat Source *E*? Although he admits having seen presentation copies signed by Bizet, he ignores it completely. Between writing out the autograph and arranging the vocal score Bizet made literally hundreds of changes, many of them of considerable importance, to notes, melodies, accompaniments, phrasing, accentuation, dynamics, words, stage directions, tempo and metronome marks. He did incorporate some of them in the autograph, but the majority appear there in other hands, including Guiraud's, as they do in the conducting score. That is what we should expect. Oeser, remarking that the conducting score makes it easier to recognize 'Kapellmeister retouches or interference by Guiraud', never quotes *E* on these points and constantly confuses it, under the term 'Erstdruck', with the full score published after Bizet's death, with which Guiraud *was* concerned. As the Court of Appeal has been known to remark when finding fault with a judge of first instance, he has so gravely misdirected himself on the relative value of the evidence that he has destroyed the foundations of his judgment.

His confusion on the whole matter of sources emerges from the statement in his preface that the French vocal scores of *Carmen* have never been altered since the first issue. That is not true; but he fails to recognize that the partial truth it contains (for many of the plates seem never to have been replaced) automatically gives them the highest claim to respect. When we recall Oeser's assumption that the authentic score must be that used at the *beginning* of the rehearsals, it is easy to see what has happened. He has summarily ejected, and either misattributed or silently suppressed, every one of the modifications and improvements introduced by Bizet as a result of hearing his music played and sung in the theatre. On page after page he ascribes them to Guiraud, the conductor, or some other anonymous bungler, even when he is forced to concede that they are in Bizet's hand in the autograph. The Alkor score flatly contradicts the composer and debases the text of the entire opera far more grossly than the old Choudens and Peters editions, which when they conflict with Oeser are nearly always correct. And it would be rash to assume that Guiraud's occasional retouches to the scoring lack Bizet's authority. Only a few examples of each type of corruption can be quoted.

While changes in orchestration can seldom be detected in a vocal score, there are passages where Bizet thinned out or silenced the orchestra in order to let the words come through. One of them occurs in the duet after the Flower Song, where he removed most of the accompaniment (a heavy crescendo) to Carmen's vital sentence 'Oui, tu m'emporterais si tu m'aimais'. Oeser restores it, though it is not even in the conducting score and parts, and was therefore cut by Bizet before rehearsals began (he also removes Bizet's direction *con islancio*). When a few bars later, as José's resolution weakens, Carmen resumes her hauting 'Là-bas, là-bas tu me suivras' at a slower tempo (*Un peu retenu,* emphasized by a changed metronome mark) Oeser rejects this as a posthumous insertion particularly damaging to the climax of the duet, thereby showing a total misunderstanding of the whole episode.

There are literally dozens of wrong tempo marks, many of them in important and familiar pieces. Oeser wags his finger at Guiraud for trying to speed up the Introduction to Act I by changing the original Allegretto moderato to Allegretto and establishing a false tradition of an excessively lively and marchlike pace; this change was made by Bizet. So was the 'falsification' of the tempo of the opening of the cigarette girls' chorus from Allegretto moderato to Allegro, and the division of the 6/8 bars in the chorus by means of dotted lines, with the direction 'Battez à 3/8'. At Carmen's first entry, where Bizet in close conformity with the drama has three changes of tempo in 22 bars (Allegretto molto, ♩ = 108—Allegro moderato,

♩. = 92, the moment of her appearance with her motif in the orchestra— ♩.= 100),
Oeser spoils this gradation by giving one tempo throughout (Allegro moderato,
♩ = 100), sweeping aside the changes as due to the conductor.

Poor Guiraud is again saddled with creating a false tradition by debasing the
tempo of the G major section of the José-Micaëla duet from Andantino moderato
to Allegro moderato, another of Bizet's changes. We are told that all tempo
modifications in the *Chanson bohème* apart from the Più animato for the refrain of
the second and third stanzas were supplied by Guiraud; Andantino quasi allegretto
at the beginning, which Oeser accepts, is Guiraud (Bizet's marking is Andantino),
the Presto in the coda, which he ignores, is Bizet.

The most disastrous corruption of tempo occurs in the finale of Act IV at the
first fortissimo entry of the Carmen-fate motif in C major (last bar of p. 359 of
current Choudens vocal score). This follows an A major chorus and fanfare offstage
(Allegro giocoso, ♩ = 116) saluting Escamillo's victory. At first Bizet continued
both chorus and fanfare against the fate motif on the pit orchestra and wrote 'Même
mouvement'. Later, in deepening the contrasts of the whole finale, he cut short the
chorus and fanfare and broadened the tempo to Moderato, confirming this with a
metronome mark (♩ = 84) and restoring an even faster tempo (Allegro, ♩ = 126)
at the renewed fanfare nineteen bars later. The improvement should be clear to the
most obtuse ears; yet Oeser—attributing it as usual to Guiraud and ignoring both
metronome marks—not only restores *Même mouvement* after the reason for it has
disappeared but argues that it is of particular importance for the architecture of the
finale. Does he seriously suppose that Allegro giocoso is a suitable tempo for this
shattering moment, and for the whole of the 3/4 section of the duet (based on the
same motif) that follows? Even if he does, Bizet did not.

All Bizet's improvements to Escamillo's *couplets* are expunged. According to *E*
the tempo should be Allegro moderato, but it is just possible that 'molto' was
omitted by accident. Oeser makes several changes to the music, both in the verse
and the refrain, altering note-lengths, removing fermatas, replacing the baritone
Moralès with the ghost tenor Andrès, making Escamillo waste his breath by joining
in the first four bars of the chorus, restoring a particularly inane two bars of
till-ready accompaniment between the stanzas, and ejecting the appoggiatura c in
Escamillo's final 'L'amour!' The latter, a clever touch of character, he damns as a
melodically unmotivated insertion by Guiraud without any authority from the
sources. In every case he is turning his back on Bizet—and he admits that one of
the changes was written by Bizet in the autograph.

This sort of thing happens in almost every number, sometimes without editorial
comment. For example we are not told the source of the ungainly accentuation of
Ex. 2 instead of Ex. 3 in the fourth bar of the duet for José and Escamillo. In fact

Ex.2

Es - ca - mil-lo!

Ex.3

Es - ca - mil-lo!

Bizet wrote Ex. 2 in the autograph but substituted Ex. 3 in the vocal score. The
opening phrase of the José–Micaëla duet has its rhythm adjusted to the weaker first
version, though Oeser once more allows that the change is in Bizet's hand. In the
card trio a manifest improvement to the string ritornello is thrown out, and Bizet's
expressive phrase to the words 'Je suis veuve et j'hérite' disappears, together with
his marking *retenez un peu*. The duet 'Si tu m'aimes' receives a wrong tempo mark
and time signature (Andantino 2/2 instead of Andantino quasi allegretto 4/4), and
Bizet's alteration to the cadence is dismissed as without authority. In the final duet
the obvious verbal improvement 'Entre elle et toi [entre nous] *tout est* fini' yields
to the poor '*C'est* fini'; Carmen's high A♭ on '*Non,* je ne te céderai pas!' and the
higher setting of her 'Je répéterai que je l'aime' are subordinated to lower originals
rejected by Bizet; while José's top B♭ at 'Pour la dernière fois, *démon!*' is attributed
to Guiraud humouring a singer and left out altogether.

Many of these corruptions—by no means all—are matters of detail that a less
than alert ear might miss in the theatre, though their cumulative effect is considerable. That qualification does not apply to a major alteration to an important melody
in Act I. Immediately after Carmen has thrown the flower and run off, the orchestra
plays a tune that returns in a different rhythm when José leads Carmen out of the
factory under arrest (it also appears at Carmen's entry in the longer quarrel scene,
a passage cut before performance). Its original form was:

Ex.4

Andantino quasi allegretto

During the rehearsals, after the quarrel scene was shortened, but before the
publication of *E*, Bizet rewrote it thus:

Ex.5

Andantino quasi allegretto

E establishes the authenticity of the later form (which is entered in the autograph,
though probably not in Bizet's hand); a glance proclaims its superiority. It does
away with the poor symmetry between the second and sixth bars; the sudden upward leap at the end of the second is far more effective after the thrice repeated a'.

Oeser, ignoring the evidence, attributes the change to a late date and obscure provenance; the only explanation he can find is a possible resemblance between Ex. 4 and a popular song of the day. It has been claimed (not by Oeser) that Ex. 5 with its threefold a' is incompatible with Bizet's style, a statement that can proceed only from ignorance; the duke's love theme in *La Jolie Fille de Perth,* the most prominent motif in that opera, begins in exactly the same way:

Ex.6

Andantino

Que vous ê - tes jo - lie, ⸺ quel-le grâce ac- com -pli - e,
Près de vous on ou - blie⸺ les beau-tés de la cour!⸺

REHASHES

From these editorial blunders it is a short step to rewriting certain scenes as Oeser thinks Bizet, Meilhac and Halévy ought to have written them. He does not actually compose new music, but he does the next best thing by conflating different versions to produce a text that Bizet never accepted. This is then equipped with bogus stage directions that sometimes fly in the face of music and drama.[8]

One of the most damaging instances occurs in the crucial scene in which Carmen throws the flower at José. The printed libretto and *E* are perfectly clear about what happens here. At Carmen's first entry, José lifts his head for a moment, gives her a glance, then *se remet à travailler tranquillement à son épinglette* (priming-pin). After the habanera Carmen breaks free from the circle of her admirers and goes straight to José, *qui est toujours occupé de son épinglette,* while the fate motif sounds in the orchestra. After seven bars it breaks off with three diminuendo bars for violas alone, against which Carmen and José have three spoken lines:

CARMEN. Eh compère, qu'est-ce que tu fais là?
JOSÉ. Je fais une chaîne avec du fil de laiton, une chaîne pour attacher mon épinglette.
CARMEN (*riant*). Ton épinglette, vraiment! ton épinglette . . . épinglier de mon âme!

On the last phrase she throws the flower in his face and runs away amid general laughter as the factory bell sounds and ·all except José depart to a reprise of the habanera refrain.

This wonderfully effective little *mélodrame* disappeared in the recitative version. Oeser, who elsewhere includes dialogue and recitative on opposite pages, banishes it to an appendix and prints in the text the full 24-bar statement of the fate motif as it occurs in the Prelude, falsifying the stage directions. Omitting all reference to José working at his épinglette, he has him raise his eyes and stare at Carmen for

---

[8] It seems possible that some at least of these misconceptions derive from Walter Felsenstein's production at the Deutsche Oper, East Berlin, to which Oeser pays fulsome tribute.

twelve slow bars while she with equal deliberation takes the flower from her corsage. This Wagnerian—indeed Tristanesque—conception is quite alien to Bizet, and it destroys the whole point of the scene. It is the refusal of José, unlike everyone else on stage, to take the slightest notice of Carmen that provokes her action. The entire habanera is an expression of this dominant trait in her character. Moreover the repetition of the whole passage, varied only in key and scoring, so soon after it has been heard in the Prelude is musically as well as dramatically banal. If (as Oeser indicates) Bizet composed it for this context (before writing the Prelude), its compression is a typical example of his dramatic concentration.

By this time the reader may begin to harbour a suspicion that Oeser has only a shaky idea of what the opera is about. That he misunderstands the very kernel of the plot is confirmed by one extraordinary feature of this edition.[9] He is convinced that Escamillo is the great love of Carmen's life, and that when she sings 'Je suis amoureuse à perdre esprit' in the Act II quintet she is thinking, not of the soldier who engineered her escape in Act I and whom she has come to meet after he has served a prison sentence for her sake, but of a man she has just coolly brushed off. To this the only adequate reply is that of the Duke of Wellington when accosted in the street with the words 'Mr Smith, I believe?'—'Sir, if you believe that, you would believe anything.'

Unfortunately this is no laughing matter; the consequences are grave. Since there is no evidence for his thesis (Carmen shows no interest in Escamillo before the Act III finale—she is merely growing tired of José's jealousy) Oeser sets about supplying some, shamelessly cooking the stage directions by inserting passages for which he can claim no authority; some of them are flagrantly at variance with the music. At Escamillo's exit in Act II he adds *Carmen suit Escamillo longtemps des yeux*. He softens Bizet's *Très retenu* at 'Je suis amoureuse' to *Un peu plus lent* and attributes Bizet's fermata before it to the conductor. (It is not quite clear how this helps Oeser's case. He talks here of the new, deeper, and more passionate emotion Escamillo has stimulated in Carmen, in contrast to her transitory feelings for José. This is flatly contradicted by what she has just said in reply to Escamillo's advances: 'Je répondrais que tu peux m'aimer tout à ton aise, mais que quant à être aimé de moi pour le moment, il ne faut pas y songer!') At Escamillo's second exit, in the third finale (refrain of his *couplets* on the orchestra in D flat), Oeser goes one better with *Carmen, en extase, le suit des yeux* and declares that Bizet's own direction—*Don José veut s'élancer sur lui, mais il est retenu par le Dancaïre et le Remendado*—contradicts the message of the music (that the D flat refrain reflects Carmen's idealized picture of Escamillo) and destroys one of the strongest and most intimate moments in the opera, the link with Carmen's simpler and purer declaration of love in the last scene.

Oeser dredges up one further piece of 'evidence' in support of his hypothesis. This is the single word 'Escamillo' sung by Carmen to a commonplace phrase (a

---

[9] A less important misapprehension, due perhaps to ignorance of the French language, concerns the change of José's rank from 'sergent' to 'brigadier' during the composition of the opera. This is not a promotion but the opposite; 'brigadier' means a corporal, not a sergeant-major. Still less does it correspond to the British rank of brigadier, as in a studio performance once broadcast by the BBC.

rising fifth and a falling tone) just after she has interrupted the duel. It occurs in Bizet's first version, and is clearly no more than a cry of recognition (she has only set eyes on the man once before). To Oeser however it is one of the most highly charged moments in the opera, and 'indispensable', since it indicates that Carmen has been in love with Escamillo for weeks. It held no such meaning for Bizet, who cut it out *before the score was copied* and therefore before pressure of any kind could have been put upon him. Oeser himself tells us this (p. 717), but that does not prevent him from later attributing the cut to Guiraud (p. 765).

It is hardly surprising after this that the superb finale of Act III is reduced to something like nonsense by the wholesale rewriting of stage directions and some manhandling of the music. At José's 'Je te tiens, fille damnée' Bizet's *saisissant Carmen* is cut. When Micaëla tells José that his mother is dying he replies 'Partons! ah! partons!' and says to Carmen 'Sois contente ... je pars ... mais ... nous nous reverrons!' Between these sentences Bizet has the direction *Il fait quelques pas, puis, s'arrêtant, à Carmen.* Oeser cuts this (except for the last two words) as a mere instruction to the stage manager. On the last syllable of 'reverrons!' the fate motif sounds in the orchestra, whereupon *Don José entraîne Micaëla; en entendant la voix d'Escamillo, il s'arrête hésitant.* This is Bizet, but it is not good enough for Oeser, who abolishes it as 'Missverständlich und der Musik nicht konform' and substitutes a preposterous *Micaëla entraîne Don José* on a diminuendo molto (*mf–pp*) chord for flutes and clarinets.

At the fourth bar of Escamillo's offstage refrain (which should begin unaccompanied—not, as in Oeser, with pizzicato chords throughout) Bizet has *Carmen veut s'élancer; Don José, ménacant, lui barre le passage* —a tremendous moment in the theatre. Oeser sweeps this away, making José merely hesitate before tamely going off with Micaëla, and three bars later completes the ruin of the finale by restoring a singularly limp and undramatic passage from a rejected earlier version with Escamillo's refrain prolonged for several bars at the cadence and José calling 'Micaëla, partons!' He refers to the removal of this as 'a very late measure of doubtful provenance'. Late it was, but its provenance is impeccable: Bizet made the change between the printing of the libretto and the preparation of the vocal score.[10] He clearly wanted a tableau at the end; he marked the cue for the curtain on Escamillo's final top F. Oeser kills the whole design by bringing down the curtain not on this superb tableau but ten bars too late, after José and Micaëla have disappeared and the smugglers started to move off.

The Act IV finale suffers most grievously of all; Oeser has introduced a whole string of anticlimaxes at the very point where Bizet's structure is most taut. One of the worst has already been described in connection with tempo marks. From the point where José stabs Carmen Bizet composed at least four versions of this finale. The first comprises four bars of chromatic scales and tremolos against acclamations from the chorus offstage, a double cry of 'Carmen!' from José, Carmen's dying reference to the card scene, José's 'Ah! ma Carmen adorée!' in G flat over tremolo

---

[10] As usual the libretto was prepared in advance of the production; it takes account of most but not quite all of the rehearsal changes. Andrès is removed from Act II but survives by oversight in Act IV.

strings (to the same phrase as in the last bars of the accepted score), the Toreador refrain in F sharp sung by the chorus off (but to different words), and a totally different end. Instead of the last twelve bars as we know them there were twenty-four. Escamillo enters and sees Carmen dead (five bars); José confesses and is arrested but does not sing 'Ah! ma Carmen adorée!' The opera ends not with four orchestral bars but with thirteen, the fate motif being built up to a big climax and then dying away to a pianissimo close in D major.

Bizet's first change (before the parts were copied) was to remove José's repeated cry of 'Carmen!' and the reference to the card scene; about the same time or soon after he changed the words of the choral refrain. In the third version he rewrote the final bars as we now have them. Oeser suggests that this was because du Locle objected to the end, though it is not clear why he should have found the shorter version any less offensive; it was Carmen's murder on the stage to which he is supposed to have taken exception. (Other changes are conjecturally ascribed to pressure from du Locle; Bizet, it seems, cannot be left to make decisions for himself.) This revision left seven bars, including José's first cry of 'Ah! ma Carmen adorée!' (which thus came twice to the same notes), between the stabbing and the F sharp chorus (Bizet does not appear to have cancelled the original stage direction in which during the chromatic scales *Carmen tombe appuyée sur son bras gauche*). (Ex. 7). His last revision removed these bars and substituted the octave fanfare on the note F$\sharp$ (Ex. 8). Oeser objects to this last revision, and begins by throwing doubt on its authenticity. He guesses that it was the outcome of a hurried conference at rehearsal, in which Bizet presumably had no part, and condemns it as in many respects injurious to the context ('in mehrfacher Hinsicht schädlich')—musically on the pedantic ground that it makes Bizet follow tonic with tonic instead of dominant (a device employed with conspicuous effect on occasion by Beethoven), dramatically because it opened the way for the stage direction in the printed score, which is attributed to the producer: *Il s'élance vers Carmen—Carmen veut fuir, mais Don José la rejoint à l'entrée du cirque—il la frappe—elle tombe et meurt. Don José s'agenouille auprès d'elle.*

This, declares Oeser, 'offends in the highest degree against Bizet's basic principles of musico-dramatic form'. But it is Bizet's own direction, as *E* (supported by the autograph) proves beyond dispute. Admittedly he changed his mind about the action here. Originally José was directed to stab Carmen just before 'damnée!' and during the chromatic scales she was to fall on her left arm and make the gesture of dealing the cards, dying before his cry 'Ah! ma Carmen adorée!' This was followed two bars later by the F sharp chorus.

In Bizet's ultimate version she dies while the chorus, with bitter irony, are singing 'Et songe bien en combattant qu'un oeil noir te regarde'. This is surely an echo of her death scene in Mérimée's novel, where José describes her last moments in these words: 'Je crois voir encore son grand oeil noir me regarder fixement; puis il devient trouble et se ferma'. It would be particularly effective if Escamillo were to emerge from the arena at that moment, but Bizet's directions are not explicit about this.

Oeser misses the double irony here and makes her die before the chorus begins.

Ex.7

Ex.8

He then rewrites all the stage directions up to the end of the opera, restoring some that occur in Bizet's *first* version, where the music was quite different. But he is left with the seven extra bars of Ex. 7 (originally associated with the recall of the card scene), in which the words and music of José's last phrase are anticipated. He accordingly snips out these two bars and leaves in the text a broken-winded progression that never occurs in Bizet at all (Ex. 9).

Three things must be said about Bizet's final revision (the substitution of Ex. 8 for Ex. 7). In the first place there can be no question about its authenticity, for it is in *E*. Secondly it is a palpable stroke of genius, since it brings José's loss of control, followed by the assault, right on top of the triumphant F sharp chorus—an electrifying moment in the theatre. Thirdly it agrees with Bizet's procedure all

Ex.9

through this finale, not only here but several times earlier, which is to simplify and concentrate: immediacy of impact was what he sought—not at the expense of musical grammar, but certainly at the expense of musical elaboration at moments of decisive action. This is one of the qualities that make him a great musical dramatist, though not of the Wagnerian stamp. Yet Oeser religiously restores all these (mostly brief) cuts and simplifications, and waters down the whole finale.

There are illuminating examples at the two points where the duet is interrupted by offstage chorus and brass (the bullfighters' march on the first cornet, not the trumpet as printed here). In the earlier version (rejected by Bizet but restored by Oeser) the voice parts are rather more complicated and there are certain differences in the words, which at the second interruption describe the bullfight in detail. Oeser indignantly ascribes the change to 'Torschlusspanik', calls it 'a renunciation of [Bizet's] stylistic principle of absolute veracity' and (in another place) 'eine barbarische Gewaltkur' that Bizet would never have undertaken except under overwhelming pressure of circumstances. He assumes that the chorus could not cope with the music; yet it is not difficult to sing, and this is the one place in the score where they were not distracted by having to act and could even have read their parts, since they are not on stage. And it is easy to see why Bizet made the change. We do not require a running commentary on the finer points of tauromachy, which will not be heard in any case, to appreciate the parallel between the struggles inside and outside the bullring. Talk about the sublime conception of the finale being 'blotted out' by the change is preposterous. On the contrary, where the more complex version runs the risk of blurring the dramatic impact, the simpler strikes home as decisively as José's dagger. Even if an editor does not agree with this reasoning, it is no business of his—indeed it is the height of editorial impropriety —to assume that a sane composer did not intend what he left in his score.

These are many other places where Bizet's stage directions are suppressed, mangled, misplaced, or otherwise disorganized: it happens at the beginning of the first, third, and fourth acts, the start of the cigarette girls' chorus and the quarrel scene, Escamillo's first entry, the finale of Act II (Zuniga should threaten José, not strike him, an act out of character; it is José, not Zuniga, whose discipline has been undermined), and elsewhere. Nor have anything like all the errors in notes, words, or tempo marks been mentioned. But enough has been said to show that the Alkor score does Bizet no sort of justice. It is not a critical edition at all but a musicological disaster of the first magnitude, an arbitrary conflation, based on random principles of selection, of what Bizet intended, what he rejected, and what the editor thinks he would have done better to write. It sometimes relegates the definitive text to an appendix and quite frequently does not print it at all. Anyone performing *Carmen* as printed here is foredoomed to misrepresent it on several levels. Until a new clean edition is published the best conductors and impresarios can do is to use the old Choudens or Peters score, remove the recitatives and ballet and any mistakes they can find, and insert (from Oeser) such of the rehearsal cuts as they think desirable.[11]

It is no pleasure to point this out, especially as the score is beautifully printed and much labour has clearly gone into its production. But it is a necessity and a duty, for an issue far beyond the feelings of individuals is involved—the integrity of a great operatic masterpiece. The editor, no doubt unwittingly, has slighted Bizet's genius and treated him as a weak-kneed nonentity incapable of knowing what he really wanted or (if he knew) of standing up for it. It is a pervading sin of the artistic middlemen of our time, as a certain type of opera producer is never tired of demonstrating, to assume an air of bland superiority and debauch the work of the geniuses whom they claim to interpret. But a stage production does not remain in print. A critical edition that betrays its standards can do infinitely more damage, since it may be accepted for generations as the composer's last word. And the present climate of musical scholarship makes it an urgent necessity to illustrate the fearful dangers of an editor taking an autograph as his ultimate source when later printed scores appeared during the composer's life.

This edition carries a preliminary notice forbidding its use for performance and its sale in France. It is not clear whether the intention is to protect the French from corruption or from apoplexy; or is Bizet still copyright there? But if the nation that produced him (and has paid him less honour than Germany) wishes to take a bloodless revenge, let it do what it should have done long ago and undertake a complete critical edition of his works. Bizet is one of France's greatest composers; much of his music is still unpublished, and the versions of several of his operas on sale in Paris today are in greater need of a drastic purge than the score of *Carmen*.

[11] In recent productions and recordings conductors have adopted all manner of expedients, including new readings of their own. Some, especially in Germany, swallowed Oeser's text whole—no doubt because, like Everest, it was there. Others rejected some but not all of the corruptions. Bernstein (New York Met. and DG recording, 1973) kept many of the worst but evolved an ingenious treatment of the Act III duel: by cutting only the 2/4 sections he got rid of the weakest music while preserving the dramatic point, that José is so far gone in degradation that he will kill the man who has just spared his life. Mackerras performed a weird version at Covent Garden in 1967, combining Guiraud's recitatives with much Oeser and passages that even Oeser rejected (including the quotation from the card scene at Carmen's death), but a well-balanced and very effective one at the Coliseum three years later. Solti, after adopting the whole Oeser hog at Covent Garden in 1973, made an interesting selection in his Decca recording (1976) and explained his views in detail in the booklet, which contains a discussion of the musical text and—probably for the first time in print—an authentic text of the libretto as Bizet set it. Abbado at the 1977 Edinburgh Festival followed Oeser in debasing the fourth (but not the third) finale and in the extended Tristanesque treatment of the flower-throwing. Haitink at Glyndebourne in 1985, in an otherwise sensitive performance, also chose the latter, and gave the A major theme (Exx. 4 and 5) in its improved and original form successively. Frühbeck de Burgos (HMV, 1970) stands alone in recording the score as it was performed on the first night.

29
Katya Kabanova

=====

When in April 1951 the enterprise of Sadler's Wells gave us the first English performance of Janáček's opera, some sections of the public and the press were manifestly baffled. Its revival in the composer's centenary year should make it clear that the difficulty lay not in the music but in the preconceptions of the listener. There is a modern danger that the work of art that fits neither the pigeon-hole nor the pillory may go by default, and *Katya Kabanova*, while it has no scandal value, does not hang comfortably on any of the traditional pegs. It has affinities with *Pelléas et Mélisande* and still more with *Boris Godunov*, not on account of its Russian subject (it is based on Ostrovsky's play *The Storm*, for which Tchaikovsky wrote a concert overture), but because Janáček, like Musorgsky, was much concerned with folk style and the rhythms of popular speech. Indeed his interest extended to the sounds of nature as a whole; he recorded in musical notation the voices of apes and walruses. But by the time the opera was written (1919–21) most of musical Europe had long turned its back on nationalism. It is true that Bartók, with whom also Janáček has not a little in common, won world fame between the wars, but the new music that made most stir was that of the expatriate Stravinsky and the doctrinaire Schoenberg and their followers. And it was the experimental rather than the national and traditional elements in Bartók that generally claimed attention. History may disturb these judgments. We have suffered a good deal from the critical heresy of judging contemporary music by the adjective rather than the noun. Some of the greatest composers of the past have been denounced as reactionaries in their lifetime.

No one could call Janáček a reactionary, but he was undoubtedly eclectic. He worked to no system, brandished no slogans, and attracted no pressure group. He inconveniently proved the continuing vitality of the tonal tradition just when it was to the interest of many to suppose it exhausted. His freedom from technical preconceptions annoys the academic traditionalist without satisfying any of the fashionable types of doctrinaire. He repeatedly does things that look wrong on paper but (except to an ear stopped with prejudice) sound right in performance; and to this must be added that stumbling-block peculiar to the born opera-composer (Verdi, for instance), the perpetration of effects that fall flat in the study but are brilliant and moving in the theatre. Although he wrote much other vocal and instrumental music of high quality, Janáček stands or falls by his nine operas. *Jenůfa* and *Katya Kabanova* alone—not to mention the three later masterpieces—are enough to place him among the few great opera composers of the century.

An instructive comparison can be made between *Katya Kabanova* and the almost exactly contemporary *Wozzeck*.[1] Both operas are intensely concentrated and tragic in tone; both handle nineteenth-century plays in a manner that owes a good deal to the modern science of psychology; both composers reveal a profound compassion for the sufferings of their chief character. But in technique and approach they are poles apart. Where Janáček combines many traditional elements in a free and empirical manner, Berg creates his stresses in the main by circumscribing a revolutionary language with the strictest logic. Janáček works outwards from his dramatic data, Berg inwards from his musical premisses. And while *Wozzeck* has not a little of the obsessional quality of Strindberg—a pity so ferocious that for some listeners it may defeat its own ends by escaping their notice altogether—Janáček treats his theme with a detachment, at once intense and ironical, that recalls Chekhov. His range of sympathy is far wider than Berg's, whose two operas are preoccupied with the sordid side of human nature. Janáček's characters—and the subjects of his operas —are remarkably varied, and although he can draw persons who are contemptible and even repulsive, like Katya's husband and mother-in-law, he never weights the scales so as to make them incredible. They are comprehended with the same vision and lapped round with the same musical essence in which the rest of the drama is distilled.

This sense of background, of the locality, physical and spiritual, in which the characters have their being, is one of Janáček's greatest (and most Chekhovian) gifts. It is doubtless connected with his peasant origin and the strong feeling of community he derived from contact with his own people and their environment. At the same time he shows an exceptional penetration into the motives of individuals, particularly of women; his portraits of Jenufa and Katya, neither of them simple characters, have an extraordinary subtlety and vitality. Katya, a passionate heroine whose power to break with her constricting environment is inhibited by her conscience, is unique in opera. Wilfrid Mellers has suggested that all Janáček's mature art springs from the intensity of his sympathy with nature and his consciousness of sin.[2] Certainly his vision of human nature is not only localized but universal. He is as free, in style and outlook, from the homespun folkiness of some national art as he is from the dreary realism of *verismo*. Although his fruit springs from good rich soil, it never tastes of the farmyard. He was in fact an experienced practical musician with a thorough knowledge of many styles and periods. In this he differs from Musorgsky, who in some of his songs was in greater danger than Janáček of allowing his interest in linguistic inflections to drain the lyrical power of the music.

It is this lyrical quality that should commend Janáček's music to a wide public, provided they do not expect the more leisurely expansiveness of Strauss or Puccini. Janáček stands in relation to those composers rather as Verdi's *Falstaff* stands to *Rigoletto*. Music and action move with such swiftness and economy that the sudden

[1] Composed 1917–22, first performed 1925.
[2] See his chapter, 'Synopsis: Innocence and Guilt in *Kát'a Kabanová*', in the Cambridge Opera Handbook on the opera, compiled by J. Tyrrell (Cambridge, 1982).

soaring phrases for the voices (and still more in the orchestra) must be caught at once before they escape. The extreme flexibility of the style forbids set pieces, and the recurring motifs, though skilfully used, do not bind the music together in a Wagnerian manner. Many technical features—the treatment of the dialogue, which may sound clipped and breathless until the ear grows used to it, the comparative absence of counterpoint, the lack of transitions, and in particular Janáček's fondness for unprepared modulations into adjacent rather than related keys—would appear at first glance rather to tear it apart. Nor does the rhythmic complexity, with a preference for compound, irregular, and swiftly changing metres (there is comparatively little common time) and a tendency to avoid accents on the first beat of the bar, always carry conviction on paper. But such suspicions are confounded in practice by the same qualities that dispel the obvious objections to *Pelléas et Mélisande*. Janáček's sensitiveness to every nuance of the drama, the shimmering and multicoloured beauty of the orchestration, which is integral and not applied, and the very personal use of harmony contribute to an impression at once unified and urgent, if not positively overpowering. Janáček's chromaticism, thanks partly to its modal tinge, is always mobile and utterly unlike the chromaticism of the German Romantic tradition from Spohr to early Schoenberg, which tends to bring movement to a standstill. Such a style of course is apt to break down in any other hands than those of genius. Even in Janáček it produces occasional incoherence; for instance the comic scenes, such as that between the mother-in-law and the drunken Dikoj in Act II, though their dramatic intention is plain, are not quite in focus with the rest. But the score is so rich in invention, psychological insight, and haunting sensuous beauty that it reduces many of the *enfants terribles* of our age to the status of nursery bogies.

30

Edward J. Dent:
A Centenary Tribute

It is not usual in this country to celebrate the centenary of a musicologist, or indeed to honour so abstruse a creature during his life. But Edward Joseph Dent, who was born on 16 July 1876 and died on 22 August 1957, was no ordinary specimen. He was the first (and for a long time the only) British musicologist of international standing, and was recognized as such everywhere. As Professor of Music at Cambridge from 1926 to 1941, the first scholar to hold the post—and, apart from Thurston Dart's brief period of two years, unfortunately the last—he broadened the narrow curriculum, prepared the way for the establishment of a full degree course after the war, and proved an inspiring teacher whose influence is far from exhausted. As one of the founders of the International Society for Contemporary Music after the First World War, he laboured long to promote understanding and good relations between a peculiarly cantankerous assortment of nationalist groups and prickly individuals, and held the presidency for sixteen years (1922–38). His books include what are still the most penetrating studies of Alessandro Scarlatti, Mozart's operas, and English dramatic music of the seventeenth century, besides more popular works whose refreshing readability should guarantee their survival for generations to come. He was the friend and biographer of Busoni. He translated nearly thirty opera librettos for Sadler's Wells and elsewhere, and although he was aware that such things must inevitably date, his translations not only proved their vitality but sometimes outshone their would-be supplanters. He was a composer, a wit, and a brilliant letter-writer.

Dent was also a highly idiosyncratic character, and in some respects a bundle of contradictions. This not only delighted his friends and students, and irritated his opponents; it coloured the tone of his more popular writings, and to some degree his approach to musical history, and is therefore more important than might appear at first glance. Not that he was ever led to suppress facts, much less to invent them. But in all historical work there is a large place for interpretation. If Dent's views were not to everyone's taste, they were expressed in a vivid and challenging form that forced his readers to reconsider their basic assumptions. He regarded this as an important objective, and few who have given serious thought to the subject would disagree with him. It is not the least prejudiced historians of the past who are read with most enjoyment today. We appreciate Gibbon, Johnson, Macaulay, Burney, Hazlitt, and others not because they are infallible but for the style and personality they bring to their work. Although Dent did not write a General History of Music, his place is alongside Burney, with whom he shared great learning, a capacity for patient research, a graceful and felicitous style, and an occasional quirkiness which after the passage of time is more likely to entertain than to trouble the modern reader.

This quirkiness arose from the circumstances of Dent's birth and background. The youngest son of a Yorkshire county family that seems to have thrown up no other artistic talent, he underwent a conventional education at Eton and King's College, Cambridge, where he began by reading Classics. His decision to embark on a musical career provoked considerable family opposition: music was not a respectable career for a gentleman, unless it could somehow be yoked with the Church. Such an association was not likely to appeal to Dent, to whom the regular church-going and sabbatarian piety of his family and class were a peculiar irritant. Similar blemishes, as he must have thought them, stained the whole climate of English musical life in the Victorian age. This was still the era of massive oratorios, not only giant Handel performances but new festival commissions from such eminent foreign composers as Dvořák and Saint-Saëns. Outside the Church all the best music was considered to be of German origin; the broad highway passed through the Viennese classics. Ten of the twelve composers in the original 'Master Musicians' series of biographies were German (the others were Chopin and Tchaikovsky). Wagner had begun to capture the more advanced spirits, and was soon to capture Dent, though he often tilted against him later. Gounod's church music was admired for its sacred qualities, as indeed was *Faust*; but the Italians, including Verdi, were condemned as superficial, if not meretricious. The rediscovery of English music of the sixteenth and seventeenth centuries had scarcely begun. Opera was ranked far below the symphony, the concerto, and the string quartet. Even Mozart seemed a childlike innocent, not to be classed with the mature masters. *Die Entführung, Così fan tutte, Die Zauberflöte*, and of course *Idomeneo* (first performed in London in 1938, by an amateur company in a tiny theatre) were strangers to the English repertory. Meyerbeer was still the giant of the operatic stage, and Covent Garden audiences—with a few exceptions—were more conspicuous for social rank, jewelled frontages, and susceptibility to high notes and vocal pyrotechnics than for musical understanding.

Dent reacted violently against all this. To the end of his life he let slip no opportunity to rail at churches and priests of all denominations (especially Roman Catholic), and to pepper a whole series of targets: reverence for the classics in general, sacred oratorios, German music (as opposed to French and especially Italian), a puritanical attitude to the theatre, pomposity and grandiloquence of every kind, commercialism, and the worship of prima donnas and posturing conductors. This was largely negative, and it would be futile to deny that it sometimes led Dent into false positions. He could not understand the high reputation enjoyed by Elgar, whom he despised as a professional musician bent on living the life of a country gentleman (a course exactly opposite to his own) and a Roman Catholic composer of oratorios to boot. When this wholesale condemnation provoked controversy, Dent took opposition as a personal affront. He detected the meretricious element

in Puccini, but failed to detect anything else. Although he was half drawn towards
Weber, he damned him for amateurishness, inability to continue an initial idea, and
uncritical imitation of Rossini. Further causes of prejudice and intolerance were
Dent's homosexual inclinations and his political radicalism, curiously blended with
a fastidious and aristocratic conservatism that remained central to his character.

Dent's revulsion from the worship of contemporary idols had however a very
positive side. It drove him to explore forgotten or undervalued aspects of musical
history, with conspicuously fruitful results. His esteem for Mozart's slighted genius
and for opera as one of the supreme forms of art led to the celebrated revival of
Die Zauberflöte at Cambridge in 1911, the first in England for many years, when
he doubled the roles of translator and stage manager. Dent was fascinated by the
theatre—spoken drama as well as opera—and unlike most English musicians of his
age, who tended to gravitate towards teaching and the organ-loft, he had practical
knowledge of it. It was natural that his most important and lasting work should lie
in the field of opera, though he made many contributions to other departments of
music. His preface to Foundations of English Opera (1928) deserves quotation for its
terse and penetrating treatment of an issue that still trips up countless musicians,
artists and critics alike:

Essential musical principles may sometimes be modified under the influence of the stage, and
the normal dramatic values are often entirely altered by the concomitance of music. There
arises therefore an operatic principle which is neither the normal musical principle nor the
normal dramatic principle. History shows us only too clearly that neither poets nor musicians
have grasped it except spasmodically and intuitively. Yet it underlies all their efforts, and the
task of the historian only becomes more interesting as it becomes more difficult . . . It is
fundamentally important that the historian of opera should always study his documents with
the eye of a producer.

Dent's first book, and in some respects his most solid achievement, was his study
of the life and works of Alessandro Scarlatti, published in 1905. This was based on
the very detailed and extensive research, nearly all into manuscript material, that
had gained him a fellowship at King's three years earlier. It is still the standard work
on the composer, and likely to remain so. When the decision was taken to reprint
it fifty-five years later (after Dent's death), the editing was entrusted to another
great English scholar, Frank Walker, who had worked in the same field and found
that Dent's discussion of Scarlatti's music required no revision at all. The book was
reproduced as it stood, with a few pages of biographical and bibliographical
addenda at the end. In his prefatory note Walker quoted a Dantean poem in terza
rima by the Italian musicologist Alessandro Longo, editor of the keyboard works
of Domenico Scarletti, describing a visit to the musicians' paradise; here the author
happily informed the elder Scarlatti that the fog obscuring his life had been
dispersed, and his music restored to currency, in 'nebbiosa Inghilterra' by 'Eduardo
Dent, un anglicano'.

The timeless quality that distinguishes Dent's best books is rare in the criticism
of any art. Most such works are preserved, if at all, by their literary style, and Dent's
was indeed lively and economical; but he also possessed the ability to pronounce

a balanced judgment, free from extravagant claims, on the music he loved best. This is equally evident in his study of Mozart's operas (1913)—the revised and shortened edition of 1947 did modify some judgments and remove a few dubious statements, but was chiefly occasioned by the fact that the battle had then been won, largely by Dent's own efforts—and in *Foundations of English Opera*, a study of the English musical theatre up to and including Purcell. This had been begun in 1914, when Dent and his associates intended to follow up the pioneer *Zauberflöte* with the first stage revival of Purcell's *Fairy Queen* since 1693. The 1914–18 war caused its postponement till 1920, and Dent subsequently rewrote the book. We are apt to forget what a recent event the restoration of Purcell's works to the theatre really is. Dent's inspiration had a great deal to do with it, before, during, and after his Cambridge professorship; for he soon infected his students and others with his enthusiasm. He edited *Dido and Aeneas* (originally for a German production in 1924) and later *The Beggar's Opera*; it was his combination of thorough historical research with practical knowledge—the two pillars on which all his scholarship was founded —that gave the movement its secure base.

The same factors were at work in the Cambridge revival of *Idomeneo* in 1939 —from which the English popularity of the work dates, long before it was produced by a professional opera house—and in the movement for staging Handel's oratorios. Dent did not originate this; it began with *Saul* at Hanover in 1923, soon followed by other works at Münster, Breslau, and elsewhere, and was introduced to England by the Misses Radford at Falmouth. *Semele*—not of course an oratorio —had been staged at Cambridge in 1925 before Dent's return as professor. But he encouraged and greatly influenced the very successful productions at Cambridge between 1932 and 1948. He declared that he never understood the oratorios until he saw them in the theatre; and this recognition of their essentially dramatic inspiration—which is obvious now, but had been hopelessly obscured by the varnish of Victorian tradition—helped to transform the entire attitude of the English musical public towards Handel's genius.

Dent had the intense professionalism of the serious scholar who began as an amateur, but he never lost the freshness of his early vision or underrated the role of the amateur performer; indeed he actively encouraged it. He wrote in the preface to the 1947 edition of *Mozart's Operas*, with reference to *Idomeneo* and *La clemenza di Tito*: 'It is characteristic of our musical life that the most interesting Mozart revivals in recent years have been the productions of amateurs.' In this spirit he translated the libretto of Handel's *Deidamia* for a group of civil servants conducted by a young engineer, and so precipitated the foundation of the Handel Opera Society. The fact that since 1955 no fewer than thirty of Handel's Italian operas have been staged in Britain[1] by various amateur and university groups owed not a little to Dent. He would not have been surprised to learn that the few productions so far in our national opera houses have left a great deal to be desired, or that in this field

---

[1] The total is now (1989) higher; only *Almira*, *Silla*, *Muzio Scevola*, and *Siroe* await their first British stage production.

Cambridge has established a palpable lead over Oxford (though Oxford awarded
him an honorary doctorate of music fifteen years before Cambridge). Dent's
enthusiasm for English opera and opera in English admitted few bounds. He
rejected out of hand the idea that operas should be sung in the original tongue, and
the clarity of diction and aptness to the voice of his own translations killed the
argument that opera in English must inevitably torture the language into grotesque
verbal inversions—though he remarked caustically that some singers seemed to
prefer the latter, becoming 'embarrassed when they realise, perhaps in the course
of a performance, that what they are singing is sense'. He expressed these views with
such fervour that some persons were understandably nettled. If his disapproval of
Glyndebourne provoked indignant explosions on the Sussex Downs, it must be
ascribed, not to serious criticism of John Christie's work, but to the old Adam in
Dent reacting against youthful memories of Covent Garden audiences dressed up
to the nines to applaud a top C or a big, big D.

Dent's serious scholarship was not confined to the books mentioned above. Early
in the century he published important articles, still valid, on Leonardo Leo and other
eighteenth-century opera composers; periodicals in several countries contain his
contributions to many kinds of musicological enquiry, some of them unexpected.
During the Second World War he wrote a pregnant little book, *Notes on Fugue for
Beginners*, that belies its dry title and is full of wise saws on composition in general;
it need scarcely be said that he regarded fugue and counterpoint not as mechanical
exercises but as means of emotional expression. He put this precept into practice in
the six unaccompanied motets he composed about the same time. Dent had creative
ambitions in his youth, but in later life he was able or willing to compose only when
he was ill. During the First War he wrote a number of songs, including a setting
of Thomas Hardy's poem 'The Oxen' (which he described as a mixture of
campanology and agnosticism); his later choice of the Book of Psalms and religious
verses by Blake and Charles Wesley may seem startling in such a committed her-
etic. It suggests—as does his surrender to the ethical idealism and sublimity of
Die Zauberflöte—that his ire was provoked not so much by religious attitudes themselves as by what he took to be the complacency and smugness of those who
propagated them. If so, this was another heritage from his youth, and one that lay
too deep for self-analysis. His statements on the subject are full of unresolved
contradictions and shaky antitheses, such as the confession 'I may not have been a
very religious man, but I do like a good fugue'. He called Palestrina the Barnby of
the sixteenth century, and was inclined to depreciate Bach for his ecclesiastical
background, his association with the organ (an instrument always apt to rouse the
rebel in Dent), and his failure to write for the theatre; but he could leap to their
defence if they were attacked.

This rogue-elephant attitude sometimes broke into his more popular books. Not
all of them, however: his short biography of Handel (1934), though superseded in
some of its facts, is still worth reading, and notable for a new theory to explain the
wholesale borrowings from other composers in the years after 1737. Dent suggested
that Handel's serious illness of that spring, which was mental as well as physical,

may have temporarily impaired his fertility of invention.[2] His Pelican book on *Opera* (1940) can be charged with a certain lack of proportion: Slavonic opera is allotted barely a page, and operetta excluded altogether, whereas opera in England receives three whole chapters, amounting to forty-eight pages, more than a quarter of the book. But Dent had a deliberate purpose in view: he wished to convert British audiences to the art he loved, and its extraordinary revival in this country during the last forty years has fully justified him. Another late work, *A Theatre for Everybody* (1945), subtitled *The Story of the Old Vic and Sadler's Wells*, written during the Second War, was largely directed to the same end, though it has a permanent historical value. Dent was able to draw on his personal acquaintance, as a director and later governor of the theatres, with many of the events and persons he describes, notably that incomparable eccentric Lilian Baylis, who did so much to overcome popular prejudice against the musical theatre as a temple of lewdness. The book may contain a few provincial judgments, but Dent's wit and curious erudition give it a quality of hilarious entertainment that leavens the lump of historical fact. In a postscript to the second impression (1946) he was able to add with justifiable pride that the first operatic première in any country after the war took place at Sadler's Wells and enriched the repertory with a work of genius, Britten's *Peter Grimes*.

One of Dent's books, *Terpander, or Music and the Future* (1926), formed part of a series designed to provoke the general reader, and contains, as one might expect, a good deal of coat-trailing. He can topple into silliness ('Sincerity is a virtue with which art has no concern'), and there are signs of that residual snobbery that his radicalism and enthusiasm for novelty could never quite quench, for example the questionable statement: 'We cannot get away from the fact that at all periods of musical history the music that made that history was in its own day the possession of a limited circle of highly cultivated enthusiasts.' Yet the same book contains the profound observation: 'We do not enjoy music as an art until we have learned to appreciate it rationally; but at the same time it cannot give us a real aesthetic emotion unless it confronts us forcibly with a further irrational element.' Another work that combines deep historical insight with deliberate provocation is his Messenger Lectures, *The Rise of Romantic Opera*, delivered at Cornell University in the winter of 1937–8. Dent made no attempt to publish them, perhaps because in his last years he was planning a substantial work on this subject. Certainly he would not have printed them as they stood. But they contain so much that is at once stimulating and new—and indeed likely to transform recognised opinion on one of the most decisive periods of musical history, which still awaits adequate treatment —that their appearance this year must be regarded as an important event.[3]

Towards the end of this work Dent drew a distinction between a course of lectures and a work of scholarship. 'The function of lectures is not to convey

---

[2] This explanation is no longer adequate. John H. Roberts has shown that 'borrowing' was an integral part of Handel's practice throughout his career.

[3] Ed. W. Dean (Cambridge, 1976).

information, which we can now obtain far better from books, but to stimulate interest in a subject.' In addressing the young, whom he always approached with a sympathy and generosity of spirit not always accorded to persons of established reputation, Dent liked to present himself as a David in the camp of the Philistines; this was perhaps how he viewed his own youth. He was anxious above all to make his students and listeners think for themselves and so train their imaginations and critical faculties; to this end he would make the most outrageous statements. Hence his hostility to the unconditional acceptance of tradition: 'our minds are rendered sluggish by the constant habit of veneration'. That his audience might be free to 'enjoy the art of today and tomorrow', he urged them 'to develop a habit of perpetual scepticism and criticism as regards all so-called acknowledged master-pieces. If you have ever allowed yourselves to reverence the great masters, I hope you will abandon that attitude, which is merely a polite mask for lazy-mindedness.'

It is easy to relate this to the iconoclastic propensities of Dent's youth, and the connection is certainly there. But it reflects the positive as well as the negative side of his complex personality, which like Busoni's (and Walt Whitman's) comprehended opposites. This denouncer of veneration and moral fervour declared that Gluck 'could only be venerated as the expression of a moral ideal; and for that he still stands even now'. He was an aristocrat who resented his upbringing and a socialist who despised public taste: 'what the general public has always wanted was to hear the greatest singers in the most trivial music'. The sensitive appreciator of the roles of Mozart's Pamina and Beethoven's Leonore indulged in bouts of rabid anti-feminism, especially if his friends showed signs of getting married. A lover of all things new and experimental, he rejected the radio and the gramophone, which 'make all orchestras sound more or less like a harmonium' (this was in 1940, not 1910). He sang the praises of modern British music in foreign periodicals, and modern Continental music in British periodicals. He was said (not without reason) to have the kindest heart and the bitterest tongue in Cambridge. He was also an inveterate leg-puller, and he achieved this with such an air of academic detachment that his victims often failed to detect it.

The international figure should not be obscured by the gadfly, if that is not too grotesque a metaphor for a man whose wily nature and elongated form earned him the nickname of 'the serpent', which he was happy to acknowledge. (According to one account he acquired it by appearing through the curtain before a performance of *Die Zauberflöte* to announce a change of cast.) Apart from his work for the ISCM, where his linguistic and diplomatic powers were stretched to the utmost (he wrote a wonderfully funny account of this in *Music Today* in 1949),[4] he was prominent in the International Society for Musicology from its foundation in 1927 and president from 1931 to 1949. Both bodies elected him an honorary life president when he retired. That alone is an indication of the respect in which he was held at a time when musicology in Britain lagged a generation behind France and Italy, and even further behind Germany, and when American musicology had scarcely begun

---

[4] 'Looking Backward', reprinted in *Selected Essays*, ed. H. Taylor (Cambridge, 1979).

to sprout wings. We were even slower to produce scholars than composers of international stature. Let us salute the great men we have.

One aspect of Dent can scarcely be revealed even now. His letters, of which many survive, are highly entertaining and full of pungent comment on the musical life of his time. They also contain pronouncements on his contemporaries, prominent, aspiring, and obscure, whose acidulated wit might wound the more sensitive relatives of those on whom his pen was laid. The letters were of course intended only for the private ear of his friends; eventually they should be made available to a wider public. And in a period when countless lesser men are dignified with a biography, it is difficult to think of many of Dent's stature who still lack this token of esteem.[5]

[5] Hugh Carey went some way towards satisfying both these requirements in *Duet for Two Voices: An Informal Biography of Edward Dent Compiled from his Letters to Clive Carey* (Cambridge, 1979).

Index

For operas based on Shakespeare plays see also pp. 252–61